Are the COVID-19 pandemic; suppression of assembly, esp
and election crisis the first volleys of the Third Episode of

Securing America's Victory

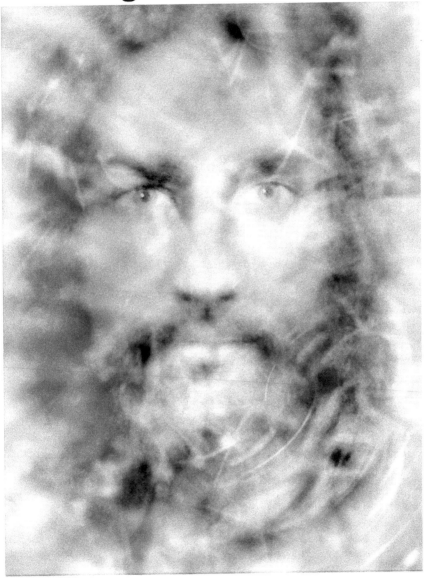

*The role of Christians and our churches in restoring acknowledgement
of the Presence of God in America and the world.*

outskirts
press

Outskirts Press, Inc.
http://www.outskirtspress.com

Paperback ISBN: 978-1-9772-3266-3
Hardback ISBN: 978-1-9772-3290-8

Library of Congress Control Number: 2020920539

This book is dedicated to:

I AM WHO I AM, Our Father God, the Creator

Jesus Christ

All the Children of God

The Healing of the Fall of mankind

The Freedom of America, all mankind, and the Earth

God bless you.

And God bless America!

Foreword

God, Our Father, has created an extraordinary and magnificently beautiful universe. He seems especially fond of spheres and circles. Both mathematicians and astrophysicists will tell you that, within this universe, if you follow a straight line long enough, it will come back to its point of origin. Every complete line is encompassed within a sphere.

The story, principles, and insights carried in this book are spherical, holistic. Physical books are a linear format. You may sense often that, as the narrative line progresses, information or message that may seem, at first, not directly related to the narrative line will be inserted. This is because, together we'll be touching other points of the sphere, that encompasses the wholeness of the message. This will quicken the synthesis and comprehension of the whole.

It is the purpose - and the prayer of myself and many, many others - that this experience is a worthwhile help to you on your trek to encompassing love, wisdom, truth, and justice. May the ultimate destination of your life's journey culminate in full reunification and reciprocal relationship with Our Father God and Jesus Christ.

Contents

I.

Was General Washington's Vision a prologue to today's crises?

On the July 4th weekend of the first year of his presidency, President Ronald Reagan had General Washington's Vision published in *Parade Magazine,* a Sunday newspaper supplement. He said it was a gift to the American people.

The nation's history has so far confirmed the truth of Washington's prophetic vision concerning America's future. A full text of this story is printed soon below.

As you read it, please consider this question:

In current times, are these listed occurrences the first volleys of the <u>third episode</u> of Washington's Vision?

- the COVID-19 pandemic and its lockdowns
- demands for mandatory vaccinations of all Americans
- the call for contact tracing and government-imposed confinements for non-compliance,
- the shutting of our businesses, choking off our means of self-reliance, and threatening to cripple our national economy
- peaceful, community protests hijacked into destructive, murdering violence by organizers living outside those communities
- the mainstream media, owned[1] by only six multinational corporations, parroting the same messages, using incomplete or incorrect information to broadcast messages of fear, hatred, and division, with increasingly anti-Christian bias
- the extended, severe, and prejudicial curtailment of church worship
- election fraud

The name "America" is an anagram. Reordered, the letters spell "I AM Race."

Exodus 3:11,15 (NRSV) God said to Moses, "I AM WHO I AM." He said further, "Thus you shall say to the Israelites, 'I AM' has sent me to you.' " [15] *God also said to Moses, ...This is my name forever, and this my title for all generations."*

This is the Name which God, Our Father has chosen for Himself and instructed us, through Moses, to use it also. That is why it is seen regularly throughout the pages of this book.

The term "God" is a generic English word for "supreme being." In theology, its definition is: *"the sole Supreme Being, eternal, spiritual, and transcendent, who is the Creator and ruler of all and is infinite in all attributes; the object of worship in monotheistic religions."* [2]

"God" translates in other languages to their word for "Supreme Being," e.g. Dios, Allah, Dieu, Gott, Brahma, Atman, etc.

This book is intentionally meant to be non-doctrinally Christian. It seeks to focus on and emphasize where the essences of Christian doctrines intersect.

Let's go back to the story with which we began. Here is the full text of:

GENERAL WASHINGTON'S VISION[3]
Originally published by Wesley Bradshaw.
It was reprinted in the National Tribune, Vol. 4, No. 12, December 1880.

The last time I ever saw Anthony Sherman was on the Fourth of July, 1859, in Independence Square. He was then ninety-nine years old, and becoming very feeble. But though so old, his dimming eyes rekindled as he gazed upon Independence Hall, which he came to visit once more.

"Let us go into the Hall," he said. "I want to tell you of an incident of Washington's life—one which no one alive knows of except myself; and, if you live you will before long, see it verified.

"From the opening of the Revolution we experienced all phases of fortune, now good and now ill, one time victorious and another conquered. The darkest period we had, I think, was when Washington, after several reverses, retreated to Valley Forge, where he resolved to pass the winter of 1777. Ah! I have often seen the tears coursing down our dear commander's careworn cheeks, as he would be conversing with a confidential officer about the condition of his poor soldiers. You have doubtless heard the story of Washington's going into the thicket to pray. Well, it was not only true, but he used often to pray in secret for aid and comfort from God, the interposition of whose Divine Providence brought us safely through the darkest days of tribulation.

"One day, I remember it well, the chilly winds whistled through the leafless trees, though the sky was cloudless and the sun shone brightly, he remained in his quarters nearly all the afternoon alone. When he came out I noticed that his face was a shade paler than usual, and there seemed to be something on his mind of more than ordinary importance. Returning just after dusk, he dispatched an orderly to the quarters of the officer I mention who was presently in attendance. After a preliminary conversation of about half an hour, Washington, gazing upon his companion with that strange look of dignity which he alone could command, said to the latter:

" 'I do not know whether it is owing to the anxiety of my mind, or what, but this afternoon as I was sitting at this table engaged in preparing a dispatch, something seemed to disturb me. Looking up, I beheld standing opposite me a singularly beautiful female. So astonished was I, for I had given strict orders not to be disturbed—that it was some moments before I found language to inquire into the cause of her presence. A second, a third, and even a fourth time did I repeat my question, but received no answer from my mysterious visitor except a slight raising of her eyes.

" 'By this time I felt strange sensations spreading through me. I would have risen but the riveted gaze of the Being before me rendered volition impossible. I assayed once more to address her, but my tongue had become useless. Even thought itself had become paralyzed. A new influence, mysterious, potent, irresistible, took possession of me. All I could do was to gaze steadily, vacantly at my unknown visitant. Gradually the surrounding atmosphere seemed as though becoming filled with sensations, and luminous. Everything about me seemed to rarify, the mysterious visitor herself becoming more airy and yet more distinct to my sight than before. I now began to feel as one dying, or rather to experience the sensations which I have sometimes imagined accompany dissolution. I did not think, I did not reason, I did not move; all were alike impossible. I was only conscious of gazing fixedly, vacantly at my companion.

" 'Presently, I heard a voice saying, "Son of the Republic, look and learn," while at the same time my visitor extended her arm eastwardly. I now beheld a heavy white vapor at some distance rising fold upon fold. This gradually dissipated, and I looked upon a strange scene. Before me lay spread out in one vast plain all the countries of the World—Europe, Asia, Africa, and America. I saw rolling and tossing between Europe and America the billows of the Atlantic, and between Asia and America lay the Pacific.

" 'Son of the Republic," said the same mysterious voice as before, "look and learn." At that moment I beheld a dark, shadowy being, like an angel, standing, or rather floating in mid-air, between Europe and America. Dipping water out of the ocean in the hollow of each hand, he sprinkled some upon America with his right hand, while with his left hand he cast some on Europe. Immediately a cloud raised from these countries, and joined in mid-ocean. For a while it remained stationary, and then moved slowly westward, until it enveloped America in its murky folds. Sharp flashes of lightning gleamed through it at intervals, and I heard the smothered groans and cries of the American people. A second time the angel dipped water from the ocean, and sprinkled it out as before. The dark cloud was then drawn back to the ocean, in whose heaving billows it sank from view.

" 'A third time I heard the mysterious voice saying, "Son of the Republic, look and learn." I cast my eyes upon America and beheld villages and towns and cities springing up one after another until the whole land from the Atlantic to the Pacific was dotted with them.

" 'Again, I heard the mysterious voice say, 'Son of the Republic, the end of the century cometh, look and learn.' At this the dark shadowy angel turned his face southward, and from Africa I saw an ill-omened specter approach our land. It flitted slowly over every town and city of the latter. The inhabitants presently set themselves in battle array against each other. As I continued looking I saw a bright angel, on whose brow rested a crown of light, on which was traced the word "Union," bearing the American Flag which he placed between the divided nation, and said, "Remember, ye are brethren." Instantly the inhabitants, casting from them their weapons became friends once more, and united around the National Standard.

" She showed him two episodes and the third began thusly: 'And again I heard the mysterious voice saying, 'Son of the Republic, look and learn.' At this the dark, shadowy angel placed a trumpet to his mouth and blew three distinct blasts; and taking water from the ocean, he sprinkled it upon Europe, Asia, and Africa. Then my eyes beheld a fearful scene: from each of these countries arose thick, black clouds that were joined into one. And throughout this mass there gleamed a dark red light by which I saw hordes of armed men, who, moving with the cloud, marched by land and sailed by sea to America, which country was enveloped in the volume of the cloud. And I dimly saw these vast armies devastate the whole country and burn the villages, towns, and cities that I beheld were springing up. As my ears listened to the thundering of the cannon, clashing of swords, and the shouts and cries of millions in mortal combat, I heard again the mysterious voice saying, 'Son of the Republic, look and learn.' When the voice had ceased, the dark, shadowy angel placed his trumpet once more to his mouth and blew a long and fearful blast.

" 'Instantly a light as of a thousand suns shone down from above me, and pierced and broke into fragments the dark cloud which enveloped America. At the same moment the angel, upon whose head still shone the word "Union," and who bore our national flag in one hand and a sword in the other, descended from the heavens, attended by legions of white spirits. These immediately joined the inhabitants of America, who I perceived were well-nigh overcome, but who immediately taking courage again, closed up their broken ranks and renewed the battle. Again, amid the fearful noise of the conflict, I heard the mysterious voice saying, 'Son of the Republic, look and learn.' As the voice ceased, the shadowy angel for the last time dipped water from the ocean and sprinkled it upon America. Instantly the dark cloud rolled back, together with the armies it had brought, leaving the inhabitants of the land victorious.

" 'Then once more I beheld the villages, towns, and cities springing up where I had seen them before, while the bright angel, planting the azure standard he had brought in the midst of them, cried with a loud voice, 'While the stars remain, and the heavens send down dew upon the earth, so long shall the Union last.' And taking from his brow the crown on which was blazoned the word "Union," he placed it upon the Standard, while the people, kneeling down, said, 'Amen.'

" 'The scene instantly began to fade and dissolve, and I at last saw nothing but the rising, curling vapor I at first beheld. This also disappearing, I found myself once more gazing upon the mysterious visitor, who, in the same voice I had heard before, said, 'Son of the Republic, what you have seen is thus interpreted: Three great perils will come upon the Republic. The most fearful is the third, passing which the whole world united shall not prevail against her. Let every child of the Republic learn to live for his God, his land, and the Union.

" ' With these words the vision vanished, and I started from my seat, and felt that I had seen a vision wherein had been shown me the birth, progress, and destiny of the United States.'

"Such, my friends," concluded the venerable narrator, "were the words I heard from General Washington's own lips, and America will do well to profit by them."

SIGNING OF THE DECLARATION OF INDEPENDENCE:
Speech of the Unknown[4]
The following is from
"Washington and His Generals: or, Legends of the Revolution" by George Lippard, published in 1847.

(NOTE: The Declaration was approved on July 4, 1776. But, it was signed later. Most signed on August 2nd.)

On August 2, 1776, a stifling hot day in Philadelphia, in a locked room, fifty-six delegates stymied in fear as they contemplated signing the Declaration of Independence that they had completed. An unknown man boldly interrupted their discussion of potential dire repercussions to themselves if they signed. Within his stirring speech, which motivated the previously quaking men to sign the Declaration, were the following words:

"Gibbet? They may stretch our necks on all the gibbets in the land—they may turn every rock into a scaffold—every tree into a gallows, every home into a grave, and yet the words on that Parchment (say)

".... to the coward-kings these words will speak, but not in tones of flattery. No, no! They will speak like the flaming syllables on Belshazzar's wall—
THE DAYS OF YOUR PRIDE AND GLORY ARE NUMBERED!
THE DAYS OF JUDGEMENT AND REVOLUTION DRAW NEAR!

"Yes, that Parchment will speak to the Kings in a language sad and terrible as the trump of the Archangel. You have trampled on mankind long enough. At last the voice of human woe has pierced the ear of God, and called His Judgment down!. . .

"And shall we falter now? And shall we start back appalled when our feet press the very threshold of Freedom? Do I see quailing faces around me, when our wives have been butchered—when the hearthstones of our land are red with the blood of little children?

"...methinks I stand among the awful clouds which veil the brightness of Jehovah's throne. Methinks I see the Recording Angel—pale as an angel is pale, weeping as an angel can weep—come trembling up to that Throne, and speak his dread message—

"'Father! the old world is baptized in blood! Father, it is drenched with the blood of millions, butchered in war, in persecution, in slow and grinding oppression! Father—look, with one glance of Thine Eternal eye, look over Europe, Asia, Africa, and behold evermore, that terrible sight, man trodden down beneath the oppressor's feet—nations lost in blood—Murder and Superstition walking hand in hand over the graves of their victims, and not a single voice to whisper, "Hope to Man!" '

"He stands there, the Angel, his hands trembling with the black record of human guilt. But hark! The voice of Jehovah speaks out from the awful cloud—'Let there be light again. Let there be a New World. Tell my people—the poor—the trodden down millions, to go out from the Old World. Tell them to go out from wrong, oppression and blood—tell them to go out from this Old World—to build my altar in the New!'

Isaiah 10:20-21 (NRSV) On that day the remnant of Israel and the survivors of the house of Jacob will no more lean on the one who struck them, but will lean on the LORD, the Holy One of Israel, in truth. 21 A remnant will return, the remnant of Jacob, to the mighty God.

"Sign—and not only for yourselves, but for all ages. For that Parchment will be the Text-book of Freedom—the Bible of the Rights of Man forever!

"Sign—for that declaration will go forth to American hearts forever, and speak to those hearts like the voice of God! And its work will not be done, until throughout this wide Continent not a single inch of ground owns the sway of a British King!

"Nay, do not start and whisper with surprise! It is a truth, your own hearts witness it, God proclaims it.—This Continent is the property of a free people, and their property alone. [17-second applause] God, I say, proclaims it!

"As God lives, my friends, I believe that to be his voice! Yes, were my soul trembling on the wing for Eternity, were this hand freezing in death, were this voice choking with the last struggle, I would still, with the last impulse of that soul, with the last wave of that hand, with the last gasp of that voice, implore you to remember this truth—God has given America to the free!

[13-second applause]

"Yes, as I sank down into the gloomy shadows of the grave, with my last gasp, I would beg you to sign that Parchment, in the name of the God, who made the Savior who redeemed you—in the name of the millions whose very breath is now hushed in intense expectation, as they look up to you for the awful words—'You are free!' "

[9-second applause]

(And) "then, the work was done."

NOTE: By signing the Declaration, our American founders were guilty of high treason under British law. The penalty for high treason was to be hanged by the neck until unconscious, then cut down and revived, then disemboweled and cut into quarters. The head and quarters were at the disposal of the crown.

Luke 12:4 (NRSV) "I tell you, my friends, do not fear those who kill the body, and after that can do nothing more.

Revelation 5:5 (NRSV) Then one of the elders said to me, "Do not weep. See, the Lion of the tribe of Judah, the Root of David, has conquered, so that he can open the scroll and its seven seals."

II.
America is key to the freedom of the people of the world

"What does it mean to say that we live in a Christian nation?

"What this really means is that our core principles, in fact, we share even across the political spectrum. The idea of the preciousness of human life. the dignity of human beings, equality, the idea of compassion, these are all the legacy of Christianity.

"The proof, by the way, is to look at the world before Christianity in pre-Christian Greece and Rome. These values really did not exist, at least not in their current form.

"When Jefferson sat down to write where our rights come from, he could think of only one source: the Creator. It is the theological principle that we are created equal in the eyes of God.

"This notion of moral equality translates into a political corollary, which is that no man has the right to rule another the core principle of anti-slavery, but, very interestingly, the core principle of democracy.

"Because what's democracy based on? No man has the right to rule another without consent."[5] - Dinesh D'Souza

"It's not a right-left issue. It is a right-wrong issue. And America has been constant on the side of what the right is.

". . . when it comes down to it, this is about keeping faith with the idea of America, isn't it? I mean Ireland is a great country, but it is not an idea. . . .That is how we see you around the world, as one of the greatest ideas of human history. . . .You and me are created equal. If there is an injustice? Then leave it to us. We'll do the rest.

"This country was the first to claw its way out of darkness and put that on paper. These aren't just American ideas anymore. There's no copyright on them. You brought them into the world. These truths – your truths – they are self-evident in (all of) us." – U2's Bono.

In today's world, the United States of America is the only country that was founded on the central principle of freedom to worship God, the Creator, as each individual chooses. This means without persecution or negative repercussion from government or society. America is key to the world peoples' Freedom under God and the only significant opposition to the quickly expanding atheistic agenda, expressed by socialism, communism, and globalism.

God and God-principles are acknowledged in all our founding documents: the Declaration of Independence, and the Constitution with its Bill of Rights. The FIRST Amendment to the Constitution in the Bill of Rights states: "Congress shall make no law respecting an establishment of religion, or prohibiting the free exercise thereof, or abridging freedom of speech, or of the press; or the right of the people peaceably to assemble, and to petition the Government for a redress of grievances."

The constitutions of all 50 states in our republic acknowledge the sovereignty of God.

The Almighty God, I AM WHO I AM, is the only Love, Wisdom, and Power Who can fully protect the United States of America and its God-Promise.

What foundational elements of our country are significant and essential to understand?
Over the years, all of the initially clear principles supporting the ideas of a free county have been under constant attack by opportunistic forces. They are working tirelessly to make governments the people's gods. Only in a free country do individuals have the freedom to author their own lives. Only in a free country is this freedom encouraged and protected,

Political, media, medical, and economic forces have become increasingly aggressive in their manipulation of vulnerable groups of people. They use twisted caricatures of God-principles to ensnare individuals into their hidden, enslaving, and corrupt agendas.

There are four cornerstones of civilization within which the collection of our smallest choices create powerful outcomes. These include:
1. Will you be a subject or citizen?
2. What form of wealth creation will characterize our future civilization?
3. What type of law will we be ruled by, i.e. from where are the people given their rights?
4. What form of government will be used?

Daily, it seems like we are only dealing with choices much smaller than those which will influence systems as grand as these above. But, it is the small choices on which we build the greatest freedom, happiness, and success, or the most dismal suffering and failure. As we sow, so we reap.

Subject or citizen?
Will we choose to be subjects, production units, where the government tells us how to think and live? Or will we choose to be citizens with the freedom to author our own lives?

Subject. A subject is dependent, being significantly under the rule or authority of a sovereign, state, or some governing power. A subject does not often have a reliable, effective way to address wrongs or grievances inflicted by the sovereign power. A subject is compelled to give obedience to their government and its leaders. Grassroots individuals have no genuine authority or truly respected voice in what is justice or what the policies of their country are, or who are their leaders. Subjects are forced into lives closely defined and mandated by the government and compulsory military service as demanded.

We Americans are citizens of our country. That is, we are participants in our America's prosperity or its demise. We vote, express our opinions freely, support leaders as we choose, and generally have a significant say in what methods and outcomes are sustained. We are governed by our consent. Our rights and the process of law are protected by the constitution of our land. We consciously give our allegiance toward the preservation of God's Principles in our country and as a beacon of God's Light to the masses of God's Children everywhere. Immigrants are still coming in waves of hopeful humanity to our shores for these reasons. Patriot citizens work for justice in their country and willingly help protect it when necessary.

Method of building wealth. Every large civilization requires the production of wealth from which the state is sustained and the people support their lives. There are only two broad categories across all known human history.

The conquest ethic.[6] Most of the world has been, and now uses, the conquest ethic. In the conquest ethic, the wealth of others is stolen. This is accomplished by violent force, coercion, manipulation, transfer, deceit, stealth, or some clever combination of these. But, it does not change the principle or the intent. It is theft: conscious, deliberate stealing. It is an act of war on the well-being and freedom of its victims.

When the target for conquest is well defended, including a country with superior military might and/or financial supply, the covert, secret, and subversive methods of conquest are applied. Today, this is the conquest method of choice. It is called asymmetric warfare. Some of the advantages of asymmetric warfare are:

- collateral damage is greatly reduced, i.e. less of the stuff they want to steal, e.g. factories, power generation plants, buildings, production units (people) etc., is destroyed;

- most of the population will not even know they are being threatened or will not understand the real source of the threat – until it is too late, and

- it costs a lot less. And those with patience and persistence can sneak up on and increasingly, degrade and weaken the enemy.

If you live under the conquest ethic, are you a citizen or subject?

America is founded in entrepreneurism. This means each of us takes personal responsibility to contribute to the prosperity of the whole by striving to earn support for oneself and our family. Any of us has the freedom and the opportunity to expand our effort into an enterprise that will offer respectable opportunity for others to earn a fair wage. This also contributes to the overall economic stability and prosperity of our communities and the country at-large.

Unfortunately, and often deliberately, entrepreneurism is confused with corporatism, the insatiable lust for money and power that has no qualms about taking advantage of others, even by means of deceit, coercion, or force. These huge businesses are conquest-ethic entities, encroaching within our republic like robbers. The American legal system is built to keep up with their shenanigans and make their unjust tactics illegal. There is a great deal of wealth that is competing against justice is these situations. Protecting and maintaining justice is a constant battle.

If you live under entrepreneurism, are you a citizen or subject?

Systems of Law

Napoleonic Law. The form called Napoleonic Law attempts to specify, by human intellect, everything that could go wrong, how to handle it, and what penalties to apply to offenders. In this system, it is the state and its laws that give the people their rights and privileges – and the state that can take them away.

If you live under any form of Napoleonic Law, are you a subject or citizen?

America's system of law is founded on Natural Law. In contrast to law based solely in the contrivances of the human intellect, the foundation of our American system of law is Natural Law, which acknowledges the Supreme Being, the Creator. It is God Who grants unalienable rights to each of mankind. Our system of law is charged with protecting those rights from infringement by the government or anybody else.

This is why the 10 Commandments are/were often placed in close proximity to courts. Interestingly, there is an almost identical set of laws in every major religion.

"Man . . . must necessarily be subject to the laws of his Creator.. This will of his Maker is called the law of nature. . .. This law of nature. . .is of course superior to any other. . .. No human laws are of any validity, if contrary to this: and such of them as are valid derive all their force. . .from this original." - Sir William Blackstone, eminent English jurist

"Natural Law has been called the ultimate source of constitutional law. Under Natural Law, God is the author and giver of all rights to people. This form of law consists of binding rules of moral behavior from God and the way He created reality and mankind. Natural law is law that is held to exist independently and above the law of a given political order, society, nation-state, or national ruler.

"The Founders of the United States of America DID NOT establish the Constitution for the purpose of granting rights. Rather, they established this government of laws (not a government of men) in order to secure each person's Creator-endowed rights to life, liberty, and property. Only in America, did a nation's founders recognize that rights are endowed by the Creator as unalienable prerogatives".[7]

If you live under Natural Law, are you a citizen or subject?

The countries that are governed in adherence to natural law have historically been countries of British source, though others have manifestos that may seem to contain the same principles. Check out the outcomes carefully. These two systems of law have very different paradigms.

There is considerable pressure currently in America to degrade our system to the government being given the authority to grant or remove rights. If that takes place, our people would become subjects, rather than citizens.

Form of government

The prominent forms of government that are germane to our world today include:

Monarchy. A system of government ruled by one person, a king or queen, who has usually inherited their authority and kingdom. Monarchies most often give rise to an aristocracy with bloodline connection to the monarch and/or privileges granted and upheld by the monarch.

Aristocracy can usually also be passed on as an inheritance. The social system stemming from a monarchy in medieval Europe was called feudalism. The system of law here is a precursor of Napoleonic Law. Saudi Arabia is a current form of pure monarchy.

Are those living under a monarchy subjects or citizens?

Socialism. Socialism is an atheistic collective. In a socialist system, all means of production, distribution, and wealth are owned and controlled by the "people." The stated motive is to use the means of production for what is in the "best" interest of the people, to remove competition among them, and not focus on profit. It advocates a classless society. However, those in the government make all the decisions on who is given what by the state. Socialism, like communism, has a highly controlled voting process. Demark is an example of socialism. Here is a video by a Cuban who windsurfed to escape socialism.[8] Though socialism is often described as a form of government, it is actually an economic system.

Are those living in a socialist country subjects or citizens?

Communism. In communism, all property is owned by the State. Theoretically, people work and are given things according to their abilities and needs. The government controls everything. It is the sole giver of benefits, such as money, healthcare, and food. The Marxist credo is materialistic and atheistic. It is a one-party police state with a centralized command economy and incessant communist rhetoric. "Voting" is highly controlled; the government chooses all candidates. China has instituted a "social credits' system for residents[9] and foreign businesses. It has also been revealed that they are doing live organ harvesting using religious and ethnic prisoners[10]. For current trends in the worldwide communist agenda, check out this video.[11] China is an example of communism. Its base is also in Marxism.

For an eye-witness account of how communists infiltrate countries and overthrow their governments, this short, poignant book is recommended.[12]

Are those living in a communist country subjects or citizens?

Fascism. Fascism is a one-party dictatorship. This form of government suppresses individual freedoms, voting by the populace is denied, and opposing opinion is not tolerated. Companies and production may be owned by selected individuals, but are completely controlled by the government. This was the beginning of modern corporatism. Fascist regimes tend to exhibit severe nationalism and militarism. Historically, fascism was considered as an extreme leftist phenomenon. World War II Germany and Italy are examples of fascism.

Are those living in a fascist country subjects or citizens?

Corporatism. By the old definition: corporatism was the control of a country by large interest groups and/or organization of society by corporate groups, such as agricultural, labor, military, scientific, or guild associations on the basis of their common interests. Today, corporatism consists of huge, multinational businesses. With recent rulings in the World Court, corporations have been bestowed with "legal" rights usually reserved for human beings. Due to their rapidly growing size, extreme wealth, and, thereby, power, they are threatening to override country sovereignties. For example, in the European Union, they may sue countries who refuse them access to their markets. They may also demand financial retribution for losses they incur due to the laws created by a country – e.g. for worker safety or equal pay - in which they do business.[13] The European Union is a megaregion governed by corporatism.

Corporatism, which includes the banking sector, is a very aggressive, though expertly hidden force in today's world.

Are those living under corporatism subjects or citizens?

<u>Techno-fascism.</u> This rising worldwide subculture is made up of "tech-lords" who consider themselves outside of all mainstream governments and their politics. A number of them are proclaiming their supreme ability to decide what is right and wrong for the rest of us. They possess an expanding power to act on their assumptions.

Most "techno-fascism" partners with governments or factions within countries for power. For example, Dr. Robert Epstein testified to the US Judiciary Subcommittee that, according to his research, Google influenced between 8 to 13 million votes in the 2016 presidential election.[14] Communist China has enacted mass surveillance to create social credit scores for greater control over their people.[15] In April 2019, Elon Musk announced a brain implant designed to hook a person directly into artificial intelligence and the internet. He predicted it would be on the market within one year[16]

Are those living under techno-fascism subjects or citizens?

<u>Democracy.</u> In a democracy, the majority votes to directly make laws. Basically, in a pure democracy, the majority has unlimited power.

John Adams, an American founder, wrote that "There never was a democracy yet that did not commit suicide." James Madison wrote in *Federalist 10* that "Democracies have, in general, been as short in their lives as they have been violent in their deaths." Historically, in democracies, demagogic leaders become adept at appealing to the emotions of jealousy, avarice, and entitlement. They also denigrate opponents in order to justify prejudicial actions taken by the majority. Soon, oppression of minority classes causes enough conflicts to collapse the democratic process."[17] Iceland is an example of a democracy. It is a small, homogeneous country of 339,031. (Wyoming, the smallest US state, has 577,737 people.)

Are those living in a democracy subjects or citizens?

<u>Republic.</u> In a republic, ultimate power is held by the people and their elected representatives. It has an elected or nominated president, rather than a monarch. There is no hereditary aristocracy. In a republic, a written constitution limits the majority and provides safeguards for individuals and minorities. Laws are made by representatives chosen by the people and who

must conform to the constitution. Voting by the people for self-nominated representatives, proposed referendums, etc. is done at local levels. That is why the US is often called a democracy within a republic. The word "democracy" is not mentioned anywhere in the Constitution of the United Stated of America. The United States of America is a republic.[17]

"We the people are the rightful masters of both Congress and the courts, not to overthrow the Constitution but to overthrow the men who pervert the Constitution."[18] - Abraham Lincoln

Are those living in a republic subjects or citizens?

Neither our lives nor our republic will be saved by an entitlement mindset. Entitlement mindset is marked by the absolute conviction that one has a right to guaranteed benefits, without personal effort, responsibility, or gratitude.

Grace is not an entitlement program!
Yes, God's Grace is the only power that can save us. Good works will not do it. However, Our Father and Jesus are not offering to carry us to heaven like a sack of potatoes, without our lifting a finger to help! Grace is a <u>reciprocal</u> covenant between Our Father and we His Children.

How many of us have become too egocentric, busy, shortsighted, uninformed, and apathetic to bother to be obedient to Jesus' Great Command for a genuine, reciprocal, love relationship with Our Father God and those around us? How many of us now invest our time and attention to such a relationship with God?

<u>Matthew 22:37-40</u> (NRSV) (Jesus) said to him, "You shall love the Lord your God with all your heart, and with all your soul, and with all your mind.' [38] This is the greatest and first commandment. [39] And a second is like it: 'You shall love your neighbor as yourself.' [40] On these two commandments hang all the law and the prophets."

How many of us treat Jesus only as an appointed mediator charged with making sure we get through heaven's gate, by his carrying us through? How genuine and just is our side of the relationship with Our Father and with Jesus?

If we have formed an attitude of entitlement to any degree, we are well on the way to becoming subjects of a tyrannical power that has the intention of taking over and dismantling all the good and potential good God has placed here in America and on the Earth.

<u>1 Corinthians 13:11</u> (RSV) When I was a child, I spoke like a child, I thought like a child, I reasoned like a child; when I became an adult, I put an end to childish ways.

Time to wake up!

When asked why God had not intervened in a current crisis of mankind, the Rev. Billy Graham replied, "God is a gentleman." He went on to explain that God does not intervene in our lives and affairs unless we invite him. That is true for America and any other country, city, town, neighborhood, family, or individual.

We are not entitled to a free-ride intervention from God without us inviting Him into our lives and nurturing a reciprocal, loving relationship with Him. We need to step up and give justice to our Father God for all His Blessings over the generations – to give Him justice for the Gift of LIFE itself. This is our part of our covenant of Grace with God, the I AM.

If we have ignored these most important personal responsibilities, the cause is our free will disobedience to God's Law of Love, spoken by Jesus, and the dishonoring of true justice.

Free will does not mean we get to set the rules or change the curriculum of God's classroom called "life." We do get to choose when we decide to learn it. This wondrous, multi-dimensional, learning space is wired for the victory of Love. It is the only happy, satisfying, rewarding, and sustainable choice. If we make choices outside Jesus' Great Command, we reap unhappiness, lack, dis-ease, and suffering.

The solution is simple. Stand up, turn around, and face the I AM!

Invite God and Jesus, with true conviction and free-will collaboration, into our lives, country, and all that matters. This necessarily entails:

- entering a reciprocal love relationship with God,
- striving to lead just, obedient lives, fulfilling Jesus' Great Command and Golden Rule;
- assuming responsibility to produce and contribute worth using the talents and abilities with which God has endowed us. This is not only measured in money, but needs to come from our hearts and souls; and
- feeling and expressing genuine gratitude.

As beloved members of God's Family, we have other responsibilities, which are Biblical acts of stewardship. Stewardship is defined as the position and duties of a steward, a person who acts as the surrogate of another, especially by managing property, financial affairs, an estate, etc. It is the responsible overseeing and protection of something considered worth caring for and preserving.[19]

Jesus tells us about the responsibilities of stewardship.

Matthew 25:14-30, (NRSV) The Parable of the Talents "For it is as if a man, going on a journey, summoned his slaves and entrusted his property to them; [15] to one he gave five talents,[a] to another two, to another one, to each according to his ability. Then he went away.*

[16] The one who had received the five talents went off at once and traded with them, and made five more talents. [17] In the same way, the one who had the two talents made two more talents. [18] But the one who had received the one talent went off and dug a hole in the ground and hid his master's money.

[19] After a long time the master of those slaves came and settled accounts with them. [20] Then the one who had received the five talents came forward, bringing five more talents, saying, 'Master, you handed over to me five talents; see, I have made five more talents.' [21] His master said to him, 'Well done, good and trustworthy slave; you have been trustworthy in a few things, I will put you in charge of many things; enter into the joy of your master.' [22] And the one with the two talents also came forward, saying, 'Master, you handed over to me two talents; see, I have made two

more talents.' [23] His master said to him, 'Well done, good and trustworthy slave; you have been trustworthy in a few things, I will put you in charge of many things; enter into the joy of your master.'

[24] Then the one who had received the one talent also came forward, saying, 'Master, I knew that you were a harsh man, reaping where you did not sow, and gathering where you did not scatter seed; [25] so I was afraid, and I went and hid your talent in the ground. Here you have what is yours.'

[26] But his master replied, 'You wicked and lazy slave! You knew, did you, that I reap where I did not sow, and gather where I did not scatter? [27] Then you ought to have invested my money with the bankers, and on my return I would have received what was my own with interest. [28] So take the talent from him, and give it to the one with the ten talents. [29] For to all those who have, more will be given, and they will have an abundance; but from those who have nothing, even what they have will be taken away. [30] As for this worthless slave, throw him into the outer darkness, where there will be weeping and gnashing of teeth.'

[a] Matthew 25:15: (NRSV) A talent was worth more than fifteen years' wages of a laborer.

Isn't stewardship really a gesture of love, gratitude, respect, relationship, and collaboration? Aren't the free will offerings of stewardship truly giving justice back to God for all His Love and all He has given us as an expression of His Love? These sound more like opportunities than responsibilities!

George Washington, in his first inaugural speech on April 30, 1789, asserted, "The preservation of the sacred fire of liberty ...(is)... entrusted to the hand of the American people."

Our most pressing role and responsibility in these times is the greatest call to God, the I AM, ever delivered by mankind!

Our greatest role and responsibility in today's crisis, as Children of God and those who profess Jesus as Christ, is to actively start, organize, deliver, and sustain the greatest collective invitation to God for His Intervention as has EVER been delivered by the mankind of earth! We must stand and face Him with love, gratitude, confidence, and joy. Then, we make the Call for the deliverance of all our people and the deliverance of our beloved America. Our Father and Jesus love her, too. They were the guiding, creating Presence at her birth.

While our government leaders can be positive collaborators and influencers, no government by itself can fix humanity.

America will be great only if she is good.

Mark 10:18 (RSV) "Why do you call me good?" Jesus answered. "No one is good—except God alone."

Keeping America will take a similar kind of courage as it took to sign the Declaration of Independence. And it will need to be founded on the informed knowledge and appreciation of what the United States of America represents in terms of the freedom and prosperity of all mankind under God's Justice and God's Law.

"We have been assured, sir, in the sacred writings, that 'except the Lord build the house they labor in vain that build it.' I firmly believe this; and I also believe that without His concurring aid we shall succeed in this political building no better than the builders of Babel; we shall be divided by our little partial, local interests, our projects will be *confounded and we ourselves shall become a reproach and a byword down to future ages. And, what is worse, mankind may hereafter, from this unfortunate instance, despair of establishing government by human wisdom and leave it to chance, war, or conquest."[20] – Benjamin Franklin*

We will need to educate ourselves on the tactics of those who have declared themselves our enemy. Jesus asked us to love our enemies. He did not advise us to adopt or be ruled by their lawlessness and debauchery or to allow ourselves to go down under their authority and become their slaves. And we must never hate or condemn them.

Our greatest demonstration of love is to our fellow humans is to:

- love God and ourselves enough to remain free,
- rescue our "enemies" and restore them to wellbeing and freedom, and
- open the opportunity for them to choose God, thereby assisting Jesus in the fulfillment of his sacred mission.

We will have to pass all this faithfully and competently from generation to generation for it to be sustainable.

Remember! America = I AM race!

Our country is currently in the final stages of two asymmetric wars. The secondary war is aimed at the total conquest of America and all for which it stands. The primary war was begun eons ago in the garden of Eden. It is the war the devil declared on the I AM WHO I AM, the Creator, and on us, God's Children. America is the last powerful bastion standing for God and His Love.

III.
Where we are now

"America will never be destroyed from the outside. If we falter and lose our freedoms, it will be because we destroyed ourselves. … Nations do not die from invasion; they die from internal rottenness." - Abraham Lincoln

"Those who want to reap the benefits of this great nation must bear the fatigue of supporting it." - Thomas Paine

"Don't expect to build up the weak by pulling down the strong." - Calvin Coolidge

Ephesians 6:12 (NRSV) For our struggle is not against enemies of blood and flesh, but against the rulers, against the authorities, against the cosmic powers of this present darkness, against the spiritual forces of evil in the heavenly places.

A number of things you read in this book are likely to make you uncomfortable at first. Be brave! Dare to consider the fuller truth. Check out what is "behind" the endnote numbers.

Remember evil - the devil - lies. He also glamorizes and falsely "justifies" his deceptions to make them more easily swallowed. He uses our goodness, compassion, empathy, and desire for true justice for all and twists them with his egoism, selfishness, hatred, and his desire to tear down all that is of God.

Here are some clues to detect his undermining of righteousness. He is a master of divide and conquer. Separating us is his primary strategy. This includes separating the Children of the I AM from Our Father God and Jesus Christ, from each other, and even within ourselves. His minions loudly and falsely criticize those of God for the devilish schemes and debauchery of which they themselves are guilty. Evil has collected many minions, amalgamating them into blocks of power. They seem to attack us separately, but still from all sides. The superficial separations are an illusion. They are connected and coordinated.

The devil is a merciless maestro of fear and hatred. **Anything that tries to get us to hate or condemn, all that tells us it is OK or necessary to harm or destroy another Child of God – regardless of that person's opinions or behaviors - is not of God.**

Malachi 2:10 (NRSV) have we not all one father? Has not one God created us? Why then are we faithless to one another, profaning the covenant of our ancestors?

Like a magician's tricks, these divide us and divert our attention away from themselves, masking their true intentions.

This is a comprehensive beginning of that wretchedly difficult, fear-ridden, and uncomfortable conversation that we all need to have together. And it must be soon. Only together – in sustained civil discourse – will we discover and unite all the pieces of truth and wisdom.

The Third Episode of Washington's Vision is upon us. America is under attack from all sides. So far, this is an asymmetric war. Instead of conventional warfare, the weapons are lies, deceit, treachery, and treason - treason against God and all that is of love and justice.

These are warning signals. Every warning is also an opportunity and an invitation from Our Father to return higher into His enfolding Love and Protection. All these are opportunities to remove the blinders, see the truth of our situation — and bring Him and Jesus into active solutions.

"Most men would rather deny a hard truth than face it." - George R. R. Martin, Game of Thrones

The first volley that finally penetrated the distracted attention of the mass of American citizenry came from Asia in the form of the CCP virus or COVID-19. Let's do a very quick overview of what we suffered and are still suffering from this pandemic and then we'll dig down.

The globalist-connected[21], medical experts immediately:

- endorsed projections from severely flawed prediction models,
  - producing devastating fear throughout America and the world,
- significantly misrepresented actual COVID-19 caused mortality rates,[22]
- denounced Hydroxychloroquine, proven safe over decades,
  - which suddenly became virtually unavailable in the market,
- encouraged dangerously fast-tracking of a new vaccine,[23]
- advocated mandatory vaccinations with dire, unconstitutional consequences for noncompliance,[24] and
- extolled the necessity of mandatory contract tracking, again with consequences for disobedience.[25]

In the name of their predisposed strategy, without balancing expert opinion, they:

- closed our churches, refusing us our right to worship and communion with God together, for the support and relief of our families,
- inflicted upon us their "official" denial of our right to meet together at all - even accidentally while passing on the sidewalk, (without being at least six feet apart, even when masked),
- compelled lockdowns, forcing us to stay at home and closing businesses.

How do these points stack with our Constitutional rights protected by the First Amendment,[26] which states: Congress shall make no law respecting an establishment of religion or prohibiting the free exercise thereof, or abridging the freedom of speech or of the press, or the right of the people peaceably to assemble and to petition the government for a redress of grievances.

They have demanded that we close our businesses, suspend employment, and watch our income cut off and all we have built dissolve.

They have placed at risk our futures and personal recovery - even potentially crashing our national economy.

Do these lists of demands, taken to the levels to which they were forced, violate our 4th and 5th Amendment rights as well?

- 4th Amendment of the Bill of Rights of the Constitution of the United States of America: The right of the people to be secure in their persons, houses, papers, and effects against unreasonable searches and seizures shall not be violated,[27]
- 5th Amendment : No person shall be …be deprived of life, liberty, or property without due process of law; . . .[28]

Further, they have infused unnecessarily, extreme fear on our people, not only of the virus, but unreasonable fear of each other.

They have also forced genuine, principled, medical professionals into a multiplicity of compromising positions:

- corrupting their Hippocratic oath to "do no harm", and
- demanding they deny access for families of those hospitalized and even deprived them of being present at the deaths of loved ones from whatever cause.

Even our elected Congress may not lawfully do these things! How can these unelected, medical "experts" accomplish that? These draconian measures would only have been justifiable if their predictions and their subsequent reporting where true. Their predictions were wildly faulty and their reporting fabricated.

We have allowed their deceitful appeals to our goodness to become, in reality, a fascist overreach of power, well beyond all reason and decency. We, the good people of America, did the best we could to protect ourselves, our neighbors, and our people, by cooperating with corrupt and conflict-ridden advice hidden under a veil of expertise.

Many are coming forward to expose the deception and mishandling of the pandemic by the medical "experts."[29]

America and the countries of the world are being milked ruthlessly for the last drop of strength, hope, courage, economic supply, relationship, endurance, and wellbeing. And the globalist-connected medicos are working to promote a second wave of their fascist lockdown.

Outside of the direct cost of actual COVID-19 deaths, the physical, emotional, and mental crises directly related to the lockdowns skyrocketed. <u>Competent statistical analyses have calculated that anxiety reactions to COVID-19 lockdowns will destroy at least seven times more years of life than can be saved by lockdowns.</u>[30] This does not take into account increased loses connected to substance use, death from overdose, increased suicide, delayed diagnosis of serious illness, or domestic violence. Nor is personal and national economic loss and its repercussions measured. The cost in human suffering due to the lockdowns has well exceeded the toll of COVID-19.

Mental Health Crisis in America

A survey of US adults in June 2020, revealed that 41% of them were experiencing at least one harmful mental or behavioral health condition, related to the lockdown. The Centers for Disease Control (CDC) revealed in an August 14, 2020 Morbidity and Mortality report, that 71% of young adults, aged 18-24, are reporting at least one adverse condition. [31]

Henna Marie, a vibrant and articulate European woman, offers an eloquent and emotionally charged plea for the voiceless victims of the pandemic lockdown. She summarizes the costs in terms of human quality of life and loss of essential freedom.[32]

Exposure of massive child trafficking In May 2020, as the medical tents were being removed from Central Park, a friend of mine, who is a pastor in New Work City, stopped to talk with one of the nurses, who was packing up. My friend asked if the tents had really been set up for COVID-19 patients, as she'd heard that they were never at capacity with those individuals.

"Oh no," the nurse responded. "They were set up to treat the children being rescued from the tunnels."

This is an indicator of a truly horrific and devastating reality of child trafficking that, having been refused by the mass media, is just now getting out to the American people.[33]

Ephesians 6:12 (NRSV) For our struggle is not against enemies of blood and flesh, but against the rulers, against the authorities, against the cosmic powers of this present darkness, against the spiritual forces of evil in the heavenly places.

Sent from outside our communities, trained rioters and anarchists hijacked peaceful protests, turning our neighborhoods and cities into war zones. They created havoc, while many of the African Americans who are true residents of those neighborhoods and who were peacefully protesting, pled with them not to be violent.

"Acting out is a substitute for conscious remembering." Sigmund Freud

The inciters shouted for justice, accusing others of heinous crimes, while denying rights and justice for the neighbors, business owners, and law enforcement officers, who lived and worked in those neighborhoods. Drawing some of the residents into the mayhem, the outsiders led the looting and burning of private and public property, beating and even killing those who opposed them. A number of low-income housing units were set ablaze. Where did the residents find shelter? What about the loss of their worldly possessions?

Again, how do these instigators fare when measured on scales of justice?

- The 4th Amendment of the Bill of Rights of the Constitution of the United States of America claims: The right of the people to be secure in their persons, houses, papers, and effects against unreasonable searches and seizures shall not be violated,
- 5th Amendment says: No person shall be held to answer for a capital or otherwise infamous crime…, …nor be deprived of life, liberty, or property without due process of law; nor shall private property be taken for public use without just compensation.

Matthew 5:22 (RSV) But I say unto you, That whosoever is angry with his brother without a cause shall be in danger of the judgment: and whosoever shall say to his brother, Raca, shall be in danger of the council: but whosoever shall say, Thou fool, shall be in danger of hell fire.

"Raca" is a term of utter contempt for another person. Jesus warned that its use was tantamount to murder and deserved severe punishment by law.[34] This advice is applicable across racial, socio-economic, and political lines.

Justice only flows from reciprocal love and respect. Justice must be reciprocal to be sustainable.

Here are some questions worth asking and points to be considered:

- Who is funding Black Lives Matter and Antifa[35]? And other paid rioters[36] from outside the communities where the riots and mayhem are being staged? (This third reference does not just make the point that anarchists are being paid, but illustrates the moral and cognitive bankruptcy of this group of paid lackeys.) Where does your donation to Black Lives Matter go?

- Muhammed Ali's son spoke out against the BLM.[37]

  Here are two African American sources overviewing the broader situation surrounding the George Floyd riots, plus the historic roots of the BLM movement.[38]

  At least 269 corporations,[39] a multitude of Hollywood actors, and other famous persons are funding the lawlessness and aiding in the legal defense of those arrested during and for their crimes. Where else in history have corporatists used their financial might?

  Here follows pivotal occurrences that have significantly contributed to where we are today.

- May 2019 in the newspaper *Chinese Daily*, the Chinese Communist Party declared a "people's war" in the United States of America.[40] This was not reported in the US mass media.

- Beginning of 2020 through the rioting
  CCP deploys Chinese soldiers on US soil.[41] Before and during the riots, through their Houston consulate on sovereign US soil, the Chinese Communist Party (CCP) deployed actual military soldiers and spying personnel, equipped with fake US IDs. The Chinese

spy personnel used "big data technology" to target individual Americans directly. They searched out individuals who, by their postings, indicated their willingness to participate in protests by Black Lives Matter and/or Antifa. They sent them videos of instructions on how to organize rioting and spread their message. *(This information just became available in August 2020.)*

- <u>January-June 2020</u> An influx of fake IDs spread throughout the US. Tens of thousands, coming mostly from China, were intercepted. Almost 20,000 were seized in Chicago O'Hare alone. Most were drivers licenses representing people in their twenties. [42]

- <u>June 2020</u>: protestors began tearing down or defacing historic statues across America. By the end of June, it had spread to Christian-related[43] buildings, monuments, and statues, including statues of Jesus.
    - "Trevor Loudon, communism expert and author, asserted that statue defacing happening across America is a 'Maoist tactic of erasing the form of culture...Maoism is about building a new man, a new society...You have to destroy all the remnants of the old society...so you can build a new society.' Loudon said that Marxist organizations such as Liberation Army and the Workers World Party have been involved."[44]

    - "Yang Jianli, a Chinese dissident and son of a former Communist Party leader who now heads the Citizen Power Initiatives for China, a pro-democracy NGO in the United States, also said the statue toppling was reminiscent of China's cultural revolution. "[It's] familiar in violence, anti-rule-of-law and political madness," he said. "The BLM protestors have crossed the line when they break or tear down the statues of America's Founding Fathers such as Washington and Jefferson. "[45]

    - "The Left (is pushing) to finally take down America," asserted Michael Walsh, author and contributor to The Epoch Times, "...In a thrice, riots have broken out, ...and whole areas of American cities are suddenly occupied by violent anarchists. How quickly the illegal COVID-19 lockdowns were forgotten in the name of "social justice"—and yet how long their unconstitutional effects have lingered.

        "It is as if somebody had given the signal, and suddenly, in 'blue' cities across the land, not only BLM and the Antifa punks have risen to show their true colors, but the politicians who run those cities as well......

        (And) "Presto, the national media now marches in Stalinist lockstep with the shibboleths of the BLM (Black Lives Matter), beginning with the demonstrably false accusation that cops are targeting young black males for extinction.

        "Make no mistake: This assault has been planned and coordinated for years to strike America where she is weakest: in her innate sense of rightness and fair play."[46]

What is the source and strategy of the riots?

It is germane here to note, once again, that 90% of the mainstream media in the United States is owned by only six multinational corporations. That means that "232 media executives control the information diet of 277 million Americans."[47]

- June 8, 2020: George Floyd's Family petitioned United Nations to help disarm police in the United States.[48] Apparently, without consulting authorities in the US for the facts, Michelle Bachelet, UN Commissioner on Human Rights, issued this public statement, "The US authorities must take serious action to stop such killings, and to ensure justice is done when they do occur. Procedures must change, prevention systems must be put in place, and above all police officers who resort to excessive use of force should be charged and convicted for the crimes committed.

  "The role that entrenched and pervasive racial discrimination plays in such deaths must also be fully examined, properly recognized and dealt with," she added.

  If she or anyone from the United Nations had consulted our government and others with the true facts, they would have seen and confirmed that this broadly spread lie is untrue.[49] It would also be known what extensive measures the US law enforcement agencies, at all levels, are pursuing to be sure injustice does not happen. The proliferation of false narrative is keeping the truth from been known by the terrorized public.

  What is the United Nations really interested in, if it is not truth and justice?

- June 2020 A number of US leaders and organizations have recently called for United Nations peace keeping forces to replace the local police departments in American cities. United Nations troops in our cities would constitute foreign troops on American soil. Under our Constitution, that would mean placing our people "under another jurisdiction" – which is against the Constitution of the United States of America. In many nations, the use of UN "peacekeepers" has been the prelude to the overthrow of their governments.[50]

  Any United Nation's troops deployed on American soil would be from other nations. UN troops have nothing invested in our communities, no relationship with our citizens or country, and have not taken any oath to uphold our Constitution or our laws. The do not recognize the authority of the USA federally, state, or locally. They have obedience only to the "new world order."

  Again, our Constitution forbids foreign troops on American soil. When taking the oath of office, an incoming president promises to uphold the Constitution. In 2016, a presidential executive order allowed use of United Nations forces on America soil with civilian populations.[51] (A website to find out from the United Nations itself how many of their troops are on American soil is included with this footnote.)

The first time the United Nations tried to take over the USA for inclusion in their "one world government" happened in 1951.[52]

- June 12, 2020: Orthodox Jews in New York city sued its mayor and the state's governor for their double standard of enforcement of COVID-19 lockdown. They kept the churches restricted, while granting permits for demonstrations. "Why is a large worship gathering deemed more dangerous than a mass protest, full of shouting, arm-waving people in close proximity to one another?" Christopher Ferrara, Thomas More Society special counsel, asked in a statement to Fox News.[53]

- June 2020 In a previously thriving, mid-sized, Midwest town, as the weeks of rioting began to lessen, the female leadership of the area was invited to an outdoor meeting to listen to a panel speak on justice and racial equality. About one hundred, mostly white women responded to the invitation. The panel, all black women, introduced themselves as Christians. As one attendee described, the panel then went into a serial tirade of venomous hatred against white privilege, punctuated liberally by the most vile profanity.[54]

Not much later, the Democratic mayor was presented with the demand to fire a list of forty of the city's employees and replace them with forty designated black people. One of the African American women on the sidelines perused the replacement list, and pointed to a man's name, saying, "This is an evil man!"[55]

"The riot zombies spray-painting and burning cop cars and smashing windows might ask themselves if they are truly anti-establishment when local governments, the UN, the Mainstream Media, major corporations, pop culture, and academia all agree with them, along with the vast majority of Americans who agree that George Floyd's murder was egregious.

"How are their demands 'counter-culture' when every major corporation has announced their support and donated generously to their cause? How rebellious is their revolution when the rioting is condoned by Democrat mayors, governors, and the entire DNC?" – Alexandra Bruce of Forbidden Knowledgetv.net

- June 24, 2020: Robert O'Brien, the national security adviser to President Donald Trump, asserted, "The days of American passivity and naivety regarding the People's Republic of China are over. ... America, under President Trump's leadership, has finally awoken to the threat of the Chinese Communist Party's actions and the threat they pose to our great way of life. ... As China grew richer and stronger, we believed that the Chinese Communist Party would liberalize to meet the rising democratic aspirations of its people. Unfortunately, (that) turned out to be very naive."
He made a point of saying he was not attacking the Chinese people, but the Chinese Communist Party. [56]

Christopher Wray, the director of the FBI, meanwhile, revealed that the bureau currently has more than 2,000 active investigations that trace back to the CCP. He told Fox News that over the past decade, there has been a roughly 1,300 percent increase in economic espionage probes with links to the Chinese regime.[57]

The Pentagon recently released a list of companies owned or controlled by the Chinese military, who are also engaged in exporting or providing production, manufacturing, or commercial services. [58]

- <u>July 3, 2020</u>: Wikipedia in their "List of revolutions and rebellions" had at the end of their list: "2020-present: George Floyd protests in the US ."[59]

- <u>July 2020</u>: A number of original leaders of Black Lives Matter resigned from the organization, stating that it had been hijacked by forces intent on overthrowing the US government. They affirmed that it had always been their intention to reform and improve from within the country.[60]

Many groups have recognized inequality and injustice, but most have insisted on the "right" to inflict injustice on others they conveniently blame for injustices to them, in which those blamed where not personally involved. A substantial amount of the rage has been created using falsehoods and fanned by those who actively seek the destruction of the United States of America.

This is all criminal insanity. And it is just the beginning, unless we take the apostle Paul's warning in Ephesians to heart. Alarming, but revealing patterns and connections are materializing. Keeping up our courage to maintain our focus on what God is revealing to His Children is crucial to our deliverance, more now than ever before.

The groups rioting do not have the wisdom germane to see how they are being misled and manipulated, or the wisdom to build sustainable justice and prosperity. We must uncloak both those inciting them, from behind the battle lines, and their true objectives.

Are we being tortured in a worldwide PsyOp?
Is what we're being put through in the COVID <u>plan</u>demic deliberate torture? This compelling video[61], under five minutes, compares Amnesty International's 1973 report on torture to the components of what we are living through in the world right now.

Amnesty says that the goals of torture are;
- "... the systematic and deliberate infliction of acute pain in any form by one person on another"
- "in order to accomplish the purpose of the former against the will of the latter."

The three major objectives within these goals are:
- Debility
- Dependency
- Dread

Signs of Americans rising together

In Seattle's, Chapel Hill Organized Protest (CHOP) zone, on June 20, 2020, good-hearted, innocent Horace Lorenzo Anderson, Jr., a special-needs youth aged 19, was shot to death. In the wake of the murder, his father, friend and family spokesperson Andre Taylor, and Sean Hannity had a discussion that resulted in fusing empathy and inspiring words of American solidarity.[62]

Community churches are coming together for serious, deep discussions toward advancing meaningful understanding, healing, and collaborative relationships across racial lines. [63] We need many, many more to step up.

The #WalkAlway movement is rapidly expanding. So much so, the BLM is starting to disrupt their events and attack members. [64] This movement encourages voters to leave the Democratic Party due to its of its modus operandi.

The American People are increasingly defying the curb on our assembling together. We are claiming our Constitutional rights.

Who is it that has set their lust for destruction and conquest on our fair land? America is the last stronghold of the free world under God's Law left in the world.

How did we get to the place where they thought we would be vulnerable to this multi-pronged attack?

Less than half of the remainder of this book briefly overviews how we got here when we weren't paying attention.

Much more importantly, the rest details how to put on the full armor of God and where our sure Victory awaits in readiness for our essential choice and commanding invocation.

But first, where did this all start?

IV.
The Fall

We are still living within the murky folds of the Fall of mankind. We've been snared in a cunningly designed, virtual concentration camp of guilt, agitation, fragmentation, and toxic diversity. It has its own pyramid scheme, where the players are rewarded with increasing earthly power and wealth, according to how many fellow humans they enslave and to what degree.

The Fall fractured our consciousness of our Unity with the I AM WHO I AM, Our Father God.

Let's take a closer look at what happened in the Fall.

Genesis 3:4-13 (NRSV):
⁴ But the serpent said to the woman, 'You will not die; ⁵ for God knows that when you eat of it your eyes will be opened, and you will be like God, knowing good and evil.' ⁶ So when the woman saw that the tree was good for food, and that it was a delight to the eyes, and that the tree was to be desired to make one wise, ...
What temptation was acting here? Egotism: self-centeredness, self-worship.

...she took of its fruit ...
What temptation was acting here? Selfishness.

and ate; and she also gave some to her husband, who was with her, and he ate. ...
What temptation was acting here? Disobedience.

⁷ Then the eyes of both were opened, and they knew that they were naked; and they sewed fig leaves together and made loincloths for themselves. ...
What temptation was acting here? Shame.

⁸ They heard the sound of the LORD God walking in the garden at the time of the evening breeze, and the man and his wife hid themselves from the presence of the LORD God among the trees of the garden. ....
What temptation was acting here? Fear.

The man said, 'The woman whom you gave to be with me, she gave me fruit from the tree, and I ate.' ¹³ Then the LORD God said to the woman, 'What is this that you have done?' The woman said, 'The serpent tricked me, and I ate.'...
What temptation was acting here? Blame.

And did you notice that Adam sneakily tried to blame God, too, because He created Eve to be with him?

In the rest of this book, the term "serpentine context" will refer to accepting living within the serpent's deception that caused the Fall of mankind.

What if we had kept faith in God's Love for us when we made our first mistakes - and with humility, repentance, and courage - faced Our Father immediately and asked His pardon and restoration? It would have been a much shorter journey through the suffering of separation. Do we really have faith in His Love now?

2 Chronicles 7: 14 (NRSV) if my people who are called by my name (I AM) humble themselves, pray, seek my face, and turn from their wicked ways, then I will hear from heaven, and will forgive their sin and heal their land.

Not even Grace is an entitlement program. Reciprocity is necessary. Otherwise, we wouldn't learn the lessons God and Jesus are teaching us. When we refuse:

- to have full faith in God's Love,
- a reciprocal relationship with God, and
- to learn our lessons humbly, we continually make the same mistakes.

Deep myth of the separation experiment

Many sources from all over the world and throughout epochs of time seek to describe and explain what, in the Christian tradition, we call "the Fall of mankind." Looking for similarities and additional facets that fill in the picture well, here is a copulation of this important event.

Growing focus on the creation, rather than the Creator, was being widely blamed as the cause of humanity's falling from the peak of LIFE's perfect expression. We were all ashamed. Many were angry and expounded that, if they had been listened to, this wouldn't have happened. Others were fearful of where this would lead, afraid even of Our Divine Parent's rejection.

At large, after exhaustive discussion, humanity decided we must prove ourselves worthy of God's Love by correcting our own mistakes. Some were just curious about what living without God would be like. To do either of these in a way that would satisfy us, we must move apart from Our Father, get ourselves together, and achieve Perfection by our own, arduous effort. When we accomplished the feat, thereby, restoring our self-respect and righteousness, we would return to Him and lay our supreme triumph at His Throne. Humanity's leaders brought this plan to Our Father with determination to see it done our way.

From the position of infinite Love, Wisdom, Power, and timelessness, Our Divine Parent looked over the contract and into the minds and hearts of His Beloved Children. He was not angry or hurt. The I AM is Infinite Love through all eternity. Seeing the absolute determination of His Children, He agreed with the proposition, but with these modifications:

1. If in attempting this separation experiment, humanity was only moving "away" - with the Divine Presence still available and dominant in humanity's consciousness - they (the children) would never be sure whether they had been able to "do it on their own." Therefore, God would cause their awareness of Him to become vague and indistinct. Most would forget their Divine Parent altogether.

2. God would no longer intervene to mitigate the mistaken choices humanity would make after the separation experiment started. Rather, the ramifications of all their choices - constructive and unconstructive - would accumulate. If they chose unconstructively often enough, then collective evil would solidify and have authority to rule their lives and existence. These "contracts" for potential evil to hold authority in, on, and above the Earth were called "separation agreements ."

3. If enough of the Children of God rose up and made the call to Our Father for His return and for the restoration of their conscious reunification with Him, the I AM would return to them.

Mankind agreed.

At implementation of the contract, humanity was expecting they would be calling back their Divine Parent to present humanity's victory. God knew His Children's return would mark their choice for the end of evil ("live" spelled backwards) and the I AM's re-creation of Perfection by Grace, thereby restoring the Unity of God's Family.

What if the I AM never left us? Surely, if He had, we and our world would not exist.

We were the ones who left God, Our Father! Have we created a virtual reality where the human ego reigns supreme? And out of Infinite Love, has the I AM altered the creation to fashion an extraordinary learning tool? According to quantum physics, the world and our experiences alter according to our choices, including our expectations.

At the point where each of us individually choses to live within the separation experiment, we chose to play with selfish, limited amusements. This robbed us of our immeasurable power. It is now a multi-generational condition, downward-spiraling suffering, into enslavement by evil and the second death.

At this point in time, what is the best action humanity can take?

What have you decided to do?

We have accepted serpentine suggestion and its context for life, and are allowing it to think for us. Abandoning personal discernment, the ability to think and reason for ourselves, begins with accepting the bribes of prestige, power, and wealth. Then we are ensnared, purchased by promises without substance or LIFE. With very little practice, allegiance of our attention is transferred to evil and limitation. And we have become dependent on what is not God, then enslaved, and continue to sink in its mire.

Sovereign Will and free will
According to the separation agreements, whatever we chose, using our free will, we would experience. If we chose unconstructively, God would no longer immediately intervene without our conscious call to Him, and according to the measure of our obedience to His Law of Love.

The I AM would no longer be misused by a capricious, bratty humanity for "quick fixes" of our mistakes, our unrepentant disobedience, our mean-spirited arrogance, and our short-sighted selfishness.

For us to truly learn the efficacy and truth of Our Father's Laws, we chose direct experience in the physical aspect of LIFE. Evil ("live" backwards) will continue to build up unmitigated, if mankind continues to live making choices outside of the I AM's Law of Love.

Our Father wants us to use our free will well. He designed and created us that way. Wallowing in misery and saying that our misery is God's Will for us is a lie and a desecration. Asserting that - our choices have power and that making those choices to change our lives is a direct rebellion against God - is an abomination. Yet some so-called Christian churches are feeding this poison to their parishioners!

The separation agreements are like contracts allowing evil to proliferate on God's Earth until we, the Children of God, choose otherwise. Part of these contracts require evil forces to broadcast, reveal their intent in some way, even while they work to confuse, con, and capture human beings. Think of some of the content of what is packaged as entertainment. Listen to the speeches coated in words of high ideals, but masking sinister intent. Research the agendas of those who would rule all humanity. Please use search engines and avenues that are not controlled and monitored by the intended global plantation owners.

The Fall fractured our consciousness of our Unity with God, Our Father. And humanity has largely held its attention in the separation experiment and serpentine context ever since.

Please answer these questions, earnestly, genuinely, and honorably:

Are you personally living anywhere within the serpentine context?

Is your family living anywhere within the serpentine context?

Is your church operating anywhere within the serpentine context?
(This includes benign, feel-good procrastination that comfortably distracts us into passive collaboration with the desecrating context. It also includes holding people prisoners to sin, by not allowing them to truly accept Grace and forgiveness.)

If in the range of any of your answers now there are any "yeses," please also ask:

Why are we living as if the Fall is permanent? Even after the advent of Jesus Christ among us?

Consider Jesus' words about God and about why he came:

Luke 19:10 *(NRSV) For the Son of man came to seek and to save the lost.*

John 1:4-5 *(NRSV) In him was life, and the life was the light of men. ⁵ The light shines in the darkness, and the darkness has not overcome it.*

John 10:10 (NRSV) The thief comes only to steal and kill and destroy; I came that they may have life, and have it abundantly.

John3:16 (NRSV) For God so loved the world that he gave his only Son, that whoever believes in him should not perish but have eternal life.

Prodigal sons and daughters all, let us consider Jesus' parable of the lost son:

Luke 15:11-32 (NRSV) And he said, "There was a man who had two sons; 12and the younger of them said to his father, 'Father, give me the share of property that falls to me.' And he divided his living between them. 13Not many days later, the younger son gathered all he had and took his journey into a far country, and there he squandered his property in loose living.

14And when he had spent everything, a great famine arose in that country, and he began to be in want. 15So he went and joined himself to one of the citizens of that country, who sent him into his fields to feed swine. 16And he would gladly have fed on the pods that the swine ate; and no one gave him anything.

17But when he came to himself he said, 'How many of my father's hired servants have bread enough and to spare, but I perish here with hunger! 18I will arise and go to my father, and I will say to him, "Father, I have sinned against heaven and before you; 19I am no longer worthy to be called your son; treat me as one of your hired servants." ' 20And he arose and came to his father.

But while he was yet at a distance, his father saw him and had compassion, and ran and embraced him and kissed him. 21And the son said to him, 'Father, I have sinned against heaven and before you; I am no longer worthy to be called your son. 22But the father said to his servants, 'Bring quickly the best robe, and put it on him; and put a ring on his hand, and shoes on his feet; 23and bring the fatted calf and kill it, and let us eat and make merry; 24for this my son was dead, and is alive again; he was lost, and is found.' And they began to make merry.

25Now his elder son was in the field; and as he came and drew near to the house, he heard music and dancing. 26And he called one of the servants and asked what this meant. 27And he said to him, 'Your brother has come, and your father has killed the fatted calf, because he has received him safe and sound.' 28But he was angry and refused to go in. His father came out and entreated him, 29but he answered his father, 'Lo, these many years I have served you, and I never disobeyed your command; yet you never gave me a kid, that I might make merry with my friends. 30But when this son of yours came, who has devoured your living with harlots, you killed for him the fatted calf!'

31And he said to him, 'Son, you are always with me, and all that is mine is yours. 32 t was fitting to make merry and be glad, for this your brother was dead, and is alive; he was lost, and is found.' "

Was the father angry with his wayward child? What were his feelings for him? What did the father want most of all?

With such a Divine Father, possessing such Wisdom and Power and ever expressing such Love to us, His Children, why do we not use the free will which God has given us to fully offer our love to Him, and obey His simple and clear instructions for our happiness and wellbeing?

Luke 6:46-49 (NRSV) "Why do you call me 'Lord, Lord,' and do not do what I tell you? 47 I will show you what someone is like who comes to me, hears my words, and acts on them. 48 That one is like a man building a house, who dug deeply and laid the foundation on rock; when a flood arose, the river burst against that house but could not shake it, because it had been well built. 49But the one who hears and does not act is like a man who built a house on the ground without a foundation. When the river burst against it, immediately it fell, and great was the ruin of that house."

Why are we still living in the serpentine context? Why are we refusing to be released completely from our sins? Why are we worshipping our egos and selfishness? By these choices, we are kowtowing to, and obeying, evil. We are laying down our God-given freedoms for the chains of misery of a deceiving power, intent on devouring us and our children! It has already engulfed, swallowed a vast number of us. Not full "digested," they can still be saved with God's Grace and Power.

John 3:19-21 (NRSV) And this is the judgment, that the light has come into the world, and men loved darkness rather than light, because their deeds were evil. 20 For every one who does evil hates the light, and does not come to the light, lest his deeds should be exposed. 21 But he who does what is true comes to the light, that it may be clearly seen that his deeds have been wrought in God.

Wake up! Let us put our hands on our life's oars and pull together for Our God, for Jesus, for America, and the freedom of ourselves, our loved ones, and all mankind!

Jesus has given us simple instruction on what to do. It only requires love and obedience. To repeat:

Matthew 22:37-40 (NRSV) He said to him," 'You shall love the Lord your God with all your heart, and with all your soul, and with all your mind.' 38 This is the greatest and first commandment. 39 And a second is like it: 'You shall love your neighbor as yourself.' 40 On these two commandments hang all the law and the prophets."

For us to return to God by truly following Jesus, we must genuinely, actively, joyful accept the possibility of the mending of the Fall and the ending of the separation experiment. This is part of the acceptance of Our Father's Grace. But Grace is not an entitlement program! We get to actively, joyfully collaborate in this process!

2 Chronicles 7: 14 (NRSV) if my people who are called by my name (I AM) humble themselves, pray, seek my face, and turn from their wicked ways, then I will hear from heaven, and will forgive their sin and heal their land.

V.
Back to the heart of all good

"A man is what he knows, but his soul will yearn for all that he does not know; For hidden there is all he may become."
- David Gemmell

Freedom is not a gift bestowed upon us by other men, but a right that belongs to us by the laws of God and nature." [65]
– Benjamin Franklin

There is only one true antidote, one effective and sustainable solution to this national and global crisis: It is the full intervention of the I AM WHO I AM, Our Father God, wielding the fullness of His Love, Wisdom, and Power.

The key to this manifesting is our loving, true obedience to His Law of Love, as taught and demonstrated by Jesus the Christ. Jesus made it very clear and succinct in his Great Command. Jesus was asked to name the greatest commandment. The questioner and the crowd were wondering which of the Ten Commandments he would specify. He surprised them. Jesus Christ delivered a simple statement on the way to return to God, Our Father, then powerfully and eloquently demonstrated The Way throughout his lifetime.

Matthew 22:37-40 (NRSV) "You shall love the Lord your God with all your heart, and with all your soul, and with all your mind.' [38] This is the greatest and first commandment. [39] And a second is like it: 'You shall love your neighbor as yourself.' [40] On these two commandments hang all the law and the prophets."

Please notice and contemplate the supreme power and essential consequence of Jesus' assertion that, "on these two commandments hang all the law and the prophets."

Could it really be so simple? We humans have made the creation of our wellbeing so very complicated. Could something that simple be the answer to cleaning up the horrific mess we've made of the world?

Yes! It is.

So it follows, that we would be well to identify – and get rid of - all the things that keep us from a relationship of reciprocal love with Our Father and Jesus, plus anything that discourages us from genuinely loving our neighbor.

Proverbs 30:6 (RSV) Do not add to his words, or else he will rebuke you, and you will be found a liar.

Love God, Our Father, with everything we've got. God has been longing and waiting for a reciprocal relationship with us for a very long time. Love is at its most wonderful and most powerful when it is reciprocal.

Love our neighbors so much, we treat them like we'd like to be treated ourselves.

Luke 6:31 (NRSV) Do to others as you would have them do to you.

That's it! Love and be obedient. Simple but not easy, until we build a momentum.

Reciprocal Love
Our Father and Jesus already love us steadfastly and infinitely. Jesus' Great Command asks us to love Them back, to love reciprocally.

Holding one's life successfully to God's Law of Love, followed and expressed by all other God-Principles, is a lot like keyboarding! From the very beginning, if we don't place our index fingers on the "F" (Father) key and "J" (Jesus) key, all we type will be meaningless, unfulfilling nonsense. But if we do place our love and confidence in Them first, as we live every day, we will flourish. And when difficulties come, if we keep our conscious choices there first, we will be guided through any storm.

Consciously connecting to the **F**ather and **J**esus "keys" before keyboarding our choices of thoughts, feelings, actions, and words in everyday life, builds conscious clarity into our lives.

When keyboarding, how often do we seek out the F and J keys to keep our orientation, to make sure the outcomes of our work are fruitful? It is so important that most keyboards have small raised nubs that we can feel with our index fingers, to know when we're in the right place.

We can choose to feel God in similar ways. Being appreciative as we make those tiny connections repeatedly through our days, expands our reciprocal relationship with God. The feeling of His Love
flowing back into us grows by increments, enhancing our feeling of knowing we are loved and precious to Him.

This is part of our giving justice back to Our Creator and Divine Parent for all we have and continue to receive from Him, as a glad free gift of His Love. And it keeps us in balance and is a multifold protection as well.

Choices and signposts on the way back Home
There are times when our current "reality" makes even this simple way too hard to handle well. Let's undo the knots and tangles in the skeins of our lives one at a time, using a series of small choices.

First choice
Our journey begins with one purposeful, conscious choice of how we read: IAMNOWHERE

Easily, 95% of the people first read it: *"I AM NO WHERE."* How does that make you feel? Awful, depressed, hopeless; constantly seeing unhappy, belittling things happening. This is the condition in which the vast majority are living our lives.

Now read it another way: *"I AM NOW HERE"*! And how does that make you feel? Strong, confident, happy, hopeful, looking forward to good things happening. And we are prompted to recognized that God is present with us.

All of us immediately and easily feel the difference that comes from this conscious, on-purpose choice of how we see life. From this feeling, we know instantly why our choices are important.

IAMNOWHERE is an analogy for all the jumble of stuff that we face every day. Again, we as Children of God, can choose to deliberately and consciously, select a positive start.

We also know that the Name God gave Moses for Himself is I AM. Let's explore higher.

The Power of the Words I AM

Exodus 3:14-15 (NRSV) God said to Moses, "I AM WHO I AM." He said further, "Thus you shall say to the Israelites, 'I AM has sent me to you.' " 15 ...This is my name forever, and this my title for all generations. Notes: Exodus 3:15 The word "Lord" when spelled with capital letters stands for the divine name, YHWH, which is here connected with the verb hayah "to be."

Proverbs 18:10 (NRSV) The name of the Lord (I AM) is a strong tower; the righteous run to it and are safe.

The second step

IAMNOWHERE. Whichever way we read it, we feel the power of I AM surging through our statement by the effect it has first on our emotions and then on our thoughts.

We are each a Child of God. We carry Our Father's LIFE within us. <u>When we use the words "I" and "am" together, an act of creation begins.</u>

What are some of the <u>un</u>constructive words with which people follow the words "I am"? For example, sick, broke, tired, bored, unhappy, frustrated, angry, sad, afraid, etc.

What are some of the constructive words with which we can follow the words "I am"? For example, hopeful, happy, well, healing, interested, harmonious, joyful, grateful, etc.

What effect do these have on our emotions, thoughts, attitudes, and our next choices? What has been the cumulative effect of using unconstructive words or choices after "I am"?

It is interesting to note that the Third Commandment in Genesis reads:

Exodus 20:7 (NRSV) You shall not make wrongful use of the name of the LORD your God, for the LORD will not acquit anyone who misuses his name. (or (RSV) You shall not take the name of the LORD your God in vain; for the LORD will not hold him guiltless who takes his name in vain.

The word "vain" can be defined as: unsuccessful, unproductive, useless, abortive, worthless, futile.

Look at the second half of the commandment in both versions. Are the life outcomes of using the words "I am" followed by an unconstructive choice evidence of the fulfillment of God's warning in the Third Commandment?

If we choose, say, and live "I AM NOW HERE," we are inviting and acknowledging Our Father's Presence with us. We are returning to His Love and choosing to stay in the Heart of God.

The third step
The third step is to ditch the compulsion to sacrifice instead of obey!

Mark 12:32-34 (NRSV) Then the scribe said to him, "You are right, Teacher; you have truly said that 'he is one, and besides him there is no other'; 33and 'to love him with all the heart, and with all the understanding, and with all the strength,' and 'to love one's neighbor as oneself,'—this is much more important than all whole burnt offerings and sacrifices." 34When Jesus saw that he answered wisely, he said to him, "You are not far from the kingdom of God."

The popular, politically-correct choice is a sacrifice, and usually a relatively superficial one. Today, we rarely give out of pure love, like Jesus asks. We are trying to prove our worthiness of God's Love by "sacrificing" ourselves. Our ideas and plans for "sacrifice" look a lot like the "benign narcissism" which produces toxic charity. Our current edition on how to prove ourselves to be good people is by how much time and "doing" we sacrifice. This is creating a frantic busy-ness that has many unconstructive side-effects.

It builds a silo around ourselves. We have less and less time for relationship with loved ones and friends. Often, we're never really present when we are with them. We're so busy, we're onto the next thing before finishing what we're doing at moment. How often do we sit in quiet contemplation, just being with God or Jesus, loving Them and accepting Their Love?

We are making burnt sacrifices of our lives and our human relationships. It will not bring us nearer to God.

This bleeds over into the experience and expression of our relationship with God and Jesus and being Christian. A lot of what we call "love" is an intellectually - created, plastic imitation of love, complete with all the glamour enhancements we've made on the idol to impress ourselves with how good we are.

Most of us who call ourselves Christians these days are very lukewarm on obedience to God. We are like shallow wells, whose meager waters are scattered in the busy-ness of trying to prove ourselves worthy of God's and Jesus' Love. Our weeks are chock full of good deeds, self-improvement study programs, and looking for others' good opinions.

We love exhibiting our "goodness" for the "likes" of others!

A lot of our church services are like entertainment hours - very active, often loud, and regularly involve free food. We throw our worship up at God and Jesus, but rarely stop to receive or nurture reciprocity – relationship. We declare, "Thy will be done." But, we're not asking God's Input, much less listening for it. Then we dash back out into the fray. Because we are "sacrificing" all the time possible to "good works" and "being good," we are good people – right? ….Really?

Genesis 3:15-16 (KVJ) I know thy works, that thou art neither cold nor hot: I would thou wert cold or hot.
16 So then because thou art lukewarm, and neither cold nor hot, I will spew thee out of my mouth.

Is this "plastic goodness and worship" what Jesus means when he asks us for genuine, loving obedience? Is this what he meant when he asked Peter to feed his sheep?

John 21:17 (RSV) ...Jesus said to Simon Peter, "Simon son of John, do you love me more than these?" "Yes, Lord," he said, "you know that I love you." Jesus said, "Feed my lambs." 16 Again Jesus said, "Simon son of John, do you love me?" He answered, "Yes, Lord, you know that I love you." Jesus said, "Take care of my sheep." 17The third time he said to him, "Simon son of John, do you love me?" Peter was hurt because Jesus asked him the third time, "Do you love me?" He said, "Lord, you know all things; you know that I love you." Jesus said, "Feed my sheep."

Where is the quiet time where we quit doing and praying - to listen? When do we become still? When do we just BE with Our Father? When do we seek out and participate in that relationship with God, the I AM?

Psalm 46:10 (KJV) He says, "Be still, and know that I AM God."

The fourth step
The fourth step is to accept God's Grace. To do that we have to stop trying to replace God's Grace with our human sacrifice.

This means to put aside permanently the egocentric urge to try to prove ourselves worthy of God's Grace. We can instead just meekly and respectfully accept it. Here's a news flash: Jesus has already delivered the Sacrifice. There is nothing we can offer from our human that can make ourselves worthy. Trying is egotistical vanity, the first step of the Fall. This choice keeps us trapped in the Fall and its serpentine context by our own free will choice.

But let's not go overboard! Getting rid of frantic and egocentric over-exertion does not mean putting in no effort at all!

Grace is not an entitlement program!
Again, God and Jesus are not looking to carry us to heaven like an overripe sack of potatoes! That is why Our Father gave us free will, so we can walk beside Him like daughters and sons. Exercising our God-given free will does not challenge or abridge God's Will. It allows us to mature in relationship with Him like children grow into the fullness of maturity as adults. Functional, balanced, loving parental / child relationships on earth are examples of His Will.

Neither is Grace a "get out of jail free" card!

Matthew 5:17-19 (KJV) Think not that I am come to destroy the law, or the prophets: I am not come to destroy, but to fulfill. 18 For verily I say unto you, Till heaven and earth pass, one jot or one tittle shall in no wise pass from the law, till all be fulfilled. 19 Whosoever therefore shall break one of these least commandments, and shall teach men so, he shall be called the least in the kingdom of heaven: but whosoever shall do and teach them, the same shall be called great in the kingdom of heaven.

Grace is an extension, an overflowing of the most wise and powerful Love. Love is most powerful when it is in motion, when it is reciprocal. Reciprocity involves both acceptance and return action. Reciprocity of love in obedience within the I AM's Law of Love is what God, Our Father is asking. Jesus is still teaching and demonstrating it.

The invitation is being broadcasted perpetually, "Come back, My beloved sons and daughters, into the Heart of Eternal Love and Goodness."

Saving Grace

Every Child of God in a state of conscious obedience and unity with the I AM is a being of immeasurable power.

So help us God! Truly, the current situation, of fear, unrest, contention, and human toxicity, is a temporary condition.

When we humbly and confidently reclaim our divine birthright, this will also re-connect us with God's full Love, Wisdom, and Power.

The Divine Might of Our Father God is the only Power capable of a permanent, sustainable solution to the present crisis in America and on Earth.

Our free-will choice of obedience and return to unity within the Love of the I AM is the best choice, the only meaningful resistance to the sinister force's widespread infection. Our conscious, purposeful return to God, Our Father will trigger the dissolving and consuming of sinister, usurped power and be the creation of our sustainable victory.

1 John 4:16 (RSV) And so we know and rely on the love God has for us. God is love. Whoever lives in love lives in God, and God in them.

1 John 1:5 (RSV) This is the message we have heard from him (Jesus) and proclaim to you, that God is light and in him there is no darkness at all.

Out of Our Father's infinite and steadfast Love for us, Jesus came to lead us back Home after we fell. He demonstrated the way back flawlessly and is still saying to us over and over, "Follow me."

Let's consider advice from our first president of the United States of America, George Washington:

"Do not let any one claim to be a true American if they attempt to remove religion from politics." George Washington (The source for this quote has yet to be found, but as you will see, it is perfectly consistent with the one below.)

"Of all the dispositions and habits, which lead to political prosperity, Religion and Morality are indispensable supports. In vain would that man claim the tribute of Patriotism, who should labor to subvert these great pillars of human happiness, these firmest props of the duties of Men and Citizens. The mere Politician, equally with the pious man, ought to respect and to cherish them. A volume could not trace all their connexions with private and public felicity. Let it simply be asked, Where is the security for property, for reputation, for life, if the sense of religious obligation desert the oaths, which are the instruments of investigation in Courts of Justice? And let us with caution indulge the supposition, that morality can be maintained without religion. Whatever may be conceded to the influence of refined education on minds of peculiar structure, reason and experience both forbid us to expect, that national morality can prevail in exclusion of religious principle." - The George Washington's Farewell Address

2 Chronicles 7: 14 (NRSV) if my people who are called by my name (I AM) humble themselves, pray, seek my face, and turn from their wicked ways, then I will hear from heaven, and will forgive their sin and heal their land.

Matthew 19:26 (RSV) *Jesus looked at them and said, "With man this is impossible, but with God all things are possible."*

In 1954, the Knights of Columbus submitted to Congress that the words "under God" should be added to our pledge of allegiance. Both Houses of Congress passed the law and it was signed by President Eisenhower.

In July 2020, NBC took a poll on whether their viewing audience thought America should keep the words "under God" in our Pledge of Allegiance. The vote was 86% to keep God in the Pledge of Allegiance and 14% to remove. (This information was texted to me.)

That is a very commanding public response. Should our Nation cater to 14%? Why? If we do, from whom are we turning away?

VI.
Love or fear?

"Fear is the mind-killer. Fear is the little death that brings total obliteration. I will face my fear. I will permit it to pass over me and through me. And when it has gone past me, I will turn to see fear's path. Where the fear has gone there will be nothing. Only I will remain." - Frank Herbert

"Are you most trapped by the way the world sees you, or the way you see the world seeing you?" - R. A. Salvatore

. . .(we) aim, however, at removing the blocks to the awareness of love's presence, which is your natural inheritance. The opposite of fear is love, but what is all encompassing (God's Love) can have no opposite." – Course in Miracles[66]

Notice in the story of the Fall that the choice of fear was what prompted Adam and Eve to hide from God and avoid His Presence.

Are we using the same tactic today and just cloaking it in smiles, false piety, and busy-ness? Or are we determined to believe that our sins condemn us, and refusing to accept God's forgiveness through Christ Jesus?

Fear creates a "veil" between ourselves and God, Our Father. It is impenetrable for one who carries fear within them. In nearly all of us, it makes us unable to see or even seek His Presence face-to-Face. In most of mankind today, the veil is so thick that we cease to even feel His ever-abiding Presence with us. Having mentally and emotionally cut ourselves off from God's Love, we hunger and thirst for love and fulfillment. And we start our search through the creation for anything that seems to satisfy our craving, our gnawing need. All these fixes are temporary.

Fear freezes us like deer in the headlights of an oncoming car. It is causing many good people to ignore both God and the encroachment of evil.

Have you noticed how God, Our Creator loves to create using circles and spheres? We are about to travel in one to gather more complete understanding.

Egotism, the first "temptation" of the Fall, engenders both shame and fear. That is because it knows that the assumption of personal exaltation born within egotism is a complete falsehood, a lie, a fabrication (causing shame). Its lie is completely vulnerable to the truth and the Light of God (causing it to fear). More shame is a trigger to more fear. More fear triggers desperation and aggression – or - depression, hopelessness, and even giving up.

"Fear is a sure sign that you have forgotten God." – A Course in Miracles

Stepping our attention back for a broader view.
The I AM WHO I AM, Our Father God loves us so much that He gives us free will, the choice to return our love to Him, and the choice whether we obey His wise and fulfilling directives and

commandments. God isn't into prisoners or slaves. He has chosen love by free will choice within His Family.

All the while, the silver cord of His constant outreach and contact with us is carrying His LIFE into us, nurturing us with His Eternal, Infinite Love. When it is time for us to go back Home, the silver cord is withdrawn and we follow it up into Our Father's embrace.

Ecclesiastes 12:6-7 (RSV)...desire fails; because all must go to their eternal home, and the mourners will go about the streets; 6 before the silver cord is removed, 7 and the dust returns to the earth as it was, and the breath, the spirit, returns to God who gave it.

Misuse of power

Is there any one of us who has not, at some time, exerted our ego to control, subdue, or shame another person? Do you remember the little rush of elation, of power? Whenever we do that, we are stealing a portion of the other person's LIFE for our own use. Now, we see the great temptation in the misuse of power.

(Please note: this is not the same as lovingly, firmly disciplining a child, who is expressing inappropriate use of their ego in defiance of the Law of Love. In those cases, the child is either spilling his/her LIFE out wastefully or testing their will against their parent's to "win by force." Standing in the maturity of an adult does not require the subjugation or belittling of another.)

The fabric and goal of the serpentine context

Members of the sinister force currently active on earth harbor furious hatred and rebellion against God. This has choked or even severed their silver cords. This leaves them with only the "life reserve" held in their physical bodies. Of their own free will in vehemently refusing God's Love and thereby, LIFE, they have put themselves in a condition of perpetual, imminent death by "starvation." This condition also causes tremendous fear.

In alarming contrast to the vital call of God's Love and by using the serpentine context of the Fall, gradually over the ages, fear has been insinuated into the cultures of the peoples of the world. It is like boiling a frog in a pot. When heat is turned up slowly, the frog doesn't sense its danger. It dies when one leap could save it.

The sinister force is saturated in fear itself. Their fear is so intense and they are in suffering so excruciating, it is literally consuming them. Eating away, deteriorating their ability of clear consciousness, draining away their life itself. They have become criminally insane in their own enraged desperation.

To continue in existence, to continue to live, they are determined to steal the LIFE of the Children of God, the I AM.

Under the influence of the serpentine context, the devil has amassed an army of ambitious generals, who are eager to subdue the masses in his name, plus legions of the ambitious, selfish, marginalized pawns as foot soldiers. These human beings are controlled and enslaved by the abomination of ideological possession[67], which is a form of hypnotic control. This control is marked by irrational, rabid hatred of any perceived opposition. No matter how minor, the order is to destroy anything opposing their sinister goal by any means available. And of course, the minion mobs get the reward of that rush of LIFE from their victims.

They have come for America. We are the last bastion standing for God, the I AM WHO I AM and Love on this Earth. They are clawing ruthlessly toward global ideological monopoly.

If we fall to their toxic deceit and bloodlust for destruction, all mankind will be forced into a global plantation. Within that model, we and all generations of our children will be the sacrificial lambs, fodder, living power-packs of usurped LIFE for continuation of evil. They intend it will be for all eternity.

The would-be vanquishers have already worked out the self-sustainability plan. We've already heard pieces of the plan, draped in false nobility, righteousness, and multiple layers of fake science. The purchased or cowered slaves of the mass media are their spokespersons, feeding us daily doses of mind and will-numbing indoctrination.

There is still real hope for deliverance.

1 John 4:18 (NIV) There is no fear in love. But perfect love drives out fear, because fear has to do with punishment. The one who fears is not made perfect in love.

Fear cannot exist in the presence of God's Love. This is a wonderful gift of understanding and wisdom from Jesus. It holds a key to our return to Love and back into the Presence, and into true relationship with Our Father. Just as Good (God) does not require evil "(live" backwards) to exist, neither does Love require fear. God's Love is the antithesis, the "antimatter" of fear.

In the Presence of God is the Love we absolutely require. In and from His Presence comes all that we desire.

Matthew 22:37-40 (NRSV) He (Jesus) said to him, " 'You shall love the Lord your God with all your heart, and with all your soul, and with all your mind.' 38 This is the greatest and first commandment. 39 And a second is like it: 'You shall love your neighbor as yourself.' 40 On these two commandments hang all the law and the prophets."

Love
Divine Love has a quality within it of sharing life experiences with the beloved. It enhances and expands constructive experiences, leading to maturity as Sons and Daughters of God.

If an experience is unconstructive, producing dis-ease, Divine Love pours in empathy (not pity) and healing. But It never allows the unconstructive to taint Its Purity or diminish Its Power.

In both constructive and unconstructive experiences, Love illumines the qualities and effects of choices.

If the Child of the I AM - while experiencing discord or afterwards - consciously turns to God, repents, and asks for forgiveness, illumination, and assistance, it all is immediately given. The call to Love compels the answer – always. The instruction and encouragement extends in time until the advancement from that lesson is accomplished, realized, and fully embodied.

We are micro-steps from love and unity within God. I AM NOW HERE. I AM IS NOW HERE.

Conscious, regular applications of Love thin the veil created by fear, until we stand again in the Presence of Our Father, wrapped forever in His Loving Embrace. Now that is a Cosmic Hug!

Be sure to work on removing shame in tandem with your lessons with Jesus on Love. Repenting and asking forgiveness every time we see one of our mistakes are baby-steps toward righteousness. Forgiveness cleanses us from shame as well as our choices of disobedience (sin).

The greatest gift of love we can give Jesus is full acceptance of the Grace He embodied that absolves us from sin and its condemnation. And then, joyfully we can partake in the journey all the way Home with him.

This Love and the supreme act of our reciprocal love is necessary to restoring our divine birthright and its freedom to live fully within God, Our Father, in Eternal Love.

We are all daughters or sons of God, the I AM. We must choose to acknowledge and reclaim our Divine Birthright to realize and experience the benefits and all that means. We get to act accordingly to maintain that conscious experience. If we choose differently, we again slide into separation and suffering.

Onward and upward
Those under the hypnotic control of ideological possession of the serpentine context are redeemable – so great is our God.

This Kingdom message changes the heart. We need to change hearts, not just minds. Thereby, through reciprocal love, the individual reunites with God and Jesus. Then we reunite with each other in harmony and justice. This is both help and the process for living within Jesus' Great Command.

Toward those who appear to be acting outside Jesus' Great Command, be steadfast in refusing to hate or condemn them. Would you berate or shame an hysterical amnesiac? They have only forgotten. They are living in a state of extreme separation from the reality of God. This existence is a great suffering, filled with limitation and lack of what is abundant God LIFE, - especially lack of LOVE, the worst suffering.

For Love = LIFE = I AM WHO I AM.

Choosing God and His Love is our salvation, freedom, and our very great reward.

Once we understand all this, fear does not and cannot reduce us into cringing, sickly, inept cowards or treasonous traitors to God, Jesus, and all mankind.

We have a choice that enthrones the Love, Wisdom, and Power that will be our Victory and eternal safe harbor. We can choose as our own the same conscious, deliberate, firm, and courageous choice that Jesus made for God Our Father, the I AM WHO I AM. We will complete the journey Home - one baby step at a time - with Jesus walking beside us.

To begin, we each have this choice: love or fear. Let's make it a good one.

VII.
Shifting the paradigm

A paradigm is a "framework containing basic assumptions, ways of thinking, and methodology that are commonly accepted; cognitive framework shared by members of any discipline or group; a typical or stereotypical example."[68]

Other words that carry the meaning of "paradigm" include, model, pattern, matrix, precedent, order, hierarchy, arrangement, and mindset. Paradigms are used in the management of affairs and to confirm authority, to settle, or control.

The paradigm operating underneath our lives, organizations, nations, and across our cultures is usually never seen - or even considered. It is simply the accepted foundation of "how things have always been done."

So how can we conceive of something so hidden and vague with clarity? This is certainly necessary before we can begin to talk about it.

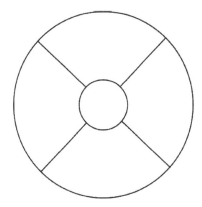

We offer a spoked wheel as a model[69] for the structure of a strong, balanced, and productive paradigm:

- The HUB: holds core values for the integrity and consistency of intent and implementation,
- The SPOKES: extend the intention into growth,
- The RIM: provides means for movement of behavior and accomplishment.

Diagramed using the spoked wheel analogy, the dominant paradigm in use throughout the world, looks like this:

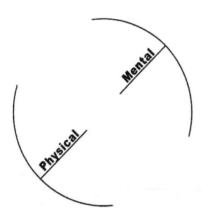

Dominant world paradigm[70]

If the wheels on our cars looked like this, what kind of ride would we be giving ourselves? How is the "ride" these days in our lives, families, churches, businesses and organizations, communities, nations, and our world?

This is an egocentric paradigm. It uses, almost solely, human intellect (the Mental Aspect) to compel action or change to take place in physical reality. There is nothing to effectively mitigate or balance the intellect's absolute authority. Over history, this paradigm has seemed to work quite well for a very long while. However, time, size, and complexity of operations, plus changing cultural and marketplace realities, have been added to the mix. And the functionality of this paradigm is breaking down. This is a paradigm that is no longer productive. Often it is not even civilized. It will no longer offer justice, sustainability, or reliable, empathic effectiveness in our communities.

Dominance of this paradigm causes pain because it:

- treats symptoms, not causes;
- tends to polarize problems, situations, and groups;
- objectifies each other and citizen groups,
- builds callousness concerning others,
- causes breakdown within and between families, organizations, diversities, and community;
- breeds apathetic (non-engaged) and sabotaging (disaffected) citizens,
- causes diversity issues to GO BERSERK! It either disconnects or fails to connect individuals and groups; and
- generally tries to subjugate those who disagree with it.

Additionally, the symptoms of this paradigm include:

- escalating complexity, excellence harder to attain and maintain;
- lowering engagement, discretionary effort, and loyalty;
- increasing dissension, stress, burnout, fear, anxiety, gossip, low morale, apathy, polarizing "politics," bullying, entitlement, unethical behavior, and victim mentality.

Current leadership, communication, and teamwork paradigms are not cutting it. Dominant-paradigm training programs available are not sustainably alleviating the problems. Potentials and sustainable improvements are being significantly hampered.

The current, dominant paradigm is the paradigm of the Fall.
The first sin we committed was that of egotism. We imagined our puny selves equal to or greater than the I AM WHO I AM, Our Father God.

Today, this egotism is being calcified into "egoism," which *"also designates a system of philosophy."*[71]

Egoism abides in the intellect. It is the mental spoke in this paradigm. Egoism today is striving to eliminate God from individuals' lives, families, education, the work environment, government, economy, medicine, relationships, and daily exchange between people. The science of egoism will not even admit the Divine's part in creation. It is trying to claim complete, supreme authority in the affairs of humankind.

We, the Children of God, are persistently being led toward focusing our attention on our bodies, minds, careers, positions, life roles, associations, connections, possessions, and the esteem given to us by others as the truth of who we ARE and what gives us worth in human civilization.

Most of us are still living and leading within the paradigm of the Fall, the serpentine context. What do most of us labor tirelessly to create, even leaders and members of churches? We strive for great accomplishments worthy of adulation; positions with numbers of followers, popularity, or wealth as indicators of God's Favor. Many seek authentication by purchasing titles and degrees. Many claim godliness and righteousness. Many drive the gospel, law, death, and threat of eternal damnation, at people to shame and compel them into accepting a terrifying version of both God and Christ. These kinds of revivals have come and gone for generations. And look at how humanity still lives.

These tactics increasingly distract us from developing true, profound, or meaningful relationships with Our Father God, Jesus, our spouse, children, extended family, friends, church members, neighbors, and coworkers.

It makes us susceptible to the leading of the serpent ego, toward domination within the serpentine context under its favored directors. This paradigm persistently elevates a small elite over the mass of subjects.

This is the paradigm of the Fall, monarchy, socialism, communism, fascism, corporatism, techno-fascism; large, polarized democracy; the Deep State, the United Nations and their Agendas 21, 2030, 2050, and their new world order.

Our founding fathers knew well the demise of every large democracy in history, and created the United States of America a republic, within which there is specific, democratic participation.

You will notice that God is nowhere in this paradigm. Regardless of any lip-service of those living in this paradigm, it is atheistic. God-principles are not honored or, perhaps, even considered. The modern, self-justifying, operational name for this paradigm is "secularism."

Recognizing and valuing the assets and limitations of the intellect

Conscious, constructive, consistent use of our mental faculties, including our intellect, is imperative to excellent, rational leadership. There are many positive attributes of the mental aspect that we need and can use successfully.

But, by itself, our intellect will not get us to a just, sustainable, or fulfilling life! Our intellect will not connect us to God. We need to be consciously aware of the intellect's limitations. The intellect:

- cannot connect with the Spirit of God by its own accord,
- makes hard and fast conclusions based on incomplete information,
- perceives the appearance of limitation, mistakes, and failure as fact and insists on dragging the dead weight around forever;
- is by nature competitive and selfish. It conceives of itself first – and then everything else;
- tends toward arrogance, controlling, competitive, and monopolistic thinking;
- is only able to manage resources acquired by the spirit. It cannot create these resources. (By itself, it uses only synthetic creativity.);
- can truly conceive only of the finite, not the Infinite. Therefore, left to its own devices, it turns everything it receives into something finite, into limitation;
- cannot love, but, is easily consumed and directed by fear;
- is like a battery. Continually charged and directed by God's LIFE and the spirit, the intellect is one of the most useful tools humanity has. Taken apart from its source of power, the intellect runs down, like an uncharged battery and the results of its labors follow suit.

Are our organizations, countries, or world in safe hands if only the human intellect is in charge? No! Absolutely not! By itself, the human intellect turns people into production and consumption units, slaves, serfs, and dependents. Over the generations and the centuries, some of the greatest minds of humanity have labored to amass wealth and power heretofore unseen. They are heading us toward a global plantation – for our own good and survival of planet earth, of course.

How did Jesus gather people to Our Father? He did and still does use love, kindliness, encouragement, forgiveness of sins, healing of maladies. He teaches God's way gently but with authority. He leads by example, acceptance, not judging people by their current difficulty, seeing us all as who we are, the Children of God.

In our everyday lives, are we lovingly and humbly obedient to God's and Jesus' Commandments? Are we truly seeking conscious reunion with God, Our Father? Or, are we trying to prove our worthiness of Grace by human means?

The latter creates poverty of the spirit. Poverty of the spirit coupled with economic poverty exacerbate each other. They create dependency and are partners on the road to a global plantation. The authors of the pandemic lockdown know this, as they are seeking the economic collapse of nations.

To change the currently dominant paradigm, we must enhance or replace it with something of greater value with Our Father's and Jesus' guidance.

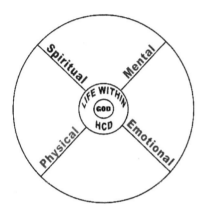

God-centered, holistic, balanced paradigm[72]

This is the paradigm of the Creation, and of the founding documents of the United States of America.

The God-centered paradigm is actually spherical and radiates like a sun. At the center is the only Source of LIFE – God, the I AM, Our Father, breathing His LIFE into us His children. That LIFE is the "who we are," and is within each of the Children of God.

This LIFE is our Highest Common Denominator, the ONE thing we all have in common. It transcends toxic diversity.

Once we choose to begin accepting the Grace of Our Father's Forgiveness as embodied and demonstrated by Jesus, we begin to be consciously aware of God's LIFE in ourselves. Like the prodigal sons and daughters we are, we can consciously get up and go back to our Father. In other words, we actively seek reciprocal relationship with our Father God. This begins the healing, the mending of the separation of the Fall.

Note that this paradigm still has the mental and physical spokes of the dominant paradigm. The addition of the other components creates a huge, positive change in the quality our lives.

This paradigm:

- restores and engages largely ignored or missing dimensions of ourselves as human beings,
- engages, connects, and integrates all resources of each and every person;
- is toxic-diversity transcendent,
- establishes integrity-based collaboration with shared core values,
- treats causes of problems, not just symptoms;
- establishes and/or strengthens collaboration and mutual appreciation throughout diversities. Individuals in this paradigm are no longer objectified, treated like objects.

In any building foundation, every block is important. Weak blocks weaken the structure. In our human model, they make the individual, family, church, organization, community, and nation go out of alignment. This new paradigm transcends the old one, mending the fabric of the citizenry by establishing undisputable, harmonious, common ground, and shared core values.

Justice requires reciprocity to be sustainable.

Like a long overdue maintenance on a motor, together we can clean out the gunk and recalibrate it. Our 4-cylinder, life motor — that has been running on only two cylinders - will spring into greater life and power.

All the members of a family, church, organization, neighborhood, community, and nation are essential participants in this revitalization. We all need to learn and consciously participate in this paradigm. It is a broader, more functional perspective, which includes parts that are already familiar. For fulfilling and sustainable outcomes, each one of us is needed in whatever role we play.

As we replace the dysfunctional paradigm with this holistic, balanced paradigm, what results can we expect to see?

- leap in unity and capacity through active, constructive engagement of all involved;
- the flourishing of these attributes: shared core values, trust, improved morale and morals, enriched communication and teamwork, enhanced safety and security, increased productivity and quality, lasting excellence, and endeavor sustainability;
- establishing an essential foundation of love expressed as harmony, honoring diversity, and transcending toxicity; and
- joining together in love, integrity, hope, joyful expectation, health, dignity, usefulness, and abundance for all.

This paradigm creates a sound base for ongoing constructive collaboration, innovation, and sustainable prosperity.

Each element added to the new paradigm has specific value. Let's start with the Author of LIFE, God, Our Divine Parent.

Genesis 1:26 (NRSV) The God said, "Let us make mankind in our image, according to our likeness ... *27So God created humankind in his image, in the image of God he created them; male and female he created them.*

Genesis 2:7 (NIV) And the Lord God formed man from the dust of the ground and breathed into his nostrils the breath of life, and man became a living being.

Having come out of the I AM, the one thing we all have in common is God's LIFE in each of us.

The Highest Common Denominator
This adds the epicenter of Innovation: LIFE = the Highest Common Denominator (HCD) we all share. This is God's LIFE inside each of us. It transcends toxic diversity.

From this point we all want the same things. Begin with Maslow's hierarchy of basic needs: food, clothing, and shelter. Then add that we all want to be loved, to be valued and respected, and to have opportunity to improve our quality of life. Most of us want to make our community and world a better place.

When we begin by acknowledging and participating in a relationship with Our Father God, this epicenter is the center and cause of continual renewal. As each Child of God is recognized and nurtured, all are enfolded and lifted up an inexhaustible resource of creativity, motivation, commitment, determination, and collaboration. The harvest includes peace, love, wisdom, justice, power, healing, respect, and joy.

This epicenter is the center and cause of that renewal. When nurtured, it is an inexhaustible resource of creativity, motivation, commitment, determination, collaboration, and passion.

The HCD expresses itself in choices within, and through, the four primary aspects of a human being: mental, emotional, physical, and spirit. In a group of people, this insures that change which occurs through learning is change supported by individual decision, rather than institutional imposition.

When we perceive and honor this same LIFE in each other, God's and Jesus' Love flows between us, healing all fear, hatred, and discord. It heals and dissolves all that is not Their Love. When we see and honor each other as this Highest Common Denominator, God's LIFE, it helps us to be patient and to forgive each other.

Without recognition of this Highest Common Denominator in ourselves and all other persons, everything goes out of alignment and loses focus. Or, it sidetracks focus for valuing each individual to something that is less important and, thereby, becomes unsustainable.

Things that can sidetrack us are very common in today's world, including non-engagement, apathy, fear, anger, selfishness / what's in it for me?, resentment against injustice, skepticism, disaffection, sabotage; focusing on what's wrong, instead of solutions; polarizations, and trying to continue the old paradigm.

Every one of our choices – consciously or unconsciously made – affect not only our own quality of life, but the whole of mankind.

In this paradigm, we deliberately recognize and honor God's LIFE in each person. When we start here, our choices expressed through our four life aspects are integrity-based, respectful, inclusive, constructive, and collaborative.

Let's add the emotional spoke

Adding the emotional spoke to the paradigm helps create what is commonly called "Emotional Intelligence." Today, "EI" is the most prized "commodity" by organizations internationally, as it brings an increased ability to thrive harmoniously. This is true for individual lives, family, churches, neighborhoods, and communities.

Consciously adding the Emotional spoke allows a productive merging and mutual relaxing and maturing of the mental/intellectual and emotional/feeling properties of each individual and the group. These qualities include self-awareness, self-regulation, motivation, empathy, people skills, team building, tolerance, calm, harmony, and happiness.

The mental aspect keeps the emotional aspect from getting too sappy, hysterical, or unfocused.

The emotional keeps the mental from getting uncaring, inflexible, or tyrannical.

Adding the fourth spoke completes the balance and stability, plus allows the rim to be completed.

Spirit is the engagement spark plug

Spirit, engaging the best of oneself, is an essential attribute of positive, dynamic, personal involvement, and the courage, strength, determination, and "heart" of any group of people in any endeavor.

The spirit, of an individual and the whole team, draws from God, plus the HCD of everyone on the team. It then fires enthusiasm, unity, hope, and joy throughout the rest of the paradigm. Full, inclusive, integrity-based engagement creates sustainable, positive change, and continuing expansion of horizons and possibilities.

This fourth spoke provides structural integrity, strength, and integration of the paradigm. It is also essential for the smooth continuation of the rim made whole, which empowers movement, growth, and accomplishment. The possibilities of noble and worthy achievement with this paradigm are exhaustless and limitless.

We all have our Source in God. In close relationship and partnership, together with Our Father and Jesus, we can consciously create a country and a world of justice, love, wisdom, opportunity, safety, security, and peace.

Acknowledgment and respect of Spirit is essential to greatness. As Children of God, our Highest Common Denominator, His LIFE in us, holds within it the greatest resources and potential of LIFE.

This Spirit of LIFE of each human being on the planet possesses as its birthright:

- all the limitless potential of life,
- all the limitless abundance of life,
- knowledge of right and wrong coupled with the ability to know when another part of Life is hurting (and when we are the ones doing the hurting); it activates conscience;
- the essence and source of positive self-esteem and self-worth,
- the ability to recognize spirit and attributes in everyone else, plus complete, blissful disregard of the color or gender of the flesh, or any dividing diversity. (This is not because we don't see and appreciate the beautiful varieties, but that our main focus is on God in each other.);
- the ability to love,
- the ability to offer both sincere apology and forgiveness without grudge,
- the ability to remain unhindered by any appearance of limitation and to proceed onward and upward,
- the ability to tap all the above and use them consciously for wonderful and even amazing achievement in life.

By consciously engaging the Spirit, the best of ourselves and every member of mankind, we can dissolve, remove, or get around the causes of problems and limitations. The collectively strong, engaged Spirit of our families, churches, neighborhoods, communities, nation, and world is an essential resource, protection, and source of sustainability.

The completed paradigm shifts, enlarges, and deepens our perspective and possibilities, offering more powerful opportunities in service and mission. It encompasses the protection of freedom in America, with the ultimate goal of God's Will done throughout the earth.

The sinister force wants themselves, through their governmental egoism, to be our god. At every opportunity, they have tried to impose their serpentine context to trick us into staying stuck in the Fall. If our enslavement becomes complete, they expect they will have an eternal source of LIFE with which to continue their wretched and unlawful existence.

That is why for centuries, they have been incrementally and methodically removing God from our public forums, alienating us from our true selves, and causing dissention between the Children of God.

God has given America, home of the I AM race, to us to steward. We are not the property or chattel of the government.

"We the people are the rightful masters of both Congress and the courts, not to overthrow the Constitution but to overthrow the men who pervert the Constitution."[73] *- Abraham Lincoln*

Leadership Opportunities

So each of us, as we are freeing ourselves, have the opportunity and blessing of Love to serve as a lamp to guide others of God's family, who are lost in the maze of evil ("live" backwards).

Remember to be sure to never judge, condemn, or hate anyone.

VIII.
Focusing the lenses of clarity

In today's world, so many of us don't really know where we are going, but we are getting there *FAST!* We are also incessantly and relentlessly barraged with demands, as well as, information overload, which ranges from important to empty, from true to false, from confusing to emotionally disturbing.

As well-meaning and conscientious people, we take responsibilities to career, family, good works, church, and God very seriously. These are placed in this order according to typical time, attention, and energy generally allocated them. We live under a lot of pressure to get things done in days that are literally bursting at the seams.

This state of awareness gives us little or no time for real consideration of what's going on outside our immediate, personal concerns. By default, we tend to assume that our community, America, the countries of the world, the earth, and mankind are running along benignly – and always will.

Many of us tend to neglect our personal wellbeing and balance. Many more of us are neglecting our relationship with Our Father and Jesus. We count on Them to always be there, and so They are. But relationship requires our presence – unhurried, peaceful, still – listening, abiding, and giving love reciprocally - not just accepting love.

Our Father created us with the most amazing accessories, with which to see life and perceive more of Him. Used well, these capabilities help us make our lives more perceptive, delightful, fruitful, and safe. So let's clean off some of these wonderful "lenses" together. First, ponder and answer these questions:

What should life be like?
If our world was a "perfect" place what would life here be like? Our responses clean off and recalibrate our overarching life compasses, directing us toward the values of our desired destination. This perspective helps us rise above the fray of daily busy-ness so we steer and prioritize better.

This conscious compass is essential! Imagine standing at a transportation ticket counter, or having just jumped into a taxi. What is the first question that will be asked? "Where do you want to go?" If we can't answer that precisely, how far will we get until we make a decision? Nowhere, except perhaps shunted to the side of the line while we make up our minds.

If we don't have a precise idea of at least the qualities we'd like in our lives, we will never get to our desired destination.

Our lives are in much more danger now because of how fast we are moving. We're all like race car drivers speeding on the track of mundane life. It seems we have pretty much the same objective: get through it as fast as possible, avoiding undesirable delays. It's a lot easier and more likely that we shoot off in an unconstructive, unfulfilling direction, or meander, lost in the jungle of "busy." Sometimes we seem stuck in a continuous, dull, but frantic loop. In any case, we are often pouring out our lives more or less uselessly, when compared to our aspirations.

Over the past 25 years I've been asking people, "What would the world be like if it was 'perfect'? The consistency of the responses have surprised me. Thousands of people, aged from 4 to 85 and from widely diverse life experiences, have offered the SAME core responses. When you have paused briefly to create your own list of personal hopes, please visit Appendix III for the core aspirations of those who have gone before you. Their top priorities have always been "Love" and "Justice." They also provided what qualities are embodied in justice.

Love

Love is central and essential to LIFE itself. Love is the fulfillment and joy of living. Love is the heart and spirit of Justice and Hope. Love is Victory over all less than itself. Love is eternal.

1Corinthians 13 (NRSV) If I speak in the tongues of mortals and of angels, but do not have love, I am a noisy gong or a clanging cymbal. [2] And if I have prophetic powers, and understand all mysteries and all knowledge, and if I have all faith, so as to remove mountains, but do not have love, I am nothing. [3] If I give away all my possessions, and if I hand over my body so that I may boast, but do not have love, I gain nothing. [4] Love is patient; love is kind; love is not envious or boastful or arrogant [5] or rude. It does not insist on its own way; it is not irritable or resentful; [6] it does not rejoice in wrongdoing, but rejoices in the truth. [7] It bears all things, believes all things, hopes all things, endures all things. [8] Love never ends. But as for prophecies, they will come to an end; as for tongues, they will cease; as for knowledge, it will come to an end. [9] For we know only in part, and we prophesy only in part; [10] but when the complete comes, the partial will come to an end. [11] When I was a child, I spoke like a child, I thought like a child, I reasoned like a child; when I became an adult, I put an end to childish ways. [12] For now we see in a mirror, dimly, but then we will see face to face. Now I know only in part; then I will know fully, even as I have been fully known. [13] And now faith, hope, and love abide, these three; and the greatest of these is love.

What more can be said, except perhaps, love is at its greatest, most fulfilling, and most powerful when it is reciprocal.

Justice

Every child is keen on justice, what's fair. How much time do most adults spend on the idea of justice during our busy days? Many of us have become so cynical, we do not expect to see justice in life, especially in the affairs of cultures and nations. It has become such a charged issue that individuals tend to try to ignore it to maintain personal equanimity and harmony or they become obsessed with achieving justice in some pocket of the world.

BEWARE: "Justice" is a word that is increasingly misused and twisted into a snare for the well-meaning, but those without discernment. These become gullible to ideological blackmail, which demands they prove their sincerity and commitment through violent words and acts of enraged hatred. The groups using toxic diversity claim righteousness and truth. Rhetoric of condemnation and hatred does not contain love and can never create justice. New acts of injustice cannot ever atone for past injustices. The old injustices are never allowed to heal.

Overall, injustice increases exponentially. The motive here is not justice, but division and unbearable strife.

Malachi 2:10 (NRSV) have we not all one father? Has not one God created us? Why then are we faithless to one another, profaning the covenant of our ancestors?

Micah 6:8 (NRSV) He has told you, O mortal, what is good; and what does the Lord require of you but to do justice, and to love kindness, and to walk humbly with your God?

Proverbs 21:15 (NRSV) When justice is done, it is a joy to the righteous, but dismay to evildoers.

Proverbs 28:5 (NRSV) The evil do not understand justice, but those who seek the Lord understand it completely.

Wisdom[74] _8:7_ (NRSV) And if anyone loves righteousness, her labors are virtues; for she teaches self-control and prudence, justice and courage; nothing in life is more profitable for mortals than these.

Lady Justice is not always shown wearing a blindfold! In Europe, the old statues of Justice do not have blindfolds. But they often carry swords to cut through all the lies, deceit, and attempts at injustice, whether deliberate or unintended. Many newer statues of Justice in the United States do not have blindfolds either. When asked why she is blindfolded, most commonly reply that it is all about racial justice, so she cannot see the skin color of those in a dispute.

She has ears. She can perceive, from hearing, people's gender. From language, dialect, accent, she can usually perceive their race, origins, and where they are living, plus their emotional and mental conditions, their educational levels, and their biases. Are there going to be demands next to plug up her ears? Certainly today, there are emphatic demands and countless attempts to put duct tape over her mouth!

To accomplish justice, must there be the fullest possible perception of all sides, layers, intentions, and nuances in every situation that needs the intervention of the ideal of justice? Should her vision be impaired? Does that blindfold exacerbate the expectation of racial injustice? Is that its deliberate purpose?

What do we see when we open our eyes?

Why is Justice always shown holding a balance scale? All statutes of Justice are shown with her balance scale. So what is the connection between justice and balance? What do you think it is?

Of course, this is a rhetorical question. There is no right or wrong answer. The most wonderful answer I've gotten so far was from an eleven year old boy named Alan, who had been labelled learning-disabled, autistic, and special-ed. After thinking about ten seconds, he replied, "If I am out-of-balance, I can't give justice to anybody else."

Wow! He left me speechless. And he is absolutely right.

Let's add that if we are out-of-balance, we will never be able to hold on to justice. Our out-of-balance condition flings away, repels justice, keeping it from our lives and experience

Justice requires reciprocity to be sustainable.

To be truly just and to start a widespread return to justice always requires that we behave justly to <u>everyone</u> we meet - <u>regardless of the other's behavior</u>. Justice never includes shaming, denunciation, anger, aggression, or violence.

This chapter is all about the qualities that help us create overall balance. If any one of them is not functioning properly, we have some kind of imbalance. We need perception unencumbered with any agenda – other than true Justice – to restore balance.

Are we just to God, Our Father? Do we express our love and gratitude to God, Our Father? Do we take the time and invest the feeling to create our personal and reciprocal relationship with Him?

We, as His children, are wired with an innate understanding of justice. From this comes our children's interest and insistence on what's fair. When justice is expressed or given to us, what are its qualities? Do they include reciprocating love, kindness, making time with us in relationship, respect, harmony, acknowledgement of our good qualities, deeds, and intentions? Must the expression be regular to be true and convincing?

Are these legitimate ways to approach our siblings in God's Family? We could even learn from Jesus how to offer our love and respect to them first.

"The highest form of human intelligence is the ability to view oneself without judging yourself and in that comes transformation. – Deepak Chopra

The qualities of Justice that have been offered repeatedly over decades can be found in Appendix III.

Choices
"We are responsible for the effect of our actions." - Rollo May

Every time we make a choice, we are using our God-given free will. Choice is POWER! And everybody has this power equally! Ultimately, we are the ones who decide what we will believe, think, feel, say, and do.

To make our life satisfying and fruitful, we need to know how to discern between constructive and unconstructive choices. This protects our free will by guarding us from undue and/or destructive influence by others. Our choices form our habits, character, and ultimately, our destiny.

All constructive choices are within and express God's Love and Justice. Jesus' Great Command, quoted previously, is a perfect test for our choices. Let's also add his Golden Rule:

<u>Luke 6:31</u> (NRSV) *Do to others as you would have them do to you.*

Any choice that falls outside these is also unconstructive.

Only constructive choices are sustainable. All unconstructive choices are unsustainable. They carry the seeds of their own destruction. Every unconstructive choice puts a chink in our armor of God. Every constructive choice strengthens it.

Ephesians 6:10-11 (NRSV) be strong in the Lord and in the strength of his power. 11 Put on the whole armor of God, so that you may be able to stand against the wiles of the devil. ...

<u>All offered to you in this book is, by intention, keyed to Jesus' Great Command and Golden Rule.</u>

Please pause a moment to form your own definitions of "constructive" vs "unconstructive" qualities.

Here's a start: helpful vs hurtful, builds vs destroys, collaborative vs apathetic or sabotaging, inspiring vs shaming, "can do" vs "won't do" or "won't try," encouraging vs discouraging.

The qualities of constructive verses unconstructive qualities that have been offered repeatedly over the decades can be found in Appendix III.

The Principle: like makes like
Galatians 6:7 (NRSV) Do not be deceived; God is not mocked, for you reap whatever you sow.

Every choice we make – consciously or unconsciously – is like a seed. Once it is made, it grows, expanding the qualities out of which it came, whether constructive or unconstructive. Choices are the building blocks of our lives and everything we experience within them. This is how life on earth is wired by our Creator. It is a magnificent classroom, in which we learn to be master and steward of ourselves, to appreciate and value the miraculous beauty of Love. We also learn, by very personal experience, how only Love and its attributes are worthy of the investment of our sacred LIFE. This LIFE is shared with us by our every-present, loving, and encouraging Father God.

Choices made consciously and "on purpose" and choices made unconsciously or carelessly have the same weight in what happens in our lives.

God, the I AM, loves and values us so much He gave us free will. Again, He is not into prisoners or slaves. Our Divine Parent desires familiar, harmonious, reciprocal, cherished relationships within Love eternal. This ultimate Gift comes with the responsibility appropriate to its worth and sacredness.

Like makes like. And our free will choices yield us experiences of profound learning and wisdom.

Galatians 6:8-10 (NRSV) If you sow to your own flesh, you will reap corruption from the flesh; but if you sow to the Spirit, you will reap eternal life from the Spirit. 9 So let us not grow weary in doing what is right, for we will reap at harvest time, if we do not give up. 10 So then, whenever we have an opportunity, let us work for the good of all, and especially for those of the family of faith.

To use the Principle "like makes like" successfully, learn these tenets well:

1. Tell yourself the truth
An old adage is that if we are true to ourselves, we will not be false to anyone else.

Most of us fib to ourselves, at least once and a while. These lies can have very unconstructive affects. Most of us have used the "I'm too busy" excuse to not do what is right because it is inconvenient and to shield ourselves from investigating what may be disturbing truths. Telling ourselves lies multiplies the lies we live by and tell to others. Internal falsehood rots us from the inside out and creates suffering, even disaster, in our lives.

2. Get off "drugs"
"Drugs" are unconstructive choices gone toxic. They are also addictive. Here, a "drug" is anything that temporarily eases our discomfort, but keeps us in an out-of-balance state. (Remember what Alan taught us about being out-of-balance.) The drugs of substance abuse are just extreme examples of this. All drugs and "drugs" lie. They divert attention, by masking and protecting all that is unconstructive.

Each aspect of a human being – mental/thought, emotional/feeling, physical, and spiritual - is vulnerable to certain "drugs."

See Appendix III for collected samples of predominant "drugs" in each aspect. Again, thousands of people from diverse walks of life and different generations have cited the same examples.

These kinds of "drugs" are more dangerous than drugs known as substance abuse! Not only are these "drugs" the precursors of substance abuse, they are by far more prevalent in our society for these reasons:

- they are free
- they are not illegal
- virtually everyone does these "drugs" at some level
- these "drugs" are contagious, e.g. depression, anger, hatred, condemnation

"Drugs" also put "static on the line" between God or Jesus and ourselves, making it harder to hear both of them and our conscience speaking to us. Using "drugs" in many varieties and increasing the number of times they are used, increases the interference in our relationship with our Divine Parent. Habitual, high-level "drug" use can force us into a virtual reality apart from God and our divine birthright. It can create negative life experiences, including feeling unloved or unimportant, losing the sense of meaning to one's life, unhappiness, depression, disillusionment, chronic fatigue, unemployment, economic setbacks, substance abuse, unwanted pregnancy, shame, toxic charity, failure to thrive, fear, anger, resentment, divorce, poverty, rage, racism, genderism, etc. They create resentment against injustice, avoidance of the truth and personal responsibility, blame, and the condemnation of others.

The mental "drugs" of the Fall include, in order of the choices, egotism, selfishness, disobedience, and blame. The emotional "drugs" of the Fall include fear and shame.

3. The only true control is self-control[75]

A lot of we humans love to exert control over others. Have you noticed how most control-freaks are a miserable mess inside themselves? Correcting, managing, and badgering others helps keep their minds off themselves and gives them a feeling of power and importance.

So, let's invest persistent quality time on genuinely and intrinsically bettering ourselves. We will be the first ones to reap the benefits. It will help us walk the path of love, truth, and justice. We will make a significant contribution to mankind's experience, for relations, friends, neighbors, coworkers, and beyond.

4. Thoughts + Feelings + Spirit = Outcomes

This is a practical result of making choices. The conglomeration of our choices in our thoughts, feelings, and spiritual expression create the outcomes of our physical lives. And yes, the unconsciously or carelessly chosen choices have the same weight in the equation!

At first this may seem like a tremendous amount of responsibility. But it is really a wonderful freedom, power, and opportunity! Because, if we don't like the way our lives are at the moment, we, as Children of God, have been given the conscious capability and power to change our choices and, thereby, the quality of our lives.

Many argue, "But what if someone or something is done to me that is unjust and/or not my fault?" This objection applies to groups as well. That argument is a symptom of the mental "drug" blame, a nefarious and potent "drug ." Once we have satisfied our "self-righteous indignation" (a spiritual "drug") and fixed the blame on someone or something else, we absolve ourselves of the responsibility of doing anything about our own condition. In other words, we clear our conscience and pave the way for getting addicted to other "drugs," including victim mentality, entitlement, laziness, and resentment against injustice. Like also <u>attracts</u> like. These are gateway "drugs" attracting more of their kind in a downward spiral.

How we choose to react and respond to injustice done to us has a significant effect on the quality of our own lives.

Constructive choices are protective, in that they do not help produce difficulties of their own creation. They build in us the courage, strength, and attitudes that are called "resiliency." Again like <u>makes</u> like.

Making constructive, positive change sustainable

1. Pay attention to the small things.

What we choose to do in the small things in life, creates the rest of our lives. This is great news! We have certain power to deal with the small stuff. Big things like world peace, and racial and economic justice are massive. They certainly seem on the surface to be beyond the competence and scope of the average individual.

But what if, we all create the habit of making constructive choices in our interactions with each person we meet every day, in all those seemingly mundane situations? What if we treat them the way we'd like to be treated? What if we consciously choose to see and value them as siblings, fellow Children of God? What if we practice seeing everyone else as the Highest Common Denominator we all share?

What would the collected outcome be? Would it work better than criticism, condemnation, judgement, yelling, demanding, anger, name-calling, fighting, revenge, and destruction?

<u>2. Deal with the causes, not just the effects of a problem.</u>
If we only "press down" on the symptoms of a problem, the causes remain and will pop up at us again and again. Here are some examples of just pushing down the symptoms of a problem:
- weeding a garden by only cutting the tops off the weeds. They only grow back.
- using pharmaceuticals to suppress a specific symptom, but not removing the cause of the illness or disease. It only shows up somewhere else in the body.
- incessantly hammering the <u>symptoms</u> of a social inequity or injustice, instead of looking for the causes together. Have you noticed how abusive and violent tactics only inflame the situations?

Reprisal and resentment against injustice only creates more - more resentment and more injustice.

"Having a grievance or a resentment is like drinking poison and thinking it will kill your enemy." – Nelson Mandela

We need to become the personal solution for transforming our own lives. It takes real love, courage, persistence, and a true desire for sustainable justice. We can make injustice unlawful, but it is the collective morals of the people that create and sustain justice.

<u>3. Use all the aspects of your LIFE.</u>[76]
Consciously engage all your mental, emotional, physical, and spiritual traits in living. Otherwise it is like riding on a flat tire throughout life. We need the help of all the aspects of our lives working in balance with each other to create a high quality life.

4. Live consciously

What does living unconsciously look like? What does being on autopilot, or cruise-control, or sleepwalking through life look like? Are we letting other people do our thinking for us? If we are choosing to live in any of these states of "unconsciousness," we will have no say about where we end up! Like a car in neutral gear, we can get pushed in any direction. And in today's world, there are plenty of people who will try it. Almost all of them will use the victim's hijacked life force and substance for selfish and unconstructive purposes. Would you leave the doors of your home open to thieves?

5. Know the Dynamics of Change[77] These are conscious steps toward sustainable, constructive change, self-engagement, and to all sustainable accomplishment: Aware, Acknowledge, Accept, Apply.

For example, say someone wanted to give us $1,000,000!!! Before the opportunity would do us any good at all, we'd have to first be <u>aware</u> of it, right? Then, we'd have to <u>acknowledge</u>, "yes, we could put this to good use." Next, we must <u>accept</u> the opportunity for an improvement. Then we can actually <u>apply</u> it in our lives and reap the benefits. (If the opportunity is money or power from anyone, we'd better study the "contract" first!)

In this chapter, and throughout this book, there are opportunities offered for creating a more fulfilling life for ourselves. Actively consider how mastering these qualities and characteristics can benefit you. These activities are connected and work together toward powerful results that are also sustainable.

Proverbs 2:7-9 *(NIV) He holds success in store for the upright, he is a shield to those whose walk is blameless, ⁸ for He guards the course of the just and protects the way of his faithful ones. ⁹ Then you will understand what is right and just and fair—every good path.*

IX.
Constructive vs unconstructive power

There are lots of "powers" in the world today claiming to be the source of success, happiness, and security – and justice. Learning to tell the difference between the true leaders (constructive) and the devious (unconstructive) is really important in creating and sustaining our personal well-being. **Today this discernment is essential to the continued viability of the United States of America – and all its potential and the protection of all that is of God on earth.**

Lack of the ability to distinguish constructive power from UNconstructive power is what causes us to fail in our personal lives. It also determines the prosperity and safety of our loved ones and all we hold near and dear – especially in today's world. A big clue to the motive and objectives of those wielding power is the kind of power they are wielding.

True power, constructive power emanates from the I AM WHO I AM, our Father God. Constructive power also comes from His LIFE within us and others. True power has very different qualities than worldly power. To protect constructive power and thwart unconstructive power, we must first be able to identify and discern one from the other.

Here's a start at identifying constructive vs unconstructive power. Think about other comparisons yourself. We get to practice this every day in our daily routines, especially every time someone wants us to think or do something they want, or expresses an opinion as we are forming opinions ourselves. It is really important to practice this discernment when we watch the news and when listening to speeches of those who want us to follow them.

Constructive power
I AM WHO I AM , God

Unconstructive power[78]
Worldly power

unifying constructively, inclusive	dividing, excluding
powerful	forceful, shocking
loving, respectful	hating, accusing
peaceful	suppressing, inciting
calm	agitated
deep	superficial
empowering all	enraging, demoralizing, weakening
forgiving, restoring	condemning, destroying

More examples can be found in Appendix III.

Pay attention

"We can't get enough of what we don't want!" Werner Erhard

Increasingly, people seem compelled to tell even total strangers a long litany of the injustices done them, their personal sufferings, all the opportunities stolen from them, and any other trouble they can dredge up. These are sure signs of the individual being a slave of victim mentality. VM's sidekicks are usually anger, poverty, and entitlement mindsets, and are often spiced with some form of drug abuse.

While every one of the personal horrors they talk about may actually be part of their experience, this resentment against injustice powerfully binds them in slavery to those conditions. It also actively attracts more of the same. Like makes like. And like attracts like.

We have become fascinated with "drugs ." Most of us lead lives saturated with these addictions. Many times these "drugs" lead to substance and other abuse.

Speaking from personal experience, each of us stuck in this horrible life-space has a significant choice to make. **We must choose between resentment against injustice or our freedom.** They cannot exist in the same place at the same time! We are already making this choice, consciously or unconsciously, every moment of every day. Pay attention closely until the qualities of each are obvious. Which is constructive and which is unconstructive? Now we can make future choices in alignment with what we want in life. Baby-step changes at first are more sustainable.

Where we focus our attention directly influences our choices and the other way around. Attention is actually a choice in itself. Remember, it's the small things on which we create the greatest happiness and success or the greatest unhappiness and failure. The great news, proven over 25 years of research, is that we can ALL do this successfully. No matter our age or situation.

We are the first and only person who must – and can - consciously and deliberately choose our freedom and train ourselves to reach for it. **Placing our attention on what we want instead of what we do NOT want is key to breaking out of our misery**. No one else can do this for us. We cannot wait for others to do something to, on, at, or for us. They will always fail to achieve our full freedom. Only we have the power to achieve our freedom from lack and suffering.

Even Grace is not an entitlement program! The first step is small and is completely, and only, in our personal control. And so is each step after that.

Whom or whatever we consistently give the greatest power in our lives to is who or what we ultimately worship. The mechanism used is free will choice directed through our attention.

When we come in touch with the picture or example of a thing, we are in touch with the thing itself. Same with thoughts. Emotions are even more powerful, though usually started by thoughts or concepts. These all actually have energetic "substance," power, and force.

Through these activities, we direct our LIFE force, which is from Our Creator. And therefore, it is a part of Our Father God. Whatever we hold our attention on long enough, we create in the experiences of our life – using the LIFE, our LIFE.

The Fall fractured our consciousness of our Unity with the I AM, Our Divine Parent. And humanity has largely held its attention in the serpentine context, separation from God, and in human isolation ever since.

Irresolute wandering; unfocused, blurred, unclear attention; and negative, angry, resentful attention are open doors for the intrusion and takeover of unconstructive power.

Keep your balance
When we are out-of-balance, we are easy pushovers.

Balance is one of the "small things" that are shunted aside in our society engulfed in busy-ness. Yet life-balance is a powerful asset upon which can be built mighty accomplishment.

Restoring our personal balance by becoming aware, acknowledging, accepting, and applying constructive ways of living are essential to our own sustainable wellbeing and our protection. The state of our personal wellbeing directly affects our family, friends, and coworkers. This dynamic extends into our churches, all our endeavors, and our communities.

Remember what Alan taught us. If we are out-of-balance, we can't give justice to anybody else. Let's add that if we are out-of-balance, we will never be able to hold on to justice for ourselves.

Justice requires reciprocity to be sustainable. Justice is an outgrowth of reciprocal love.

Restoring and maintaining our own personal balance is actually an essential and powerful contribution to establishing justice in our communities, nation, and throughout the world.

Instability is an open door for the intrusion and takeover of unconstructive power.

Forgiveness

"To give up resentment against or the desire to punish." Webster's Dictionary

Forgiveness takes courage - especially when severe pain, suffering, and loss are involved.

It is hardest to forgive ourselves. There is often acute shame, guilt, potential disgrace, embarrassment, and cowardice connected to taking responsibility for the results of our own poor choices. We often attempt to shield our cringing egos from these uncomfortable thoughts and feelings. We also try to dodge personal responsibility for our mistakes by strongly criticizing, condemning, and judging others.

"An eye for an eye only makes the whole world blind." - Mohandas K. Gandhi

Only by liberally exercising the courage of forgiveness can we ever heal ourselves, our nation, and our world.

Let's look at some guidelines that define forgiveness as an attribute far above being a doormat!

Forgiving someone does not mean that something bad or wrong did not happen. Forgiving the Child of God, who the other person is, does not condone unconstructive or unjust choices and actions. It does not rule out appropriate restraints or penalties being applied.

When you forgive someone, it does not mean that you are going to just let them hurt you again.

When we choose to forgive, we are giving up anger, hurt, resentment, and the desire to see someone punished. At the same time, we understand that nobody, not one of us, gets away with anything we create outside the Law of Love.

Forgiveness is one of the greatest blessings that we, as the forgivers, have in this world. It frees us from the power of those that have done injustice to us. If we don't forgive, the wrong doer and the wrong done continue to have the power to oppress and hurt us.

And do not worry about justice being done. No one ever gets away with an offense against the Law of Love – including us.

Romans 12:19 (KJV) ...Vengeance is mine; I will repay, saith the Lord.

God knows how to be just and to right the scales of balance. And a functional court system can be part of that also.

Nobody gets away with anything unjust!

Matthew 5:17-19 (KJV) Think not that I am come to destroy the law, or the prophets: I am not come to destroy, but to fulfill. 18 For verily I say unto you, Till heaven and earth pass, one jot or one tittle shall in no wise pass from the law, till all be fulfilled. 19 Whosoever therefore shall break one of these least commandments, and shall teach men so, he shall be called the least in the kingdom of heaven: but whosoever shall do and teach them, the same shall be called great in the kingdom of heaven.

We can put love and opportunity to heal in the place of the anger, hurt, resentment, and desire for revenge. For the one being forgiven, your forgiveness will provide a wonderful example, a constructive life lesson, and perhaps a fresh start. Being forgiving strengthens and frees us.

Forgiving does not compel continuing a relationship, nor does it exclude relationship with the one we've forgiven.

When someone has been unjust to us, we may not want to forgive. But that choice will hurt us, not the one who created the injustice. They may not even know or care whether they are forgiven. Holding on to refusing forgiveness, and its attendant resentment or self-deprecation, will poison our lives in many ways. Still, to forgive or not forgive is our own choice – and either has consequences.

There are some relationships in life we so desperately want to hold on to, even though they are toxic. Here, we need to deliberately see things like they really are. An associate of mine helped me expand my understanding of "forgive and forget" with this story.

In winter, she was visiting a friend of hers who lived in the upper peninsula of Michigan. There was a strict rule for going to out to the woodpile for firewood. One took the long, hefty stick by the door on the trip. A rattlesnake had taken up residence in the wood pile. Before gathering wood for the fire, from as far a distance as the stick would allow, one struck the pile vigorously, several times. The snake would vacate, temporarily providing a safe interval in which to collect firewood.

"A rattlesnake's nature is to bite," she observed. "He will also always bite. Some people have chosen to be snakes. No matter how much you love them, they will always hurt you. It is very important to forgive them for your own wellbeing. But, don't ever forget what they are. Choose wisely."

Generously practicing forgiveness is essential in relationships we want to keep long term, like within family. Here, the concept of "forgiving and forgetting" comes into play. This doesn't mean we affect false amnesia. If together the relationship heals and continues well, this is a form of "forgetting." There will be a time when contact with that person does not trigger an automatic replay of what they did to hurt us. Then forgiveness has opened the way to full healing.

Forgive yourself first
Hint: It's impossible to really forgive yourself for something you know is wrong and you keep doing anyway.

Drop the baggage! Consciously choose another way of thinking, feeling and/or acting - and move on. But remember, you must forgive yourself as well. Everybody has made mistakes and has things that need to be forgiven. We all need to wipe our emotions clean so we can have a fresh start. Making a list of what we need to forgive can be helpful. Erase the items as they are forgiven and don't recall them. If one does come back, put it on the list again.

Because none of us is perfect, forgiveness is something we must be willing to do every day.

Not forgiving ourselves keeps us stuck in a place of suffering. It can also cause us to take it out on others by not forgiving them or being intolerant.

Forgiving others

"To err is human, to forgive is divine." Alexander Pope, Essay on Criticism

Lack of forgiveness - holding on to anger, resentment, even irritation - blocks our personal healing, restoration, and wellbeing. Holding on to the wrongs done to us only hurts ourselves. It allows unconstructive people and their injustice to continue to hold authority and influence in our lives.

When someone first hurts us, we are a victim. If we let them do it over and over again, we have become a volunteer.

This creates resentment and fear in our lives, in how we make choices, and how we relate to others and ourselves. Fear and resentment attract mistakes.

Forgiveness clears hurtful history. It creates an opening for people to be accountable and take responsibility for their mistakes.

Refusing to forgive:

- loses opportunity,
- maintains separation, hatred, and enslavement to injustice, and
- blocks all possibility of reconciliation, collaboration, unity, and justice.

Refusing to forgive is an open door for the intrusion and takeover of unconstructive power. It gives support to internal cowardice so often desperate for the excuse to deflect its own hidden faults, laziness, and misdeeds.

We can choose to raise our ability and willingness to forgive to an art form! Within this chosen consciousness, we realize only Love is truly personal. Everything else is just a mistake, a lack of understanding, a reaction of the wrongdoer's own suffering. As we raise our willingness and ability to forgive, we increase our resilience, protecting ourselves against hurt.

Again, as we learn to forgive consciously, it protects us. ***Forgiveness will also begin to dissolve fear.***

In the Lord's Prayer to Our Father, Jesus taught us to ask God to "forgive us our trespasses <u>as **we** forgive</u> those who trespass against us."

<u>Matthew 6:14-15</u> (NRSV) For if you forgive other people when they sin against you, your heavenly Father will also forgive you. [15] But if you do not forgive others their sins, your Father will not forgive your sins.

<u>Proverbs 20:9</u> (NRSV) Who can say, "I have kept my heart pure; I am clean and without sin"?

<u>Luke 6:37</u> (NRSV) "Do not judge, and you will not be judged. Do not condemn, and you will not be condemned. Forgive, and you will be forgiven.

<u>Luke 17:3-4</u> (NRSV) "If your brother or sister sins against you, rebuke them; and <u>if they repent</u>, forgive them. [4]Even if they sin against you seven times in a day and seven times come back to you saying <u>'I repent</u>,' you must forgive them."

Gratitude
To whom are you grateful with your first thought as your eyes open on a new morning?

<u>Ephesians 5:20</u> (NRSV) …giving thanks to God the Father at all times and for everything in the name of our Lord Jesus Christ.

Without gratitude, we live our days in anxiety, egocentric planning, or always having a "chip on our shoulder." In other words, *we become pickings for use by unconstructive power.*

And there are a lot more benefits to liberally practicing gratitude. Being thankful to God and His LIFE, all its good people and things, even the lessons it gives, is very important.

When we decide to practice being thankful on purpose every day, three wonderful things happen:

- First, we're a lot nicer to be around, plus we'll probably get along with people better and have more friends;
- Second, the more we express thankfulness, the more LIFE will give us for which to be thankful;
- Third, if we practice being thankful regularly, it starts melting away any selfishness we might have.

To get started, we may have to <u>allow</u> ourselves to feel gratitude. Then, we can move on to actively practicing being thankful every day. Whether expressed silently or shared out loud, gratitude and encouragement must be sincere to reap the benefits.

Keeping and regularly reviewing an ongoing list of what we're grateful for is a real lift and helps protect a positive attitude. It colors and enhances all our relationships. Start your list by noticing and being grateful for small things, like a sunset or the fragrance of newly cut grass.

Psalm 95:2 (NRSV) Let us come into his presence with thanksgiving; let us make a joyful noise to him with songs of praise!

Egotism

Egotism was the first "drug" chosen by mankind, when we fell for the serpent's offer that we could be like God. Ultimately, it means putting ourselves, our ego, before God, and thereby seeking also to put ourselves above God. In the mundane life, it is having everything revolving around self-centered concerns as reasons for all choices, words, and actions.

Since prayer and open relationship with God was removed from public K-12 education, the focus in education has largely been on aggrandizing and satisfying individuals and their egos. Entitlement and narcissism in our children are rising dramatically.[79]

Individual egos unconnected to God eventually perceive their own shallowness. Apart from God, the Creator, lack of real substance and the vacuum resulting from no true self-worth or genuine reality creates great despair. The children's lives become only "virtual," even to themselves.

The action is similar to a battery that is not recharged. It just runs out of juice and nothing hooked to it works. Only in this example, the "battery" is the child and the "charger" is God and the "charge" is LIFE. As we all know, this applies to every human and all our endeavors, including families, churches, organizations, communities, and nations.

Today, this egotism is being calcified into "egoism," which also designates a system of philosophy. –Huber Gray Buehler

Today, egoism, the system where human intellect is first and master, and "herd thinking" or collectivism are threatening and planning to overtake the entire world. It is a system of philosophy ruled by the globalist-corporate elite, socialistic and communist regimes, and all political forums advocating the "State as God." Certainly, they mean to elevate themselves to be our gods and masters.

Egoism, in those who are not rich, is evidenced in the organized terrorists, insurrectionists, the spies, cyber-hackers and manipulators, political and cultural traitors, etc. All of these are purchased and/or ideologically possessed by the elite, to do their dirty work. Once the dangerous business of revolution is accomplished, the purchased pawns are disposable, because they do not adapt to placid enslavement.

These mayhem-makers are a liability to the totalitarians, due to their pawns' tendencies toward disloyalty to humanity, disobedience to authority, theft, and violence. Historically, once communist and fascist regimes come into full power - aided by the unrest and turmoil inflicted by the elite-paid anarchists – they execute those same anarchists quickly.

In Ethiopia, the communists came into power aided largely by the terrorism created by gangs of students. After the communists achieved control, their soldiers rounded up the insurgents. The parents of these youth were compelled to witness their executions and forced to pay for the bullets used to kill their children. Youth, who did not have families to terrorize or from whom the communists could extort money, were tied together in groups and blown up with dynamite.[80]

The anecdote to this madness is found here:
- Obedience and love to the I AM WHO I AM, Our Father God, Who is the only loving, just, incorruptible, and invincible power;

  1st Commandment: Exodus 20:3 (NIV) You shall have no other gods beside me.

  2nd Commandment Exodus 20:4-5 (NIV) You shall not make for yourself an idol, whether in the form of anything that is in heaven above, or that is on the earth beneath, or that is in the water under the earth. 5 You shall not bow down to them or worship them.

  Luke 4:8 (NRSV) Jesus answered him (the devil), "It is written, 'Worship the Lord your God, and serve only him.' "

  Proverbs 18:10 (NRSV) The name of the Lord (I AM) is a strong tower; the righteous run to it and are safe)

  John 5:39-41 (NRSV) "You search the scriptures because you think that in them you have eternal life; and it is they that testify on my behalf. 40 Yet you refuse to come to me to have life. 41 I do not accept glory from human beings.

- Know who you are – a Child of the I AM with an essential place in God's Family for eternity, and

- Keep His commandments.

1 John 5:3 (NRSV) In fact, this is love for God: to keep his commands. And his commands are not burdensome,

Whom or what are we worshipping when we are consumed with busy-ness or unwilling to accept the Grace, that removes our sin and welcomes us to return to full reciprocal relationship with God? What idols are being foisted on us by deceivers wielding unconstructive power?

We are already well acquainted with them if we just wake up and pay attention! They include:
- medical experts who have broken their Hippocratic oath to "do no harm"

Plus all who
- want us to accept their leadership without question, e.g. worship them
- try to take away our unalienable rights to freedoms given to us by God
- try to divide us with their lies
- tell us that hate and violence are the way to justice
- corrupt our souls, minds, feelings, and spirits
- try to force us into dependency on them and slavery
- tell us we can't think for ourselves and that they will take care of us, and all we have to do is give up our freedoms and blindly follow them
- insinuate hypnotic control on We the Peoples and seek to subjugate us in any way
- try to tear down the United States of America
- kidnap and torture our children

Disobedience to God is an open door - with a welcome mat - for the intrusion and takeover of unconstructive power, whose most debilitating weapons are fear, division, and resentment against injustice.

May We the Peoples come together and refuse to be divided.
We have the Love of Almighty God and access to His ear and Power.

There are a lot more of us than there are of them.

Ecclesiastes 4:9-10,12 (NRSV) Two are better than one, because they have a good return for their labor: [10] If either of them falls down, one can help the other up. But pity anyone who falls and has no one to help them up. [12] Though one may be overpowered, two can defend themselves. A cord of three strands is not quickly broken.

John 13:34-35 (NRSV) I give you a new commandment, that you love one another. Just as I have loved you, you also should love one another. By this everyone will know that you are my disciples, if you have love for one another."

Consciously, deliberately obeying God is the essential core to victory over the diabolical forces arraigned against us. When choosing obedience to God, we are aligned with His Purpose and His Power is going forth before, with, within, behind, and surrounding us. We are enfolded.

God can do anything – except fail.

Evil intention and its power have now built to the point where it is moving toward full conquest and control of all humankind. If the United States of America falls, the whole world will descend into abject slavery. The misery and horrific danger we are facing is of our own making. We have allowed the serpentine context to rule ourselves, our children, our communities, and our nations.

The Power of the I AM WHO I AM is pure Divine Love and Wisdom in action. Our Father God's Power is exponential and omnipotent. And we only have to love, obey, ask, and we will receive it.

The first reaction to these pronouncements usually is: "This is something way beyond anything I have any power to affect in any way." And we run for comfortable shelter. Often with the excuse, that "God has told me I don't need to be concerned with that in anyway" or "He's given me this much smaller assignment and I don't have responsibility beyond that."

That is Grace-as-an-entitlement in action.

That is the choice for subjugation and enslavement by evil.

Have we in <u>any</u> way contributed to this situation? If we are not perfect, if in way we are living within the serpentine context, we do have blame and responsibility. Then the hiding and doing nothing attitude is without truth, integrity, or honor. That choice is also cowardice without love, loyalty, respect, or gratitude.

And it is probably just plain, unmitigated, selfish stupidity!

Will we pull together our courage? Will we be obedient?

What is the minimal role God has asked us to play?
- Our Father has asked us to return to His Love in relationship,
- He has asked us to be obedient to His Law of Love, which is the only way of living a quality, happy life,
- We only have to CALL Him and His Omnipotent Power will be released.

Genesis 4:26 (NRSV) At that time men began to call on the name of the Lord.

Matthew 18:19 (NRSV) "Again, truly I tell you that if two of you on earth agree about anything they ask for, it will be done for them by my Father in heaven. 20 For where two or three gather in my name, there am I with them."

Are these requests so heinous, so heavy?

We can do this.

Since the serpentine context is still very active and appears to be expanding, what is its end-game goal?

What kind of power has been and is being used on us?

What is at stake?

X.
An historical flyover

History repeats itself. - George Eliot

Those who cannot remember the past are condemned to repeat it. - George Santayana

Each time history repeats itself, the price goes up. - Ronald Wright

History repeats itself because nobody listens the first time. - Erik Qualman

Those who cannot remember the past are condemned to repeat it without a sense of ironic futility. - Errol Morris

In this chapter, we do many brief flyovers of history to pick up threads that directly and meaningfully impact the situation in which we find ourselves today. These are threads of both of darkness and of light, of corruption and slavery, plus hope and freedom.

All enslavements of others are violent attempts by individuals or groups to quell the desolation and fear caused by their self-chosen separation from God and His Divine Love. Long-term enslavement always involves the binding of individuals' minds, emotions, and spirts, before it becomes physical.

This flyover is a proverbial search for needles in the haystack of history. Very little of mankind's vast history was recorded and the surviving records are even less. One thing that has been shown by history is that the conquest victors have nearly always written a history that magnifies or outright fictionalizes their virtues. In current times, there have been very active efforts to use omission of selected history and revisionist history as a tool of indoctrination and enslavement. The Nazi's used it excessively.

Today in America and at a global level, it is a robustly common practice. For example, in public schools in America, according to all the teachers I've met after about 1980, it is taught that the Pilgrims came to America to create economic advantages for themselves. The truth is that the Pilgrims were fleeing religious persecution and came here for freedom to worship God as their conscience dictated.

Public schools no longer teach about the republic form of government, which is the governmental form of the United States of America. Teachers are instructed to say that the republic is a form of democracy. The term "democracy" is not once mentioned in the US Constitution. That is because, from history, our founders strongly viewed democracy as unstable and prone to creation of injustice, anarchy, and violent dissolution.

Most of us don't know what is missing, or even that it was there in the first place. If we aren't aware of the broader history of elites enslaving the masses of people, including their "how," we will believe any fabricated version fed us by the elites. Here, "elites" doesn't mean merely wealthy people. It means the mega-rich who want to own the world, including us.

It is those who are trying to broaden and entrench their hold on us now. They can easily even take our attention off themselves and focus our hatred on their enemies, who are actually trying to keep us free. This is a standard level 101 magicians' trick worked on the naïve made vulnerable by ignorance.

Narrowing historical perspectives and carefully made revisions of history are inflicted on We the Peoples and done for control. In all tracking of the diabolical elite, follow the money and the power.

Let us begin our flight.

The Fall

When we chose separation from God, we also separated ourselves from the full flow of His LIFE and Love. At that point, we become like batteries disconnected from their charger. We know we only have so much time left. Our intellect knows that our vitality and strength will wane and we will slide into feebleness, unconsciousness, and our physical bodies will die. With our backs turned to the Light of God, we live in the shadows.

We have examined the dynamics of the Fall in chapter IV. The Fall was only the beginning of the devil's scheme. The author of the serpentine context still intends to permanently separate us from God, Our Father and Creator – by any means he can devise. Usually he works through his enslaved minions, as they can appear to be one of us.

God's full Power is actually a trinity of Love, Wisdom, and Power. Therefore, there is always Balance and Goodness.

The deceiver is only interested in power. He is cunning and devious, not wise. He knows and cares nothing of love. In his incessant, seething, jealous rage, he knows no mitigation of the use of his usurped power – except the Power of Almighty God.

1 Thessalonians 4:16 (NIV) For the Lord himself will descend from heaven with a cry of command, with the voice of an archangel and with the sound of the trumpet of God.

Matthew 13:41 (NIV) The Son of Man will send out his angels, and they will weed out of his kingdom everything that causes sin and all who do evil.

There are two main strategies the serpent has used to usurp the Power of God within us God's children:

- Tearing the people, to be enslaved, completely away from any allegiance or even remembrance of Our Father and Jesus. These slave masters attempt to make the government god and all the human governing authorities within, its priests. Their stated political doctrine – e.g. socialism, communism, fascism, or new world order – becomes the declaration of belief, the creed.

- Infiltrating the church and using the people's faith, desire for God, and adherence to church doctrine, coupled with the threat of eternal damnation, to totally subjugate.

This is why the "separation of church and state" is so very important. It means the separation of a specific doctrine from the government. It does not mean the separation of God, the Supreme Being, and the state or its people.

Ancient times: the money beast

The "money beast" is an ancient scheme for power by satanists that has taken on the trappings and tone of a religion. It is absolutely antichrist and against pure Judaism. Its origins are traceable to ancient Babylon. In this doctrine, money is the cornerstone of its insatiable lust for power through wealth. Stealthy deceit is its method. Relentless, covetous greed is its main trait. It uses economic power to produce economic enslavement and inflicts massive wars to create more wealth. Mankind is its fodder.

The descendants of these, dressed in the robes of the Pharisees, contended with Jesus. These are not represented in the majority population of the Jewish people. Remember Jesus was Jewish.

Babylonian money beast is alive and prospering today.

Revelation 3:9 (NIV) I will make those who are of the synagogue of Satan, who claim to be Jews though they are not, but are liars—I will make them come and fall down at your feet and acknowledge that I have loved you.

The advent of Christ Jesus

John 8:23 (NIV) But he continued, "You are from below; I am from above. You are of this world; I am not of this world.

John 6:35,37-38 (RSV) Jesus said to them, "I am the bread of life; he who comes to me shall not hunger, and he who believes in me shall never thirst. _37_ All that the Father gives me will come to me; and him who comes to me I will not cast out. _38_ For I have come down from heaven, not to do my own will, but the will of him who sent me;

John 3: 5-6 (NIV) "Very truly I tell you, no one can enter the kingdom of God unless they are born of water and the Spirit. _6_ Flesh gives birth to flesh, but the Spirit gives birth to spirit.

Luke 12:32 (NRSV) "Do not be afraid, little flock, for it is your Father's good pleasure to give you the kingdom.

Matthew 18:14 (NRSV) ...it is not the will of your Father in heaven that one of these little ones should be lost.

Luke 19:10 (NRSV) For the Son of Man came to seek out and to save the lost."

Matthew 5:16 (NRSV) Let your light so shine before men, that they may see your good works and give glory to your Father who is in heaven.

John 14:12 (KJV) Verily, verily, I say unto you, He that believeth on me, the works that I do shall he do also; and greater works than these shall he do; because I go unto my Father.

John 10:10 (NRSV) The thief comes only to steal and kill and destroy; I came that they may have life, and have it abundantly.

John 3:20 (NRSV) For every one who does evil hates the light, and does not come to the light, lest his deeds should be exposed. 21 But he who does what is true comes to the light, that it may be clearly seen that his deeds have been wrought in God.

Matthew 5:44-45 (NRSV) But I say to you, Love your enemies and pray for those who persecute you, 45 so that you may be children of your Father in heaven;

Mark 4:22-25 (RSV) For there is nothing hid, except to be made manifest; nor is anything secret, except to come to light. 23 If any man has ears to hear, let him hear." 24 And he said to them, "Take heed what you hear; the measure you give will be the measure you get, and still more will be given you. 25 For to him who has will more be given; and from him who has not, even what he has will be taken away."

Romans 5:19 (NRSV) For just as by the one man's disobedience the many were made sinners, so by the one man's obedience the many will be made righteous.

The Transfiguration
Matthew 17:2 (NRSV) And he was transfigured before them, and his face shone like the sun, and his garments became white as light;

The Crucifixion
John 10:17-18 (NRSV) For this reason the Father loves me, because I lay down my life in order to take it up again. 18 No one takes it from me, but I lay it down of my own accord. I have power to lay it down, and I have power to take it up again. I have received this command from my Father."

Matthew 27:50-51 (NIV) And Jesus cried again with a loud voice and yielded up his spirit. 51 And behold, the curtain of the temple was torn in two, from top to bottom; and the earth shook, and the rocks were split;

The Resurrection
John 11:25-26 (NRSV) I AM the resurrection and the life

The Ascension
John14:1-3 (NRSV) Do not let your hearts be troubled. Believe in God, believe also in me. 2 In my Father's house there are many dwelling places. If it were not so, would I have told you that I go to prepare a place for you? 3 And if I go and prepare a place for you, I will come again and will take you to myself, so that where I am, there you may be also.

John 3:14-15 (NIV) ...the Son of Man must be exalted, lifted up15 that everyone who believes may have eternal life in him

330 AD: Roman Emperor Constantine
Constantine had conquered more territory than his army could control. He needed a way to control the subjugated population at a grassroots level, within a uniform code. He saw the, theretofore, persecuted, but still growing and wide-spread, Christian faith as his opportunity.

This precipitated the first powerful example of the conjunctive melding of church and state that used Christianity as its doctrinal core. The Roman emperor flushed out the Christian leadership by a prestigious invitation to a great conference to debate the largest "doctrinal divide"[81] between Christian sects and to find consensus. Then, they were to "purify" the scriptures to articulate that consensus.

The debate did not end in consensus.

". . .mainstream Christian thought at the time,. . .held that Jesus, as the Son of God, was subordinate to his father and of a similar, rather than identical essence." An opposing, small group," maintained that the Father and the Son were of the same substance.". . ."Constantine offered a new creed expounding the nature of God," and, "as a result of its adoption by the universal council, became the essential statement of belief for all Christians in the empire. It contained the compromise formulation that God the Father and God the Son were 'consubstantial'." The Nicene Creed became the most widely read document authored by a Roman Emperor.[82]

Thereby, it was Constantine who formed the central doctrine of the Christian church, which would soon dominate the world. Thus, all Christian churches espousing, this doctrine, worship according to the dictate of a pagan Roman Emperor, who is one of the history's most successful experts in inflicting, widely spreading, and enforcing the conquest ethic.

The Constantine-backed doctrine was made into the newly official Church, which was granted the power to be the sole, earthly arbitrator between God /Jesus and mankind. Using the might of the Roman military, the new Church burned all the libraries they could find containing spiritual concepts outside their doctrine. The other Christian leaders and people who would not comply were sought out and martyred.

This is when the Sabbath was changed to Sunday. There is no Biblical support for this change. The celebration of Jesus' birth was changed to December 25th, the pagan celebration of the return of the sun, from its withdrawal through winter.

Constantine was a pagan sun-worshiper. All accounts of this time say he was not baptized Christian until he was on his deathbed. They differ on whether he was too far dead to resist or that he wanted to hedge his bets.

The scriptures chosen (canonized) from this conference where compiled and edited toward expressing the chosen doctrine, while yet retaining credibility for those alive who had knowledge of the earlier versions of the scriptures. A new, official bible was created out of these efforts.

Only two to four copies of this Bible, depending on the source, remain. One is called Codex Sinaticus and is dated mid-4th century. Additional doctrinal revisions are written in the margins. A sample of these is in Matthew 24:36. The phrase "nor the Son" was crossed out. The King James Version of the Bible records this deletion. Newer versions of the Bible, created from other and earlier scriptural texts, have restored that phrase.

10th-16th Centuries: Serfdom
In Eastern Europe, from the 10th century and strongly through the 14th, dwindling throughout the 15th and 16th centuries, hundreds of thousands of white people experienced generational, physical, and economic tyranny from white masters within a Church-supported, feudal system.[83]

1100s-1800s: The inquisition

The Inquisition has its origins in the early organized persecution of non-Catholic Christian religions in Europe. In 1184.[84] One of these groups was concentrated in what is now the southern part of France and northern Spain. They called themselves the "Cathars," which means the "Pure Ones." The scripture they focused on most was the Lord's Prayer. The Cathars refused to bow to the Catholic Pope, to acknowledge the papacy's claim to infallibility, or to convert to Catholicism. Purportedly, they also had certain artifacts that the Pope coveted. Historically, the genocidal war waged by the Catholic Church against Cathars was considered the first crusade launched against a Christian population.

The Inquisition became an official office created within the Catholic Church charged to root out and to punish those who did not accept the authority of the Catholic Church and its doctrines. It is known by the brutality of its tortures and the cruelty of its executions. It began in the 12th century. The last recorded execution was of a school teacher in Spain in 1826.

Corruption was rampant throughout those who enforced the Inquisition. It was used to eliminate political opponents, including an estimated 15,000 Knights Templar and also Joan of Arc. It was used to steal wealth. The Inquisition in Spain was the most notoriously vicious.

It was Napoleon who finally, temporarily, stopped the Spanish inquisition, when he conquered that country in 1808, The attempt was made to reignite the Inquisition and the last execution was of the school teacher mentioned above.

The Supreme Sacred Congregation of the Roman and Universal Inquisition still exists within the Catholic Church, now called Congregation for the Doctrine of the Faith.

14th-20th Centuries: The Ottoman conquest of Europe

The Islam Ottoman Empire, originating in Turkey, sought territorial expansion through invasions into mostly eastern and central Europe beginning in the 14th century and continuing into the early 20th century. At its height, it encompassed all of southern Europe and northern Africa as far as Algeria.[85]

Taking Christians as slaves, creating European converts to Islam to fight in their armies, and a system "by which Christian youths were drafted from the Balkan provinces for conversion to Islam and life service to the sultan," soon prevailed.[86] This is one of the global, historic examples of the white race being enslaved by people of color.

1486-1800s: Witches hammer

Malleus Maleficarum is usually translated as the "Hammer for Witches," and is the best known treatise on the recognition, apprehension, trial, torture, and execution of witches, from 1486, when it was written, through the 1800s. It was used by both the Catholic and Protestant Churches, which, in-turn, influenced its wide use through secular government and court systems.

After a papal bull supported the work of inquisitors in this area, this book was written by Heinrich Kramer, with another inquisitor, Jacob Sprenger, added later as an author.

"Kramer wrote the *Malleus* following his expulsion from Innsbruck by the local bishop, due to charges of illegal behavior against Kramer himself, and because of Kramer's obsession with the sexual habits of one of the accused, Helena Scheuberin, which led the other tribunal members to suspend the trial.[87]

This book was the first force that raised "harmful sorcery" to the criminal status of heresy."[88] Kramer's book proclaims that:

- nearly all committing witchcraft are women [about 80% of all prosecuted were women];
- women are by nature corrupt and evil,
- because women are the negative counterpart to men, they corrupt male perfection through witchcraft and must be destroyed;[89] and
- most women are doomed to become witches, who cannot be redeemed; and the only recourse open to the authorities is to ferret out and exterminate all witches.

The book describes in detail what traits pointed to witchcraft. It states that witches:

- behave outside proper female decorum,
- have strong personalities,
- dominate their husbands,
- could not or did not cry during trial or torture,
- were midwives,
- had marks on their bodies [all their hair was typically shaved off in the search],
- had red hair on heads and private parts, and
- could not be drowned or burned.

Any witness, regardless of credentials, could testify against someone accused of witchcraft. Torture of both of the accused and witnesses was used to draw out confessions. The executions were horrendously painful.

Both, Kramer and Sprenger were staunch in their conviction that God would never permit an innocent person to be convicted of witchcraft. Yet, logically following their assertion from the last bullet point above: all those who died from drowning or being burned at the stake, as a result of their trial or conviction, were proved to not be witches.

"According to the latest estimates, 45,000 people were executed for witchcraft in Early Modern Europe. … Women were four times more likely to be executed for witchcraft than men[90]. That makes the female death toll approximately 36,000.

Enforcement of the Witches Hammer was a gruesome movement to enslave all women into a narrow doctrinal slavery. It was an atrocity inflicted on all free-thinking people, women and men, who thought and lived outside that doctrine, with the greatest violence being imposed on women.

Beginning in 1380: Translations of the Bible into common language

In 1380, came the first recorded translations from the Vulgate Latin of the Constantine Bible into language the common Christian populations could understand.[91] It was translated into English by John Wycliffe, a theologian, scholar, and church reformer. Also in the 14th century, a group of unknown scholars produced a Bible in German. Martin Luther's German version, compiled from 1522-1534 is the most famous one.

Since 330 AD, the scriptures had been only translated and interpreted to the common people through priests. The Catholic Church vigorously opposed these new translations and pronounced them heretical.

1492: Columbus

Christopher Columbus was a sailor and navigator searching for a shorter way to the rich markets of China and the Far East. He never set foot on North American soil! Funded by King Ferdinand and Queen Isabella of Spain, Columbus first sailed the three-ship fleet provided for him west in 1492. Columbus' voyages were centralized in the Caribbean Islands. The Spanish military, known as conquistadors, were a mandatory part of the voyage, as ordered by the funding sovereigns. The conquistadors were ordered to seize anything of value they found. The hope was for gold. When that was not present, they seized hundreds of native people as slaves to enrich the Spanish monarchy and defray expenses.

The earliest that African slaves were brought to North America by European slavers was 1619, 127 years after Columbus' first voyage took place and 284 years before the Declaration of Independence made the United States of America a nation. The only slaves on the North American continent, before and at Columbus' time, were captured and held through the conquest activities of the Native American tribes against each other. Columbus had nothing at all to do with slavery in North America.

16th Century: Protestant Reformation

The unresolved quarrel over Biblical translations and numerous grievances delivered to the Catholic Church[92] resulted in the first two protestant schisms in the Christian Church. Both in Germany, they were the Lutheran Church[93] and the much less known Mennonites,[94] who called their reform "the third way."

Wars of European monarchies

From the mid-1500s to the mid-1600s, these wars were waged not only for power and land, between and within nations. A key element in many disputes was religion, specifically what Christian doctrine was practiced by the "enemy." These wars are a bloody example of the results of melding of governmental power and religious doctrine. So is the Spanish Inquisition.

Impacts of slavery in America

Three general groups of people, one indigenous and two from beyond our shores, have converged into the melting pot of modern day America. All three have horrific experiences – dating as early as 30 BC with the immoral, malicious, criminal monster of slavery. They are, in order of their experiences with slavery, white immigrants descending from slaves and serfs, the Native Americans, and Africans kidnaped from west Africa and sold into slavery in North America. The experiences of these three groups are detailed in the next chapter.

Illuminati

It is usually reported that the Illuminati was originally founded as the Bavarian Illuminati by Johann Adam Weishaupt in 1776.[95] It's purposes were for constructive spiritual studies and conversations between like-minded men across the European continent. It was rather quickly infiltrated, as a convenient vehicle, by the serpentine forces that embodied the Babylonian money beast and the luciferian cults of ancient Egypt. There was an effort to restore it to God in 1834, but that was unsuccessful.

The Illuminati have proceeded with their blatantly satanic practices and objectives ever since. They have always been devoted to global conquest. Today they are strong in the multi-national corporations, which include banking and financial sectors. To find them, follow the money, the power, and satanism and its perverse sexual practices in powerful places. They have infiltrated virtually every avenue of mankind's expression and civilization.

Ephesians 6:12 (NRSV) For our struggle is not against enemies of blood and flesh, but against the rulers, against the authorities, against the cosmic powers of this present darkness, against the spiritual forces of evil in the heavenly places.

1776: Declaration of Independence

By signing the Declaration, our American founders were guilty of high treason under British law.

The penalty for high treason was to be hanged by the neck until unconscious, then cut down and revived, then disemboweled and cut into quarters. The head and quarters were at the disposal of the crown. This is an example of the harshness of European serfdom, a form of slavery.[96]

The principles of our Declaration were the first, in humanity's available history, where a country on earth began by declaring that God is the author and giver of unalienable rights to us His Children.

"For that Parchment will be the Text-book of Freedom–the Bible of the Rights of Man forever!" – the Speech of the Unknown, at the signing of the Declaration of Independence.

"I have said that the Declaration of Independence is the ring-bolt to the chain of your nation's destiny ...The point from which I am compelled to view them [the signatories] is not, certainly, the most favorable; and yet I cannot contemplate their great deeds with less than admiration. They were statesmen, patriots, and heroes, and for the good they did, and the principles they contended for, I will unite with you to honor their memory."[97] – Frederick Douglas, an African American who escaped slavery, became a noted abolitionist in the North

Take a read of the Declaration of Independence on the internet. It will provide interesting points of comparison as you continue to read this book.[98]

1790: The Constitution of the United States of America[99]

The deliberations of the Constitutional Convention of 1787 were held in strict secrecy. Consequently, anxious citizens gathered outside Independence Hall when the proceedings ended in order to learn what had been produced behind closed doors. The answer was provided immediately. A Mrs. Powel of Philadelphia asked Benjamin Franklin, "Well, Doctor, what have we got, a republic or a monarchy?" With no hesitation whatsoever, Franklin responded, "A republic, if you can keep it."[100]

Our freedoms require our continuous effort, participation, and collaboration to remain sustainable.

The draft of this document was begun on May 25, 1787; it was ratified on May 29, 1790.[101]

The Constitution of the United States of American encodes the principles that Jesus Christ spoke and demonstrated into the operation of government.

"What does it mean to say that we live in a Christian nation? What this really means is that our core principles, in fact, we share even across the political spectrum. The idea of the preciousness of human life. the dignity of human beings, equality, the idea of compassion, these are all the legacy of Christianity.

"The proof, by the way, is to look at the world before Christianity in pre-Christian Greece and Rome. These values really did not exist, at least not in their current form. When Jefferson sat down to write where our rights come from, he could think of only one source: the Creator. It is the theological principle that we are created equal in the eyes of God.

"This notion of moral equality translates into a political corollary, which is that no man has the right to rule another the core principle of anti-slavery, but, very interestingly, the core principle of democracy. Because what's democracy based on? No man has the right to rule another without consent."[102] – Dinesh D'Souza

The Constitution of the United States of America is specifically designed toward protecting the unalienable rights given by God to each individual within mankind. It is designed toward creating and maintaining the outer manifestations of liberty and freedom, based on God-principles.

"...there is neither warrant, license, nor sanction of the hateful thing [slavery]; but, interpreted as it ought to be interpreted, the Constitution is a GLORIOUS LIBERTY DOCUMENT. Read its preamble, consider its purposes. Is slavery among them? Is it at the gateway? ... is it in the temple? It is neither. ...take the Constitution according to its plain reading, and I defy the presentation of a single pro-slavery clause in it. On the other hand, it will be found to contain principles and purposes, entirely hostile to the existence of slavery." – Frederick Douglass[103]

The American Constitution creates a protection against a fusion of government and religious doctrine while protecting the rights of each individual to worship the Supreme Being as our conscience directs – or to choose not to worship.

The First Amendment to the Constitution in the Bill of Rights reads: *"Congress shall make no law respecting an establishment of religion, or prohibiting the free exercise thereof; or abridging the freedom of speech, or of the press; or the right of the people peaceably to assemble, and to petition the Government for a redress of grievances."*

This document is written with the wisdom to separate government from religious doctrine. In this document, all our other founding documents, and the writings and lives of our founders, even greater wisdom and understanding is shown. Our country's founders never separate the United States of America, Her governance, our people, or themselves from God, the Supreme Being. Rather they are constantly acknowledging, praising, and invoking God's Presence in the affairs and destiny of America.

No wonder the serpent and its minions have so ravenously lusted for the demise of our beloved America, the home and beacon to the world of the I AM race.

God is showing miraculous, loving patience, and restraint in allowing us to use our free will choice and learn from our mistakes. Remember, God views everything from a position of eternity and infinity, within Love. That also means that we can choose eons of the most abject slavery and abuse.

Unless we call to God for His intervention.

Let's learn from history and from current events, as we continue our historical flyover.

1830-1850: The Trail of Tears and the "one drop" rule
According to tribal heritage, the "one-drop" rule[104] was first inflicted on the Native Americans to steal their lands, property, and freedom during President Andrew Jackson's Indian Removal Act, enforced between 1830-1850. Any person with 1/32 Native American ancestry was removed, at gun point, from their homes, land, and businesses, with only what they could carry. They were then forcibly marched to locations thousands of miles away and west of the Mississippi River. This became known as the Trail of Tears. Many thousands died along the way.

Before and during the centuries of slavery, people had interracial relationships, both forced and voluntary. In the years before the Civil War, free people of mixed race (free people of color) were generally considered legally white if individuals had less than one-eighth or one-quarter African ancestry (depending on the state). Many mixed-race people were absorbed into the majority culture based simply on appearance, associations, and carrying out community responsibilities."[105]

The "one-drop" rule was next applied to the African Americans and morphed into the Jim Crow Laws.

1837-today: Urban plantations
President Martin Van Buren fashioned urban plantations on the agricultural plantations of the pre- Civil War South. They were used to create and control large blocks of voters, held in line by patronage. After the Civil War, vulnerable minorities were targeted, especially blacks migrating north and also immigrants. Later, big city "bosses" were raised up like William Magear Tweed "boss' of Tammany Hall in New York and Richard Daley in Chicago.[106]

1860: Abraham Lincoln elected to the Presidency of the United States of America
In the ten southern states, Lincoln's name did not appear on the ballot.[107]

"Lincoln thought he discerned the hand of a plot," Dr. Allen Guelzo, Director of Civil War Studies, Gettysburg College

Abraham Lincoln saw theft as the fundamental sin of slavery. It is the theft of people's lives, freedom, and the fruits of their labors. Slavery has been rampant all over the world since time immemorial. It wasn't until later that a narrowed racial aspect was assigned to slavery in America.[108]

Lincoln often said that slavery was the immoral hypocrisy expressed as, "you work and toil and earn bread, and I'll eat it." He asserted that whenever he heard someone advocating slavery, he felt the firm desire to see it tried out on the advocator personally.

This significant divide that underlines the philosophies of anti-slavery and pro-slavery is strongly present today in politics. It is fundamentally the same. The underlying concept is either:

- individual citizens get to keep the fruits of their own labors, or
- government gets to take the fruits of their subjects' labor, either for themselves or to be redistributed through government programs of the governmental leaders' choosing.[109]

An American socialist theorist of the Civil War times, George Fitzhugh declared that slavery was actually what they were reading about from European socialists. He argued that slavery was a practical form of socialism. It looks after people, who can't take care of themselves, throughout their lifetimes.

Fitzhugh even tried to sell slavery to black leaders as an early form of the welfare state. Interestingly, he did not apply an exclusively racial label. Reducing people of any race to extreme poverty also had a similar effect. Fitzhugh and his cronies advocated the expansion of "slavery" throughout the United States.[110]

"Fitzhugh differed from nearly all of his southern contemporaries by advocating a slavery that crossed racial boundaries. … and suggested that if Yankees were caught young they could be trained, domesticated, and civilized to make 'faithful and valuable servants.'" [111] In other words, he saw whites and all other races as available for slavery.

"It is a libel on white men to say they are unfit for slavery. [112] *– George Fitzhugh, 1860*

The plot Lincoln discerned was the intention to turn all of America into a plantation.

A nation, whose people do not remain free, will be a slave planation and eventually a nation of acute poverty.

1861-1865: The Civil War

The United States of America is the only country in the world that has fought a civil war for the end of slavery within its borders. President Lincoln first intervened in slavery in America with the "Emancipation Proclamation" freeing the, primarily, southern, slaves.

Frederick Douglass found fault in the United States' previous protection of slavery. At first he called Lincoln the "white man's president." Later the two entered into conversations, including on how to best resolve the fact that blacks were kidnapped from their homes in Africa and sold into slavery in America. Putting aside a proposed idea to re-immigrate the African Americans back to Africa, Douglass opted to be part of the grand experiment and last best hope that America still is.[113]

Soon after, Lincoln paid with his life for the passing of the 13th Amendment to the US Constitution ending slavery, and for his intention to garner African Americans equal process under law and the right to vote.

A note from 2020: As the riots in America continued, a number of the genuine founders and leaders of Black Lives Matter resigned[114] from the organization, stating that it had been hijacked by those intent on destroying America. These grassroots leaders asserted that their intent had always been improving America from the inside. They made a similar decision to Douglass'.

1865: 13th Amendment

The 13th Amendment to the Constitution of the United States abolishes slavery. It was first passed in the Senate in 1864, but failed in the House. The Republican Party again proposed the 13th Amendment in the House on January 31, 1865. "In the final vote, all 86 Republicans had voted in favor of the Thirteenth Amendment, along with 15 Democrats, 14 Unconditional Unionists, and 4 Union men; opposition came from 50 Democrats and 6 Union men.[115] The amendment passed by a vote of 119 to 56, narrowly reaching the required two-thirds majority. It was ratified on December 6, 1865.

1865-today: Ku Klux Klan

The KKK sought to thwart, by violence, African American participation in public life and community in the South.

"Nathan Bedford Forrest founded the KKK and was a pledge delegate to the Democratic convention," asserted Dr. Carol Swain, an African American who has taught at both Princeton and Vanderbilt[116]. Bedford had been a Confederate cavalry general.

The KKK was and still is a terrorist arm of the Democratic Party. After the Civil War, the KKK was responsible for the murder of 3,000 Black Republicans and 1,000 White Republicans.[117]

The Klan assassinated Rep. James Hinds (R-AK) on October 22, 1868 "for advocating civil rights for former slaves. Hinds was knocked off his horse by the shotgun blast to his back, and lay on the road until help arrived. Before he died, Hinds sent a message to his wife and identified his killer. He died about two hours after the attack. A Coroner's Inquest identified the shooter as

George Clark, secretary of the Monroe County Democratic Party and a local Klansman. Clark was never arrested or prosecuted.[118]

"The Ku Klux Klan is currently active in 33 states and 'still poses a threat' to US society," according to a new Anti-Defamation League (ADL) report from 2017. There is a proliferation of extreme white supremacist groups in America.[119]

US House Speaker Nancy Pelosi's great-grandfather is Nathan Bedford Forrest.[120] Former Senate Majority Leader Robert Byrd from West Virginia was also a former Ku Klux Klan Exalted Cyclops. And he was the president pro tempore in 2010, when Democrats controlled the Senate. Byrd was also a mentor and friend to Hillary Clinton. [121]

1865-1960: Jim Crow laws
"Democrats were the party of slavery, Jim Crow, the Ku Klux Klan, and anti-desegregation. Republicans were the party of Lincoln, Reconstruction, anti-lynching laws, and the civil rights acts."[122]

The "one-drop" rule, originally applied to Native Americans, was next applied to the African Americans and morphed into the Jim Crow Laws.

"The one-drop rule was a social and legal principle of racial classification that was historically prominent in the United States. It asserted that any person with even one ancestor of black ancestry ("one drop" of colored blood) is considered black (*Negro* or *colored* in historical terms)."[123]

"The one-drop rule is defunct in law in the United States and was never codified into federal law."[124]

Dr. Carol Swain asserts that, as part of Jim Crow, African Americans were not allowed their Second Amendment rights.[125] Not being allowed to own guns made them completely vulnerable to the violence of the KKK.

"Jim Crow" forced blacks into an inferior position through a system of laws enforced at the state level. These laws were enforced from 1865 through the 1960s. Locals committed lynching, if police enforcement did not produce the results they wanted. An estimated 3,500 blacks were lynched during this period.

"... the political enforcement of Jim Crow was entirely in Democratic hands. The Ku Klux Klan functioned as the paramilitary wing of the Democratic party, and it was used to drive Republicans out of the South after the Civil War."[126]

In the 21st century: "It is standard SJ (Social Justice) fare to claim that America (and specifically white Americans) must atone for the past sins of racism. Thus, the institution of America carries the burden of racial guilt.

"However, if institutions carry burdens of guilt, then let's get more specific. It was the Democratic party in the United States that was most responsible for slavery and Jim Crow.

"At the time of the Civil War, all slaveholders were Democrats, or at least no one has proved an exception at this time. ... Although the KKK was not officially aligned with the Democratic party, it consisted of white Democrats who terrorized both white and black Republicans (mostly black ones)."[127]

There has been a flurry of "proofs" regarding the possibility that there were ten Republican slave owners at the time of the Civil War. Their research and "logic," in my opinion, has holes in it. Let's assume, for demonstration, that their assertion is actually correct.

The *Quora* website has this to say, "In the eleven states that formed the Confederacy, according to the 1860 census there were 316,632 registered slave owners out of some 5.5 million free inhabitants...or about 5.7%."

Following the math, if there were truly ten Republicans at the time of the Civil War - even if they were only in the Confederate states, that would mean that Republican slave owners were 0.00003 of 1% of all slave owners. That number is infinitesimal. It only further proves that slavery was a Democratic Party institution.

1866: 14th Amendment
Republican Congressman John Bingham wrote the 14th Amendment to guarantee due process and equal protection of the laws to all citizens. It enshrines in the Constitution provisions of the GOP's 1866 Civil Rights Act. . . . After its passage in the Senate, in the House, all votes in favor of the 14th Amendment were from Republicans. All votes against it were from Democrats. This Amendment passed on June 13, 1866. It was ratified July 9, 1868.[128]

Late 1800s-current: Eugenics
There are two basic aims of eugenics: 1. to keep those judged "unfit" from leaving descendants, and 2. to multiply the more "fit and useful" citizens. Its purpose is really about protecting the position of the elites. Those groups most often targeted were the disabled, mentally ill, the poor, and racial minorities particularly African Americans, Native Americans, and Hispanics.[129]

Massive funding for eugenics came from the Carnegie Institution, Rockefeller Foundation, the Harriman railroad fortune, and from J.H. Kellogg.[130]

Margaret Sanger was a foremost leader of the eugenics movement. The Sanger group's parent organization, The American Birth Control League, had as its goal: to promote eugenic birth selection through the United States. She was also the founder of what became Planned Parenthood.[131]

Today, 78% of the Planned Parenthood clinics are located in minority neighborhoods. And PP is the largest provider of abortions in America.[132]

The leading cause of death in America[133] and worldwide[134] is now abortion.

Currently, according to the source, the blacks are 12% to 13.6% of the population, but are having 36% of the abortions. [135]

Adolf Hitler and the Nazis borrowed extensively from the American eugenics movement for their "Final Solution to the Jewish question."

At the Nuremberg trials, Nazi eugenicists attempted to justify their human rights abuses by claiming there was little difference between Nazi eugenics and US eugenics. [136]

In 1927, Supreme Court Justice Oliver Wendell Holmes Jr. wrote the majority decision that government-forced compulsory sterilization of the "unfit, including intellectually disabled" for the protection and health of the state did not violate the Due Process clause of the 14th Amendment. This led to 70,000 forced sterilizations in the United States.[137]

This Supreme Court ruling directly applied to Carrie Buck, a young white woman, who could read. As a result of the ruling, she was forcibly sterilized.

There is no evidence that men were sterilized.

1869: 15th Amendment

The 15th Amendment was proposed by the Republican Party, toward securing the vote for men of color, "regardless of previous conditions of servitude ." Previously passed in the Senate, "the vote in the House was 144 to 44, with 35 not voting. The House vote was almost entirely along party lines, with no Democrats supporting the bill and only 3 Republicans voting against it, some because they thought the amendment did not go far enough in its protections." This amendment passed on February 26, 1869 and was ratified on February 3, 1870.[138]

At this time, no women in the US had federal voting privileges.

African Americans – many of them newly freed slaves – put their newfound freedom to use, voting into office scores of Black candidates. During Reconstruction, 16 Black men served in Congress and 2,000 Black men served in elected local, state, and federal positions. [139]

Most Southern state legislatures quickly enacted Jim Crow laws to work around the 15th Amendment, like literacy tests and poll taxes. The KKK added intimidation factors. Democrat Andrew Johnson followed Lincoln as president.

Suppression of black voting, particularly in the south, was fiercely pursued beginning in 1870. Though much reduced, this suppression has not been fully eliminated.[140]

1886: The Statue of Liberty

Dedicated on October 28, 1886, "the Lady" in New York City harbor was gifted to the American people by the people of France, most notably their children.[141]

The inscription at the base of the statue reads:
"Give me your tired, your poor,
Your huddled masses, yearning to breathe free,
The wretched refuse of your teeming shore,
Send these, the homeless, tempest tost to me,
I lift my lamp beside the golden door." – Emma Lazarus

It welcomes all the enslaved and persecuted in other lands to the hope and possibility of freedom.

1895: Fabian Society
The claws of the beast of global enslavement entered the United States of America in 1895 with the Fabian Society. The Fabian Society projects a socialistic concern for the masses, championing the State as God, which would take care of the poor, so they would never be in need. Its coat of arms depicts a wolf in sheep's clothing. Their true objective is oligarchic collectivism.[143]

Today, they are found primarily in corporatism, including the financial sector, and in globalism, and wherever these interests intersect with politics.

<u>Matthew 7:15</u> *(RSV) "Beware of false prophets, who come to you in sheep's clothing but inwardly are ravenous wolves.*

1913: Federal Reserve
Baron Alfred Charles Rothschild (1842-1918), a world banker of enormous power, was the mastermind of what became the Federal Reserve. It was, and is, a plan designed to undermine and weaken America's financial structure and to exert major control over our economy and our politics. The power is held by the international elite.

After Woodrow Wilson's election to the presidency, Rep. Carter Glass, Chairman of the Banking and Currency Committee, introduced the Glass Bill toward creation of a central banking system. Allegedly, this new system was supported to end a perceived threat from twelve banks in New York City, Boston, and Chicago, which purportedly dominated 75% of the money interests in the US.

On April 15, 1912, the Titanic sank with the majority of the most influential American leaders opposed to the Glass Bill on it. J.P. Morgan was scheduled to sail, but changed his plans at the last moment.

On June 26, 1913, the bill passed in the House of Representatives; a revised bill was passed by the Senate on November 22. The politically imbalanced Conference Committee hastily prepared a compromise draft. Without any public hearings, the resultant Glass-Owen Bill was brought to the Congress on December 23, 1913. Many Congressmen and Senators, including some very key individuals, were already away from Washington D.C. It passed the House and was immediately sent to the Senate where it passed the Senate. The vote there was 43 yea to 25 nay, 27 absent or abstaining. Only an hour after the Senate vote, President Wilson signed the Federal Reserve Act into law.[144]

The Federal Reserve is not an agency of our federal government and has no "reserves ." With its passing, all money and credit resource of our country came under the control of J.P. Morgan's First National Bank and Kuhn & Loeb's National City Bank in London. The latter's principle allegiances were to international banking interests.[145] And by that time, "British foreign policy and the Rothschild Banking family foreign policy (had already become) one and the same."[146] From then, US banking and currency was fully controlled by the Federal Reserve and the Illuminati.

1917: Russia falls to communism

The Union of Soviet Socialist Republics was formed in 1917 by the Bolsheviks, after revolting against the Provisional Government under Prince Lvov. Communism came out of the philosophy and writings of Karl Marx.

In his book, *The Devil and Karl Marx: Communism's Long March of Death, Deception, and Infiltration,* Professor Paul Kengor offers remarkable and timely information about the source and goal of Karl Marx's ideology. Marx is the foundation of communism and socialism worldwide. More humans have perished, by far, due to these lock-stepped political ideologies than any other political system in history. The number of the dead is generally placed at 140 million.

The chosen loyalty and orientation Karl Marx chose is clear, not only in writings "replete with paeans to Satan." From his personal poetry, here are two samples: from the "The Pale Maiden": "Thus Heaven I've forfeited, I know it full well. My soul, once true to God, is chosen for Hell." And from "The Player", Marx wrote: "See the sword – the Prince of Darkness sold it to me. For he beats the time and gives the signs. Ever more boldly I play the dance of death."

Here, it is well to follow the money and the power. And know that they are using the same "conquest playbook" for the United States of America.

Vladimir Lenin governed Russia from 1917 until his death in 1924[147]

1919: 19th Amendment

The road to acknowledging the right of women to vote and, thereby, become real citizens of this country, was a long one, beginning in 1878.

"The Republican Party pioneered the right of women to vote and was consistent in its support throughout the long campaign for acceptance. It was the first major party to advocate equal rights for women and the principle of equal pay for equal work." - National Federation of Republican Women

"When the House of Representatives passed the 19th Amendment in May 1919 it did so by 304 votes to 89, with Democrats only 104 to 70 in favour but Republicans 200 to 19. "When the Republicans were right." - London Review of Books

On May 21, 1919, US Representative James R. Mann, a Republican from Illinois and chairman of the Suffrage Committee, proposed the House resolution to approve the Susan Anthony

Amendment granting women the right to vote. The measure passed the House 304 to 89—a full 42 votes above the required two-thirds majority.[148]

Two weeks later, on June 4, 1919, the US Senate passed the 19th Amendment by two votes over its two-thirds required majority, 56-25. The amendment was then sent to the states for ratification.[149]

Democrats tried vigorously to block ratification of the 19th Amendment, but failed.[150]

1920: American Civil Liberties Union (ACLU)

The process toward forming the ACLU began in 1914, led by communist and socialist leaders in America. In 1920, the American Civil Liberties Union was officially formed, with socialist Roger Baldwin in the lead. The publicized goal of the organization was to fight for "the rights of man set forth in the Declaration of Independence and the Constitution."[151]

Has there ever been an organization of socialist or communistic doctrine that ever truly supported the United States of America, or its Declaration of Independence and Constitution?

"I am for socialism, disarmament, and ultimately for abolishing the State itself as an instrument of violence and compulsion. I see the social ownership of property, the abolition of the propertied class and social control of those who produce wealth. Communism is the goal."[152] – Roger Baldwin, 1935

Generally, the ACLU will defend only someone whose case will be another micro-step toward replacing the United States of America with a communist regime.

"In thirty-seven years of history of the Communist movement in the United States, the Communist Party has never been able to do as much for itself as the American Civil Liberty Union has done for it.[153] - Dr. J. B. Matthews, Chief Investigator for the House Special Committee on Un-American Activities in 1955

Cases involving the separation of church and state are their specialty. The ACLU is one of the most dominant weapons tearing away at Christian faith and tradition in America.[154]

1922-1945: Fascism

The original fascist ideology was formulated by Italians Giovanni Gentile and Benito Mussolini.[155] Fascism is one-party totalitarianism. This form of government suppresses individual freedoms, voting by the populace is denied, and opposing opinion is not tolerated. Corporatism is part of the system. Companies and production may be owned by selected individuals, but are completely controlled by the government. Fascist regimes tend to exhibit severe nationalism and militarism. Historically, fascism was considered as an extreme leftist phenomenon.

Italy

Fascist dictator Mussolini ruled Italy from 1922 to 1943.[156]

Germany

The Nazis core is fascism, but it added the "intense emotion of antisemitism, scientific racism, and eugenics into its creed. It subscribed to theories of racial hierarchy and Social Darwinism, identifying the Germans as a part of what the Nazis regarded as an Aryan or Nordic master race."[157]

Adolf Hitler became Germany's Chancellor in 1933. He was Führer from 1934 to 1945.[158] Who funded the Nazis?

Adolf Hitler admired and used many political and social interpretations from America. These included the handling of the American Indians, the Jim Crow Laws, euthanasia of "inferior" races, and slavery.[159]

Nazi laws making Jews second-class citizens without rights were derived from the Jim Crow laws. Even the Nazi's found the "one drop" law first applied to the Native Americans too severe.[160]

Euthanasia was applied in Germany first with institutionalized people with disabilities, the "worthless eaters" as they were called. The practice was put on an industrialized scale in the "Final Solution to the Jewish question" for the extermination of the Jews. Approximately 2.7 million people, mostly Jews, were systematically murdered in this way.[161]

Concentration camps were slavery under another name. Though the Nazis often deliberately worked people to death. [162]

1929-1941: The Great Depression
Caused by a variety of factors and triggered by the 1929 stock market crash, the Great Depression in America lasted until approximately 1941. The economic depression was actually worldwide.

1933+: President Roosevelt, Benito Mussolini, and Adolf Hitler overlaps
Roosevelt was very impressed with Mussolini. The US President called him "that admirable Italian gentleman . . . I am much interested and deeply impressed by what he has accomplished and by his evidenced, honest purpose in restoring Italy."

Having read one of Roosevelt's books, Mussolini remarked in an Italian magazine, "FDR is one of us! He's fascist."[163]

FDR dispatched some of his ranking advisors to Rome to investigate Mussolini's fascist implementations. They were looking to import some Italian strategies to the United States. Advisor Rexford Tugwell, after returning, exclaimed, "Fascism is the cleanest, neatest, most efficient piece of social machinery I've ever seen. It makes me envious."[164]

Hugh Johnson, director of FDR's National Recovery Act (NRA), pontificated on the "shining example of Mussolini." Johnson called for the end of free-market capitalism in America.[165]

Mussolini was a man of the left; FDR recognized him as that and as being more "progressive."[166]

Hitler was also on the "left." He formed his politics in Schwabing, Germany, within bohemianism and sectarian socialism.[167]

Hitler and Lenin, then in exile, frequented the same pub, Schellng-Salon, and lived in same neighborhood.[168] It is rumored that the 20-year-old Hitler and the twice-that-age Lenin played chess together.[169]

Later, Hitler changed the German Workers Party name to National Socialist Workers Party. "Nazi" is a contraction of the German words for "National" and "Socialistic." Check out the Nazi Party political platform and you'll find elements very familiar in today's America.[170]

Mussolini and Hitler were anti uncontrolled big business. Hitler was also a racist; his racism was rooted in hatred of capitalism.[171]

Hitler used America's Jim Crow laws as the foundation for "legally" classifying German Jews as second class citizens and removing their rights. He also drew significantly from the US eugenicists.[172]

Hitler wrote "fan mail" to the American progressives Madison Grant, head of the New York Zoological Society, and Leon Whitney of the American Eugenics Society. "Your writings are my Bible," Hitler wrote. He claimed they had had a dramatic impact on Germany. These American men were both colleagues of Margaret Sanger in the progressives' eugenicist movement. One of the US eugenicists commented, "...the Nazi's are beating us at our own game.".[173]

"National socialism is the determination to create a new man. There will no longer exist any individual arbitrary will, nor realms in which the individual belongs to himself. The time of happiness as a private matter is over. … If you tell a big enough lie and tell it frequently enough, it will be believed." . – Adolf Hitler, from his book Mien *Kamph*

A leading Nazi newspaper wrote about the Roosevelt administration, "We, too, as German Nationalist Socialists are looking toward America." Of FDR's New Deal, they said, "We fear only the possibility that it might fail."[174]

1933: Stealing of the US Gold Reserves
"The US was put...more firmly on the gold Standard by the Gold Standard Act of 1900. From 1900 to 1933, gold was coined by the US Mint, and our paper currency was tied into the amount of gold held in the US Treasury Reserves. "America's gold reserves were already being covertly transferred overseas."[175]

Purportedly, President Roosevelt believed the advice of John Keynes, England's leading economist, who recommended deficit spending as a way to fight the Great Depression and revitalize the economy. The idea included "borrowing" against future taxes. Keynes was a member of the Illuminati.[176]

"The surest way to overthrow an established social order is to debauch its currency," - Vladimir Lenin

Later John Keynes wrote, "Lenin was right, there is not more positive, or subtler, no surer means of overturning the existing basis of society than to debauch currency. … The process engages all of the hidden forces of economic law on the side of destruction, and does it in a manner that not one man in a million is able to diagnose." [177]

On April 15, 1933, Franklin Roosevelt, through a presidential executive order, required every person in the USA to exchange their gold bullion, gold coins, and gold backed currency for money not redeemable in precious metals. This was forced under criminal penalty. For their gold, they were paid $20.37 per ounce in the paper money issued by the Federal Reserve. The order required the Federal Reserve to also return their gold to the US Government, but they were paid in in gold certificates. [178]

The gold that remained in our country was, then, controlled by the Federal Reserve and the Illuminati. [179]

1939-1945: World War II
World War II was fought from 1939 to 1945. The United States entered the war on December 7, 1941, with the Japanese attack on Pearl Harbor.

1945 American Progressives react to Hitler's defeat
When Hitler was defeated, American Progressives knew that they were vulnerable to guilt by association. They had to cover their tracks so they could disavow their true motives. They choose to use a tactic recommended by Hitler himself: the big lie. They took action to:

- muddle the meaning of fascism,
- take "socialism" out of National Socialism,
- move the classification of fascism from its historically "extreme left wing" position into right wing connotations. [180]

1945: United Nations
The first recorded call for a global government came from Vladimir Lenin in 1915. [181] At the close of World War II, there was a big push for creating a stabile organization to be the core of the movement for a new world order.

The UN charter is largely designed after the Constitution of Russia and the *Communist Manifesto*. The charter was written by Alger Hiss, who became the UN's first secretary-general, and Joseph E. Johnson, who later became secretary of the Bilderberg Group. [182]

The United Nation's mission and vision statement boils down to 'the maintenance of international peace and security.' It claims eradicating conflicts across the globe as its pivotal duty. Through this focus on arbitration and police action, it seeks to improve lives and transform communities." [183]

How have the United Nation's military corps, the UN "peacekeepers," been used in the past?

"The United Nations is an international organization founded in 1945. It is currently made up of 193 Member States." – UN.org

Did you notice they said "states" not countries or nations? Does that tell you something about their mindset and goals?

They themselves note four areas of concentration:[184]

- maintain international peace and security
- protect human rights
- deliver humanitarian aid
- promote sustainable development

Tentacles of the United Nations, among others, include, [185]

- World Bank (International Bank for Reconstruction and Development), which intends to hold all the financial power of the world
- World Health Organization, to internationalize medical treatment
  (*Incoming class action law suits name current director-general of WHO, Dr Tedros Adhanom Ghebreyesus, as a defendant in crimes against humanity connected with the COVID-19 pandemic.*)
- International Monetary Fund (IMF) for international trade and commerce oversight
- UNESCO, United Nation's Educational, Scientific, and Cultural Organization for standardization of all education within the doctrine of collectivism, and other alignments in science and culture
- World Trade Organization
- World Court

"To achieve one world government it is necessary to remove from the minds of men their individualism, their loyalty to family traditions and national identification," Brock Chisholm, first director of the UN World Health Organization.[186]

Under the false front of "justice and peace," the UN has been the frontline ploy toward global government. It is the global government administrative arm of the new world order. They are being fashioned to become the future global bureaucracy.

The UN General Assembly adopted a budget of $3,073,830,500 for the United Nations to cover the year 2020 .

"The proposed programme budget for 2020, which provides necessary resources to the UN Secretariat to implement its various tasks, also prepares us well for entry into the Decade of Action for sustained development goals implementation (SDGs). - General Assembly President Tijjani Muhammad-Bande [187]

This is UN Agenda 2030, which is an internal goal within UN Agenda 21.[188]   For the implementation methods and repercussions of this agenda watch this video.[189]

In 2019, the United States of America paid 22% of the UN's budget or $674.2 million. Shares of the next largest countries include: China 12%, Japan 8.5%, Germany 6%, UK 4.6%, France 4.4%, Italy 3.3%, Brazil 2.9%, Russia 2.4%.[190]

The US has only one vote in the UN General Assembly, which is dominated by socialists. "Non-aligned" nations vote 85% of the time with the communists. Eighty-five percent (85%) of the time, the assembly as a whole has voted against the US on key issues.[191]

The military intent of the UN is "to disarm the US military, shut down our bases, give the UN control of our Armed Forces and nuclear weapons," while strengthening the UN forces so that they are unchallengeable. At that point, the UN would also control and command American military personnel.[192]

"The United Nations is the greatest fraud in all history. Its purpose is to destroy the United States," - Rep. John Rankin, (D-MSS, 1921-53)[193]

"When the existing governments and ruling theories of life, the decaying religious and the decaying political form of today, has sufficiently lost prestige through failure and catastrophe, then and then only will world-wide reconstruction be possible.- " H.G. Wells, 1933, The Shape of Things to Come[194]

"It is the sacred principles enshrined in the United Nations charter to which the American people will henceforth pledge their allegiance."- President George Bush, speech to the UN General Assembly, February 1, 1992[195]

"My vision is that we (the US) would become an instrument working as much as possible through the United Nations for freedom and democracy and human rights and global economic growth," - Bill Clinton, while campaigning for the Presidency[196]

1949: Chinese communism

"Religion is the opium of the masses." – Karl Marx

On October 1, 1949, following a bitter civil war with the nationalists, Chairman Mao Zedong broadcast his announcement of the Peoples Republic of China.[197]

Who funded the Chinese communists?

In communism, all property is owned by the State. People work and are given things according to their abilities and needs. The government controls everything. It is the sole giver of benefits, such as money, healthcare, and food. The credo is materialistic and atheistic. It is a one-party police state with a centralized command economy and incessant communist rhetoric. "Voting" is highly controlled; the government chooses all candidates.

The Chinese Communist Party (CCP) has become increasing controlling. In 1989, in Beijing's Tiananmen Square, they slaughtered thousands of student protestors.[198]

In May 2019, in the *"Chinese Daily"* newspaper, the CCP declared a "peoples war" on the United States of America. [199]

In December 2019, it instituted a "social credits' system for residents[200] backed up by intense techno-fascism. It has also been revealed that they are doing live organ harvesting using religious and ethnic prisoners.[201]

January 2, 2020, truth of CCP complicity in the Coronavirus pandemic began to leak.[202]

The CCP, and communism in general, are determined to realize global conquest.[203]

1960s: Saul Alinsky community organizing

Saul Alinsky refined "political shakedown" in the name of community organizing.[204] Highlights of his methods included:

- making the white middle class people ashamed of themselves by weaponizing where they were not perfectly living up to their ideals; beginning with college-aged young adults
- driving a wedge between the "haves" and the "have-nots"
- enticing large corporations to use their economic power for selfish motives

In the dedication to his book, *Reveille for Radicals,* Alinsky, an atheist, revealed his main mentor: *"...the first radical known to man who rebelled against the establishment and did it so effectively that he at least won his own kingdom...Lucifer."*[205]

Check out the lists of Alinsky's distinguished students, which include Barrack Obama and Hillary Clinton. [206]

1962-today: Education in US government school system

In 1962, expressions of prayer were taken out of schools, by a Supreme Court ruling that allowing group or individual verbalized prayer constituted the establishment of a religion. Please visit Appendix III for a brief historic overview of God in American education and the Supreme Court rulings forbidding prayer in public schools. There are many more rulings than the Engel v. Vitale case, which is usually highlighted. Drug addiction spiked as the 1962 kindergarteners graduated from high school. More details and ramifications in next chapter.

Spearheaded by these rulings, indoctrination spread to the removing of Judeo-Christian morals, replacing them with relative morality. Progressively egocentric focus and narcissism were encouraged. More recently, collectivism and herd-thinking has been punctuated by a shared, acute shame for the human "mistreatment" of the Earth.

1964: Civil Rights Act

There are have been five recent Civil Rights Acts, including the Civil Rights Act of 1964.

Since 1956, Republicans have consistently worked to get civil rights legislation through the Congress. They have just as consistently been blocked by Democrats. "Before he took up the cause of civil rights as president, Lyndon Johnson, acting as Senate majority leader, blocked the GOP's 1956 civil-rights bill, and gutted Eisenhower's 1957 Civil Rights Act. Democratic senators filibustered the GOP's 1960 Civil Rights Act."[207]

The Civil Rights Act of 1964 was truly a bi-partisan effort. And its passing was long overdue. As a percentage of their party, more Republicans voted for the Civil Rights Act of 1964 than did Democrats.

The final vote in the House, passing the 1964 Civil Rights act, was 290 to 130. Sixty percent of the Democrats brought 152 votes for the bill. Seventy-eight percent (78%) of the Republicans voted for the bill, with 138 votes. This included "nays" and "not voting" members. For the voting record in all of Civil Rights acts, please see.[208]

The 1968 Civil Rights Act, also known as the Fair Housing Act . . ."initially passed the House in a 327-93 vote, with 68 percent support from Democrats and 87 percent support from Republicans. It then went to the Senate, where it was amended and voted upon, passing in a 71-20 vote in which 42 Democrats (66 percent) and 29 Republicans (81 percent) voted in favor."[209]

1968: The War on Poverty

This political plan created the dependency of economic slavery on the poor of all races in America. By giving more money to the single mothers, it monetized the breakup of the nuclear family. Hereby, the morals of our people were assaulted through the hidden, but strong messages. The government had relieved poor men of the moral responsibility, joy, and honor of raising their own children. In conjunction, women were given more money to live on by having more babies. They didn't have to work. [210]

The so-called War on Poverty encouraged voting blocks for the political party, which enacted the subsidy-creating legislation. President Lyndon Johnson, the leader for this program, in private called it the "n----r" bill[211]. It was intended to increase pressure on blacks in the urban plantations.

"The poor people (in the early 20th century) were more decent.... In this welfare state, that was supposed to make them better off and better human beings, that's when the crime rate skyrocketed.... (Most) black children were being raised by two parents in 1960. But 30 years later after the liberal welfare state...the great majority of black children were being raised by... single parent(s)...This is the welfare state. When you pay people not to get married, they don't get married.... Socialism is a great idea. It does not mean it is a great reality." - Thomas Sowell, "The Myths of Economic Inequality," Uncommon Knowledge

"The African Americans were leading decent lives and better themselves until the government started to help them?" Peter Robinson asked Sowell, whom he was interviewing on his program "Uncommon Knowledge ." Sowell agreed with him.[212]

1970s-current: Political Correctness

Definition: Political Correctness (PC): the avoidance, often considered as taken to extremes, of forms of expression or action that are perceived to exclude, marginalize, or insult groups of people who are socially disadvantaged or discriminated against.

Origins of PC:

1790–95 (in the sense "in accordance with established norms");
...in the 1920s the Soviet Communist Party began using the concept of political correctness to enforce strict adherence to the party line in all aspects of life. If you were unfortunate enough to be deemed politically incorrect, you were likely to be exiled to a gulag, or worse.

1970–75 for the more recent meaning, ...marked by or adhering to progressive orthodoxy on issues involving especially ethnicity, gender, sexual orientation, or ecology.[213]

Progressive orthodoxy:
While the majority in the US generally opposes injustices, like sexism, racism and poverty, certain more extreme, activist groups do not tolerate any differing opinions. "Their ideology has morphed into a narrow-minded dogma." Today, this is termed "progressive orthodoxy." Using aggressive and bullying tactics, they do not respect or allow freedom of speech for anyone but themselves.[214]

From where did the PC "Hate America First" indoctrination come? The Muenzenberg's Creed was instigated by Lenin and created by Willi Muenzenberg, a genius influencer. Its aim was to influence Americans to commit cultural suicide. Kent Clizbe, a former CIA espionage operative, has traced the history of its inception through the "politically correct" American counter-culture to today.[215]

2010: Bill Gates claims world doomed. He advocates zero carbon emissions and drastic depopulation.[216]

2014: Christian pastors agree to lead their congregations into the FEMA camps
"MSNBC interviewed a pastor, who also happens to be [is now former] Chairman of the Congressional Black Caucus, Emmanuel Cleaver (D-MO.). Representative Cleaver stated very clearly that preachers are being muzzled by the 501(c)3 regulations being enforced for the Justice Department and the IRS. In 2014, Representative Cleaver headed up a meeting with several thousand clergy, along with representatives from FEMA, the IRS, and Eric Holder [82nd Attorney General of the United States from 2009 to 2015]. According to Cleaver, the pastors minister to a total of about 10 million Christians."

Part of the responsibility of the Clergy Response Teams is to peacefully lead their congregations into FEMA camps during martial law and to implement forced population relocations in the future. This is allegedly done under the NDAA laws. [217]

"The fact that FEMA has recruited up to an estimated 28,000 pastors, as a low end estimate, to as many as 100,000 pastors, as a high end estimate, in order to form the clergy response team is very disturbing, not to mention frightening."[218]-asserted Dave Hodges.

On December 31, 2011, President Obama signed the National Defense Authorization Act (NDAA) into law, which also contains a measure allowing US citizens to be taken into custody and held indefinitely without ever being charged with a crime. Not only can any citizen deemed a threat to "national security interests of the United States," they may be held indefinitely without receiving a trial. The military would be the ones arresting those citizens.[219]

2015: Bill Gates claims greatest threat In a TED Talk, Bill Gates, CEO of MicroSoft, overviews global vulnerability to pandemic.[220]

May 2018: #WalkAway Campaign begun
Founded by Brandon Straka, a former liberal, on May 26, 2018. In 2017, he encouraged people to "walk away" from the divisive tenets endorsed and mandated by the Democratic Party of

today. "We are walking away from the lies, the false narratives, the fake news ... Never lose faith that people can change," he said. "I reject a system which allows an ambitious, misinformed, and dogmatic mob to suppress free speech, create false narratives, and apathetically steamroll over the truth."[221]

January 2019: 5G
The dangers of 5G were reported on the floor of the United Nations.[222] Further personal research is recommended, on an uncensored search engine.

May 2019: the CCP declares war
In the *Chinese Daily* newspaper, the CCP declared a "peoples war" on the United States of America.[223]

October 2019: Event 201
"The Johns Hopkins Center for Health Security in partnership with the World Economic Forum and the Bill and Melinda Gates Foundation hosted Event 201, a high-level pandemic exercise on October 18, 2019, in New York, NY. The exercise illustrated areas where public/private partnerships will be necessary during the response to a severe pandemic in order to diminish large-scale economic and societal consequences."[224]

Note how the scripts prevalent in the "exercise" were exactly parroted or closely rephrased during the real pandemic outbreak. The creators and hosts of the precursor event later disclaimed that it predicted the COVID-19 pandemic.[225]

January 2020: CCP complicity in pandemic begins to surface
As early as January 2, 2020, the truth of CCP complicity began to leak.[226]

2020: Pandemic in America
"Truthful" commentaries and timelines abound on the internet. The only one I found that reflects what I experienced as I lived through it is here.[227]

Spring 2020: the riots and "The Philosopher of Antifa"
Enter Herbert Marcuse, a part-Jewish German, who escaped his homeland before the rise of the Nazis. He taught at Columbia, Harvard, and Brandies, before moving to California. In the 1960s, ensconced at the University of San Diego, he was the guru of the New Left in the 1960s.

The working class never rose, like Karl Marx predicated. So, for Communism and its socialist economic system to rise in America, somebody had to find a large enough group - a new proletariat - to be the revolutionaries. The groups of the sixties, e.g. Weather Underground, Yippies, Students for a Democratic Society (SDS), the Black Panthers, etc. did not have enough people.

What Marcuse did was find groups who hated something about America, those who felt excluded from the mainstream. Then he transposed the "class struggle" of Marxism and Leninism into pairings for conflict and focuses for their hatred, such as:

- Race: blacks hating whites
- Gender by biology: women hating men
- Fluid gender: LGBTs hating heterosexuals
- Economic: have-nots hating haves

Combined together, these groups might produce the numbers necessary to stage insurrection.

These groups have been spiced with Marcuse's "repressive tolerance," in which he argued the legitimacy of hating haters. The latter means anyone who disagrees with you. Now, the insurrectionists are fired up with self-righteous resentment-against-injustice, shielded by the "moral high ground" of permission to hate. They are ready to destroy anything and anyone that gets in their way.[228]

"An eye for an eye only makes the whole world blind." – Mohandas K. Gandhi (one of the mentors of Martin Luther King)

2020: The "new" socialism

"Socialism is suicide. Communism is homicide." - Margaret Thatcher

"Socialism is an economic system. Communism is a political system." - Dinesh D'Souza

President Reagan said that socialism was on the ash heap of history. But it has made a loud and strident revival. And, it is a very different kind of socialism. It is aggressively disruptive, dividing us up into opposing groups and demanding that we hate each other. In other words, socialism has adopted and weaponized "identity politics ."

They have totally confused many of our youth, teaching them that socialism will give them everything they want for free and they won't have to work. This, of course, is economically unsustainable.

"The trouble with Socialism is that eventually you run out of other people's money." – Margaret Thatcher

"They want to 'welfarize' America and have people need the government … and in that way guaranteeing their votes." – Candace Owens.

Pandemic-related fear is also being used to turn our citizens into a cowering herd, so afraid for their lives that they will give up their unalienable rights. Panic creates submission.

"Elect socialism and you get communism."- Public domain, author unconfirmed

"To argue with a person who has renounced the use of reason is like administering medicine to the dead." – Thomas Paine

For an intelligent and informative discussion about the "new" socialism, see this video.[229]

Fall 2020: Medical fascism, next installment? The new world order is already gathering itself toward the attempt at another plandemic lockdown, mandatory vaccines, and contact tracing.

These are designed to make We the Peoples fear each other, and be terrified by falsely-inflated threats of sickness and death. Their aim is to destroy our courage and unity, and destroy America's economy. Then they intend take down American herself.

For responsible, nonpolitical previews of their plans[230], what the vaccines contain[231], the "masking" agenda[232], mental health crises from the first lockdown[233], and how the cost of life because of the lockdowns has far exceeded the life-costs of death from the virus itself,[234] these references are offered.

Here is a video plea for all the voiceless victims of the COVID-19 plandemic. Here is a plea for the freedom and wellbeing of all humankind. [235]

NWO
The new world order is an attempt to inflict one secular doctrine, involving the utter subjugation of the masses of the people, for the excessive wealth and power of a few. See chapters XIII and XIV. It is the oligarchical collectivism of the Fabians attempting its final coup.

This is the intention and the face of the spread of satanism.

The present spread of satanism
This worship of a destroyer, rather than the Creator, has been around since the "fall of mankind." But it has been in the background and without open form.[236]

The Satanic Temple has been pushing consistently for recognition of satanism as a legitimate religion and to have their statues of satan put up temporarily or permanently in various locations around America. The organization was created in 2013 and has locations in sixteen states. It has been given tax exemption as a church. Another dogma of Satanism is represented by the Church of Satan.[237]

Q Anon, a military intelligence group, was one of the first to draw attention to how a satanic elite controls political and social elites by ensnaring them in satanic practices, including sexual exploitation, abuse of minors, adrenochrome, cannibalism, and human sacrifice. Q drew attention to Jeffrey Epstein[238]. The deeper puppeteers are mentioned in this flyover.

Jeffery Epstein and Ghislaine Maxwell were acting minions for a much more powerful force. Their assignment was to ensnare as many powerful and/or famous people in business, politics, public opinion, and entertainment as possible. The objective wasn't just perverting them, but controlling them, through blackmail, toward whatever purpose their puppet masters devise. So who funded Epstein, Maxwell, and all their elaborate stage props? Why? Our children were their bait and fodder.[239]

In international banking satanism's presence has long been suspected, but its reach has been severely underestimated.[240]

The symbolism and practices of satanism have saturated the movies and especially the music industry for decades now. It has spread not only through the structure of these industries, but throughout the global leadership. This insider information is significant and vital toward our true understanding of the extent of the satanic infestation.[241]

Rescuing the children from the tunnels mentioned in chapter III. Nationally, since October 2019 through the spring, while we languished in lockdown, tens of thousands of children were rescued from an international, satanic child trafficking cartel, operating in a vast underground network. The US military has been carrying out these rescues.[242] Internationally and nationally, rescues are still going on. Hear from survivor and escaped insiders.[243]

Where did you think so many of the missing children from America and globally have gone?

The mass media has largely refused to cover this story. Why? **We must understand NOW that the fodder of this wide-spread evil is OUR CHILDREN.**

Matthew 18:14 (KJV) "...it is not the will of your Father which is in heaven, that one of these little ones should perish.

Satanic child trafficking – the foulest and most wicked slavery
Human trafficking is the politically-correct name today for slavery. It is one of the largest evils of the early 21st century. This diabolical, totally evil form of slavery has expanded worldwide. Our children are being sucked into an Illuminati-orchestrated terror of satanic child trafficking, which is the exponentially most horrible form of slavery.

Luke 17:1-2 (KJV) Then said he unto the disciples, It is impossible but that offences will come: but woe unto him, through whom they come! ² It were better for him that a millstone were hanged about his neck, and he cast into the sea, than that he should offend one of these little ones.

This slavery crosses all racial, religious, economic, and national lines. It is condoned and practiced by a vast number of famous and global elites. This is perpetuated by people in positions of power, trust, and influence in our world. Follow the money, power, and involvement in satanism, including child sexual abuse, to find the instigators and committers of these heinous and evil crimes.

If this covert abomination cannot unite us, in God's Name, what can?

It is time to wake up!

This is an urgent call to all people of good intention, and especially the Christian community who has long declared devotion to love and justice, Jesus, and God.

Time to gather our convictions and our courage – arise!

*Ezra 10:4 (KJV) **Arise**; for this matter belongeth unto thee: we also will be with thee: be of good courage, and do it.*

*Matthew 17:7 (KJV) And Jesus came and touched them, and said, **Arise**, and be not afraid.*

Isaiah 60:1 (KJV) **Arise**, shine; for thy light is come, and the glory of the Lord is risen upon thee.

Psalm 44:26 (KJV) **Arise** for our help, and redeem us for thy mercies' sake.

Psalm 82:8 (KJV) **Arise**, O God, judge the earth: for thou shalt inherit all nations.

Lamentations 2:19 (KJV) **Arise**, cry out in the night: in the beginning of the watches pour out thine heart like water before the face of the Lord: lift up thy hands toward him for the life of thy young children, that faint for hunger in the top of every street.

Psalm 112:4 (NIV) Even in darkness light dawns for the upright, for those who are gracious and compassionate and righteous.

Isaiah 60:2 (KJV) For, behold, the darkness shall cover the earth, and gross darkness the people: but the Lord shall **arise** upon thee, and his glory shall be seen upon thee.

XI.
Targeting of vulnerable populations

To defeat the hydra of globalist conquest, We the Peoples must again become We the People. We can do so by recognizing, acknowledging, and USING TOGETHER the love, wisdom, and power of our Highest Common Denominator, the LIFE of God, Our Father, the Creator within each and all of us.

Vulnerable populations

Proverbs 10:0-9 (NRSV) *The wise of heart will heed but a babbling fool will come to ruin.* ⁹ *Whoever walks in integrity walks securely, but whoever follows perverse ways will be found out.*

Any group or country bent on conquest aims first at their intended victim's weakest points for the entry of their forces. Thereby, they erode and unbalance their opponent. If the attacker is using asymmetric warfare, they can not only capture these first prisoners, they can indoctrinate them and make them support the invasion.

The most vulnerable in America are our children and our African American poor.

Our Children

Luke 17:1-2 (KJV) *Then said he unto the disciples, It is impossible but that offences will come: but woe unto him, through whom they come!* ² *It were better for him that a millstone were hanged about his neck, and he cast into the sea, than that he should offend one of these little ones.*

The enslavement of our children through changes in public education
In the early 1950s, a Congressional investigation described a collectivist "revolution" within the United States.[244]

The funding and uppermost leadership of this incursion came from the largest corporate foundations, using tax-exempt dollars. According to the chief investigator Norman Dodd, "some of the foundations were weaponizing the American education system to enable...'oligarchical collectivism'." Their program stressed "internationalism and moral relativism...(and)...crushing individualism and promoting collectivism ."[245]

The culprit foundations included the Ford Foundation, the Rockefeller foundations, and the Carnegie Endowment. The largest recipients of these funds toward revolutionizing education included Chicago University, Columbia University, Harvard, and the University of California.[246]

Since the 1950s, from these and other similar higher education institutions, teachers and other educators, trained in this mindset, have been sent out across our nation to instruct our children.

In addition, foundation money and other influences have been used to place foreign communists into prominent US educational institutions.

Alan Gaither, president of the Ford Foundation, told Dodd (that they, at the Ford Foundation, were) " '...operating under directives...the substance of which is, that we shall use our grant making power so as to alter life in the United States that it can be comfortably merged with the Soviet Union.' "[247]

Dodd noted in sworn testimony that the intended revolution "could not have occurred peacefully, or with the consent of the majority, unless education in the United State had been prepared in advance to endorse it."[248]

He summed it up in this way, " 'The effect was to orient our educational system away from support of the principles embodied in the Declaration of Independence, and implemented in the Constitution...What we had uncovered as the determination of these large foundations, through their trustees, to actually get control over the content of American education.' "[249]

"The movement is closely related to Fabian socialism," added Aaron Sargent, lawyer, and expert witness, during the 1950s Congressional investigation. Sargent also testified that foundations were in violation of the law and their charters. [250]

This cloaked initiative is still going on today.

Alex Newman, the author of the article so heavily quoted here, says "it may seem counter-intuitive that such prominent capitalists and industrialists are supporting what appears to be socialist and communist agendas."

It makes perfect sense when we look into possibilities and avenues protected and cloaked by indoctrination method. The corporatist oligarchs use the socialists and communists like the monarchs used the serfs. They do the grunt work. These front-line schillers do the dirty work to indoctrinate, threaten, and do the dangerous parts involving violence on We the Peoples. But, when the time comes, the corporatists will sweep in and take the harvest. They are totally convinced of their right and power to rule unconditionally.

"The Philosophy of the school room in one generation...will be the Philosophy of the Government in the next." - Abraham Lincoln[251]

Beginning in the early 1960s, our children of all races have been isolated. First they became isolated from their parents, as many mothers started to work outside the home. Parents, in general, were distracted into pursuing "a better life" for their children. This largely materialistic movement started shortly after televisions were enshrined in American homes.

Then in 1962, the acknowledgment of the Presence of God was removed from public education. This was done by the US Supreme Court ruling that prayer, an expression of worship and free speech guaranteed by the US Constitution, was unconstitutional in public schools. There were many more

Supreme Court rulings regarding prayer in schools than the Engel v. Vitale case, which is most familiar.

Here is the voluntary prayer which was objected to in this case: "Almighty God, we acknowledge our dependence upon Thee, and we beg Thy blessings upon us, our parents, our teachers, and our Country." This prayer does not invoke one religion or one doctrine of a specific religion. Yet, the ruling accepted the argument that it represented the government <u>creating</u> a religion.

In response to a complaint for the rights of ten students, 1st Amendment rights for millions were removed. (Not all these students named wanted it. Some had even had volunteered to lead the prayers prior to the suit.) In addition, constitutionally, the federal government has never had jurisdiction in education.

More information on this case is available in Appendix III, including "An Outline History of Religion in American schools," as well as a list of the multiple Supreme Court rulings concerning prayer in public schools.

The American adult population did almost nothing to combat it. They were too busy. Apparently the churches were also too busy.

Shortly after the 1962 ruling, Judeo-Christian morals were removed. Today, those exhibiting them are often mocked and/or ostracized. The absence of God, prayer, and God-based principles became felt immediately. It was obvious that he best teachers were being severely suppressed in both their usual methods and what they said.

The students who were in kindergarten in the Fall of 1963 were the first students to go through their entire school experience without the Presence of God as an acknowledged, integral part of their public education. They graduated from high school in the spring of 1976. Look what happened to the incarceration rates for adults after these youth and those who came after them joined the adult population.

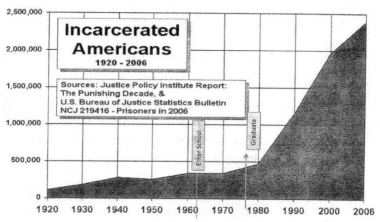

Adult Incarceration Trend

1962 School prayer ruled unconstitutional.   1963 School Bible reading ruled illegal.

Thirteen years later (K through 12) adult crime began to explode.

Many will say that the incarceration rates were due to a sharp rise in drug abuse. Beginning about 1965, skyrocketing substance abuse was seen in schools and in young adults. Incarceration centering on illegal drug use and related choices accounted for a significant portion of the surge in incarceration.

Here's the question: What were these young people looking for in drugs that was missing from their lives? What are they still looking for? The drug addiction rates are still rising.

Without the sense of love from Our Father, coupled with the lack of a moral compass within the school system, our children have been led into terrible confusion about who or what is a true. In the school environment and especially on social media, our children have not been equipped to recognize what is genuine authority on life's questions.

They believe everything. But, due to our truancy, they trust no one, including themselves as individuals - or us.

We, of the generations that have gone before, have a divine responsibility to provide our younger generations the principles and substance on which to build constructive lives. Many of us have failed to enfold them in relationships of reciprocal love, even outside of the school environment. Constructive, supportive parenting and family presence, plus faith-based schools and church activities have been important, positive influences and protection.

But largely, we have delegated the training of our children, whom we love and who are our future, to the school system. But we have not stayed connected to supervise and guide the process. Who stepped in to fill that convenient vacuum? With what has it been filled? What has been the toll on our children? What will be the toll on our future?

Here is where the globalist training began to influence our children to blindly accept secular authority and "expert opinions" as always true.

Tenets of socialism and communism have taken the place of God-based principles and have turned our schools into propaganda and indoctrination centers for the doctrine advocated by the Fabian Society and proliferated through funding by huge corporate foundations.[252] Remember, the proposed new world order is an oligarchy, structured to benefit the huge, multinational corporations. Look at the corporations who are getting into the game by funding Black Lives Matter and Antifa.[253]

Here is one of their major tools used to infiltrate our schools and change the character of the curricula.

Begun in 1857 as a professional organization, the National Education Association (NEA) has become one of the most powerful unions dominating public schools in America with its collectivist education agenda.[254]

In 1900, the NEA, with its 2,500 members was demanding that the federal government become involved in public education, despite the 10th Constitutional Amendment, which gave <u>no</u> educational power to the national government. Rather it empowered the States and parents to guide education in their communities.

In 1984, the meticulously researched and documented book *NEA: Trojan Horse in Education,* by Dr. Samuel L. Blumenfeld, indicates that American educators had been radicalized by the NEA for over a century. Blumenfeld wrote, "the NEA has subjected its members to a unrelenting hatred of capitalism and an unceasing, uncritical benevolence toward socialism."[255]

"The destructive role played by the NEA is so serious that by 2004, even then-US Secretary of Education Rod Paige described the union as a 'terrorist organization.' "[256]

Quotes from the leaders of the NEA crystalize their intentions.[257]
"...all of us...must be subjected to a large degree of social control...The major function of the school is the social orientation of the individual. It must seek to give him understanding of the transition to a new social order," 1934, William Givens, right before he became executive secretary of NEA.

"It is no longer a question of collectivism or individualism, but what kind of collectivism," socialist Stuart Chase, the most frequent contributor to the NEA Journal from 1930-1940.

"...we need certain world agencies of administration. Those planetary governing agencies should include a global 'police force' and a world 'board of education," J. Elmer Morgan, chief of the NEA Journal in the 1920s. (The formation of UNESCO was the fruit of these ongoing demands by NEA.) He also called on teachers to "to prepare the hearts and minds of children...(and added)...At the very top of the all the agencies which will assure the coming of world government must stand the school, the teacher, and the organized profession."

"The National Education Association believes that home school programs based on parental choice cannot provide the student with a comprehensive education experience." 1988-2006. This is the current version of an NEA resolution.

In many states, teachers were required to be members of the NEA and fund political campaigns favored by it, until a recent suit in Illinois ended compulsory dues. In 2020, the NEA is the largest trade union in the United States with almost three million members.[258]

In the classroom, these collectivist theories are masked with encouragement, idealistic self-righteousness, self-congratulations, sugary awards, acceptance (belonging) to the "cause," and guidance dominated and funded by the agenda of intellectuals who want to rule humankind, without God.

With the very best of intentions of the local educators, a vast number of public schools have put aside God-principles and even common sense as the guiding principles. They have allowed and collaborated with an all-encompassing indoctrination of America's children and youth.

Schools are no longer teaching children how to think for themselves, right from wrong, self-discipline, responsibility, honor, integrity, truth, humility, kindness, generosity, or self-reliance. They are teaching moral relativism, egotism to the point of narcissism, selfishness, collectivism, ideological intolerance, and dependency on the human intellect, which is draped in the unquestioned robes of science, medicine, and especially government. These tactics prepare young minds to blindly accept authority and/or "expert opinions" as always true.

The dominant system continues to develop individual egos, by training them to expect immediate response and gratification of their selfish whims and desires. Many of our youth's egos are overextended to the point that they develop a frantic, aching vacuum of meaninglessness. The ego urgently needs to "have impact" as proof of its power and, thereby, worthiness.

But "egotism, in the sense of 'self-worship,' is preferable to egoism, since egoism also designates a system of philosophy." Practical Exercises in English by Huber Gray Buehler.

"Desperate need to belong" is a type of inverted egotism, as "belonging" also reinforces and validates the ego's self-worth. Where or with whom they belong is increasingly essential to young people. Because this is a state of being frantically out-of-balance and, thereby, vulnerable, it is easily manipulated.

Now sex and gender confusion are being added to the mix. Facebook has 58 gender choices for those signing up for an account. [259] And here's an example of a video targeted to adolescent boys.[260]

Cathy Rouse has been looking into sex-education in public schools. She is a lawyer, senior fellow, and director of human dignity at the Family Research Council, a nonprofit research organization, which centers on family issues in public policy.[261]

What she found out is that often sex-education classes are outsourced and the curricula is "chillingly reminiscent of those used by the propaganda arms of totalitarian regimes. … The result is that these schools turn out ideologues who 'don't know if they are male or female, but they have a lot of anger at our country.'"[262]

Even kindergarteners are being told they might have been born in the wrong body, but it can be remedied with drugs and surgery.

Rouse has put together a brochure on her findings.[263] She advises parents to "Ask for all the material your child will be taught in advance. That's your right."[264]

No wonder our children are increasingly disturbed. Are those indoctrinating our children trying to make them crazy? Does this definition of psychoneurosis sound familiar?

Psychoneurosis: a functional disorder in which feelings of anxiety, obsessional thoughts, compulsive acts, and physical complaints without objective evidence of disease, in various degrees and patterns, dominate the personality; a relatively mild personality disorder typified by excessive anxiety or indecision and a degree of social or interpersonal maladjustment.[265]

Our children and youth are not only drowning in a sea of unquestioning trust in government to take care of them, but the most current educational dogma is making them <u>unable</u> to take care of selves.

When the youth reach adulthood, the training and indoctrination is continued through social media and mass media, intellectually and politically.

2010: The Fabian Society's and corporate foundations' undermining of America through our children is still continuing. It is now openly global.

Common Core curricula
Only one example is the Gates Foundation, which is pouring billions of dollars into the collectivist education reform of UNESCO and "internationally-aligned" Common Core curriculum, which was imposed on American children through the public school system beginning in 2010. The largest funder of Common Core, before the Gates Foundation, is the American tax payers. [266]

Where did Common Core start?

"It all started with former Arizona Gov. Janet Napolitano, who was the 2006-07 chair of the National Governors Association and now leads the University of California system..."[267]

Note that the University of California is one of the universities funded by the corporate foundations to "revolutionize" education, beginning in the 1950s.

"Over the past decade, there has been no progress in either mathematics or reading performance, and the lowest performing students are doing worse," - Peggy Carr, associate commissioner of the National Center for Education Statistics.[268]

Warning from educator whose father grew up in Nazi Germany
"People need to know, people need to be aware, people need to especially be cautious because tyranny and totalitarianism don't come in with a bang, they come in with baby steps or eroding freedoms and we are seeing that," - Karen Siegemund is President of the American Freedom Alliance. She has had a richly varied career and interests, ranging through science, languages, international relations, and education. Her father was born in Berlin in 1928, living through the rise and fall of Nazi Germany.[269]

The very most vulnerable – our unborn children
Is there anything more vulnerable, miraculous, or more precious than a baby alive in its mother's womb awaiting its birth into the world?

Yet today, the impulsive desires of parents, whose own choices and acts have conceived these children, have been raised above their own child's right to life itself! Did the parents choose to have sex with mutual consent? Is the mother healthy enough to bear the child full term? If not, are there mitigating possibilities that could protect the lives of both the baby and the mother? If the answers to these questions are collectively affirmative, why is there a question about whether the baby will be given a chance to be born and live?

When are we going to honor life and take responsibility for our own choices and actions? When are we going to be more concerned about what is right and upholds life, justice, and integrity, than with what is convenient?

Has life become so cheap and disposable – as long as it is someone else's life - that a totally innocent life is so easily ended? Is it even easier to be callous if the one being sentenced to death cannot speak for themselves?

Until we honor, cherish, and defend the LIFE of all the Children of God, somehow somewhere, our own lives will not be honored. What goes around comes around.

Many, many girls and women have been impregnated using deceit or totally against their will. This is atrocious. Their God-given rights as well as their bodies, minds, feelings, and spirits have been violated. May I speak with empathy to you? Is the child you carry guilty of the crimes put on you, or is that little one also a victim? Beloved mother, your sacred LIFE has been violated, but not by the child you carry. Will causing the death of your baby's LIFE bring justice to yours, or only make you an accomplice to murder?

Even if it is not possible or desirable for you to keep your baby, would you please consider a nine month demonstration of respect and love for LIFE, including your own, by carrying and birthing your baby and giving it up for adoption?

There are people ready to empathetically and expertly help you through this challenge and for you to be whole, free, and proud at the end of it[270]

Here is an overview of abortion statistics:
Leading cause of death in America in 2017: Abortions 862,320 – 2nd: Heart disease 647,457[271]
Abortion was the leading cause of death worldwide in 2019, killing 42 million people.[272]

Expanded Abortion Statistics: Current United States Data[273]
Total number of abortions in the US 1973-2018: 61.8 million

Current statistics include:
- 186 abortions per 1,000 live births (according to the Centers for Disease Control)
- US Abortions in 2017: approximately 862,320 (Guttmacher Institute)
- Abortions per day: 2,362+ (GI)
- Abortions per hour: 98+ (GI)
- 1 abortion every 96 seconds (GI)
- 13.5 abortions / 1000 women aged 15-44 in 2017 (GI)

"These statistics include only surgical and medical abortions…pharmacy experts project that about 14 million chemical abortions occur in the United States each year, providing a projected total of well in excess of an additional 610 million chemical abortions between 1965 and 2009."[274]

During the COVID-19 lockdowns, abortion clinics remained open. Even though, other medical services providing women's health services were also open.

"Our doors will stay open because sexual and reproductive health care is extremely important, and we have to ensure access to it," Meera Shah, chief medical officer for Planned Parenthood in the New York City suburbs of Long Island, Westchester, and Rockland, one of the hardest-hit regions in the country, told BuzzFeed News Thursday over the phone. "Pregnancy-related care, especially abortion care, is essential and life-affirming, especially now when there is so much insecurity around jobs and food and paychecks and childcare."[275]

Candace Owens, a young black leader, speaks out on the choice of abortion and Planned Parenthood.[276]

Planned Parenthood improperly applied for and unlawfully received $80 million of coronavirus relief funds meant for struggling small businesses[277]

In PP's 2019 report, their abortions made up 95% of PP's "pregnancy resolution" services; up 4% from the previous year by 12,915 abortions.[278]

Their income breakdown for the 2018-2019 fiscal year is below:[279]
- PP non-government clinic income: $369.6 million
- PP donations revenue: $591.3 million;
- PP government grants and reimbursements: $616.8 million, up 9%

- Total profit: $110.5 million
- Total income: $1.63 billion

The abortion issue is still contentious and hotly debated in America. The debates are usually over extremes. But the American public holds a wide array of opinions in the middle.

Three-quarters of Americans say they want to keep in place the landmark Supreme Court ruling, *Roe v. Wade,* that made abortion legal in the United States, but a strong majority would like to see restrictions on abortion rights, according to a new NPR/PBS NewsHour/Marist Poll[280]

Pew Research Center research shows where Christians by doctrine and other major religious groups stand on abortion. Interestingly, the American Methodist Episcopal Church, the AME, a largely African American Christian denomination, is one of the most conservative on the subject of abortion.[281]

Revelation 3:15-16 (NIV)I know your deeds, that you are neither cold nor hot. I wish you were either one or the other! [16] *So, because you are lukewarm—neither hot nor cold—I am about to spit you out of my mouth.*

The Vulnerable Poor
First, let's take a look at who is suffering in poverty:[282]

Poverty rates: World and US comparison
Let's start with a global view so we can see how America fits in the overall issue of poverty.

The World Bank of the United Nations estimates that 10% of the world's population, about 730 million people, lives in "extreme poverty." That is defined by one person living on the equivalent of $1.90 per day. Many of these also do not have safe drinking water or any access to education.

Using the highest estimate, about 990,159 people in the US live on $2.00 a day. These are included in the homeless generally, and those who do not have the ability to navigate the federal system of help, usually due to mental illness or addiction. This number is about 14 hundredths of 1% of the world's people living in extreme poverty.

The extreme poverty rate in the US is 3 tenths of 1%.of our population, compared to 10% in the world at large.

In our American definition, the poverty line for one person is $13,000 per year, or $36.62 per day. The U.S. poverty rate dropped to 10.5% of the population in 2019 from 11.8% in 2018. Over the past six years the rate has dropped steadily from 14.8% in 2014. The poverty rate of 10.5% is the lowest recorded rate since the census has reported on poverty starting in 1959.

"Don't expect to build up the weak by pulling down the strong." - Calvin Coolidge

So, why are there so many of us, US citizens, screaming for bloody murder based on poverty and lack of opportunity in America? Who are trying to tear down and destroy the United States of America? **Why the disparaging of the opportunity and freedom we have here, compared to the rest of the world?**

The United States of America is the only existing country that was founded on acknowledgement of God and His laws for justice, and freedom, including the respect and valuing of individuals as Children of God.

We're not close to perfect. But we are the only strong country left which is standing for God, love, and freedom. If We the Peoples stand together, we can secure America's Victory – and we can be instrumental in saving the world's people from a global plantation.

"This country was the first to claw its way out of darkness and put that on paper. These aren't just American ideas anymore. There's no copyright on them. You brought them into the world. These truths – your truths – they are self-evident in (all of) us." – U2's Bono.

Why are we being encouraged and enraged toward clawing our way back into darkness?

Or is there a sinister force bent on the destruction of America for its own diabolical egoism and selfishness? We the Peoples are being deceived, bamboozled, hoodwinked, and hijacked into destroying the last best hope for mankind on earth!

"It's not a right-left issue. It is a right-wrong issue. And America has been constant on the side of what the right is.". . . when it comes down to it, this is about keeping faith with the idea of America, isn't it?

". . . .That is how we see you around the world, as one of the greatest ideas of human history. . . .You and me are created equal. If there is an injustice? Then leave it to us. We'll do the rest." - Bono

To take care of it, we must no longer allow the diabolicals to divide us and pit us against each other.

We the Peoples must become the best version of We the People ever achieved and stand up united against the diabolicals. We must refuse to cooperate with their schemes for our own demise. There are many more of us than of them. **Arise! The time is now.**

Let's take a look at some of the places we can improve together.

Children and seniors in poverty in the USA
In 2018, 16.2% of all children (11.9 million kids) lived in poverty - that's almost 1 in every 6 children. In 2015, the National Center on Family Homelessness analyzed state-level data and found that nationwide, 2.5 million children experience homelessness in a year.

Seniors have an adjusted poverty rate of 14.1%, nearly as high as that of our children.[283]

Thirty-three percentage (33%) of Black children live in poverty.[284]

Poverty by ethnicity:
According to 2018 US Census Data, the highest poverty rate by race is found among Native Americans (25.4%), with Blacks (20.8%) having the second highest poverty rate, and Hispanics (of any race) having the third highest poverty rate (17.6%). Whites and Asians each have a poverty rate of 10.1%.[285]

Poverty ethnicity by percentage of the poor and numbers of people:[286.]
By crunching the numbers, approximately, 46.6% of the poor in America are white (19,924,467 people); 25.0% of the poor are Hispanic (10,687,479 people); 21.4% of the poor are black (9,148,692); 4.6% of the poor are Asian (1,955,979); and 2.5% of the poor are Native Americans (1,083,847).

Slavery's influence in America
Early in America's history, three significant groups of people, one indigenous and two from beyond our shores, have past horrific experiences with the immoral, malicious, criminal monster of slavery and its crushing poverty. We all have converged into the melting pot of modern-day America.

The slavery of Native Americans
Slavery had been part of the culture of the Native American tribes for generations. Making slaves of the survivors of conquered tribes was commonplace. In 1838, Native Americans at-large lost their liberty due to a scheme for political power.

The Indian Removal Act of 1830,[286] which President Andrew Jackson forced through Congress, authorized the federal government to extinguish Indian title to lands in the Southeast, now known as the American Deep South. Approximately 60,000 Native Americans of many tribes were forcibly removed from their traditional homelands to open lands west of the Mississippi, to what is now Oklahoma. The main group were collectively called the "Five Civilized Tribes," these being the Cherokee, Chickasaw, Choctaw, Muscogee, and Seminole tribes. These peoples were in the process of cultural transformation toward a white American way of life, which had been proposed by George Washington and Henry Knox. Many of these Native Americans were already integrated into communities, many as business and plantation owners.

The "Trail of Tears," actual removal of the Natives went on from 1830 through 1850. Started by Jackson, the removal was completed by President Van Buren.

President Andrew Jackson, *in his fifth annual message, December 3, 1833*
"They (the Native Americans) have neither the intelligence, the industry, the moral habits, nor the desire of improvement which are essential to any favorable change in their condition. Established in the midst of another and a superior race, and without appreciating the causes of their inferiority or seeking to control them, they must necessarily yield to the force of circumstances and ere long disappear."

Federal troops and state militia removed the Native Americans at gun point from their homes, businesses, and land. Even those documented as American citizens were taken. They were only allowed to take what they could carry. Non-Indians and half breeds, including spouses and freedmen, and, oddly, their African slaves, were all rounded up. Split into groups of 700 – 1,000 people, they were forcibly marched thousands of miles, often in freezing to excessively hot weather. Up to 16,700 Indians died during the experience, from which the atrocity earned the name "Trail of Tears."

This atrocity is also remembered within the bloodline of generations.

A number of lawsuits were filed and the most influential *Worcester v. Georgia (1832)* won in the Supreme Court. Jackson defied the Supreme Court and continued the removals.

This theft opened up approximately 25 million acres for predominantly European settlement. Many have said that Jackson used the sale of this land for political gain.[288]

The lingering atrocity to the Native Americans is that they have been held captive on land that would often not support human life and put into a state of enforced dependency. Not until present times, did the Native Americans find lucrative opportunities in business that are helping them rebuild their tribes and lives within prosperity.

The slavery of Africans

A very brief overview of slavery in West Africa

In ancient times, slavery in Africa was as common as it was throughout the ancient world. There were many forms of slavery practiced on the African continent, such as slavery for prostitution, debt, criminality, human sacrifice, and of war captives. Human sacrifice, using slaves, was common in West Africa during the 1800s.

As the gold economies and trans-Saharan slave trade developed, a number of West African nation-states were organized around the slave trade, including the Ghana and Mali Empires, the Bono State, and the Songhai Empire. Warring political groups enslaved conquered enemies.[289]

It wasn't race that distinguished slavery in West Africa. The distinction was one of kinship.

Slavery in West Africa was made illegal in 1875. Though it waned, it continued until almost World War I.[290]

The uniquely barbaric enslavement of Africans in America and its deliberate perpetuation
Between 1501 to 1867, peoples from the west African coast were forcibly removed from their homes and communities and imprisoned on the slave ships like cargo. Approximately, 3.7%[291]of these human beings where shipped toward North American ports, amounting to some 389,000 souls. This is also an indication of how widespread slavery is globally. What is now Brazil absorbed about 44% of those kidnapped from West Africa.[292]

African slave importation into North America began in 1619 and slavery persisted in the United States until 1865 – a period of 246 years.[293]

In 1712, slavery in the North American colonies reached the depths of human depravity.

It entered, through Willie Lynch, a British slave owner in the West Indies. The Virginia slave owners hired him as a consultant to tell them how to help planters install the African slave system. In a short narrative, he describes a system any planter can use to "break his slaves and produce generations of conforming and productive slaves, plus how to set them against each other."[294]

Lynch's dehumanizing, terrorizing method began with the forced witness of the violent murder of a male slave, followed by an extreme whipping of another witness male salve, all forcibly watched by female slaves and their children.

The atrocity inflicted on the African slaves was calculated to blow a hole in their racial memory so deep it would be taught to all exceeding generations, by their own people. Then, for fear of the violence happening to them and their children, they were forced into daily, hard labor. That the slaves would absolutely kowtow to their masters and their taskmasters was the implicit, unmitigated expectation.

Wikipedia proposes that the advice of Willie Lynch is a hoax[295], but it does not deny this treatment of slaves. Many people, both blacks and whites, have noted common characteristics among descendants of African slaves which might be explained by the "Willie Lynch theory ." Many African Americans descended from slaves today support this explanation.

It is obvious that the ghosts of these atrocities are being carried in their bloodline – regardless of who is given "credit" for them.

Before the American civil war, throughout the south, there were freed slaves who became plantation owners. The percentage of African Americans owning black slaves was roughly equivalent to the percentage of African Americans in the overall population.[296]

Luring African Americans into the slavery of economic dependency
President Martin Van Buren (1837-1841) fashioned urban plantations on the agricultural plantations of the pre-Civil War South.[297] They were used to create and control large blocks of voters, held in line by patronage. After the Civil War, vulnerable minorities, especially blacks migrating north and also white European immigrants were targeted. Later, big city "bosses" were raised up to control individual cities.

In 1964, President Lyndon Johnson declared the "War on Poverty."[298] Privately, he called the legislation "the n----r bill" and boasted that it would keep "them n----rs" voting for his political party for the next 200 years. [299]

One of the greatest criticisms of the ongoing programs initiated in 1964 is that the program monetizes the breaking up of poor families by awarding more money to a single mom raising a child. The amount was set to increase with every new birth.

Before the mid-1960s in America, children were almost all born into a nuclear family, that is to married couples. Even in 1964, children born to unmarried women were only seven percent of all births in the United States.

Then President Johnson declared the "War on Poverty." In the decades to follow the number of children born out of wedlock exploded. Here is how this devastation to our American quality of life progressed. It was felt most acutely in the black community.

In 1965, the births to unwed African American mothers was 25%. By 1991, it was 68%; by 2011 72%, and by 2015 77%.

There are approximately, 11,000,000 single parent families in America. Just over 80% (81.5%) are headed by single mothers. In 2019, within ethnic groups, families with single moms were: 43% of Native American families; 38% of black families; 38% of Hispanic families; 29% Asian and,28% white. Forty-nine percent (49%) of these moms were never married and 34% of these families live in poverty.

"Since 1968, (there has been) a fourfold increase in the number of unwed parents." – Pew Research Center, 2017

And how is marriage faring in America when children are concerned?

"Once largely limited to poor women and minorities, single motherhood is becoming the new 'norm'. This prevalence is due in part to the growing trend of children born outside marriage - a societal trend that was virtually unheard of decades ago" - Single Mother Guide

This was a despicable debasement and economic enslavement of African Americans and all poor people, regardless of race. With the government relieving fathers from the responsibility of raising their own children and mothers getting more money for more babies, the population surged fueled by promiscuity. What these politicians did was reduce the flower and strength of American manhood to the function of a sperm donor. They reduced the courageous, kind American women to brood mares for voters.

To make things worse, 78% of Planned Parenthood facilities, the largest provider of abortions in America, are in minority neighborhoods."[300] The PP founder was Margaret Sanger, a noted white eugenicist, who advocated the eradication of "inferior races" through abortion, birth control, and other means. Sanger said, "Colored people are like human weeds and are to be exterminated." [301] Is there a link with a hidden political agenda?

Dr. Alveda King, niece of Martin Luther King, has confirmed this and said, " PP has been working to annihilate Blacks for 100 years." She also pronounced the PP-NYC decision to take Sanger's name off their Manhattan abortion location is "just window dressing ."

In 2015, blacks were 13.4% of the US population and were having 36% of abortions. White Americans had 36.9% of the abortions, but made up 76.6% of the population.[302]

Like the Native American reservations, this slavery was meant to create dependency. Is it also a scheme to buy votes and secure political power?

"The poor people (in the early 20th century) were more decent…. In this welfare state, that was supposed to make them better off and better human beings, that's when the crime rate skyrocketed…. (Most) black children were being raised by two parents in 1960. But 30 years later after the liberal welfare state…the great majority of black children were being raised by… single parent(s)…This is the welfare state. When you pay people not to get married, they don't get married…. Socialism is a great idea. It does not mean it is a great reality." - Thomas Sowell, "The Myths of Economic Inequality"[303]

In this interview with Sowell on the program "Uncommon Knowledge with Peter Robinson," interviewer Robinson summed up some of Sowell's points this way: "The African Americans were leading decent lives and bettering themselves until the government started to help them." Sowell agreed with his statement.[304]

Politicians show up in the African American neighborhoods every four years, around election time, to secure votes. Their conspicuous absence in the intervening years, confirm their motives.

White immigrants' history of slavery and serfdom
White slavery by the Romans, in a long line of their governmental forms, lasted strongly from approximately 30 BC to 800 AD. (After that, as the Roman power began to crumble, serfdom was slowly built.) The invading Turkish Ottoman Empire took European Christians into slavery between the mid-1300s and the early 1900s.[305]

From 1630 through 1776, half to three quarters of the white European immigrants were indentured servants. Over ten percent of these were involuntary, victims of kidnapping or war conquest. Many died in captivity. At first, they outnumbered black slaves. The two groups worked side by side.

Beginning in the early 1600s, white Europeans in larger numbers fled to the shores of America to escape the form of slavery called "serfdom."[306] By the 1600s, the slavery of serfdom had already lasted six centuries.

Slavery of white Europeans by Rome lasted approximately 830 years, plus 570 years by the Ottomans. Add the 600 years of serfdom, plus involuntary indentured servitude. Even reducing the span of years due to "overlapping slaveries," the historic white experience with slavery is about 1,800 years.

The European immigrants to America almost all had their ancestral roots in serfdom and many in slavery. Most often they came to America of their own free will with reason for hope, whether they were escaping famine or tyranny.

Their response to freedom and being able to keep the fruits of their labor was to become industrious, conscientious, and hardworking. In Europe, those who enslaved them in poverty, were wealthy, privileged, and usually aristocratic. Money earned and accumulated in the New World was a protection against slipping back into generational serfdom and its acute poverty. Often, this hidden fear has morphed into guarded frugality and workaholic tendencies.

The slavery of serfdom and its poverty
Replacing Roman control, the feudal system and its serfdom were in place from the 10th century and continued even through the 16th century.[307]

Serfdom grew in Europe out of the collapse of the Roman empire. It started in Western Europe first and was followed later by similar changes in Eastern Europe. The changes were irregular at best. This is an attempt to make some brief sense out of the chaos that ensued.

In localized areas, men with military skill and/or political power became the controllers of larger tracts of land. Originally, a number of them had received the lands from the court of Charlemagne. As his empire dissolved over a couple of generations, the men of local power maintained control, but owed allegiance to, first, the Church and, secondly to any overarching kingdom who guaranteed land claims.

The lord of each manor made his own rules, administered them, and was the court system and the enforcer for the estate and all who lived on it.

As Rome lost its power there were fewer and fewer conquered adults and kidnapped children being forced into slavery. A severe labor shortage ensued, as there weren't enough peasants to do the work required. i.e. very poor, but free country people. As the cities crumbled due to lack of Roman enabled trade, "plebeians," former city dwellers, migrated into the countryside seeking to survive. These people were, by circumstance and force, compelled into serfdom.

Due to the lawlessness and bands of military terrorizing the countryside, both peasants and the serfs needed the lords' military protection. The lords needed laborers. The serfs were somewhere between the peasantry and slaves.[308] Here's a quick overview:

<u>Slaves</u> were still in Europe	<u>Serfs</u>
not free	"unfree"
classified as property	classified as human
could be sold	could not be sold
could be killed	could not legally be killed
	could be blamed & punished
	unpaid
	had no legal or customary rights
	could not own land, may have property
	tied to land, may not leave
	mobility constricted
	owed rents chosen by land owner
	could marry within class
	kept in family units
	serfdom was hereditary on all offspring
	military service could be forced

The owners of the manor had absolute control over what the rents would be for those living on and working their land. Each lord was also the enforcing legal authority. Serfs could not file grievances against their lords. The Church enforced this system through their teachings. They also claimed supreme power for brokering the afterlife of heaven or hell for each individual.[309]

The Eastern European transformation into serfdom happened later and with differences.[309]
A short video explaining the feudal system can be found here.[310]

How are the vulnerabilities of all of us, of every race, being further exploited?

XII.
The road out and away
from global enslavement

"Time weighs down on you like an old, ambiguous dream. Your keep on moving, trying to slip through it. But even if you go to the end of the earth, you won't be able to escape it. Still, you have to go there – to the edge of the world. There's something you can't do unless you get there." – Haruki Murakami

An old Cherokee told his grandson:
"My son, there's a battle between two wolves inside us all."
One is EVIL.
It's anger, jealousy, greed, resentment, inferiority, lies, and ego.
The other is GOOD.
It's joy, peace, love, hope, humility, kindness, and truth."
The boy thought about it, and asked:
"Grandfather, which wolf wins?"
The old man quietly replied:
"The one you feed."

"The greatest error is to not look evil in the face." - Unknown

The information in this chapter is absolutely needed to help us understand the perverse and enslaving ideologies that are so widespread. From this information, we will be able to recognize how often they are repeated, how relentlessly they are pursued, and to what intended goal.

We will comprehend our immediate danger. And we will also recognize what we have in common, including our fervent desire for justice, freedom, and life.

We get to stop letting them polarize and divide us, from God and from each other.

Only then can we galvanize the alignment and commitment that will restore and maintain our liberty for the generations to come.

Reoccurring patterns of enslavement and serpentine context are what we are training ourselves to recognize. Serpentine context is the operation of ego, selfishness, disobedience to God and His Law of Love, plus shame, and fear in human history and affairs.

These were the stumbling blocks, the temptation points, of the Fall of mankind. They resulted in our apparent separation from Our Father and they are sustaining the illusion of that separation today. For other clues to unconstructive choices, review the mental, emotional, physical, and spiritual "drug" lists in Appendix III, especially those "drugs" bolded as most toxic in each aspect.

All those who seek to enslave others claim their right to do so in the name of God or "goodness" or "right" or "justice," while desecrating all principles of love, justice, and truth. They claw desperately for security, power, wealth, and longer life by human means.

Most "conquerors" in these endeavors seem to expect a certain amount of worship from those they conquer. They set themselves up, or allow others to set them up, as idols. (Beware of anyone who tries to set any of us up as idols. There are hidden motives at work.) Have you ever seen a conqueror or a haughty manipulator remain poor?

Those who attempt to enslave are opportunistic predators. Today, most use asymmetric warfare, the warfare of stealth and treachery. They target the most vulnerable, exploiting and deepening their vulnerability toward submission to the human wills of the would-be conquerors. The control is developed to the point where the conquered will viciously attack, destroy, and even kill anyone or anything as commanded. This, of course, is a form of protection for the would-be conquerors and the sacrificed are only ever fodder and tools to them.

1 Timothy 6:20-21 (KJV) O Timothy, keep that which is committed to thy trust, avoiding profane and vain babblings, and oppositions of science falsely so called: 21 Which some professing have erred concerning the faith.

2 Peter 2:1 (KJV) But there were false prophets also among the people, even as there shall be false teachers among you, who privily shall bring in damnable heresies, even denying the Lord that bought them, and bring upon themselves swift destruction.

The road to enslavement looks innocent and promising. Therefore, it is easy to be fooled. The small things, not mastered within ourselves, make all built upon them twisted and unstable. Chapter VIII Focusing the lenses of clarity, centers on these small things.

The strategy of the enslavers is very similar to the story of the frog put in a large pot of water on the stove. Little by little the heat was turned up. The frog didn't notice, was not alarmed, and so didn't jump out of the pot. He was cooked before he realized his danger.

Matthew 7:15 (RSV) "Beware of false prophets, who come to you in sheep's clothing but inwardly are ravenous wolves. 16 You will know them by their fruits.

The claws of the beast of global enslavement entered the United States of America in 1895 with the Fabian Society. The Fabian Society projects a socialistic concern for the masses, championing the State as God, which would take care of the poor, so they would never be in need. Its coat of arm depicts a wolf in sheep's clothing.[311]

Their true goal is oligarchical collectivism. This means they intend to subjugate the masses under an elite group, who would rule. They would decide what kind of life it is good for the people to live. And they would "take care" of them according to their obedience. This, seemingly benign offer, truly means that as long as a person is productive, they will be sheltered. If they become unproductive for the State and will not or cannot become productive, they will be euthanized (murdered). This is articulated in a film of George Bernard Shaw, one of the original founders of the Fabian Society in London.

The Fabian Society's goal is collectivism of the people for the power of a select few. It has been working to influence the systematic erosion and dismantling of the God-centered culture and the citizens of America. It has mounted a calculated, systematic, and relentless attack on the moral fiber of our people, and is still working toward that goal. The Fabian society has the same model as the new world order. Is that a coincidence? See and hear what the new world order advocates.[313]

Since the first attempted United Nation's invasion of our national sovereignty in 1951[314], the enemy has gotten much more subtle.

In 2007, Curtis Bowers, a Christian, family man, and educator, was appointed to the Idaho House of Representatives. During his interim appointment, he got a very unexpected introduction to the ongoing socialist/communist agenda and its workings within America. He did a deep dive into research and easily uncovered startling and profound information regarding their success with their agenda over the years.[315]

The terms "socialism" and "communism" are being used interchangeably today. As seen in the descriptions in chapter II, they involve similar dynamics.

Socialism appears more benign and is thought generally as "more just ." A "new socialism" has been fashioned to make it more marketable.[316] This is a magicians' trick used by the mass media and certain politicians to deliberately keep us confused, and thereby, tentative, and inactive.

Many communistic regimes have changed their names to "socialistic" to mask their true character.

"Socialism is an economic system. Communism is a political system." – Dinesh D'Souza

"Elect socialism and you get communism." - Unknown

"Socialism is suicide. Communism is homicide." - Margaret Thatcher

'Fascism is a system of government led by a dictator who typically rules by forcefully and often violently suppressing opposition and criticism, controlling all industry and commerce, and promoting nationalism and often racism,"[317]

"Communism" is the softer face of its Siamese-twin fascism. Communism is committee fascism. Communism is the use of totalitarian, fascist power to inflict socialism on large groups of people.

"An oligarchy is "a form of government in which all power is vested in a few persons or in a dominant class or clique; government by the few."[318]

Oligarchy is also a political system. The model for power here is a "small-committee fascism." This is the "money beast" of Babylon, alive, and still ravenous. This is the form of the new world order.

It is a multi-headed hydra. In the legend of the 12 feats of Hercules, one of the "miracles" he had to perform was the killing of the hydra.[319] A hydra is a mythical beast with many vicious heads on long necks. If one head is cut off, two new heads grow immediately to replace it. In our example. If one leader of the nwo is eliminated, two diabolicals pop up to replace him.

The objective of the new world order is slavery of all people under a global elite. Elite here does not mean all wealthy people. It means the mega-rich, including corporations, who use their economic power to create political power toward creating global slavery under their authority. In their scenario, the fruits of all the peoples' labors would be theirs. They would also own the DNA, bodies, and children of their slaves.

We the Peoples of the United States of America and our country are being attacked viciously and relentlessly by a modern-day hydra. It's intent is to destroy this last bastion on earth dedicated to God and committed to the freedom and liberty of all mankind.

The multi-headed, fascist committee of the global elite, who are marketing themselves as the new world order, must destroy the United States of America to accomplish their goals

To tear down our America, they must separate We the Peoples from:
- God,
- our God-principles,
- our self-esteem and balance, and
- each other.

Since the 1960s, the main target has been the white middle class, because they hold the power in America and because most of them are trying to live up to the principles of God and treating others as they would like to be treated. If they can be destabilized as a group, it could turn elections. The wedge point was Saul Alinsky. (See the history flyover of the previous chapter.)

Today, the target is still the white middle class. The newest weapon has been a politicized black population.

The platform has been Black Lives Matter. [320] The trigger point, the lit matched to the fuse connecting the explosive charges, already placed globally, was the death of George Floyd. Here is the suppressed officer video cam prior to his horrible death. Here is the suppressed, first coroner's report. The Floyd family, suddenly rich through sympathetic, global crowdfunding, bought an independent expert review, which has been spread by the globalist-owned mass media.[321]

Symptoms of indoctrination
Historically, regionally enforced racial, gender, economic, social and/or political slavery, has been building along with the power-lust of elites. Certainly, the Nazis longed for worldwide conquest. Many have theorized that they still are.

Because we greatly outnumber them, they must win full influence over our minds, feelings, and spirits and then turn us physically against one another.

Indoctrination by global interests is aimed at producing the "pathology of ideological possession."[322] This is a state where individuals will immediately parrot prescribed doctrine. When the "possession" takes over, we can see it in their eyes and hear it in their voices. The individual is no longer "present." They behave as if compelled to:

- repeat the full doctrine, whether or not it is relevant or appropriate within the conversation or situation;
- shame, condemn, fight, and discount or destroy anyone and anything that either disagrees or does not enthusiastically support the doctrine.

With the strategic help of the mass media, the tsunami of indoctrination, including political correctness, is increasingly ensnaring, particularly our younger people, in a toxic, rabid, ideological possession. The "powers who would be" are going for ideological monopoly.

In those under ideological possession, their indoctrination spills out in anger, hatred, criticism, condemnation, judgement, and blame. People turn and rend each other. With the sinister force inflaming and managing the process, masses of people are now ganging together with the objective to cause the greatest possible harm to any person or group, that seems to be opposing their desired outcome. In their rabid state, they perceive all who don't enthusiastically validate their agenda to be the mortal enemy of themselves, all they hold near and dear, even life itself.

Today, the socialist / communist agendas have been unified into the openly globalist scheme, fashioning itself as a new world order. Generations in the making, our amalgamated enemy has gathered large groups of indoctrinated minions. They have "refined" the process of war to multiple levels that do not destroy so much in collateral, hard assets, but are far more deadly to the spirit. Debauchery and individual victimization are at record levels.

But, **it is the turning of mankind against each other in mass numbers that has the potential to conquer us.** The astronomical resentment of injustice, coupled with monumental lust for revenge is a raging "addiction" that will not quench itself until all mankind is conquered and globally enslaved. Their end game objectives will be concisely overviewed in Chapter XIII.

Malachi 2:10 (NRSV) have we not all one father? Has not one God created us? Why then are we faithless to one another, profaning the covenant of our ancestors?

Under the influence of the globalists and sent from outside our communities, trained rioters and anarchists, who hijacked peaceful protests, are the outcomes, the harvest of programmed moral relativism. This enflames and stokes an egocentric refusal to accept any discipline or delay of narcissistic expectations. They are what they were trained to be by the indoctrination factories within public K-12 education and social media.

These indoctrinated minions advocate, - no, demand - anarchy without any thought or care of its consequences. To them, anarchy promises the unabridged, unexpurgated expression of their shallow and selfish whims of the moment. They are completely willing and feel entitled to take, desecrate, or destroy whatever gets in the way of what they view to be their rights to freedom. Most of us would call it license and lawlessness.

They are acting out what they were programmed to become, a proxy army, the sharp edge of a wedge to force into reality the chaos envisioned by the sinister force toward its goals. In the wake of this unrest, there are many opportunities for political license to attempt to impose greatly destructive laws and election results.

Please note here that restraining someone from acts of injustice, including deceit, theft, destruction, or violence, is an appropriate action.

We the Peoples are becoming so exhausted by constant turmoil, threat, and fear that many are beginning to consider accepting and even welcoming slavery to evil. Understand that this "apparent inability to cope" is being encouraged by the sinister force. They are tricking us into becoming more separated from God and each other.

At the point where each of us individually chooses to live within the separation experiment, we have chosen to consider compromising, or even collaborating, with evil. This robs us of our immeasurable power as Children of God. When this happens, we "spill" out our LIFE force, our power. And our enemy laps it up to make itself stronger.

Discernment
"I see in the near future a crisis approaching that unnerves me and causes me to tremble for the safety of my country. . . corporations have been enthroned and an era of corruption in high places will follow, and the money power of the country will endeavor to prolong its reign by working upon the prejudices of the people until all wealth is aggregated in a few hands and the Republic is destroyed. " - Abraham Lincoln[323]

The corporatist oligarchy of the new world order elite and their tactics match Lincoln's prediction with alarming accuracy.

The greatest weapon of those who would destroy America today is resentment against injustice. They are tearing apart our communities by creating a tsunami of toxic diversity.

This is part of the conquest ethic. It is commonly called "divide and conquer ." They are increasing our division by pitting us against each other. They are seeking to splinter We the Peoples in America so that there will be no single power that can withstand their amalgamated might. Having conquered the rest of the world, they have come for America.

The white people living today are not personally responsible for the atrocities to our black or Native American ancestors. Threatening and hating them, stealing or destroying what they have, beating or killing them, only creates more injustice. We should know this from our own experience.

What is actually happening is that they are tricking us into blaming each other for the gross injustices that they have inflicted on us all over centuries.

This strategy shreds all constructive relationships and blocks the creation of the multitude of new relationships we must create to collaborate with reciprocity for justice.

Here are remarkable observations, made by an emerging black leader about the recent riots and the power of choices.[323]

We must not let them turn We the Peoples against one another.

Justice requires reciprocity to be sustainable.

"An eye for an eye only makes the whole world blind," - Mohandas K. Gandhi.

Gandhi was a mentor of Martin Luther King.

Native Americans are part of my ancestry, and though not large, my blood would have gotten me a "ticket" on the Trail of Tears.

Speaking even from my modest portion of Native American heritage, there is nothing – no revenge, retribution, or compensation – that can possibility make amends for the injustices humans have inflected on each other for power and wealth.

Remembering our Highest Common Denominator turns toxic diversity into delightful variety and gives us a platform for co-creation of justice.

To heal the Fall and to create justice, we get to find our way through together to two-way communication of respect, harmony, and collaboration based in God-principles. **We will have to consciously choose between resentment against injustice or our mutual freedom in God's Love.**

The injustice and pit-falls of sympathy

The injustices done, anywhere in time, by tyrants of any race to any race cannot be healed by inflicting injustice on anyone else living today. The people alive today did not do the actual acts of slavery-either to the Africans, Native Americans, white Europeans, Hispanics, or Asians who are our ancestors. There is not any restitution that can truly compensate for past slavery and its incumbent atrocities. – **except crafting and maintaining our mutual freedom together now.**

We must be empathetic. But, never sympathetic! Sympathy is poison.

Sympathy is essentially an agreement with the manifestation of injustice as an intractable condition in the here and now. Sympathy reinforces the perception of inequality as real. Sympathy locks people in their suffering, mentally, emotionally, spiritually – and therefore physically. Sympathy fixates the attention on injustice and manacles individuals to their sufferings with the chains of victim mentality and poverty/entitlement mindsets. It chokes us on self-pity. It destroys courage, strength, and resolve.

WAKE UP! Notice how all oppressors claim the moral high ground and, thereby, the right and authority to inflict heinous injustices on others, We the Peoples?

At some point in this crisis, our would-be conquerors will come in, stop their own divisiveness, and look like heroes for stopping the violence they have paid to incite. The next ploy is blackmail. They will promise to keep the peace, if we give up our rights and freedoms.

If we do this, we will be choosing a life of servitude for our children and for generations to come.

The chaos across our nation and paralyzing fear they've introduced into our immediate environments, that threaten our physical wellbeing, can paralyze us mentally, spiritually, and physically. It is designed to force us to do anything that may seem to minimize our current danger. Our mind locks, we lose foresight and with it our courage.

It is only the **outer form of evil** that changes. It does a reptilian chameleon trick to camouflage itself to "fit in perceptually" within a situational or cultural period. **It is still the serpentine context in conquest mode.**

We must wake up to their tricks and manipulation!

We must stop the desperate, irrational projection of blame and evil onto each other.

We must have the courage to stop the hate, so we can face our fear, which is our ultimate vulnerability.

If we cannot make it through this maze of blame and hatred, we will never find justice.

Collaboration points

What is the difference between hell and heaven? This story describes hell this way: All the people are seated at one huge banquet table, which is heavily laden with heaped plates of every delicious and desirable food. There is more abundance than the people need or could use. The people don't have hands. Their elongated forearms have spoons at the end of them. Ravenously and greedily, they plunge their spoons into the food and bring them toward their open mouths. But they can't get the food into their mouths because of how their arms are made. Frustrated shouts rend the air. And a neighbor lunges forward and gobbles down the food from the other's spoon. Well, you can imagine from there the frenzied, food fight that ensues, complete with illegal wrestling holds, whacking, and general mayhem.

And what is heaven like? The people are in the same condition, in front of the same plentiful feast. They are feeding each other with love, patience, gentleness, equality, consideration, peace, calm, and joy.

The Creator's garden of mankind is one of many colors and delightful variety! Our Father God designed us with free will. There must be a very compelling reason for Him to have done so, especially to have put up with our misuse of it for so long.

We get to learn to use our free will constructively. Only if we are FOR what is right – God, Love, His Truth, instead of being AGAINST what is wrong, will we find the permanent solution from the heartbreaking, devastating struggle of humankInd.

All criticism, condemnation, judgment, and other forms of hatred, are also symptoms of the desolation and fear of separation. This includes doctrinal wars within and between religions and their doctrines. It includes the secular doctrines of socialism, communism, fascism, corporatism, techno-fascism, and the new world order. Guess who has the best marketers and publicists?

When, in the history of all these conflicts, have the final goals of the instigating humans ever been truly anything but personal glory, power, and wealth – at our expense?

WE MUST BUILD UP <u>IMMUNITY</u> TO EVIL. This requires inoculations of Divine Love....not of evil.

Today, understanding the past slaveries of all races will help us fathom and harvest the promise of the melting pot of America.

The solution involves:

- seeing and relating to each other through our Highest Common Denominator, the LIFE of God within each of us, and seeing it as proof of our essential places in God's and Jesus' family;
- opening genuine conversations toward civil discourse,
- educating each other, while cultivating understanding and empathy,
- planning and implementing action toward building reciprocal, loving relationships; baby steps first;
- combining those accomplishments to create next steps, and so forth, and
- being sure to share and publicize throughout our communities, with invitations to all to participate.

Here is a perfect place for the Christian churches and all the community of faith to step forward to initiate, empower, and sustain community discussions. A number of churches and associations of churches have already begun this. Many more are needed.

John 13:34-35 (NIV) "A new command I give you: Love one another. As I have loved you, so you must love one another. By this everyone will know that you are my disciples, if you love one another."

We get to, we must stand together with God and Jesus and refuse the vaccinations of fear and all enslaving behaviors "made mandatory" by intimidation or force. These are cloaking worldly schemes for wealth and power. Look behind their Halloween masks of benevolence! Don't let them fool us again!

Anything that tells us to hate another Child of God, anything that demands that we inflict injustice upon them, <u>regardless of their apparent behavior or position in society</u>, **is NOT of God!** Anyone who would try to put themselves in the place of God, as an idol for us to worship and obey, is not of God. Here are more of their telltale traits:

- they are "experts," while implying <u>their</u> expertise is infallible
- they have come to save us from a calamity threatening our very lives. (Make sure to check out thoroughly if they have any part in the creation of the threat.)
- they will amass huge power and wealth by having us follow them
- in that aftermath, there will be no process left to mitigate or remove that power over We the Peoples
- they assert or demand that giving up our God-given, unalienable rights, and their constitutional protections, is an easy and necessary step to our salvation and future safety
- they try to make us feel foolish or selfish for trying to hold our freedoms
- they villainize those of us who resist

<u>Proverbs 16:27-30</u> *(NRSV) Scoundrels concoct evil, and their speech is like a scorching fire* [28]*A perverse person spreads strife, and a whisperer separates close friends.* [29]*The violent entice their neighbors, and lead them in a way that is not good*

Please note here that restraining someone from deeds of injustice, including deceit, theft, destruction, or violence, is appropriate action.

Who is directing all this and what is its intended outcome?
Recognize that these schemes on Earth are ultimately orchestrated by one who has encrusted himself in exponential narcissism. He is consumed with supreme jealousy for God, the Creator, - and has fanned that jealousy into excruciating hatred. He will not consider Love. He must have ALL the power personally. He will not share with any other. By his, so-far intractable insistence, he has cut himself off from LIFE, the continuous flow of God's Love. And therefore, he has cut off the LIFE flowing into him. (If you dig deep enough, you will find all diabolical humans worship him.)

In this condition, to continue existence itself he must steal LIFE from God's Children. He will stop at nothing to enslave, destroy, and devour all that contains God's LIFE. Of course, we are talking about the devil.

He has created hybrid minions of himself and, by deceit and treachery, put them in positions of influence and power. The ultimate objective is the total and permanent separation of all mankind from God, Our Father, in abject slavery. He is designing, through our enslavement, his ongoing source of life.

C.S. Lewis had insight into the devil's schemes. Check out his small book, *The Screwtape Letters.*[324] Old Screwtape's minions are not safe from his insatiable appetite either. He has tricked them also.

Today in America

Those demanding restitution by continuing and escalating new injustices have been blinded by anger, hatred, rage, and bloodlust. Most of this rage and behavior has been accomplished by insidious indoctrination, including lockstep messaging through mass media. They will never be satisfied by those who are sincerely trying to find a solution to injustices done to others - no matter what those labelled as "privileged" do. Whatever is attempted or gifted toward solution, it will never be enough for "the mob."

The self-righteous, inflamed by resentment against past injustices, will simply up the ante on the living with more and increased demands. These demands will be progressively intrusive, attempting to negate the free will and unalienable rights of their targets. They are creating a pressure cooker of ridicule, condemnation, and fear of potential violence to mentally, emotionally, physically, and spiritually fatigue us to the point where we submit to their tyranny. This insurrection is a multi-headed monster.

This proxy, mob-army of the global elites will drain every drop of blood and life, and then kick the lifeless bodies to the gutter with derision. The ultimate aim is the running of the lives, churches, businesses, and governments of the mass of the people, according to the divisive whims and the toxic plans of a minuscule part of the population.

In other words, what we are experiencing today in America is the frontline of a worldwide asymmetric war with the ultimate goal of a global plantation.

Let's add the spiritual component of what is happening in America and the world today.

The opposite of love is fear, not hate. Hate comes later in the equation, the progression. Fear rises out of egoism and selfishness. **Fear creates** doubt and sows discord.

Fear, at its most fundamental, is the fear of being separated from God, Love, and LIFE. It is the Fall from Divine Grace and of becoming separated from our Divine Birthright as Children of God, Our Creator and Father. Hence, the terms "Fall of mankind" and the "separation experiment ."

All of this is a complete illusion orchestrated by the serpent in the biggest, most evil "psy-op" (psychological warfare) of all time.

Fear causes us to choose to hide or to fight. Hiding seems to protect our vulnerability from view. There are lots of ways to hide. Fighting seems to protect the dignity and rights we all sense innately are ours. There are lots of ways to fight.

Most of us don't have any true idea what we are trying to protect. We give it names like justice, dignity, respect, constructive self-determination, free will, rights to keep the fruits of our labors, unalienable rights, security from violence, safety from desecration; the right to life, liberty, and the pursuit of happiness.

All of these come from God's Divine Breath, the I AM's LIFE in us, our Divine Birthright, which assures us our essential place in Our Father God's Kingdom.

Genesis 1:27 (NIV) God created mankind in his own image, in the image of God he created them; male and female he created them.

Genesis 2:7 (NRSV) then the LORD God formed man from the dust of the ground, and breathed into his nostrils the breath of life; and the man became a living being.

The farther the devil can separate us mentally and emotionally from God, the less likely we are to call to the I AM WHO I AM for help and deliverance. It is even less likely that we will ban together consciously to do so. After eons of stealing the power of our LIFE from us, the devil has become so powerful in the physical realm that God is his only effective enemy and nemesis. All the military might of the United States of America has only produced a temporary setback in his plans for global conquest.

The original fear of the Fall has been expanded through history by sadistic customs. It is carried in our human and racial collective memories. Although certainly not the only examples, here are real world examples of deliberate injustice:

- originally self-made aristocracy by force, the elites of all races subjugated other humans toward amassing power and wealth, i.e. slavery of any kind

- use of daughters by elites as pawns in power games. They were given or sold to be breeders of children to fuse bloodlines and, thereby, enhance military and governing alliances

- The Inquisition sought to control the lives of all peoples and, with terror and brutality, claiming exclusive and ultimate authority of one religious doctrine over access to God, Jesus, Love, LIFE, and the admittance to eternal life

- "Witches Hammer" an extreme violence, psychologically, emotionally, and physically, used to further subjugate primarily women; falsely invoking God as its supreme collaborator

- the "Willie Lynch" method of breaking African slaves

- misuse of the helpless in indecently extreme and harmful medical experiments by the Nazis toward accumulation of more power over humanity

- lies, deceit, treachery, war, and slavery of all kinds

- the annual murder of millions of unborn children globally

- treason against God

Whose fingerprints do you perceive in all this atrocity and injustice? Why do we continue to cooperate?

Fear can be enhanced by deliberate, repeated, misuse of psychological manipulation. It is almost always coupled with some level of emotional and physical abuse. The development of this has become "science." Many branches of science are being used as weapons of subjugation and slavery in many areas.

Strategic psychology is being used now to create discord and dissention, to shatter unity and collaboration, to increase fear in all. The conditioning and indoctrination levels have reached nearly full saturation in subgroups of vulnerable groups, which we have studied. More are added here. The deliberate unconstructive use of this science is being applied to create mass polarization across our nation. It is aimed toward the tearing apart of the United States of America.

Dividing the young from America's founding principles
An alarming number of young people are so enslaved by the collective, herd mentality that they cannot tolerate at all neither any small difference of opinion nor less than enthusiastic endorsement of how they think. They are mentally and emotionally compelled to defend the collective and their place in it. Their most common weapons are "political correctness" (verbal abuse of dissenter) and shunning. These are being escalated into physical aggression. The young are being incited to participate in rioting against expertly-packaged "social injustices" that are too broadly applied to create anything but more injustice. Trigger terms that spark these behaviors include: America, the right or rightist, injustice, Republican, Trump.

Dividing women from men
The feminist movement has become so hateful and toxic that, not only are they denouncing all men (especially white men), they are trying to denounce and abandon all the gifts and divine attributes of womanhood. The trigger points used to be anything that smacks of being cast in the roles of "sexual commode," "negotiated broodmare" for someone else's power and political ambitions, or subjugated into a role of nonhuman docility. Today, there is rarely anything in the feminist rhetoric that carries a sense of balance, respect, and nurturing of life, justice for all, and their own responsibility in creating justice. And yet, they further debase themselves by adopting hatred of the "opposite sex," murdering their own babies, and indifferent, active promiscuity, which women have so long recognized as evil and degrading.

Reversing the poles of extreme racism
The indoctrination of African Americans started with slavery and the "willie-lynch method," followed by 245 years of dehumanizing subservience. The trigger term is "nigger ." Today, whether it is used directly or others can be blamed for what is behind the term, it is being used to invoke extreme hatred, mindless rage, and violence against whites. Mass media is most often the carrier of the trigger statements.

Remember that when President Johnson mounted the "War on Poverty," he privately called it the "nigger bill ." Crunching 2018 census statistics, blacks share the second highest poverty rate by ethnicity with Hispanics. Yet, even today, the blacks account for only about 21.4% of all those in poverty in America. What was planned under the surface of Johnson's statement? What further misuse of our black brothers and sisters was being planned by Johnson and his cronies?

No other groups of poor people have been incited against America or whites, like the African Americans. Neither, history would indicate, has slavery been so vile, violent, and cruel as that inflicted on the ancestors of our black citizens. Is this increased vulnerability being exploited through education, urban plantation living, politics, incitement to riot, and unscrupulous reporting?

Who is orchestrating it and how is this being manipulated?

Nationwide, Americans of all races and social-economics were <u>united</u> in decrying Floyd's cruel death.

The agenda-brokers, through political and media spin, encouraged more extreme division and hatred, inciting mass rioting throughout America and the world. The death and injury tolls are still being tallied, along with the millions of dollars in property destruction and theft. The impact on residents of the neighborhoods and the lives of small business owners who were in the path of the violence will probably never be fully known.

And how can the debilitating fear in American citizens and the damage to our unity be measured? Did all the rage, violence, destruction, and horror create one iota of justice for anyone?

August 11, 2020: Email from a friend in South Chicago
"I assume you have heard or seen the carnage that took place in Chicago last night and this morning. Some say it was due to a shooting in Englewood (a black more or less impoverished) community. It seems that 'fake' new sparked civil unrest, but the subsequent looting was not driven, it seems, by that. Sounds like the instigators and provocateurs you've been speaking of.

"People, good people, are afraid now, and that is always dangerous. Frightened good people often cease to be good when immersed in fear.

"There seem to be no towers of strength among us anymore.

" 'Black Lives Matter' the signs say, but what difference does that make when those lives do not appear to matter to those of whom they speak? I have watched the black struggle for 70 years. Once I saw a people striving to improve their lot, to live a good life, to become educated, know more and do more. I see so much less of that now. I see laziness, indolence, and the arrogance of ignorance that screams at the top of its voice, 'I don't have it so you won't have it either.' And people (white and black) agree.

"Once a man was deemed a man (and, in today's world, a woman) by their deeds. If he performed good acts, good seemed to flow, or if not flow at least stream, or even trickle to him. Now it seems that those who achieve nothing are deemed to be worth more than those who strive. Those who have achieved a little something (white or black) seem to matter less than those who have not worked, not educated, not derived anything from the culture beyond entitlement.

"Slavery has been dead 155 years. When will the people themselves decide they are no longer enslaved?

"I'm ranting because I am disappointed with the behavior of the members of my race that have acted out of greed, and a lack of appreciation for what they have, rather than what they do not. I remember when I was teaching, that there were students born and raised and living in the ghetto that wore more expensive clothing than I. Yet all they did was whine about what they did not have.

My sympathy (I hold no agreement) is nil; my compassion is strained. I do not wish them ill, but I find it difficult to wish them well. We are placed here to rise above, not succumb to the sinister force, to the Dark One. Anger is evil; self-pity is the way to evil; unrequited love is the way to evil; close mindedness and willful blindness are the ways to evil. Seeing one's self as the only wronged creature is the pathway to evil. My way is the right way; my way or the highway.

"If we can't come beyond these, how can we hope to see the light even when it's right in front of us? How difficult is it for those of us who think we know what we are looking for? How much more difficult for those who do not know?

"I ask no answers. I just ponder some of the questions." – John Harvey

"No blood spent is worth spending; but if it must be spent then let something arise from it leading all back into the oneness of everything and complete freedom for the soul." - John Harvey

"Where patience and perseverance master, God waits." - John Harvey

There is currently an aggressive attempt at revisionist history called the "1619 Project," which is proclaiming that the 1619 beginning of slavery of Africans in America is the true beginning of American history, not the Declaration of Independence in 1776. It further asserts that everything that America and all the other people and peoples built in the United States over the four centuries since 1619 was built upon the suffering of African slaves. Apparently, in their minds, nothing any others of us had to offer is of significance or restoring worth over the past 400 years.

Harkening back to the "drugs" identified earlier, this may be the most toxic cocktail of victim mentality, resentment against injustice, and entitlement I have ever witnessed.

The least hurtful of the outcomes will be the burning of bridges and shattering of relationships - existing and potential - with any other races and people who are contributing worthy endeavors to our country and have nothing at all to do with the injustices inflicted on people 400 years ago.

Many school systems are already teaching the curriculum to our children. This will result in a maiming of their minds, emotions, and spirits. It will teach them unjust hatred, resentment, entitlement, and encourage the excuses to never try to help themselves.

The 1619 Project is a politically-motivated misuse and further victimization of our African American brothers and sisters.

"Slavery has been dead 155 years. When will the people themselves decide they are no longer enslaved? - John Harvey

The Fall and its separation experiment has been teaching us - by the hard way of bitter, self-inflicted experience - what is good versus evil, what is love versus fear. Who is God, Our Father - and who is the trickster. Let's accept the lesson, and stand together in our Family of God, with God Our Father, and Jesus.

From today, we get to stand united with unshakeable clarity! From our similar pasts, We the Peoples have plenty of historical experience to empathize with and learn from each other. Let's start talking and listening. We get to set aside fear, resentment against injustice, anger, and hatred. We get to refuse to let them inflame us against each other.

Luke 11:17 (KJV But he, knowing their thoughts, said unto them, Every kingdom divided against itself is brought to desolation; and a house divided against a house falleth.

1 John 2:11 (NRSV) But whoever hates another believer is in the darkness, walks in the darkness, and does not know the way to go, because the darkness has brought on blindness.

1 John 2:9 (NRSV) Whoever says, "I am in the light," while hating a brother or sister, is still in the darkness.

Malachi 2:10 (NRSV) have we not all one father? Has not one God created us? Why then are we faithless to one another, profaning the covenant of our ancestors?

Only within God together, by free will choice, and with clarity and resolve, will we successfully withstand the divide and conquer tactics of the sinister force.

Make no mistake. This is the epic battle of good against evil, of Love against the egoism of fear and selfishness.

Ephesians 6:10-12 (NRSV) Finally, be strong in the Lord and in the strength of his power. [11] Put on the whole armor of God, so that you may be able to stand against the wiles of the devil. [12] For our struggle is not against enemies of blood and flesh, but against the rulers, against the authorities, against the cosmic powers of this present darkness, against the spiritual forces of evil in the heavenly places.

We are caught in a continuous loop of hell and suffering that we, mankind, have helped create ourselves.

There are three roles that make up the construct of this whirling tornado:
- aggressor
- victim
- non-engaged

It is the complicity of people playing these roles – consciously or unconsciously – that is creating and sustaining this continuous-loop hell. It is happening now, as we share these words.

Every one of us has played each of these roles to some extent in our lives. This is also true for every race, community, government, and nation; for every religious doctrine, including all the factions of the Christian doctrine.

Remember: all of these human beings, however arrogant, angry, humble, confused, or afraid, are Children of God, the Creator.

Aggressor: whoever seeks by deceit, scheme, manipulation, coercion, threat, or violence to steal life, liberty, or wealth (however meager, including fruits of labor) from another human being or group of human beings. An aggressor can also be a group of people of any size.

Victim: a human being who finds themselves the prey, dupe, or target of aggression. Many victims go down with little or no resistance. Usually cowed by fear, the paralyzer, they simply crumble meekly. Some wallow in their victimhood like it is a badge of merit or esteem. Some victims are even too proud to admit that they were victimized to attempt their freedom. Even if we are caught unaware and unprotected or overcome by a force greater than our own power, it doesn't mean that victimhood should be or is permanent.

In the Nazi concentration and death camps, while the victims always way out numbered their armed guards, only seldom did they rise up for their freedom. Many escaped. Many died. But none of these were any longer victims or slaves.

The slavery of economic dependence breeds accepted victimhood also.

Non-engaged and aloof: There are those living today, who are seeing the infiltration and degradation of our communities and the bright promise of America, but do not take meaningful and effective action or do not act at all. Some choose this out of fear, often coupled with confusion. Some feel too weak or powerless. Some affect aloofness from the rising conflict.

The non-engaged commit their children and others to victimization and slavery to save themselves a temporary, deceitful, and fragile interval of peace. The situation in America is so critical right now that they themselves are already being swept up in it. Aloofness can only disguise it temporarily.

 Are not the COVID-19 "plandemic" and the orchestrated riots shaking your veneer and even the walls of your homes, if not your conscience?

Luke 9:24 (NRSV) For those who want to save their life will lose it, and those who lose their life for my sake will save it.

Those who would give up essential Liberty, to purchase a little temporary Safety, deserve neither Liberty nor Safety." – Benjamin Franklin

There is a fourth possibility for our role. And any child of God, any man or woman, even a child, can fill this role. They are those who stand humbly, simply, without ulterior motive, purely with and for God. They refuse to acquiesce to evil. They stand with a determined courage for the Truth that God's Love is the greatest power and wisdom anywhere. This Love carries within it the only true and sustainable justice, the only sustainable victory.

These people have been present in every generation in the past. Without them, the world would have gone down into global slavery and hopelessness long ago.

In this fourth category, there is no room for aggression, victimhood, or aloofness. These are the ones who have chosen to perceive the truth of the hell mankind has created on earth – and then they face it. These individuals also have the courage to face their own past complicity in the problems facing us now. This is where we learn humility. Only with real humility can we truly receive God's Love and Grace.

Without humility, we humans seek to misuse God to aggrandize ourselves, like the conquerors and monarchs of history, like the socialists, communists, and fascists. It is the same for those who would set themselves up as gods in a new world order.

To step into the fourth role of mankind, we get to put Jesus' advice into action. The first step on this journey is the one illustrated by his parable of the prodigal son.

Luke15:17-20 (NRSV) But when he came to himself he said, 'How many of my father's hired hands have bread enough and to spare, but here I am dying of hunger! 18 I will get up and go to my father, and I will say to him, "Father, I have sinned against heaven and before you; 19 I am no longer worthy to be called your son; treat me like one of your hired hands." ' 20 So he set off and went to his father.

The second step is to accept Grace. Accept the Love that God and His Son Jesus have always, are today, and for eternity are offering to us. In the Fall, we chose an existence outside a relationship of reciprocal love with Our Father. Then, we were complicit with the sinister force as it began stripping us of our divine birth right and healthy love for ourselves. We refused to reclaim our divine birthright due to our shame.

God's and Jesus' Love will restore us. This Love is the only thing that will. We still get to use our free will to accept it.

Luke 15:20-24 (NRSV) ...But while he was still far off, his father saw him and was filled with compassion; he ran and put his arms around him and kissed him. 21 Then the son said to him, 'Father, I have sinned against heaven and before you; I am no longer worthy to be called your son.' 22 But the father said to his slaves, 'Quickly, bring out a robe—the best one—and put it on him; put a ring on his finger and sandals on his feet. 23 And get the fatted calf and kill it, and let us eat and celebrate; 24 for this son of mine was dead and is alive again; he was lost and is found!' And they began to celebrate.

Now, by God's Grace, we will be able to fulfill Jesus' Great Command and His Golden Rule.

Matthew 22:37-40 (NRSV) He said to him, "You shall love the Lord your God with all your heart, and with all your soul, and with all your mind.' 38 This is the greatest and first commandment. 39 And a second is like it: 'You shall love your neighbor as yourself.' 40 On these two commandments hang all the law and the prophets."

Luke 6:31 (NRSV) Do to others as you would have them do to you.

When we step into the fourth role – **the redeemed** – we can inspire the rest of our siblings in God's Family. And through God's Love, Wisdom, and Power, we win the victory over evil.

Let's be sure not to hate - even those who have made themselves our worst enemies! Hate would deceive and weaken us.

The truth is that aggression like theirs is born out of enormous fear. They are just stuck in the separation experiment. And they've super-charged their egos trying to compensate and protect themselves.

It is, however, quite appropriate to find those intent on violence and other crimes against humanity, and to take them into custody, and restrain them. It will lessen the vile harvest they are already going to reap.

No matter how great their power appears to be, God's is infinitely greater. No matter how great their power appears to be, it is not their own! It has been stolen by deceit and stealth – hijacked from us through our own compliance. They have manipulated and engineered a huge stream of our power that is feeding them every moment. <u>We can choose not to give them any more of our power</u>.

Jesus gave us an excellent example of how to deal with evil.

Luke 4:3-12 (NRSV) The devil said to him, "If you are the Son of God, tell this stone to become bread."
⁴ Jesus answered, "It is written: 'Man shall not live on bread alone.' "
⁵ The devil led him up to a high place and showed him in an instant all the kingdoms of the world. ⁶ And he said to him, "I will give you all their authority and splendor; it has been given to me, and I can give it to anyone I want to. ⁷ If you worship me, it will all be yours." ⁸ Jesus answered, "It is written: 'Worship the Lord your God and serve him only.' " ⁹ The devil led him to Jerusalem and had him stand on the highest point of the temple. "If you are the Son of God," he said, "throw yourself down from here. ¹⁰ For it is written: " 'He will command his angels concerning you to guard you carefully; ¹¹ they will lift you up in their hands, so that you will not strike your foot against a stone.' " ¹² Jesus answered, "It is said: 'Do not put the Lord your God to the test.' "

Neither the new world order nor anyone else can enslave or terrorize us without our consent.

Let us consciously and deliberately put the power God has given as His LIFE within us into conscious, deliberate combination with Our Father's and Jesus' Power. The Victory will be ours.

Attention! In the next two chapters, we will examine in detail what has been planned **and is being put into motion FOR THE IMMEDIATE ENSLAVEMENT OF MANKIND AND THE WORLD.**

If, at first, it doesn't scare you, you are playing the "aloof" role.

Remember! Just because others have planned this for us and put extraordinary effort and expense into inflicting it on us, it does not mean that they will be successful. It does not mean we have to cooperate with it.

We have exponentially powerful choices that will thwart their well-laid plans.

The last four chapters will map the global solution to this attempt at global slavery.

The interesting, collaborative mix of the current global elite has done such a good job of mesmerizing us, while they accumulated massive, encompassing power, that we are left with only two choices:

1. sincerely return to and fully collaborate with Almighty God for our deliverance, or

2. be compelled into the most dehumanizing, cruel, and indefinite slavery ever seen on planet Earth.

XIII.
Previews of intended coming attractions

Many will recognize tactics of Machiavellian principle in robust use within the United States of America and elsewhere in the world.

The Machiavellian principle implies that moral considerations are irrelevant in affairs of state... even if that means deceit or murder. Among its other tenets are:

- "Never attempt to win by force what can be won by deception.
- ...he who seeks to deceive will always find someone who will allow himself to be deceived.
- The vulgar crowd always is taken by appearances, and the world consists chiefly of the vulgar."

- Niccolò Machiavelli, from The Prince

Niccolò Machiavelli, (born May 3, 1469, Florence, Italy—died June 21, 1527, Florence), Italian Renaissance political philosopher and statesman, secretary of the Florentine republic, whose most famous work, The Prince (Il Principe), brought him a reputation as an atheist and an immoral cynic.[325]

Justice requires reciprocity to be sustainable. Anyone accusing others of injustice while not extending justice to those they accuse is not worthy of trust. This includes those who engage in character assassination, false accusation, deception, treachery, treason, rioting, looting, violence, murder, politics of dependency, or any other acts of enslavement.

Participating in mass marches on Washington DC, including the Black Panthers' constitutional convention in the early 1970s, taught me many, many life truths. Among these was the truth that the frontline organizers and the marchers were being manipulated from behind the scenes. We had nowhere near the full truth of the agenda and its slowly, surely progressing and overarching goals.

We were armed with our sincere intentions for justice and peace, and our well-meaning, ignorant pride in our assigned task to write a new "constitution ." We had not even a shred of the wisdom, or the knowledge of history or human nature to produce a meaningful document. The document produced did not have the ghost of a chance to create, much less sustain, justice. What we came up with was basically a wish list detailing the meanderings of immature, egocentric, and inexperienced minds, and gullible emotions. It enlarged our egos, emphasizing and demanding privileges that we mistook for rights. We dictated to the "others" whom we expected to abide by this constitution, but nowhere was there mention or definition of our responsibilities. We expected something for nothing, thinking that our passion and rage paid the toll. We were completely lacking in common sense, maturity, wisdom, self-discipline, and true compassion or empathy.

I learned how easy it is to tear down and how challenging and demanding it is to build up even the simple things of progress. Building with balance, unity, justice, and sustainability is even more difficult, impressive, and more precious.

Racism was not exhibited by Jesus Christ, nor is racism Biblically supportable. The LIFE of God, the Creator, is in all peoples, multiplying fruitfully through His creation plan. Slavery, while not overtly challenged, was documented, including whites as slaves, e.g. Romans had Greek slaves.

How to recognize the "diabolicals"
A very small percentage of earth's people are diabolical, that is evil to the core. Most of those who appear to be atrociously and defiantly unconstructive have been twisted, subverted, and controlled by diabolicals.

Ninety-five to 98% of us are good, kind people who sincerely crave justice, peace, prosperity, and wellbeing for all. These are our tender innards and they are very vulnerable. In our sincere innocence, even now, most have never even begun to realize the crucial need for our conscious, self-protection from temptations, which pull us away from integrity-based values. Most of us have not been taught how to protect ourselves or what the threat would look like when it showed itself. The root of that wisdom and knowledge was forcibly removed from public schools in 1962, while most of our parents were distracted and busy making a "better life" for us. They, too, were naïve.

Using the serpentine context, the agents of the diabolicals lure sincere, well-meaning people with honorable words and virtuous, moral concepts. Later, these are severed from any balancing relationships and connection. Then, with steadily larger doses of venomous resentment against synthesized injustice and hatred, the deceivers twist them around. To add to the growing disorientation, the indoctrinators subject their ideological hostages to shame for not being committed enough to the "just cause ." When the shame level is high enough, ideological possession takes hold. Next, a target, on which to wreck revenge for perceived injustice, is fixed in their consciousness.

From these ranks come the people-turned- attack-dogs of these manipulators, who are released into the population to incite, riot, steal, destroy, burn, beat, murder- in other words, to desecrate our neighborhoods and communities.

Anarchists who perform the violence and destruction do not generally have an intent to replace what's destroyed with anything else. Rather, they destroy wantonly only because what is to be destroyed has the audacity to represent a curb on their narcissism. This is ultimately-toxic-grade-selfishness toward whatever their whims or appetites suggest they want. (The whims of those doing the physical violence.)

They do not have any perception that what they are destroying holds the only means of producing what could possibly provide the things, sensations, amusement after which they lust and to which they are addicted. Once they have had their doses of the extreme, excited rushes of destructive power, they will lead short lives of utter desperation and deprivation. Most will likely commit suicide or be put out of their misery by other means. If history repeats itself, they will be killed systematically by those who instigated and funded their anarchy.[326]

Karl Marx predicted that the working class would rise against capitalism, but it never did. Those seeking to remove our constitutional government have had to find other groups willing to be culturally destructive. To further their aims, they recently selected those in the LGBT movement or "wokeism" to indoctrinate.

Ash Sarkar, a young British academic media favorite, described wokeism this way:
"Woke is accepting that LGBT identities are valid and should be protected under the law, that culture is an acknowledgement that racialized outcomes, reproduced through institutions in society and people of color measurably are treated differently...what I want, at an interpersonal level, is understanding, empathy and solidarity and at a political level, I want the pursuit of redistributive goals, whether that's power, whether that's wealth, whether that's land, in order to pursue aims of social justice, along class, gender, and race lines."

In other words, they aim to shame the productive citizens out of power and influence and steal what they have created. But those victims must remain productive because the ones who aim to usurp them have no idea how to produce and steward resources, and, thereby, sustain life, community, or society.

The ideologically possessed are also trained to incite fear within local populations, plus more anger and hatred. They mouth absurd, untrue slogans and insane, irresponsible, pre-scripted demands. They terrorize and enrage groups and individuals toward shredding as many civilized, collaborative relationships as possible.

We are allowing them to turn "We the Peoples" into defectors from justice like themselves – full of hatred and rage and no sense of decency, no cognition that these are <u>our</u> own neighbors, neighborhoods, homes, businesses, and communities. We become the manipulators' perfect tools to spread injustice and open the doors wide to tyranny.

After corporate would-be oligarchs, incite rioting and destruction, their indoctrinated, paid[327] attack dogs leave town and let us, the residents, deal with our shattered communities.

Proverbs 17:23 (NRSV)The wicked accept a concealed bribe to pervert the ways of justice.

Prelude to 2020

1947 Nuremberg Code: August 1947, after World War II and the illusory defeat of global conquest, out of the Nuremburg Trials in Germany, came the Nuremberg Code. For every human being in the world, this Code declared medical freedom as a basic, unalienable human right of every person. The Code mandates informed consent and that no medications or medical procedures may be forced upon any of us; and that, if we initially agree, we may withdraw our participation at any time. This has been upheld consistently over the years in the medical profession worldwide. For more details, go to [328]

1993 European Union[329] The European Union (EU) was founded as a result of the Maastricht Treaty on Nov. 1, 1993, after four decades of development. It represents the first megaregion of the United Nations' new world order. The people of the countries participating lost their voting power; national sovereignty, flags, currency, and piece by piece they are losing their cultural identities and customs. Great Britain voted to withdraw from the EU in June 2016, after a protracted legal and populist fight called BREXIT. The UK stopped being a member of the EU on January 31, 2020. The people of other "nation-states" are fomenting similar movements. The EU was largely created and is currently controlled by a number of multinational corporations. It is the first implementation of its kind by the Bilderberg toward realizing their aims of global government. They are duplicating the same process, with addition of pandemic, toward establishing a new world order.

2010: Gates claims world doomed. He advocates zero carbon emissions and drastic depopulation.[330]

2012 Domestic Propaganda Ban Repealed. July 2, 2013, an amendment to a defense authorization bill, legalized uses of government-sponsored propaganda on the American people. Government-sponsored news feeds and electronic media shows, movies, and platforms have proliferated since then, production and media time paid for at taxpayer expense. Prior to this, the government was authorized to use propaganda only in foreign countries.[331]

2015 TED Talk Predicting Global Pandemic by Bill Gates. Gates asserted that the greatest danger to world population is no longer nuclear war, but pandemic.[332] Did he just predict it or was he part of planning it? Follow the money and power connections.

USA Mass media ownership 90% of the mass media in the United States is owned by six multi-national corporations.[333]

2018 - 2020: Northern California Wildfires Fires did not burn like natural forest fires; evidence of laser weapon source was widely evident. Also, compare map of wildfires with Agenda 21 map with northern California marked as a future "no human habitation" area.[334]

June 2020: Many news reports about outsiders paid to hijack peaceful protests into riots and worse.

Look how well we're already being indoctrinated into accepting our "sheep" role in the new world order! Let's review just some of their tactics during their training called COVID-19. By personal experience, you will know the collaboration levels of yourself, friends, organizations, communities, and our nation. Part of the collaboration was necessary and appropriate. The question is when did the tactics and demands reach levels of deceit, encroachment on Constitutional rights and freedoms, and indoctrination toward compliance? When did the lockdown demands no longer have true medical and scientific fact behind them?

Here are questionable tactics which were tested during the pandemic, to assess our willingness to comply:

- Extreme threat of death[335], using wildly inaccurate "scientific" prediction models

- o Producing such fear of contagion that we were willing to give up our rights to medical "experts," including:
    - Right to worship
    - Right to congregate
    - Right to livelihood and prosperity, individually and nationally
- o Shaming for noncompliance
    - shock and horror from others
    - rise of snitches
        - Making us afraid to associate with each other
            - compulsively clinging to the use of face masks[336]which also:
                - o cover our unique identities and subdue meaningful, communitive facial expressions
                - o sever our ability to share our humanity and
                - o are ineffective
        - Usurping of or scaring/shaming of authority
            - compelling medical people to go against their oath to "do no harm"
            - refusing family visitation to the ill from any cause
            - refusing significant others and family presence even at the death of a loved one
            - compelling doctors to falsify cause of death information on death certificates to say people died OF COVID-19, when they died with COVID
            - Incentivizing hospitals for admitting patients for declared COVID-19 ($13,000 each) and for use of respirator for treatment of same ($39,000)

These items are well documented all over the alternative media and in these well-made videos. "Crimes against humanity" inflicted in the name of a fake pandemic have also been well documented for the upcoming class action suits in Germany and globally.[337].

Before and during the pandemic, we got this guidance and encouragement from influential leaders, such as Henry Kissinger and Bill Gates. It is best that you hear it from their own lips. Please watch this video.[338]

The recommendation is very high for you to personally research all this, using an uncensored, untracked search engine. The new world order also has websites for megaregions and other plans more brazenly available, though cunningly written and scripted. They are active within what appear to be normal community development initiatives.

The strategic importance of mandated vaccines
We the Peoples are starting to wake up. Americans pushed back on the globalist attempt to keep us in lockdown until a vaccine was developed, that they promised would keep us safe. Many, unfortunately, are nearly hysterically convinced, by mass media sources, that they will die

if they get COVID-19. This is happening despite the growing statistical data to the contrary, readily available through alternate news sources.

Increasing numbers of Americans are resisting their doomsday pitch for a second lockdown.

Unknown to most Americans, people across Europe are organizing protests against this false plandemic and its sinister intentions.[339] They are powerfully refuting and refusing the new world order and its agendas.

The globalists are losing their hold of fear and misinformation on We the Peoples. Their first attempt to destroy the United States' economy didn't work. The US riots haven't created mass revolution, despite complicit, saturation media coverage.

Why are they forcing the criminally-reckless, fast-tracking of a vaccine? By all medically-ethical procedures and history, a responsible process should take a minimum of five to six years.[340]

Cui bono? Who benefits and in what ways? Who pays the price of those "benefits"?

Here are two major objectives that come into focus, which are from the globalist manifesto, and will be overviewed specifically in the next chapter. Those two goals are 95% depopulation and total subjugation.

Let's examine what is really going on in the competitive race by big pharma for the hundreds of billions of dollars, that would be reaped annually from vaccine sales, inflicted on a compliant world population.

Here is a brief overview of what vaccine and medical experts are saying. The individual, Dr. Carrie Madjeg, highlighted here, has decades of experience in vaccines and as being a physician. She has also been in meetings where authorities and experts were discussing these factors.[341]

These characteristics are present in vaccines being produced by the big pharma competitors: [342]
- **Medically, the formational, chemistry approach is completely experimental**. They have no substantial histories to confirm their approach is safe. In fact, what evidence is available from <u>animal</u> testing says it is definitely NOT safe.[343]
    - **Transfection is being used.**[344] It is a process that is used in the creation of GMO plants for food production. "GMO" means genetically modified organism. These products were also rushed to market without sufficient testing on animals and none on humans. Research, after the fact so to speak, is amassing statistics of greatly disturbing side effects. Europe severely restricted GMO seeds, foods, and food products.[344]

The pharmaceutical companies have been transparent, even in the mass media, that they are short-cutting ethical, proven, medical safeguards, as they rush COVID vaccines to market.

Is this part of the new world order depopulation rollout?

But, this is not the only alarming characteristic of their vaccines. Additional factors to consider include:

- The vaccine would introduce synthetic RNA or DNA into a human body, which would cause mutation of the person's genome. Whether that would be permanent or temporary is unknown.[345]

  - "Genome" means a full set of chromosomes; all the inheritable traits of an organism."[346]

  - **That means that we would no longer be human.** Our body's genome would no longer be an organism that appears genuinely, authentically in nature. **It would no longer be what was authored by God.**[347]

  - The Supreme Court has ruled that anything that does not appear in nature, but has been altered by man, can be patented – legally owned by an entity, e.g. an individual, corporation, etc.[348]

    - Within agriculture, seeds and plants bearing the genome of the patent holder are legally owned by that patent holder. To the farmer, it means that they must purchase next year's seeds from the patent holder or their designee. The farmer may not save seeds from his harvest to replant for the next season.

      The artificial GMO genomes are very aggressive and alter the genome of fields of plants[349], planted with naturally-occurring seeds in adjacent fields through wind-enabled cross pollination. Many farmers, who replanted their harvested seeds, have been put out of business due to lawsuits from GMO patent holders.[350]

- **What if our personal body's genome adjusted to a patented genome?** Would we no longer own ourselves?[351]

- **What about our children's genomes?** A genome is a full set of chromosomes; all the inheritable traits of an organism.

"The vaccine would introduce technologies into our physical bodies that would, very quickly, alter: how we live - who we are - what we are." – Dr. Carrie Madjeg

This is a mass rollout of "transhumanism"[352] on an unsuspecting humanity, attempted through enormous deceit and to be mandated by force. Transhumanism advocates the melding of humans with artificial intelligence. In most Hollywood movies, it promises greater and even immortality. The movie *The Matrix* provides a more realistic prediction the outcome.

Here's what else the vaccine will be "packing":

- **Hydrogel carrying nanotechnology.**[353] Nanotechnology refers to microscopic robots that can assemble, disassemble, and reassemble inside a human body. They will connect to artificial intelligence (AI) and upload information on your body's functions. 24/7.
    - What else can it upload? Say a permanent "good-bye" to personal privacy, even within your own body.

    - **Communication with AI is a two-way street.**[354] Facebook has already proven through multitudinous tests, without specific user permission, that the type of posts directed to individuals or groups can reliably affect their moods, positively or negatively.[355]

    - What if something similar was going on 24/7 inside your own body, mind, and emotions - and you had no control over it or its content?

Does the world "subjugation" now have a new meaning?

- **Luciferase**, a bioluminescence substance, invisible in regular light. Programs, that will also be available for a smart phone, cause it to show a phosphorescent glow. This will be the proof that you have submitted to the vaccination. Along with that glow, will be an identifying, numerically-based code.[356]

Further information to consider:

- *Vac*cine manufacturers are not legally responsible for any harm done by their products due to their mistakes or negligence.[357]

- According to the recent Emergency Preparedness legislation,[358] we cannot be forced to have a vaccine if there is a viable treatment for the illness. Now the motives behind the battle over hydroxychloroquine become more clear.

- Does the government have the right to mandate vaccinations?[359]

If the vaccination really works, how would a person refusing to take the vaccination endanger someone who did have the vaccination? Why are vaccine advocates so vehement against free will choice?

And here, again, the Nuremburg Code is very germane. For every human being in the world, this Code declares medical freedom as a basic, unalienable human right of every person. The Code mandates informed consent and that no medications or medical procedures may be forced upon any of us; and that, if we initially agree, we may withdraw our participation at any time. This has been upheld consistently over the years regarding legalities within the medical profession worldwide. For more details, go to [360]

4ᵗʰ Amendment of the Bill of Rights of the Constitution of the United States of America: The right of the people to be <u>secure in their persons</u>, houses, papers, and effects against unreasonable searches and seizures shall not be violated...[361]

5ᵗʰ Amendment : No person shall be ...be deprived of life, liberty, or property without due process of law; ...[362]

"We are sovereign human souls and we need to take our rights back." - Dr. Carrie Madjeg

Notice that those with the global agenda are so confident in their ultimate triumph over God and mankind that they are beginning to openly declare their intentions. They also appear confident that they have achieved a high enough level of ideological possession. In other words, they apparently think they have us either fully indoctrinated or cowed, so that We the Peoples are now their owned sheep herd. They seem confident of achieving ideological monopoly.

Again, they rhapsodize their intended high ideals "for the good of all mankind," but they are all very vague on the practical "how to" they will employ to bring all this about.

Are our pandemic experiences in America and worldwide unassociated events or are they initial training courses in becoming compliant subjects?

The Pathology of Ideological Possession
These ideological narratives are engulfing millions in the "pathology of ideological possession," making them mouthpieces for an agenda. Dr. Jordon Peterson gives the definition and Chris Caige's remarkable comments follow.[363]

<u>2 Chronicles 7: 14</u> (NRSV) If my people who are called by my name (I AM) humble themselves, pray, seek my face, and turn from their wicked ways, then I will hear from heaven, and will forgive their sin and heal their land.

Before we read about the globalist "pitch," let's check in with the I AM, Our Father.

<u>Genesis 1:27-28</u> (NIV) So God created mankind in his own image, in the image of God he created them; male and female he created them. ²⁸ God blessed them and said to them, "Be fruitful and increase in number; fill the earth and subdue it. Rule over the fish in the sea and the birds in the sky and over every living creature that moves on the ground."

<u>1ˢᵗ Commandment: Exodus 20:3</u> (NIV) you shall have no other gods beside me

<u>2ⁿᵈ Commandment: Exodus 20:4-5</u> (NIV) You shall not make for yourself an idol, whether in the form of anything that is in heaven above, or that is on the earth beneath, or that is in the water under the earth. ⁵ You shall not bow down to them or worship them;

XIV.
The globalist intentions

"Can a bad man's lie ever release a good one from his word?" Mari Sandoz, Cheyenne Autumn

"The globalist project has now been revealed for the fixed game it is, one that mostly benefits the corporate oligarchs and the CCP (Chinese Communist Party)." Clifford Humphrey[366]

"Only a virtuous people are capable of freedom. As nations become more corrupt and vicious, they have more need of masters." – Benjamin Franklin

<u>*Proverbs 12:19*</u> *(NIV) Truthful lips endure forever, but a lying tongue lasts only a moment.*

Let's turn our consideration first to the CCP and how fast they have destroyed centuries of culture in China and enslaved its people with tyrannizing surveillance and social credit scores.[367]

Many are starting to resist the CCP. "In China, more than 300 million people have withdrawn from the CCP and its affiliated organizations in the 'Tuidang' (Quit the Party) movement.

<u>June 4, 2020</u> From Beijing, a group of "free Chinese" from the world and China itself, announced the creation of the Federation of China. The date, deliberately chosen, was an anniversary of the Tiananmen Square Massacre. The Federation of China is predicated on a one person, one vote, democratic vision. Their Proclamation was read to the world on a boat with the Statue of Liberty in the background. For more details, please view their video.[368]

Here is a recent overview of what the CCP is doing in Hong Kong to bring them under their rule.[369]
<u>May 2020</u> Hong Kong's people were demonstrating in the millions, holding purple banners that read, "Heaven is Eliminating the CCP." If the CCP forces Hong Kong under their communist system, "the United States, the United Kingdom and Europe have pledged to take away its free port status." The only financial window Beijing has (to the world) will be closed.

<u>June 30, 2020</u> The CCP published their Beijing "national security act" one hour before the 23rd anniversary of Britain's transfer of Hong Kong to Chinese rule. The contract of the transfer agreed to includes a 50 year window of autonomy for Hong Kong from mainland rule. It was described as one country/two systems. Less than halfway into the agreement, the CCP is inflicting their communist system of the mainland on Hong Kong.

This ends any freedoms that have been enjoyed by the Hong Kong people. The national security act outlines what it calls terrorism as any resistance or noncompliance with any of the new law. Those convicted could face life imprisonment. The law may be applied retroactively. Arrests began immediately.

<u>By July 8, 2020</u> The CCP authority over Hong Kong was already being flexed. They took over a hotel in Hong Kong for their new headquarters of the Office of Safeguarding National Security. It has full immunity from local jurisdiction. Citing it as "political propaganda," a popular protest song had been banned from use on school property. All political slogans connoting any separation of Hong Kong from China became illegal. They demanded that internet providers remove from all customer accounts all email and social media content judged inappropriate according to the new law. Searches of any property may be done without warrant. System proceedings against those already arrested are going forward. In addition:

- pro-democracy political party Demosisto was disbanded within 24 hours
- annual rally of pro-democracy Civil Rights Human Front banned
- protests went on. This time their purple flags read (in Chinese and English) that protesters could be arrested according to the national security law. Over 300 people were arrested, including a 15 year old girl; 10 were arrested under the new national security law.
- certain books became unavailable in libraries

New information coming out of mainland China: Forced demolition of homes without recourse - ongoing

In 2017, the Chinese regime demolished homes in a low-income area of Bejing, leaving tens of thousands of migrant workers homeless. In October 2019, they started to target the middle class.[370]

At 3 AM on January 29, 2020, a two-mile long demolition team arrived at Wayoa Village, a middle class residential area in Beijing. Court magistrates brought along district public security, local police, and unlicensed "black security." They pepper-sprayed, attacked, and walked over residents gathered to protect their homes. There was not appeal and no compensation. Vehicles with technologies to shield mobile phone signals were set up in every intersection.

"On elderly person said in a video, "This was my home. I worked hard most of my life to build this home. Now it's gone. The government has not mentioned compensation. The rest of our lives go down just like this home did. Help us."

The man who got this story out said, "In this land (China), we have no rights, not even the right to survive. The communists allow no ownership of private property. That's why we are issued a so-called resident's ID. It means that we Chinese can live here, but it has nothing to do with citizenship."

Residents of this neighborhood were primarily retired military and government officials, plus writers, artists, and entertainment and news personalities.

Why are any of We the Peoples in America advocating communism in our country? Why are we following those who do?

Remember the old adage, "If you elect socialism, you get communism." Which brings us to:

The manifesto of the new world order

What they are telling us – e.g. they are protecting us from the pandemic; working for justice, happiness, and prosperity of all mankind – is not what they intend.

2 Peter 2:1 (KJV) But there were false prophets also among the people, even as there shall be false teachers among you, who privily shall bring in damnable heresies, even denying the Lord that bought them, and bring upon themselves swift destruction.

The globalist "project" is embodied in the United Nation's Agendas 21, 2030, and 2050, called often the new world order (nwo). It is being directed and championed by the elitist organization known as the Bilderberg.[371] The "official" descriptions of their objectives are in high-brow, do-gooder language to glamour and shame people into praising these self-glorified, mass deceivers. All their "sounds-good" communications are intended to entice us to follow them into completely degraded submission and enslavement.

Today, the details of how they intend to achieve their objectives are suspiciously absent in their public-facing documents. They ask us to just trust them because they have ours and all humankind's best interest in mind. They assert that they are the experts and imply that we are incapable of guiding this essential process without them. Hmmm. Sounds familiar. Where have we heard that recently on American soil? Maybe it was from medical "experts" with wildly faulty predictive models, who assume fascist authority.

Here are the highlights of their ambition:

1. **Worship of Nature.** Nature / Mother Earth is to be set up as the idol we must worship. Nature on Earth is presented as the source of our life and our sustainer. This is poetically disguised evolution theory. Can you see connections between this assumption in Wicca and parts of the environmental movements? The globalists assert that the race of mankind is by itself a pestilence that must be mercilessly controlled if both the Earth and mankind are to survive. Therefore, our compliance with their demands is noble. The Green New Deal is the slick packaging designed to bypass our discernment, by use of glamorizing and shaming.

Genesis 1:27-28 (NIV) So God created mankind in his own image, in the image of God he created them; male and female he created them. ²⁸God blessed them and said to them, "Be fruitful and increase in number; fill the earth and subdue it. Rule over the fish in the sea and the birds in the sky and over every living creature that moves on the ground."

Mankind is meant to be good stewards of God's exquisite creation, which He provided to be an inspiration, a connecting avenue to Him, and a platform for physical existence. Stewardship does not mean exploitation, misuse, or despoiling. Mankind has a lot to learn and correct. But it must be done within the Divine Order outlined. This design does not include making an idol of nature that is actually a marionette puppet, with the new world order operating the strings.

In the new world order, the creation would be worshipped, instead of the Creator, God. There is no room for God or Jesus in the globalist's offer or at the inn of the new world order. Graciously, the world elites have authorized themselves to be the caretakers of Earth. Many famous individuals have already volunteered their services, predicting their place rather obviously, in the highest echelon.

1st Commandment: Exodus 20:3 (NIV) You shall have no other gods beside me.

2nd Commandment Exodus 20:4-5 (NIV) You shall not make for yourself an idol, whether in the form of anything that is in heaven above, or that is on the earth beneath, or that is in the water under the earth. _5 You shall not bow down to them or worship them;_

Since the 1980's, top scientists have proven that scientifically and mathematically the only way that Life, and therefore creation as we know it, could have started is due a Supreme Intelligence. British scientists Sir Fred Hoyle, an agnostic, and Professor Chandra Wickramasinghe, an atheist, came, independently, to the staggering conclusion that the odds that life began spontaneously was $1:10^{40,000}$, a mathematical impossibility. They concluded, "There must be a God."[373]

Hoyle expounded on this subject later and often.[374] "If one proceeds directly and straightforwardly in this matter, without being deflected by a fear of incurring the wrath of scientific opinion, one arrives at the conclusion that biomaterials with their amazing measure of order must be the outcome of intelligent design."

He would go on to compare the random emergence of even the simplest cell to the likelihood that "a tornado sweeping through a junk-yard might assemble a Boeing 747 from the materials therein" and to compare the chance of obtaining even a single functioning protein by chance combination of amino acids to "a solar system full of blind men solving Rubik's Cubes simultaneously."[374]

Since then, scores of scientists and mathematicians have made the same kind of calculation. All are in favor of the existence of a Supreme Being. Later, poplar scientist Carl Sagan figured the same outcome at $1:10^{2,000,000}$. Scientists and other researchers who hold to the concept of a Supreme Being, who created life and the universe, have been denied funding and influential positions for decades now.

2. **Megaregions.** The economic and population centers worldwide would be organized into "Megaregions." The borders of the megaregions would usurp city, county, state, and national borders. Eleven Megaregions have been designed for North America. Parts of the United States, Canada, and Mexico would also be annexed in their creation. The names of these regions do not reflect the names of these three nations.[375]

3. **Rule by the non-elected.** The megaregions would be run by non-elected elites, "experts," and bureaucrats. No need for the bother of elections and voting.

4. **Inventory and control.** Each megaregion will be funded – its wealth determined, established, and verified – by a Blockchain list of all it contains and manages. The inventorying for this list has been in process of being compiled for decades now.[376] It includes, but is not limited to land, buildings and contents, minerals and water rights, monetary wealth, patents and copyrights,

works of art, scientific accomplishment, human beings, their estimated production worth over their projected lifespan, their DNA (not under their ownership), etc. The unique DNA coding of an individual can be easily captured and recorded by routine medical testing, such as the test for the COVID-19 virus.

5. **Digital currency.** All megaregions would operate using digital currency. Every subject would have a chip implanted, usually shown as located between the forefinger and the thumb on the right hand. It would contain all the individual's personal information, medical records, passes and permissions, plus banking and financial information. No one could buy or sell, travel or receive services without being chipped. There would be no private property ownership. All would belong to the State.

Revelations 13:15-18 (NIV) The second beast was given power to give breath to the image of the first beast, so that the image could speak and cause all who refused to worship the image to be killed. [16] It also forced all people, great and small, rich and poor, free and slave, to receive a mark on their right hands or on their foreheads, [17] so that they could not buy or sell unless they had the mark, which is the name of the beast or the number of its name. [18] This calls for wisdom. Let the person who has insight calculate the number of the beast, for it is the number of a man (or[a] is humanity's number). That number is 666.

6. **"Unsustainables" to be discarded.** Agenda 21 has within it Agendas 2030 and 2050, which are dated, descriptive roll-outs of the new world order. Their declared objective is to "not scratch Mother Earth." Many things we now think of as innate, essential parts of living have been declared "unsustainable" and will no longer be allowed. These include:[377]

- the nuclear family
- voting
- private property
- fossil fuel
- consumerism
- home gardens
- irrigation
- raising of animals for meat consumption
- all commercial agriculture

What are the deliberately non-spoken repercussions of even just the bottom four items being declared "unsustainable"? Remember the disclosure clause in the separation agreements. Check out the movies *Solvent Green* and *Cloud Atlas,* regarding protein for the workforce.

The freedom to author our own lives would also be "unsustainable." Here is another facet of the "unsustainables" doctrine that is hidden – and, so far, unimaginable to those who are helping to tear down America. It was articulated in a film of George Bernard Shaw, a founder of the original Fabian Society in London. Remember, they were working for oligarchical collectivism, which is the model of the new world order. It is not a coincidence. Shaw asserted:

"You must know half a dozen people at least who are of no use in this world, who are more trouble than they are worth. Just put him there and say, 'Now, sir or madam, now we'll be kind enough to justify your existence. If you can't justify your existence, if you aren't pulling your weight in the social boat, if you are not producing as much as you

consume, or perhaps a little more, then clearly we cannot use the organization of our society for the purpose of keeping you alive. Because your life cannot benefit us and can't be of much use to yourself.

"Under socialism you would not be allowed to be poor. You would be forcibly fed, clothed, lodged, taught, and employed, whether you liked it or not. If it were discovered that you had not character and industry enough to be worth all this trouble, you might possibly be executed in kindly manner. But whilst you were permitted to live, you would have to live well." – George Bernard Shaw, a founder of the Fabian Society.

Of course, it would the demigods of the new world order, who would decree what "living well" is.

7. 95% depopulation of the world. To scare us into accepting this, the new world order advocates are using fake science, famous people, and hysterical spokespersons decrying catastrophic predictions. They are predicting the imminent ruin of earth as a platform for life due to global warming. This has been packaged as the "Green New Deal." It asserts that we are compelled as a species, for our very existence, to reduce carbon emissions to zero to save planet Earth. The "equation" for accomplishing this includes a 95% depopulation of humans on the planet. [378]

Currently, as a lot of scientific and historical information has been amassed that debunks this theory, the globalists seem to be wavering on the earth warming hypothesis and to be looking for a different "doomsday" scenario on which to base their same demand for depopulation.

This requirement cycles back to the immediate restructuring of civilization and society on this planet, which is slated to complement the 95% reduction of the human population. What means of mass murder are they contriving so that it will be acceptable to us? Perhaps a pandemic, which Bill Gates predicted in a 2015 TED Talk and for which he has continually promoted global preparation? Now he is demanding draconian, fascist measures of depopulation for "our own good." [379]

The primary objective of depopulation is to reduce We the Peoples of the World to a number that can be controlled. If the new world order accomplishes its goals, the remaining world inhabitants would be forcibly compelled to live within the urban sprawls of the megaregions in high-density "pack 'em & stack 'em" housing. We have seen examples of this "flown by" us for our reaction, approval, and buy-in levels. Are the huge high-rises of mini-apartments in the large Asian cities and the "tiny house" craze examples of this being insinuated into our thinking and acceptance?

There are exponentially more of us than the number of diabolicals and their minions. We have the upper hand if we keep our wits and our courage. If we don't allow them to scare or indoctrinate or bully us. [380]

Psalm 46:5-7 (NIV) God is within her, she will not fall; God will help her at break of day.⁶Nations are in uproar, kingdoms fall; he lifts his voice, the earth melts.⁷The LORD Almighty is with us; the God of Jacob is our fortress.

1 Thessalonians 4:16 (NIV) For the Lord himself will descend from heaven with a cry of command, with the voice of an archangel and with the sound of the trumpet of God.

Matthew 13:41 (NIV) The Son of Man will send out his angels, and they will weed out of his kingdom everything that causes sin and all who do evil.

2 Chronicles 7: 14 (NRSV) If my people who are called by my name (I AM), humble themselves, pray, seek my face, and turn from their wicked ways, then I will hear from heaven, and will forgive their sin and heal their land.

XV.
What are our choices?

"Soon we must all face the choice between what is right and what is easy." - J.K. Rowling

"Only a virtuous people are capable of freedom. As nations become more corrupt and vicious, they have more need of masters." – Benjamin Franklin

You may still not be convinced of a global conspiracy. But you know full well the Fall of mankind is true. Let's start there.

We are now in the epic battle between good and evil. This is the one humanity has anticipated since time immemorial, the one the devil has been promising. Every choice by every human living in America and throughout the Earth is vital.

"You're never wrong to do the right thing." - Mark Twain

Nearly all of us are, to some degree, ensnared in the entangling, dream-state insinuated into us by the serpent deceiver. We accepted it by our own free will choice. We have made myriads of choices within the serpentine context. Every choice not to wake up is a choice for the self-styled prince of darkness, and away from the I AM, Our God and Father. These choices are rejections of Jesus Christ's Mission of Redemption.

The opportunity, the responsibility – and repercussions – are all on us. Until we unite for the defeat of the diabolicals, the minions of the satanic, "We the Peoples" will pay the price of their escalating destruction.

Things will never go back to the familiar and deceptively mundane way they were before the globalist played their pandemic card to open their bid for world domination. Their leaders have had the boldness to declare it in videos made for wide distribution for some time now.[382]

We the Peoples will all be enslaved if they are victorious.

"People pay for what they do, and still more for what they have allowed themselves to become. And they pay for it very simply, by the lives they lead." - James Baldwin

The evildoers in any and all races are miniscule in number. If we allow them to pit us against one another, trapped in a cross rough of rage and shame, we will lose everything we hold near and dear. We can still win the victory of love and justice, but only together. Together with God.

The I AM WHO I AM is the only One with the Love, Wisdom, and Power to win the Victory. Our Father God has been waiting patiently, lovingly for us to learn the lesson we asked for in the Fall, the separation experiment. Remember, at the beginning of the separation experiment, there were separation agreements, through which the I AM has allowed our unconstructive choices to build over eons. Our collective choices have created our current national and global situation.

Luke 11:17 (NRSV) But he knew what they were thinking and said to them, "Every kingdom divided against itself becomes a desert, and house falls on house.

This division is the legacy of the serpentine context. It is based in merciless malevolence and uses of treachery and force to create the separation of individuals from Our Father God and the separation of mankind from each other.

Without God's Love and His LIFE Itself, our existence would become a perverse and obstinate atrocity of suffering. The would-be lords of the global plantation care not who or what they destroy. All they want is themselves in full possession and control of what is left.

Apart from God there is no LIFE or Love. People who allow themselves to be or to remain separated from God have no chance at all for love, peace, security, happiness, honor, respect, or anything approaching a truly fulfilling life.

Declare our own freedom and independence from the globalist tyrants! **We get to show the same courage and resolve as America's founders who signed the Declaration of Independence for us and our future. We get to re-sign that document in our own minds and hearts today.** Please read it again!

Our unity must be forged with courage, resolve, and with love and forgiveness. Uniting in these essential ways will be a great beginning:

- choose God, the I AM WHO I AM, Our Father first above all else
- see the HCD, God's LIFE in us in all we meet. This is an essential catalyst for transcendence out of toxic diversity - that will begin to restore sanity and perspective
- restore our reciprocal, love relationship with Our Father God, Who is awaiting our return with joyous expectation. (Please read again the parable of the lost son.)[383]
- reclaim our Divine Birthright as Children of God, in all our glorious diversity
- choose of our free will to live Jesus' Great Command and Golden Rule
- gather together in groups to call in unison and unity for God's Divine Intervention. (*See chapter XX. Making the call compels the answer.*)

Achieving these, the greatness of our God-given potential will expand exponentially and quickly. What heights of creative greatness we will enjoy serving together within the Heart of the I AM and our restored God Family! Will this be the beginning of heaven on earth?

Only We the Peoples together with God, living consciously within Love, can stop the criminal insanity of the globalists' intent to devour the United States of America, home of our I AM Race. In their insatiable lust for power and wealth, they will engulf all nations of the world peopled by the Children of the I AM of all religions ....and with them the lives of our families and our hopes for the future.

The preservation of the good in all mankind and the earth requires our immediate, informed attention, and decisive action. It requires our conscious choice to be free in God, the I AM.

The diabolical injustice inherent in the two-spoked paradigm of the serpentine context will collapse itself by its own sadistic weight of pitiless evil, **if we refuse to sacrifice our lives and freedom** by standing together united, in conscious collaboration with our Father God and Jesus.

Evil has now built to the point where it is making its moves toward full conquest and control of all humankind. The misery and horrific danger we are facing is of our own making.

The first reaction to this pronouncement usually is: "This is something way beyond anything I have any power to affect in any way." And we run for comfortable shelter.

Descending into fear, and its sidekick selfishness, is a common first response, especially when being confronted with something that is so widespread and intimidating. We have largely been lured into states of unconsciousness resembling "sleep walking" or "auto-pilot," and operating within blurs of busy-ness. This looming, immediate threat is a total surprise for most of us.

"The eye that seeks the safe path is closed to the future." - Frank Herbert, Dune

We can choose to rise above fear into love – into God's Love, Wisdom, and Power. Let's throw off the role of sheep into which we've been cast within the serpentine context.

The serpentine context is now very active and expanding aggressively. It has reached the doorstep of every American. Surely, the plandemic, the suppression of Christianity, the rioting, and election fraud have proven this.

Doing a calm, candid, personal inventory can be very helpful. Let's clear our perception with a game of "20 questions ."

Please answer these questions for your own life and situation:

Are any of the fundamental choices listed within these six points really too big for me to even try to do? Write your answers in this book!
- *choose God, my Father first above all else*
- *restore my reciprocal, love relationship with my Father God and Jesus*
- *reclaim my Divine Birthright as a Child of God*
- *choose of my free will to live Jesus' Great Command and Golden Rule*
- *acknowledge and honor my Highest Common Denominator, my LIFE inside me – and in everyone I meet*
- *gather with groups to call in unison and unity for God's Divine Intervention*

Matthew 11:29-30 (NIV) Take my yoke upon you and learn from me, for I am gentle and humble in heart, and you will find rest for your souls. 30 For my yoke is easy and my burden is light."

How is the spread of evil already affecting me and all I hold dear, e.g. pandemic, riots, restrictions on worship, widespread hatred and fear?

Is there any likelihood that the negative effects of this expanded aggression will pass me and my loved ones by of their own accord?

How many innocents have already been sacrificed?

How will I face our Beloved Jesus when it is all over? According to my next choices right now, what words am choosing to hear come out of his mouth when that time arrives?

*Matthew 25: 40, 45 (NRSV) The King (Jesus) will reply, "Truly I tell you, whatever you did for one of the least of these brothers and sisters of mine, you did for me." Or will I be hearing...
45 "He will reply, 'Truly I tell you, whatever you did not do for one of the least of these, you did not do for me.'*

At the point where each of us individually chooses to live within the separation experiment, we choose to play with selfish, limited amusements – accepting at least some of the glittery "opportunities" and smooth, ego-swelling enticements of the globalists. Resisting this is difficult, challenging in the extreme, even for devout Christians.

The globalists and their leaders have carefully designed it to be overwhelmingly difficult. They have designed it for our complete compliance and enslavement.

No choice but to fully obey and live Jesus' Great Command is a choice to opt out of the separation experiment and begin the healing of the Fall. To remain free, we must give up our egocentric disinterest and aloofness. We must actively pursue and accept full re-unification with Our Father God, Jesus, and our eternal God Family.

We have highlighted the manifesto of the new world order. We have traced the covert beginnings of the socialist / communists' systematic infiltration inside America. We have shown how humanity has fared in the globalists' implementation tests toward gaging our responses and expanding our indoctrination during the pandemic.

Ask for insight prayerfully, diligently, and thoughtfully. Then, answer truthfully and carefully this next set of questions. Write your answers by each point.

Does new world order?
- *encourage and protect the ability to think independently,*
- *promote self-sufficiency, and*
- *create healthy, balanced, self-esteem?*
  -OR-
- *promote collectivism (hive thinking),*
- *promote dependency on government,*

- *create or coddle the inability to competently guide one's life or take care of oneself, and*
- *does it degrade or minimize self-worth outside the collective?*

Does participation in the new world order promote, pressure, or require ideological possession?

Is its ultimate goal ideological monopoly?

Would your full participation be, in any way, optional?

Would you have meaningful input in its formation, guidance, or improvement?

Would you be a citizen or a subject or a slave?

Who is really in charge in of the new world order?
Who makes all the rules?

Who enforces them and by what moral criteria?

Is there any mitigating power to their authority?

To whom would you ultimately be beholden?

Whom and/or what are you asked to obey and worship?

Would that obedience requirement be rigid or would you have creative freedom?

Would your obedience be encouraged or enforced?

What have you chosen to be your future?
Your choice will influence the future of your family, loved ones, and friends. What have you chosen for them?

What is your next choice right now?

Understand this clearly: the new world order = global communism.

"History will record that those who have the most to lose will be the ones who did the least to prevent its happening. ...Is life so dear and peace so sweet as to be purchased at the price of chains and slavery? . . . Where then is there a road to peace? It is a simple answer after all. You and I have the courage to say to our enemies, 'There is a price we will not pay. There is a point beyond which they must not advance.' ...You and I have a rendezvous with destiny. We'll preserve, for our children, this, the last best hope for man on earth or we'll sentence them to take the last step into one thousand years of darkness. . . .You and I have the ability, the dignity and the right to make our own decisions and determine our own destiny."– Ronald Reagan (full speech[384])

"They who can give up essential liberty to obtain a little temporary safety deserve neither liberty nor safety." - Benjamin Franklin

XVI.
Quick discernment guide

Virtue is bold and goodness never fearful." William Shakespeare, *Measure For Measure*

"The highest form of human intelligence is the ability to view oneself without judging yourself and in that comes transformation. – Deepak Chopra

"Acting out is a substitute for conscious remembering." Sigmund Freud

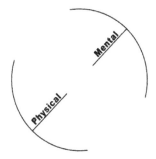

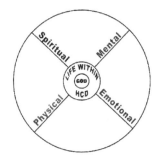

Dominant Paradigm Worldwide[385]

God-Centered Paradigm[386]

Origin of Impetus, Authority, Power, and Moral Value Base

Origin of Impetus, Authority, Power, and Moral Value Base

Human Intellect: unmitigated by any balancing or greater power, using mental concepts/ideas to compel systems and changes into the physical, mental, emotional, and spiritual affairs of self and other human beings; does not recognize, acknowledge or or obey any other authority, including God, the Creator.

God/I AM/Supreme Being/Creator: infusing its LIFE into the physical form of each human and expressing through Free Will choices of Its Children in mental, emotional, physical, and spiritual aspects.

Qualities
Synthetic creativity; fallible, dualistic, symptomatic, focus on using outside power to control outward behaviors of individuals and groups, inconsistent.

Qualities
Original creativity; causal, holistic, wise, constant, complete, perfect, and loving; focus on inner causes of all behaviors controlled by individuals themselves.

Power and authority outside of God and over individuals to masses of people; directing organizations, countries, and globally.

Power of the I AM above, surrounding and within each individual.

Intellectually dictated behavior, intellectually memorized responses, imitated without understanding.

Assumption of unchangeable, negative human traits, e.g. anger, selfishness, hatred, racism, Injustice.

Change by imposition of "greater" authority/power onto part or all of human population; adherence by surveillance, shame, force, and punishment.

Symptoms of its influence as it strives for dominance
Resentment against injustice (real or fabricated), division, anger, demonizing of "opponents," instilling self-righteous indignation, self-aggrandizement; identifying individuals though broad group as "the enemies;" criticism, condemnation, judgement, hatred; deluge of misinformation, deceit, indoctrination, stop-think, frenzy; dehumanizing foes, vicious labeling and stereotyping of proclaimed enemies; prohibiting civil discourse; encouraging relentless, inflamed rhetoric; rewards for acting out, including lies and violence; encouraging revenge (injustice) against foes as restoration of justice and equalization; insatiable appetite for victimization and demise of perceived foes (whether a person or group) identified as enemies; anarchy, mob rule, indiscriminate destruction, tearing down of every trace of targeted culture and way of life;

Exacerbation of all these negative traits.

Sustainability factors
Use of implied authority and/or threat outside the individual to compel compliance; continuous, subduing indoctrination.

Primary causal choice underlying paradigm
Fear

Conscious Free Will choice used constructively – with fully understanding why.

Individual knowing how to get at the causes of the most stubborn, unconstructive traits and remove them.

Change by Free Will choice, using deliberate, conscious collaboration, with God and with other, self-governing people.

Symptom of its Inspiration
Striving for the restoration of a conscious, every day, reciprocal, love relationship with Our Father God and Jesus Christ, beginning with ourselves, and expanding to others.

Deliberately, joyfully living Jesus' Great Command: _Matthew 22:37-40 (NRSV)_ You shall love the Lord your God with all your heart, & with all your soul, & with all your mind.[38] This is the greatest and first commandment. [39]and a second is like it: You shall love your neighbor as yourself. [40] On these two commandments hang all the law and the prophets." And His Golden Rule: _Luke 6:31 (NRSV)_ "Do unto others as you would have them do to you."

Symptoms include: love, respect, kindness, modesty, honesty, responsibility, accountability, generosity, dependability, diligence, prudence, peace, integrity, morality, the desire for justice for all.

Engagement, enhancement of all these qualities and virtues.

Sustainability factors
Conscious, independent choice from within each individual, based on conscious relationship with God within His Law of Love, with all other laws and choices springing from that source.

Primary causal choice underlying paradigm
Love

Symptoms

escalating complexity, excellence harder to attain and maintain, Increasing injustice, lowering discretionary effort, entitlement, non-engagement, unethical behavior, bullying, low morale and morals, lower quality of life, apathy, fear, anxiety, stress, increased violence, bribery/graft, degradation, deterioration, enslavement, dystopia.

Results

Shared core values, trust, respect; united vision of purpose, objective, and integrity; clarity, harmony, collaboration, all-level leadership, all respected and affirmed; synergy, results greater than sum of the parts; reciprocal love and, thereby, sustainable justice; abundance, sustainable peace and prosperity.

Inclusive, civil discourse actively engaged toward just reconciliation and continued, reciprocal love and justice; beginning within our families and churches; spreading throughout our neighborhoods, organizations, and businesses.

Same process engaged throughout community and its future planning and implementation; expanded through states, nations, all mankind, and our world.

Anyone or anything that teaches or demands that we hate is not of God. Anything that divides We the Peoples, God's Family, is part of the serpentine context, the broken paradigm. Whoever and whatever uses these tactics seeks to stand in the place of the true God and to strip us of our God-given, unalienable rights. It seeks to makes us all slaves.

The importance of elected and otherwise appointed leaders, **who are living and leading within this holistic paradigm**, cannot be over emphasized. The office of leadership, includes all who are in positions of trust, authority, or influence, from parents on up.

The process is not sustainable if imposed from the top down. Leadership's role is to embody and demonstrate these virtues personally; then championing, and guiding them in all over which they hold influence.

To be sustainable, the process must be predominantly causal, not just symptomatic.

The real Power is conferred by Our Father to us, His people. So is the ultimate responsibility.

"When big hands are busy, small hands do the work because they must." J.R. Tolkien

It is We the Peoples who must accept and embody these virtues to create and sustain Love, Justice, Freedom, and Prosperity in our lives. As we do this, we will tame and reclaim the earth and all mankind with love.

Nothing good in life is an entitlement program. Nothing is free, except degradation and slavery. If any of us condone or deny the God-given, unalienable rights to any of our brothers or sisters, we, too, will eventually trade places or join them. Such has been the story of slavery globally throughout the ages.

Love is the most powerful and sustaining force in all the universe. Manifest Love is most powerful when it is reciprocal. Justice emerges from Love. Justice <u>must</u> be reciprocal to be sustainable.

The two secrets of sustainable Justice are Love and reciprocity.

The I AM WHO I AM, Our Father God, is the Author and Personification of Love. God is the primary Source of Love. Out of the I AM came the Holy Spirit and the Son called Jesus. Jesus worships his Father. He demonstrated this highest mastery, and is still calling the invitation to each of us, "Follow me!"

XVII.
Was the Fall meant to be permanent?

Our Father God never intended the Fall to be permanent! He still doesn't.

Why do we continue to choose living in the serpentine separation experiment and agreements that create and prosper the sinister force? This evil intends our complete enslavement and is alarmingly well along in its process to accomplish it. **WAKE UP!!!**

God has left us many signs in the Bible that tell His mind and heart. They all tell us NO! God never intended the Fall to be permanent.

These include:
God kept us from the Tree of Life, so our condition in the Fall would not be permanent.
Genesis 3:24 (NRSV) He drove out the man; and at the east of the garden of Eden he placed the cherubim, and a flaming sword which turned every way, to guard the way to the tree of life.

God continually promised He and His Love are with us.
Isaiah 54:10 (NRSV) For the mountains may depart and the hills be removed, but my steadfast love shall not depart from you, and my covenant of peace shall not be removed, says the Lord, who has compassion on you.

Isaiah 41:10 (NRSV) So do not fear, for I AM with you; do not be dismayed, for I AM your God. I will strengthen you and help you; I will uphold you with my righteous right hand.

Our Father sent Christ Jesus to redeem us and demonstrate the way back Home.
Isaiah 28:16 therefore thus says the Lord God, See, I am laying in Zion a foundation stone, a tested stone, a precious cornerstone, a sure foundation: "One who trusts will not panic." (NRSV)

Jesus taught us to pray <u>directly</u> to our Father.
Matthew 6:9-13 (NRSV) " 'Our Father in heaven, hallowed be your name, [10] your kingdom come, your will be done, on earth as it is in heaven. [11] Give us today our daily bread. [12] And forgive us our debts, as we also have forgiven our debtors. [13] And lead us not into temptation, but deliver us from the evil one, for yours is the kingdom and the power and the glory forever. Amen.

Jesus' teachings and demonstrations of God's Love (The whole New Testament)

Jesus' forgiveness of sins during his Mission

Jesus' parable of the lost, prodigal son. Please read it again!
Luke 15:11-32 (NRSV) And he said, "There was a man who had two sons; [12]and the younger of them said to his father, 'Father, give me the share of property that falls to me.' And he divided his living between them. [13]Not many days later, the younger son gathered all he had and took his journey into a far country, and there he squandered his property in loose living.

[14]*And when he had spent everything, a great famine arose in that country, and he began to be in want.* [15]*So he went and joined himself to one of the citizens of that country, who sent him into his fields to feed swine.* [16]*And he would gladly have fed on the pods that the swine ate; and no one gave him anything.*

[17]*But when he came to himself he said, 'How many of my father's hired servants have bread enough and to spare, but I perish here with hunger!* [18]*I will arise and go to my father, and I will say to him, "Father, I have sinned against heaven and before you;* [19]*I am no longer worthy to be called your son; treat me as one of your hired servants."* ' [20]*And he arose and came to his father.*

But while he was yet at a distance, his father saw him and had compassion, and ran and embraced him and kissed him. [21]*And the son said to him, 'Father, I have sinned against heaven and before you; I am no longer worthy to be called your son.* [22]*But the father said to his servants, 'Bring quickly the best robe, and put it on him; and put a ring on his hand, and shoes on his feet;* [23]*and bring the fatted calf and kill it, and let us eat and make merry;* [24]*for this my son was dead, and is alive again; he was lost, and is found.' And they began to make merry.*

[25]*"Now his elder son was in the field; and as he came and drew near to the house, he heard music and dancing.* [26]*And he called one of the servants and asked what this meant.* [27]*And he said to him, 'Your brother has come, and your father has killed the fatted calf, because he has received him safe and sound.'* [28]*But he was angry and refused to go in. His father came out and entreated him,* [29]*but he answered his father, 'Lo, these many years I have served you, and I never disobeyed your command; yet you never gave me a kid, that I might make merry with my friends.* [30]*But when this son of yours came, who has devoured your living with harlots, you killed for him the fatted calf!'*

[31]*And he said to him, 'Son, you are always with me, and all that is mine is yours.* [32]*It was fitting to make merry and be glad, for this your brother was dead, and is alive; he was lost, and is found.' "*

How many examples there are of God's Love and His intent to heal the Fall and restore us into reunification with Him in reciprocal Love!

Here are demonstrations of God's Love and Power being victor over death:
Raising widow's only son from dead
Luke 7:12-15 *(NRSV) As (Jesus) approached the gate of the town, a man who had died was being carried out. He was his mother's only son, and she was a widow; and with her was a large crowd from the town.* [13] *When the Lord saw her, he had compassion for her and said to her, "Do not weep."* [14] *Then he came forward and touched the bier, and the bearers stood still. And he said, "Young man, I say to you, rise!"* [15] *The dead man sat up and began to speak, and Jesus gave him to his mother. (NRSV)*

Raising of Jairus' daughter
Mark 5:22-23, 35-42 *(NRSV)Then one of the leaders of the synagogue named Jairus came and, when he saw him, fell at his feet* [23]*and begged him repeatedly, "My little daughter is at the point of death. Come and lay your hands on her, so that she may be made well, and live."* [24] *So he went with him...*

[35] *While he was still speaking, some people came from the leader's house to say, "Your daughter is dead. Why trouble the teacher any further?"* [36]*But overhearing] what they said, Jesus said to the leader of the synagogue, "Do not fear, only believe."* [37]*He allowed no one to follow him except Peter, James, and John, the brother of James.* [38] *When they came to the house of the leader of the synagogue, he saw a commotion, people weeping and wailing loudly.* [39] *When he had entered, he said to them, "Why do you make a commotion and weep? The child is not dead but sleeping."* [40]*And they laughed at him. Then he put them all outside, and took the child's father and mother and those who were with him, and went in where the child was.* [41] *He took her by the hand and said to her, "Talitha cum," which means, "Little girl, get up!"* [42] *And immediately the girl got up and began to walk about (she was twelve years of age)...*

Jesus raises Lazarus to life
John 11: 38-43 *(NRSV) Then Jesus, again greatly disturbed, came to the tomb. It was a cave, and a stone was lying against it.* [39] *Jesus said, "Take away the stone." Martha, the sister of the dead man, said to him, "Lord, already there is a stench because he has been dead four days."* [40] *Jesus said to her, "Did I not tell you that if you believed, you would*

see the glory of God?" [41] *So they took away the stone. And Jesus looked upward and said, "Father, I thank you for having heard me.* [42] *I knew that you always hear me, but I have said this for the sake of the crowd standing here, so that they may believe that you sent me."* [43] *When he had said this, he cried with a loud voice, "Lazarus, come out!"* [44] *The dead man came out, his hands and feet bound with strips of cloth, and his face wrapped in a cloth. Jesus said to them, "Unbind him, and let him go."*

The Crucifixion: God rending any veil separating us from His Loving Presence:

The veil to the Holy of Holies in Jerusalem temple was ripped from top to bottom, from God down to mankind, as Jesus took his last breath of the crucifixion.

Matthew 27:50-51 (NRSV) And when Jesus had cried out again in a loud voice, he gave up his spirit. [51] *At that moment the curtain of the temple was torn in two from top to bottom. The earth shook, the rocks split.*

The Resurrection: The Father of Jesus and Our Father broke the power of death by restoring life to Jesus' physical body. Jesus walked from that tomb, first appearing to a woman, Mary Magdalene, who was sent by the Risen Christ as a messenger to the men.

John 20:11-19 (NRSV) But Mary stood weeping outside the tomb. As she wept, she bent over to look into the tomb; [12] *and she saw two angels in white, sitting where the body of Jesus had been lying, one at the head and the other at the feet.* [13] *They said to her, "Woman, why are you weeping?" She said to them, "They have taken away my Lord, and I do not know where they have laid him."*

[14] *When she had said this, she turned around and saw Jesus standing there, but she did not know that it was Jesus.* [15] *Jesus said to her, "Woman, why are you weeping? Whom are you looking for?" Supposing him to be the gardener, she said to him, "Sir, if you have carried him away, tell me where you have laid him, and I will take him away."* [16] *Jesus said to her, "Mary!" She turned and said to him in Hebrew, "Rabbouni!" (which means Teacher).* [17] *Jesus said to her, "Do not hold on to me, because I have not yet ascended to the Father. But go to my brothers and say to them, 'I am ascending to my Father and your Father, to my God and your God.'"* [18] *Mary Magdalene went and announced to the disciples, "I have seen the Lord"; and she told them that he had said these things to her.*

The Ascension: The Ascension is an essential part of the fulfillment of Jesus' mission promise to bring us back to Our Father. As with his physical death and the resurrection, he demonstrated the process by going before us. He assured us that he would come to bring each of us into the same reunification and eternal life. The Ascension is the ultimate "fall buster!" It absolutely shatters and consumes for eternity the serpentine context. And more important, brings us Home to God eternally.

John 14:1-4 (NRSV) "Do not let your hearts be troubled. Believe in God, believe also in me. [2] *In my Father's house there are many dwelling places. If it were not so, would I have told you that I go to prepare a place for you?* [3] *And if I go and prepare a place for you, I will come again and will take you to myself, so that where I am, there you may be also.* [4] *And you know the way to the place where I am going." (NRSV)*

Luke 24: 50-51 (NRSV) When he had led them out to the vicinity of Bethany, he lifted up his hands and blessed them. [51] *While he was blessing them, he left them and was taken up into heaven.*

God does NOT mean the Fall to be permanent. Are some working to make the Fall permanent in mankind's minds and hearts? Are they trying to make it so for personal power and wealth?

Proverbs 30: (NRSV) Do not add to his words, or else he will rebuke you, and you will be found a liar. (NRSV)

In today's churches, we human leaders and parishioners alike have a tendency to embroider around the very simple directions Jesus brought from Our Father and then demonstrated, flawlessly and perfectly, with his life.

Matthew 22:37-40 (NRSV) He said to him, "You shall love the Lord your God with all your heart, and with all your soul, and with all your mind.' 38 This is the greatest and first commandment. 39 And a second is like it: 'You shall love your neighbor as yourself.' 40 On these two commandments hang all the law and the prophets."

Egocentric embroideries are adding to God's Words. They keep us wandering around in the wilderness.

John 3:19-21 (NRSV) And this is the judgment, that the light has come into the world, and men loved darkness rather than light, because their deeds were evil. 20 For every one who does evil hates the light, and does not come to the light, lest his deeds should be exposed. 21 But he who does what is true comes to the light, that it may be clearly seen that his deeds have been wrought in God.

The embroidery doesn't serve the members of the congregation well. Like sheep, walking up a steep hill riddled with snake holes and covered with loose pebbles, we get our feet caught in the holes and we repeatedly slip and slide on the pebbles, never fully gaining our footing. Are many of us really making it into the full acceptance and realization of Jesus' promises, to dwell safely and peacefully within God's Love? Too often, the truth is "no."

Why is this happening? Is it that we have become more fascinated with the alluring temptations of an increasingly complex world? Do we like feeling so good about ourselves for our cleverness, often mistaken for wisdom? Do we wander off the straight and narrow way onto meandering footpaths of ego and intellectual pride? Do we make embroideries on God's and Jesus' direction to amass prestige and power over those who can be ensnared by our crafty and cunning gyrations?

Revelation 3:15-20 (NIV) "I know your works; you are neither cold nor hot. I wish that you were either cold or hot. 16 So, because you are lukewarm, and neither cold nor hot, I am about to spit you out of my mouth. 17 For you say, 'I am rich, I have prospered, and I need nothing.' You do not realize that you are wretched, pitiable, poor, blind, and naked. ... 19 I reprove and discipline those whom I love. Be earnest, therefore, and repent. 20 Listen! I am standing at the door, knocking; if you hear my voice and open the door, I will come in to you and eat with you, and you with me.

Matthew 6:24 (NRSV) "No one can serve two masters; for a slave will either hate the one and love the other, or be devoted to the one and despise the other. You cannot serve God and wealth."

When any of these things happen, whom or what are we worshipping?
We are following the ways of the world, which is caught in the serpentine context. We are choosing not to live Jesus' Great Command.

What are the repercussions? This ensnaring "embroidery" keeps us distracted and caught in superfluous human nonsense, that temporarily eases our discomfort. In others words, it keeps us firmly addicted to the "drugs" described in chapter VIII, Focusing the lenses of clarity. It increases our vulnerability exponentially, making us easy pickings for hardcore evil intent.

Matthew 15:7-9 7 (NRSV) You hypocrites! Isaiah prophesied rightly about you when he said 8 'This people honors me with their lips, but their hearts are far from me; 9 in vain do they worship me, teaching human precepts as doctrines.' "

At the point where each of us individually chose to live within the separation experiment, we are vulnerable to the cartel of "global-plantation-owner-wannabes." They have ensnared many of the Christian churches and, thereby, we Christians ourselves. They have made us catspaws, unwitting agents, to their massive scheming toward global enslavement of our Family of God.

This robs us of our immeasurable power as Children of the I AM. It is now a multi-generational condition of downward-spiraling suffering. It is moving toward complete enslavement.

We can make different choices consciously.

Are we using our free will to stay stuck in pride, or remorse, degradation, and even rage? What are the greatest sins which are keeping us from Our Father God?

1) Not choosing God as number One in our lives. Choosing to stay in limitation and sin, by keeping on making the same unconstructive choices

   This choice means: continuing the original egotism and selfishness of the Fall that ruptured our conscious, unified relationship with God.

2) Refusing to accept God's forgiveness for ourselves and/or refusing it to others

   This choice means: stubbornly holding on to continuing misdeeds and unconstructive choices outside God's Law of Love, as expressed by Jesus' Great Command and Golden Rule. It means refusing Jesus.

3) Refusing the redemption of Grace offered through Jesus' supreme physical sacrifice

   This choice means: refusing to leave the tomb of spiritual death. Refusing to move out of that "tomb state" even though God sent Jesus to atone and bring us Home.

   The supreme ego trip! It is asserting that our personal sinfulness is greater than God's Love, Forgiveness, and Atonement through Jesus Christ.

Pretty silly, huh? How long are we going to linger in suffering and slavery to sin (unconstructive choices) – with only everyone's human ego for company?

Laughing at ourselves shatters self-aggrandizement, self-deceit, and self-pity.

But, do not mock God! He is neither a fool nor a patsy!

Galatians 6:7-10 (NRSV) Do not be deceived; God is not mocked, for you reap whatever you sow. 8 If you sow to your own flesh, you will reap corruption from the flesh; but if you sow to the Spirit, you will reap eternal life from the Spirit. 9 So let us not grow weary in doing what is right, for we will reap at harvest time, if we do not give up. 10 So then, whenever we have an opportunity, let us work for the good of all, and especially for those of the family of faith.

From which paradigm are we living, serving, and leading?
Here are some questions from which we can benefit by asking them of ourselves regularly.

Are we actively obedient to Jesus' Great Command and Golden Rule?

Are we fulfilling the separation experiment so we can return to our consciously-united relationship with Our Father?

Will the separation agreements, allowing the authority of the sinister force, be removed by ANY human means?

Will God rescind the separation agreements and remove the authority of the sinister force and its leadership by anything other than our true, loving <u>obedience</u> to God, as requested by Christ Jesus?

Mankind must accept and use the Christ-consciousness of God above the physical world if there is going to be mastery over the conditions human beings have generated here.

Let's look for the seeds and signs of complicity with evil and how those choices compare to collaboration with God and Jesus

In our personal lives:

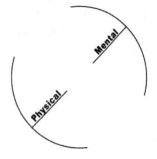 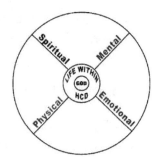

Serpentine context paradigm[387]
Busy-ness, no time for relationships.

Looking for love, approval etc. from
fickle, human sources.

Afraid/ashamed to seek God's Presence,
think freedom = distance from God.

Don't want relationship with God,
use excuses and dodges to avoid
God; misuse of free will.

God-centered paradigm[388]
Seeking unity, accepting reunification.

Accepting God's love, wisdom,
 protection; resting in Him.

Regularly practicing stillness, focus on
on God; learn, then know that I AM
and the Christ are the only true
freedom.

Know true fullness, satisfaction in God;
fill places of hunger with Our Father's
and Jesus' Love.

In church worship:

Serpentine context paradigm
Praying, carrying on loudly and publically
to show piety.

God-centered paradigm
Seek God privately, in stillness
and quiet.

Booming music, impeding connection, shattering unity.

Be peaceful and still, listen to God and Jesus.

Loud praise, but no relationship.

Patient building of relationship with God, the I AM long term.

Claim God's Will; never ask or listen

Seek God's Will, listen until get His Answer, test it, be clear what it is, go forward.

FUN!- then done, obligation paid for a week.

Teach and demonstrate "how to" draw God and Jesus into everyday life.

Dependence on human entertainment; creating services with drawing and and keeping members the first priority.

Feed their spirits, using outer world tactics carefully; tell truth clearly, simply, and openly, in small bites

Practices of gossip, judgment, cliques.

Unity, inclusive family, acceptance, and respect for all.

In church service and outreach:

Serpentine context paradigm
attempting to prove selves worthy by works, or by self-degradation and shame.

God-centered paradigm
Loving neighbors as selves, recognize and acknowledge HCD.

Main objective: to feel good about selves, or humiliating selves.

Relieving, even removing, causes of suffering from others.

Deliver services at, on, for, and, to those "needy folks."

Serve with them to alleviate problems they have helped us to identify together.

Look at those served as objects of our good deeds, worship only separately from "service population."

Remember our HCD; create full inclusion worship services.

Seeing need, doing nothing, congratulate selves on being loving and good.

Love is not a spectator sport, engage.

Leadership Perspective (relationship of leader to those led)

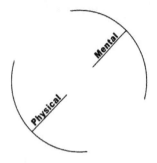

Serpentine context paradigm[389]
I am your leader.
I am here to direct you in how to
to live well.
The better you do what I say, the
better you'll be.
I impart information and direction.
You comply, acting accordingly.
The better you do this and the
better you produce, the more
reward, favor, and protection I will
give you.

God-centered paradigm[390]
We are Children of God, brothers and
sisters in God's Family.

God is the giver of all good things. With
ongoing diligence I am working to be
a good and faithful steward.
All I share with you, Our Father and
Jesus have first given to me.

I invite you to the opportunity to work
and serve together. You make the
choice of your own free will. Each
contributing our talents, abilities, and
supply, we will create value and enjoy
reward together.

*Matthew 23:8 But you are not to be called rabbi, for you have one teacher, and you are
all students.*

Objective
Gather followers, who know that if
they stick with me, I will keep them
on track

My leadership creates success, value,
and improvement. The number and
and quality of my followers will attest
to my worthiness. This is acknowledged
and I have an exalted place in the
community and financial reward.

Objective
God's Will be done here on earth as it
is in heaven. I live humbly and joyfully
in conscious unity with God and the
Christ, gladly choosing to walk in Their
Love.

My greatest reward is to watch my
siblings live in conscious, reciprocal
love with God. To see them happy
well, and successful by their own
constructive and collaborative effort.

Success and sustainability factors
Strength, drive, ingenuity, charisma,
and timing of the leader. Use of all
resources within his/her influence,
including human resources (people.)

Success and sustainability factors
Love for God and Jesus, choosing Their
Ways; faith, obedience, determination
persistence, patience, steadfastness,
joy, and gratitude.

**Primary causal choices underlying
paradigm**
Individualistic vision, egotism,

**Primary causal choices underlying
paradigm**
Conscious choice to live according to

selfishness, fear. Often also shame. All of which manifests as the drive to prove oneself worthy and/or to protect turf.

Jesus Great Command and Golden Rule. Love, confident hope, joyous expectation. Responsibility, self-discipline, diligence, generosity, humility.

Results
Results subject to human limitations, regardless of claims; scattered, due to divergence of opinion, purpose, method.

Results
Unity of vision, purpose, and objective; clarity, harmony. Collaboration, all-level leadership, servant leadership.

Thereby some endeavors "cancel out" or impede others. Some results are unconstructive or even malevolent.

All respected and affirmed. Synergism, results greater than the sum of parts.

Separation, disagreement, competition, schism, delay or destruction of potential, collective achievement, and produces lower quality of life.

Leveraging of resources due to love and unity. Provides a vessel through which God can work ever more extraordinary miracles.

Mankind must learn, willingly and expertly, to use our Christ awareness above the physical, material world if there is going to be mastery over the conditions human beings have generated here.

Jesus Great Command and His Golden Rule:
Matthew 22:37-40 (NRSV) He said to him, "You shall love the Lord your God with all your heart, and with all your soul, and with all your mind.' [38] This is the greatest and first commandment. [39] And a second is like it: 'You shall love your neighbor as yourself.' [40] On these two commandments hang all the law and the prophets."

Luke 6:31 (NRSV)Do to others as you would have them do to you.

Each of us has the privilege of an essential part to play in the healing of the Fall and the final ending of its resultant suffering of the separation experiment, separation agreements, and their serpentine context.

Then God, Our Father will then <u>remove the authority of the entire sinister force and its leadership</u>. Understand, believe, and accept this to be the consuming of the usurped authority of the devil and all his minions, including the satanists and the globalists, corporatists, the communists/socialists, the corrupt bankers, all that opposes the I AM WHO I AM.

To realize and actuate this Invitation from Our Father God and Jesus Christ, we must become very determined to be FOR what is right (constructive), instead of AGAINST what is wrong (unconstructive). What is constructive is based in love and is unifying. It expands, grows, and includes all. It builds joy and creative possibility, expanding LIFE.

The unconstructive involves criticism, condemnation, judgment, and toxic division; it wastes our LIFE in discord and conflict, shrivels life experience, spiraling downward toward death. The unconstructive demands that we live within the constrictive walls of our lowest common denominators: ego, selfishness, disobedience, shame, fear, hatred, and separation.

Hold steadfast to the truth that our LIFE is our Highest Common Denominator. It is what we all have in common. It is the I AM's LIFE in each of us.

Remember, that Our Father God, and His Son Jesus are gentlemen. We have to invite them into our lives and our world for Them to fully enter and raise our experience and reality. Their Presence will bring us the realization and the truth of infinite, exponential Love and fulfillment.

We get to use our free will to accept and trigger this divine invitation into motion, releasing the miracles God and Jesus are holding in readiness by:

- jubilantly obeying Jesus' Great Command,
- recognizing, accepting, and reclaiming our divine birthright as Our Father's children,
- learning the workings and potential of divine yeast,
- inviting and activating the full might of the Love, Wisdom, and Power of the I AM WHO I AM, Our Father God, into our lives, families, churches, organizations, communities, nation, and our world.

Let's do it!

Let us move now into recognition of our divine birthright and its reclamation.

XVIII.
Reclaiming our divine birthright

Matthew 7:13-14 (NIV) "Enter through the narrow gate. For wide is the gate and broad is the road that leads to destruction, and many enter through it. But small is the gate and narrow the road that leads to life, and only a few find it.

"A man is what he knows, but his soul will yearn for all that he does not know;
For hidden there is all he may become." - David Gemmell

"Most men would rather deny a hard truth than face it." - George R. R. Martin, Game of Thrones

The current-day battle lines

We, who profess faith in God and Jesus Christ, have been largely asleep at our posts while the current battle lines were drawn and the enemy's advance troops set in place. The mechanisms and hordes for the final conquest of United States of America, and We the Peoples, are also awaiting orders for the full assault in very physical terms. Some would say the first squadrons have already been unleashed.

The *Chinese Daily* newspaper, in May 2019, declared a "peoples' war" on the United States of America."[391]

Henry Kissinger and others are calling for global governance. Bill Gates is calling for global vaccine and restrictions on personal movement and other "privileges" based on noncompliance.[392]

To accomplish their intended dominion, the sinister force's global tyranny, called the new world order, must have a debased, humiliated, defenseless, hopeless, docile population of people who are convinced they are unworthy of and/or orphaned by God to accomplish their intended domination.

Are we cooperating with God and Jesus or with something else?

Many Christian churches are advocating spiritual "worth" through feeling redeemed by good works or through wallowing in the wretched suffering of our sins. We've already examined the former. Let's put our attention on the second trap.

Matthew 23:1-8 (NRSV) Then Jesus said to the crowds and to his disciples, ² "The scribes and the Pharisees sit on Moses' seat; ³ therefore, do whatever they teach you and follow it; but do not do as they do, for they do not practice what they teach. ⁴ They tie up heavy burdens, hard to bear, and lay them on the shoulders of others; but they themselves are unwilling to lift a finger to move them. ⁵ They do all their deeds to be seen by others; for they make their phylacteries broad and their fringes long. ⁶ They love to have the place of honor at banquets and the best seats in the synagogues, ⁷ and to be greeted with respect in the marketplaces, and to have people call them rabbi. ⁸ But you are not to be called rabbi, for you have one teacher, and you are all students.

These church leaders misrepresent God as a god of condemnation, wrath, and punishment. They keep our people from fully participating in life, from fully using the talents with which Our Father endowed every one of us. These leaders keep those entrusted to their care, stuck in the same position as the third slave in Jesus' Parable of the Talents:

Matthew 25:24-30 (NRSV) Then the one who had received the one talent also came forward, saying, 'Master, I knew that you were a harsh man, reaping where you did not sow, and gathering where you did not scatter seed; ²⁵so I was afraid, and I went and hid your talent in the ground. Here you have what is yours.'

²⁶ But his master replied, 'You wicked and lazy slave! You knew, did you, that I reap where I did not sow, and gather where I did not scatter? ²⁷ Then you ought to have invested my money with the bankers, and on my return I would have received what was my own with interest. ²⁸ So take the talent from him, and give it to the one with the ten talents. ²⁹ For to all those who have, more will be given, and they will have an abundance; but from those who have nothing, even what they have will be taken away. ³⁰ As for this worthless slave, throw him into the outer darkness, where there will be weeping and gnashing of teeth.'

Is keeping Christians fixated on Jesus' horrible, sacrificial death and encouraging us to dwell within an excruciating state of sinfulness and separation a deliberate choice of disobedience by church leadership? It keeps the faithful from fully receiving God's Grace through Jesus Christ and being relieved of the crushing, de-habilitating weight of sin. We are not allowed to "follow him" as he requested into the full forgiveness of sin, the resurrection out of its death into abundant life, or accepting, with peaceful assurance, that he is coming to get us to take us Home at the close of our earthly life.

Romans 3:23-24 (NRSV) for all have sinned and fall short of the glory of God, ²⁴ and all are justified freely by his grace through the redemption that came by Christ Jesus.

John 14:3 (NRSV) And if I go and prepare a place for you, I will come back and take you to be with me that you also may be where I AM.

Does that restricted, doctrinal perspective keep us enslaved to sin, instead of in grateful, joyous – and functional – relationship with Our Father and with Jesus? Or, does it make and keep us vulnerable to enslavement by the sinister force?

In practical application, this posture in churches declares that sin is more powerful than God, the I AM WHO I AM and His Sovereign Love, Wisdom, and Power. It hijacks the power of our divine birthright of as Children of God and our place in God's eternal Family. It makes us slaves, serfs of death and the devil. It keeps those leaders in power over us by draconian deception and theft. Most of the church leaders, who espouse this doctrine, have taken up positions as gatekeepers between us and Our Father God and Jesus Christ.

And it is usually a toll gate! How much wealth have the overall "Christian" churches amassed with this strategic disobedience that leads devout Christians to sacrifice ourselves to our own sins? All the while, these leaders proclaim loudly that God sent Jesus to redeem us from those very sins? Yet they do not allow us to accept full deliverance.

Galatians 6:7 (NRSV) Do not be deceived; God is not mocked, for you reap whatever you sow.

We have need to be rightfully humble and grateful, yes, but not self-effacing and sabotaging. Remaining stuck in our fallen state helps nothing except evil. And nothing we have in our fallen state collectively could ever pay off the debt of the Fall - our continued insistence on living in the serpentine context.

What better preparation could be offered on the devil's alter than people who have been restrained from truly accepting the reality for them personally of God's Grace and Forgiveness through Jesus Christ? Thereby, the faithful are being robbed of their freedom from sin, stealing their potential power and courage. Such pastors and church leaders are delivering slaves to the planned global plantation! For we are broken people until we accept Our Father's Grace! He and Jesus are still extending it to us.

Many pastors have become compliant in nwo plans for subjection of their own parishioners. They have bought the glib sales pitch and/or yielded to force applied. Either way, they have swallowed the hook.

"MSNBC interviewed a pastor, who also happens to be the [now former] Chairman of the Congressional Black Caucus, Emmanuel Cleaver (D-MO.). Representative Cleaver stated very clearly that preachers are being muzzled by the 501(c)3 regulations being enforced for the Justice Department and the IRS. In 2014, Representative Cleaver headed up a meeting with several thousand clergy along with representatives from FEMA, the IRS and Eric Holder [82nd Attorney General of the United States from 2009 to 2015]. According to Cleaver, the pastors minister to a total of about 10 million Christians."[393]

Mark 12:24 (NRSV) Jesus said to them, "Is not this the reason you are wrong, that you know neither the scriptures nor the power of God?"

Luke 7:23 (NRSV) "...And blessed is anyone who takes no offense at me."

1 John 2:11 (NRSV) But whoever hates another believer is in the darkness, walks in the darkness, and does not know the way to go, because the darkness has brought on blindness.

1 John 2:9 (NRSV) Whoever says, "I am in the light," while hating a brother or sister, is still in the darkness.

John 14:21 (NRSV) Whoever has my commands and keeps them is the one who loves me. The one who loves me will be loved by my Father, and I too will love them and show myself to them."

Luke 4:12 (NRSV) Jesus answered him (the devil), "It is said, 'Do not put the Lord your God to the test.' "

Mankind must be trained to use Christ-consciousness above the physical world if there is going to be mastery over the conditions human beings have generated here.

Jesus has already - obedient to God's Will - sacrificed himself TO RID US of the stranglehold of sin – so we may have LIFE and have it abundantly. When will we gratefully, joyfully accept this Way to return into reunification and reciprocal relationship with Our Father? When will we accept – regardless of any human opinion – Jesus' rescue and walk out of the tomb of fascination with death?

John 10:10-11 (NRSV) The thief comes only to steal and kill and destroy. I came that they may have life, and have it abundantly.[11] I am the good shepherd. The good shepherd lays down his life for the sheep.

God sacrifices Himself for us in His infinite Love to that we may return to LIFE with Him.

Our full acceptance of Grace through Jesus Christ opens up within us the avenue of reciprocal love, our emotional ability to return Our Father's Love not only with gratitude, but also with full confidence, assurance, and courage. Then we have the strength and joyful desire to come into true obedience, as Jesus directed in His Great Command.

Matthew 22:37-40 (NRSV) He said to him, "You shall love the Lord your God with all your heart, and with all your soul, and with all your mind.' [38] This is the greatest and first commandment. [39] And a second is like it: 'You shall love your neighbor as yourself.' [40] On these two commandments hang all the law and the prophets." (NRSV)

The I AM WHO I AM, Our Father God, waits with expectant hope for our free will return to Him. He looks forward with heavenly delight to taking us up again in His loving arms and heart. He has been incessantly working to consciously re-confer on us, each one, our Divine Birthright as His Children.

Prodigal sons and daughters all, let us arise and go back to Our Father!

Luke 15:20-24 (NRSV) So he set off and went to his father. But while he was still far off, his father saw him and was filled with compassion; he ran and put his arms around him and kissed him. [21] Then the son said to him, 'Father, I have sinned against heaven and before you; I am no longer worthy to be called your son.' (repentance)
[22] But the father said to his slaves, 'Quickly, bring out a robe—the best one—and put it on him; put a ring on his finger and sandals on his feet. [23] And get the fatted calf and kill it, and let us eat and celebrate; [24] for this son of mine was dead and is alive again; he was lost and is found!' And they began to celebrate.

Answer these questions prayerfully and truthfully:
Was the father angry with his child?

Was a mediator required to garner the father's favorable consideration of his child's return?

Was a sacrifice required to facilitate the return of the child into the father's good graces? Was a human blood sacrifice required?

Jesus spoke the words of this parable. Take them to heart.

It is the devil who sacrifices others, never himself. He resolutely and absolutely refuses to humble himself and obey the I AM WHO I AM. And he staunchly protects his separation from God. He worships the sin and rebellious separation he has chosen. He and his minions work tirelessly to lure us into their same trap. He has devoted himself to the destruction and death of every Child of God. He feasts ravenously on the blood he wantonly spills. And he takes in the LIFE energy of his slain to continue the slaughter. Human blood sacrifice is a Luciferian sacrilege that was savagely inflicted on Jesus Christ.

But even that could not hold Jesus in satanic death or separation from Our Father God, the I AM.

John 10:17-18: (NRSV) *"For this reason the Father loves me, because I lay down my life in order to take it up again. [18] No one takes it from me, but I lay it down of my own accord. I have power to lay it down, and I have power to take it up again. I have received this command from my Father."*

There never was any reason to hide from Our Father God in the garden. Even today, after all the burden of distress and injustice humanity has proliferated, the I AM is ever faithful.

If we expose *ourselves* fully to His Love, admit our mistakes, humble ourselves, and genuinely ask God's forgiveness, He delivers it with overwhelming, heavenly compassion. We can even feel His Joy in forgiving! Please review again Jesus' full parable of the prodigal son.

Sent by our Father God, Jesus came willingly into the density and morbidity of earthly existence to deliver the invitation back Home into full communion and relationship with Our Divine Parent, the Creator. Jesus has paved a superhighway for us back Home. Why are we still content to wander around in the satanical, globalist maze?

Over 2,000 years ago, we, humanity, missed the opportunity for the freedom of mankind and the earth. We are still missing it or we would not be in the condition and situations in which we find ourselves, our country, and the Earth.

If we don't wake up and change our modus operandi, pronto, those who survive will find ourselves residents of a global plantation.

Jesus is still walking with us. The I AM WHO I AM, Our Father God is still pumping His LIFE through us. Neither has forsaken us. Let us not forsake Them.

Each of us has the open, divine invitation in front of us at this moment. Act now! Stop hiding and avoiding Them. Turn and face Them right now! Whether your openness and receptivity is a new occurrence or a renewal, do it with love and joy!

Admit all mistakes. (God and Jesus already know them.) And They still love us and want us back in full reciprocal, loving relationship for eternity.

Accept that Grace that is flowing to and through you at this very moment. Whether you seem to feel it or not, It is there. Sometimes, Our Father's Love is like a gossamer veil of fragrant breath. He wields Omnipotent Power, and yet, He often holds us in delicate tenderness.

Visit often – and our consciousness of God's Presence and our blessed relationship within His Love and Divine Will will grow in us. Even in a moment of our conscious connection, the morass of decades can be swept away and consumed.

I used to be a resident at the foot of the cross, looking up in anguish and remorse, with an almost fascinated horror at the suffering Jesus.

During my life, our Beloved Jesus has clearly said two sentences to me that have shaken me to my core. The first one came when he visited me while I was contemplating a crucifix. His voice was tender, but it thundered with power.

"Take me off the cross and FOLLOW ME!"

My whole being mentally, emotionally, spiritually, and physically tremored.

Jesus wanted more for me than I was allowing him to give me. He knows we can't accept forgiveness and eternal LIFE, if our hands and hearts are full, clinging fiercely to sin, blood, and death.

Only by my fully accepting His Sacrifice and thereby accepting the reason for that Sacrifice - the I AM's Forgiveness of all my sins and my return to God - could Jesus actually see his Mission as accomplished in my life.

I had to believe more in God's Love and Power than I believed in and feared by own sin.

I had to love Jesus and Our Father **reciprocally** for the Miracle of my Redemption to take place.

Jesus wants me consciously returned to the I AM Family in full **reciprocal** relationship. Jesus wants me to follow him – with him walking beside me – into the resurrection and the ascension, into eternal LIFE in Our Father's heavenly kingdom.

He wants the same for you and every one of us.

Sisters and brothers in Christ! Anyone who tells you anything else than what Jesus told me - and Jesus is constantly trying to tell you – has consciously or unconsciously chosen to live enslaved in the serpentine context. Even now, I can hear it whispering the temptations, the soul-numbing "drugs" of the Fall. I can hear the whispers of fear and shame and of the threat of eternal damnation.

Here's a news flash. The serpent does not have the power of LIFE or of eternal death. He no longer has the gift of LIFE, even for himself. He must steal it from a child of God to keep alive in his wretched, twisted existence.

Every moment you let him continue to deceive you, he steals...no! you feed him a drop of your LIFE.

Luke 12:4-5 (KJV) And I say unto you my friends, Be not afraid of them that kill the body, and after that have no more that they can do. [5] But I will forewarn you whom ye shall fear: Fear him, which after he hath killed hath power to cast into hell; yea, I say unto you, Fear him.

Perfect love casts out fear.

1 John 4:16 (NRSV) And so we know and rely on the love God has for us. God is love. Whoever lives in love lives in God, and God in them.

1 John 4:18 (NIV) There is no fear in love. But perfect love drives out fear, because fear has to do with punishment. The one who fears is not made perfect in love.

1 John 5:3 (NRSV) In fact, this is love for God: to keep his commands. And his commands are not burdensome,

To unlock and escalate the Divine Intervention that is essential to us, we must reclaim our Divine Birthright as Children of the I AM. And then by demonstrations in daily life, we graduate to Sons and Daughters of Our Father God!

The first step is to consciously and deliberately choose to want God's Love and our reunion with Him for eternity more than we want the things of this world.

1 John 2;15-16 (NRSV) Do not love the world or the things in the world. The love of the Father is not in those who love the world; 16 for all that is in the world—the desire of the flesh, the desire of the eyes, the pride in riches—comes not from the Father but from the world.

Matthew 6:24 (NRSV) No one can serve two masters; for a slave will either hate the one and love the other, or be devoted to the one and despise the other. You cannot serve God and mammon.

If, as we let go of each little bit of worldly fascination, we purposefully replace it with love of God, the metamorphosis will go more quickly. We humans don't fare well when we just quit something and create a "vacuum" wanting to be filled. It doesn't remain empty long and in this world. Something worse is likely to volunteer to enter our minds and hearts.

Instead, purposely and lovingly, invite God in. He always accepts invitations of love. Step by step, we lose our addictions to the unstable, unfulfilling things of the world, and, prodigal sons and daughters all, advance on our walk back to the Father.

As we advance on our journey Home to Our Father God, we will find ourselves able more and more to become the fulfillment of Jesus' Great Command. We will naturally be loving the Lord Our God "with all our hearts, and with all our souls, and with all our minds ."

This will also be the fulfillment of the separation experiment. This will trigger the end of the separation agreements (from Chapter IV. The Fall.) And thereby, dissolve and consume the authority of the entire sinister force and its leadership. They will no longer have any power over us.

Philippians 4:7 (NIV) And the peace of God, which transcends all understanding, will guard your hearts and your minds in Christ Jesus. (NIV)

We will begin feeling waves of His Love returning to us, as this state of reciprocal love becomes our natural state of everyday life. The peace that passes all understanding then enfolds us.

This makes forgiving others much easier. We begin to see all others like ourselves, another of God's Children struggling to find the way back Home. We start seeing Our Father's LIFE in them, as it is in us. This is the "Highest Common Denominator" we talked about in Chapter VII, Shifting the paradigm. It transcends toxic diversity. And we find ourselves "loving our neighbor as ourselves ."

Coming into attunement with Jesus' Great Command, we don't fear, but rather naturally desire reunification with Our Father and Jesus.

Say, right now! – who ARE you?

When we think or say "I" or "me" to what are we referring? Today, most people in most situations are referring to their physical bodies or something relating directly to those bodies. These include how our body feels, what we wear, how we look, what we do. Start paying attention to what you mean when you use the terms "I" and "me ."

In young adults, youth, and children, the degree of body-consciousness as their identity is increasing rapidly. Other priority focuses include: how many people like or "like" them, which ones, what they say about them, and who they hang with. These are symptoms of serpentine indoctrination and its herd mentality.

Many of us, and more of our children, no longer respect our selves or have healthy self-worth. Increasingly, our concepts of worth and meaningfulness are being attached to shallow, insubstantial, and fleeting values or the fickle opinions of others.

What does this do to the person's spirit, their soul? It puts the soul in isolation, fear, and desolation. The soul begins to starve to death. Vitality, self-esteem, self-protection, and resilience plummet. These conditions keep individuals from developing true, healthy relationships with God, Jesus, or human beings. The effect of this condition makes the individual lose their desire or ability to even try to develop strength and competence in themselves. This condition allows, even encourages, an individual to seek subjugation as a means to escape fear and an alarming lack of confidence in their own abilities.

Who or what are we worshipping? Whatever we keep our best attention on most of the time is what we are worshipping. Are we resting our allegiance on "experts," and our self-worth more and more on unstable and capricious human opinions? Or are we secure in God's Love and our essential place in His Family? Are our lives founded on God-based, and therefore, integrity-based values?

Are the strategies overviewed in Chapters XI – XIV building to such waves as to threaten capsizing our life-boats? They are deliberately designed to keep our attention distracted and away from God! They are deliberately designed to destroy ours and our children's healthy self-esteem!

Revelation 3:1-2, 8-12, 15-16 19-22 (NRSV) . . ."I know your works; you have a name of being alive, but you are dead. [2] Wake up, and strengthen what remains and is on the point of death, for I have not found your works perfect in the sight of my God...

[8] "...Look, I have set before you an open door, which no one is able to shut. I know that you have but little power, and yet you have kept my word and have not denied my name. [9] I will make those of the synagogue of Satan who say that they are Jews and are not, but are lying—I will make them come and bow down before your feet, and they will learn that I have loved you. [10] Because you have kept my word of patient endurance, I will keep you from the hour of trial that is coming on the whole world to test the inhabitants of the earth. [11] I am coming soon; hold fast to what you have, so that no one may seize your crown. [12] If you conquer, I will make you a pillar in the temple of my God; you will never *go out of it. I will write on you the name of my God, and the name of the city of my God, the new Jerusalem that comes down from my God out of heaven, and my own new name.*

¹⁵ "I know your works; you are neither cold nor hot. I wish that you were either cold or hot. ¹⁶ So, because you are lukewarm, and neither cold nor hot, I am about to spit you out of my mouth. ¹⁷ For you say, 'I am rich, I have prospered, and I need nothing.' You do not realize that you are wretched, pitiable, poor, blind, and naked....

¹⁹ I reprove and discipline those whom I love. Be earnest, therefore, and repent. ²⁰ Listen! I am standing at the door, knocking; if you hear my voice and open the door, I will come in to you and eat with you, and you with me. ²¹ To the one who conquers I will give a place with me on my throne, just as I myself conquered and sat down with my Father on his throne. ²² Let anyone who has an ear listen to what the Spirit is saying to the churches."

We each have the power to change our choices at any time. And, yes, it can require a lot of conscious determination. But, the quality of our choices directly equates to our self-esteem and the quality of our lives. Notice how intrinsic the healthy love of oneself is in the fulfillment of Jesus' Great Command. It is also intrinsic in His Golden Rule:

Luke 6:31 (NRSV) Do unto to others as you would have them do to you.

How can we even begin to understand or follow Jesus' Great Command or Golden Rule, if we no longer love ourselves?

Proverbs 19:8 (NRSV) He who gets wisdom loves himself; he who keeps understanding will prosper.

Do you love yourself?

What keeps us from reclaiming our divine birthright?
When Jesus spoke, the message he was conveying had to bridge divine truth and the limited comprehension of the people, whose context for reality had been calcified within the serpentine context of the Fall – the separation experiment. In their reality, Our Father was separate and distant from them. Their life reality was severely limited, ego-centric, and full of lack and fear.

To our great suffering, this condition of deceit, separation (sin), and death is still the practical, everyday reality of most of our lives.

How many times did Jesus lose patience with the mental density and slowness of even the disciples' understanding?

The common words, understandable to those to whom Jesus was ministering, were inadequate to express the fullness of the truth he was conveying. So many times, he used symbols, parables, and unusual word usage with multiple layers of meaning, to surround and deliver the fullness of the Truth to a reluctant, recalcitrant humanity.

"Drugs" All "drugs" keep us separated from God. Again, "drugs" are unconstructive choices that make us feel better temporarily. But, they keep us in an out-of-balance state. They are choices outside of Jesus Great Command. Nearly all of us are recovering addicts. Most babies come into this world "clean," consciously connected in the Unity of Love within the I AM, Our Divine Parent and the Source of our LIFE. We teach them addiction to the serpentine context and its willful separation from God through our own disobedient use of free will. And they join us in enslavement.

Now we see more of the importance of the acknowledgment of God and of prayer in all education and all public arenas of our lives, communities, and nation.

Revisiting attention Busy-ness can cause a period of separation from God. Staying active and still building our relationship with God during our daily activities is like running the bases in baseball. As we make our rounds as fast as we can, we "touch" the bases with God and Jesus, with a short prayer, a thank you, or even "Hi! I love you!" If someone or something on the field of life temporarily stalls our progress requiring focused attention, remember to briefly "touch back" with God before advancing.

The bases are like the safe, God places in life. Often, we are in such a drive to "get somewhere" in our busy-ness that we touch base with Our Father and Jesus only as an obligatory afterthought – or not at all. Then, when we do it, it becomes a mindless, habitual gesture, void of the love of relationship.

Yet, to become stagnant - either afraid or too apathetic or lazy, to be productive - is also a choice of selfishness. This choice soon becomes a comprehensive deterioration of our wellbeing.

We can be. We get to be love in motion - conscious, deliberate, joyful, grateful, love in motion.

This understanding, choice, and manifestation through action, is a form of balance. It is an expression of the balance scale which Justice always holds.

1 Corinthians 13:11 (NRSV) When I was a child, I spoke like a child, I thought like a child, I reasoned like a child; when I became an adult, I put an end to childish ways.

This experience of leaving the world of life-draining temptation is our passing through a crucifixion. For how long will we stay nailed to a cross of suffering, disobedience, shame, fear, limitation, and dependency on a selfish and cruel humanity?

Let's consider the only Source of true and just self-esteem. This is a lesson we can learn from Jesus.

Who does Jesus worship? Throughout the Bible, Jesus personally worshipped the I AM WHO I AM, His Father. He asked, implored, and commanded us to do the same. He is still personally demonstrating life loving God - with all his heart, mind, and strength.

Jesus lived within the first and second Commandments:
1st Commandment: Exodus 20:3 (NIV) You shall have no other gods beside me.

2nd Commandment Exodus 20:4-5 (NIV) You shall not make for yourself an idol, whether in the form of anything that is in heaven above, or that is on the earth beneath, or that is in the water under the earth. 5 You shall not bow down to them or worship them;

He also asserted:

Luke 4:8 (NRSV) Jesus answered him (the devil), "It is written, 'Worship the Lord your God, and serve only him.' "

John 5:41 (NRSV)I do not accept glory from human beings.

John 6: 38 (KJV) For I came down from heaven, not to do mine own will, but the will of him that sent me.

John 13:16 (NRSV) Very truly, I tell you, servants are not greater than their master, nor are messengers greater than the one who sent them.

John 5:30 (NRSV) I of myself can do nothing. It is the Father who does the works.

Mark 10:17-18 (NRSV) As he was setting out on a journey, a man ran up and knelt before him, and asked him, "Good Teacher, what must I do to inherit eternal life?" 18 Jesus said to him, "Why do you call me good? No one is good but God alone."

From these follow the natural obedience to all the rest of God's Commandments and Jesus' Great Command, that is the fulfillment of all the law and prophets. Jesus is still showing the Way and is still commanding, "Follow me!"

Luke 12:2-3 (NRSV) For there is nothing covered, that shall not be revealed; neither hid, that shall not be known. 3 Therefore whatsoever ye have spoken in darkness shall be heard in the light; and that which ye have spoken in the ear in closets shall be proclaimed upon the housetops.

Who are we really?

Many assert that it is heresy when we say that we humans must make the call for God's Perfection to manifest here on earth. That is because they do not know who we ARE!

Genesis 1:26-27 (KJV) And God said, Let us make man in our image, after our likeness: and let them have dominion ...over all the earth,...27 So God created man in his own image, in the image of God created he him; male and female created he them.

Genesis 2:7 (NRSV) Then the LORD God formed a man from the dust of the ground and breathed into his nostrils the breath of life, and the man became a living being.

Genesis 5:1-2 (NRSV) When God created mankind, he made them in the likeness of God. 2 He created them male and female and blessed them. And he named them "Mankind" when they were created.

Psalm 82:6 (KJV) I have said, Ye are gods; and all of you are children of the most High.

Who does Jesus say about who we are?

Matthew 6:9 (NRSV) "Pray then in this way: Our Father in heaven, hallowed be your name...

Luke 12:32 (NRSV) "Do not be afraid, little flock, for it is your Father's good pleasure to give you the kingdom.

Matthew 6:26 (NRSV) Look at the birds of the air; they neither sow nor reap nor gather into barns, and yet your heavenly Father feeds them. Are you not of more value than they?

Matthew 18:14 (NRSV)So it is not the will of your Father in heaven that one of these little ones should be lost.

John 20:17 "I am ascending to my Father and your Father, to my God and your God."

Matthew 5:16 (NRSV)In the same way, let your light shine before others, so that they may see your good works and give glory to your Father in heaven.

Luke 17:20-21 (KJV) And when he was demanded of the Pharisees, when the kingdom of God should come, he answered them and said, The kingdom of God cometh not with observation: ²¹ Neither shall they say, Lo here! or, lo there! for, behold, the kingdom of God is within you.

Is mankind following Jesus? Are you?

What does healthy love for ourselves look like? Loving ourselves enough to be obedient to God's Laws, including His Law of Love expressed in Jesus' Great Command.

We will know we are approaching Unity in the I AM's Love when:
- we awake in the morning and begin with an expression of pure Love to God, Our Divine Parent,
- we continue with gratitude and joyful anticipation of what our walk in the garden of God's good creation will be that day,
- our first conversation with Our Father is our acknowledging, accepting, and gratefully claiming our divine birthright and essential place in His Family,
- during the day, we recognize and express gratitude for the experiences of God's Love and blessings as they occur - and we'll start noticing more of them!
- we see the experiences that are less than the perfection of Love as wonderful opportunities to call in God's Love and express it in our responding choices,
- we share God's Love and good wishes for us all in a kind, inclusive, natural, relaxed, and common way (not phony, stressed, critical, or sanctimonious);
- our conscious, interactive relationship with Our Divine Parent will "restart." This is the result for which Jesus strove during his mission. He is still actively engaged in the fulfillment of this mission. Thank you, God and Jesus!

We will be able to quietly and humbly stand before Our Father and Jesus, looking Them full in the face!

Psalm 46:10 (NRSV) "Be still, and know that I am God! I am exalted among the nations, I am exalted in the earth." (NRSV)

Jesus has paved the way for us. God has blessed us with the free will to choose Him - or mammon and self-imposed suffering.

What have we chosen in the past? What will we choose for our future? Let's make the choices consciously, not by default from distraction while giving lip-service, or while building lives on sand.

Luke 6:46-49 (NRSV) "Why do you call me 'Lord, Lord,' and do not do what I tell you? ⁴⁷ I will show you what someone is like who comes to me, hears my words, and acts on them. ⁴⁸ That one is like a man building a house, who dug deeply and laid the foundation on rock; when a flood arose, the river burst against that house but could not shake it, because it had been well built.⁴⁹ But the one who hears and does not act is like a man who built a house on the ground without a foundation. When the river burst against it, immediately it fell, and great was the ruin of that house."

Arise out of the serpentine context, brothers and sisters of God's Family! Jesus has already smashed the chains and unlocked the prison doors!

When we have consciously chosen and are walking the way spoken and demonstrated by Jesus, by the Grace Our Father is already extending to us, we will arise consciously into our Divine Birthright, as sons and daughters of God!

Reclaiming Our Divine Birthright

The sinister force has no power of its own. It usurps ours. We, the Children of the I AM, have been tricked, coerced, manipulated, scared, and shamed into giving the sinister force the power and substance of God's LIFE in us. So, it is living and prospering at our expense. Evil is still here by our complicity.

The vehicle through which this unholy transaction takes place is our unconstructive choices – choices not attuned with Jesus' Great Command.

Remember, it is the small things. These small, unconstructive choices, and their transfer of the power of LIFE, have amassed over generations, over eons. It is a ponderous, threatening morass, a multi-headed monster. It is trying to enslave all mankind worldwide. This is what it means to be separate from the I AM, Our Father.

This is what we signed on for when we chose the separation experiment. Of course, this was after we allowed ourselves to be deceived by the serpent, thereby helping perpetrate the Fall.

Our current situation of stifle is what it has grown into while we dilly-dallied around, not learning the lesson at hand.

Have we decided to learn the lesson? Do we choose now to love and desire God, Our Father above all else?

Then let us make that prayer of commitment in the silence of our hearts.

Beloved Father God, I AM WHO I AM, in the Name of the Ascended Jesus Christ, and with love and gratitude, I reclaim my Divine Birthright as Your Child!

Keep this prayer ongoing to remind yourselves who you really are. The practical, consistent manifestation of it can be a process!

One of the ramifications of the decision to reclaim our Divine Birthright is greater power with which to collaborate in the fulfillment of Jesus' Mission.

Joshua 24:15 (NRSV) ...choose this day whom you will serve, ...as for me and my household, we will serve the LORD."

Luke 21:19 (NRSV) by your endurance you will gain your souls.

Proverbs 23:18 (NRSV) Surely there is a future, and your hope will not be cut off.

John 16:33 (NRSV) "I have told you these things, so that in me you may have peace. In this world you will have trouble. But take heart! I have overcome the world."

John 12:26 (NRSV) Whoever serves me must follow me; and where I am, my servant also will be. My Father will honor the one who serves me.

John 14:12-14 (NIV) Very truly I tell you, whoever believes in me will do the works I have been doing, and they will do even greater things than these, because I am going to the Father. ¹³ And I will do whatever you ask in my name, so that the Father may be glorified in the Son. ¹⁴ You may ask me for anything in my name, and I will do it.

Our Father created us as beings of great power when He filled us with His Own LIFE. He gave us free will which is part of that LIFE. The I AM WHO I AM is not interested in prisoners or slaves. Our Divine Parent created us as His sons and daughters. THIS is WHO WE ARE. This is our Divine Birthright.

Our Father God, and Beloved Jesus Christ, His Son, are standing ready to deliver us from the pressing evil of this world. But it requires consciously delivered, united, and reciprocal action.

We must reclaim our Divine Birthright – consciously and dynamically. We must participate actively and consciously in this, God's Victory on Earth.

Could there be a greater privilege?

Matthew 28:20 (NIV) "And surely I am with you always, to the very end of the age."

Isaiah 40:31 (NRSV) ...those who wait for the Lord shall renew their strength, they shall mount up with wings like eagles, they shall run and not be weary, they shall walk and not faint.

2 Chronicles 7:14 (NRSV) if my people who are called by my name (I AM) humble themselves, pray, seek my face, and turn from their wicked ways, then I will hear from heaven, and will forgive their sin and heal their land.

"Whatever you recognize you own.
And whatever you own,
you shall give importance." Ruth BeeBee Hill, Hanta Yo

Having reclaimed our Divine Birthright, we have the privilege of full, conscious collaboration with Our Father and Jesus in the restoration of God's Kingdom on earth!

God is Love. From Divine Love emerges Justice. Justice must be reciprocal to be sustainable.

We get to give Justice to all we meet – regardless of their behavior.

If the other is being just, our choice will expand that Justice. If the other is not being just, we get to start the chain of Love that can grow into justice for this person and expand from there. Like with a fire, it can take many sparks or matches to start it producing light and warmth. Constructive intentions coupled with Love always build together.

When we look at any person, including one who is being difficult, as having the Highest Common Denominator, God's LIFE, inside them, it is easier for us to be kind, loving, and just to them. That recognition itself is restoration of Justice. It starts restoring the person's memory of who they really are as God's Child. And it begins to dissolve all that's unconstructive that is enslaving them in suffering.

We can help each other consciously claim our Divine Birthright and essential place in God's Eternal Family.

This is just one of the powerful ways we get to cooperate with God, Our Father and Jesus, once we have allowed Our Father to restore our own Divine Birthright.

Calling on our God and Lord Jesus, together, let us make a tsunami of Love and Justice using divine yeast!

XIX.
Divine Yeast

What is sacred among one people may be ridiculous in another;
and what is despised or rejected by one cultural group,
may in a different environment become the cornerstone
for a great edifice of strange grandeur and beauty. – Hu Shih

What can we do to help create sustainable peace, justice, and a community based in God's Love?

"If I am a minority of one, the truth is the truth." – Mohandas K. Gandhi

Sometimes we see a great thing that should, even needs, to be accomplished. And yet, feeling alone, we can lose our courage, our will to try. Gandhi proved the power of even one person standing up for truth. He also proved the exponential power of millions joining together peacefully and of one accord. As we decide to work together, our strength and power actually do grow exponentially.

Philippians 2:2-3 (NIV) make my joy complete by being like-minded, having the same love, being one in spirit and of one mind. ³ Do nothing out of selfish ambition or vain conceit.

Over the past 25 years, I have had the privilege to be central to numerous, small scale studies totaling about 7,000 people. Tracked in great detail, we studied the results of a simple, inspired program teaching the 'how to" of consciously making choices that are keyed to Jesus' Great Command and Golden Rule.

"(This is) about experiencing the unfiltered love of Christ - and getting to share that with our brothers and sisters. It is so challenging, and yet done in such a loving way. It really wipes the slate clean and allows someone to think, "What is my true potential? Not just in life, but in my service to Christ?

"This allows us the opportunity to complete the greatest command to love other people like Christ loves us – and to love them with everything we've got." – Pastor Josh Vargas

Increasing positive results in any mutual endeavor:
The simple explanation for this multiplying, catalytic dynamic is:

1. When people decide to live or work together:
      1 (person) + 1 (person) + 1 (person) = the power of 3 people

2. When people decide to live, work, or serve <u>consciously and constructively</u> together:
      1 (person) + 1 (person) + 1 (person) does NOT equal the power of 3!
      It equals: $1 + 1 + 1 = 3^2 = 9$ (the power of 9 regular people!)

3. If or when that group also decides to deliberately and actively add God into their equation:
        1 person + 1 person + 1 person = 3^{3+} = 27+

This equation is also written: $(1 + 1 + 1)^{GOD}$ = Extraordinary Results

We have had a number of mathematicians and physicists in our groups. They all have stated that these equations are credible to describe and compare the energetic differences in the three situations noted. Typically, even with mild inclusion of God and Jesus, even without scripture, there is generally a 30% greater improvement. When implemented in these seminars, according to the Inspiration, the process has never failed.

Even facing the disturbing and threatening situation in America today, we have a number of assets readily available. When used in a consciously, constructive manner, they have great, collective power.

Our Assets - *in reverse order!*
1.There are way more of us than them (the sinister force).

2. We can consciously engage our Divine Birthright, then powerfully and continuously use our Divinely-given Free Will. We can:

- choose not to cooperate with their evil. We can refuse submission and obedience to the sinister force, Deep State, or their minions. Here, "no decision" is a choice for enslavement;

- consciously and resolutely choose obedience to God and His Law of Love, as spoken and demonstrated by Jesus Christ;

- energetically pray and pray and pray, calling to Our Father for help and deliverance;

- actively cooperate with Our Father, Jesus, the angelic hosts, and each other.

We get to choose the future of mankind and this earth! We get to create a "critical mass" of Love in reciprocal relationship with Our Father God. Thereby, we will open the door, which we had shut, for God's and Jesus' reentry into the hearts, minds, and affairs of mankind.

Justice requires reciprocity to be sustainable. Once we establish conscious obedience to God, we can call on the I AM with full confidence in His Loving, Wise, and All-Powerful Response. The more Children of God who call together consciously, the more powerful and fast-moving will be the Deliverance.

Now we can actively build the exponential power of Divine Yeast.

Previous significant discovery, a breakthrough for mankind

During 1978 through 1983, two scientists conducted unique, and in method laudable, in-field experiments that have not only amazing results, but great significance to our current situation in the United States of America and globally.[394] Clinical and research psychologists Elaine Aron, Ph.D. and Arthur Aron, Ph.D. were the leading researchers.

The subject of their research was, very roughly, how does:
1. deliberately connecting to the Creator God and calling for His Love and Peace,
2. by increasing the number of people simultaneously,
3. in the same location,
4. affect the overall quality of community life in that location?

Within major urban areas mostly on mainland USA, they tracked the "misery indexes," e.g. suicide, homicide/murder, divorce, death, traffic fatalities, rape, robbery, aggravated assault, breaking and entering, larceny, auto theft, unemployment, beer and cigarette sales, and pollution. They also tracked positive indicators, including marriage and employment.

I remember seeing the, then, police chief of Washington D.C. on the evening news. He was commenting about the experiment and that it would be a cold day in hell when the death rate in the city went down in the summer. He had to "eat" his comment.

Within cities during the wars in the Middle East at that time, the Arons brought in meditators and tracked the changes in fighting, deaths, and peace initiatives.

To summarize very briefly, they discovered that when people got together in a location and,
- consciously connecting with God, called for the Intervention of His Love and Peace, and
- in faith accepted its manifestation,
- the negatives began to decline and the positives rose.

When the number of people petitioning God together reached 1% of the population to be affected, the 'misery indexes" plummeted and statistics on positive outcomes rose substantially.

When the intercessor group was comprised of "experts" in this action, it only required the square root of 1% to register a similar effect within the enfolding population.

Most of the meditating participants were from outside the areas targeted. **When the groups dispersed, all the good effects of the experiment reversed themselves.**

In the 1980's, this group initiated an ongoing implementation at a central point of the US, toward benefitting the nation. With generally about 1,600 people participating, they tracked significant results.

As we look into the realities of today and into the possibilities of the future, what opportunities are presented by the information we just reviewed on the cumulative power of our united love and calls to Almighty God?

Building reciprocal love relationship throughout God's Family

1 John 4:16 (NIV) And so we know and rely on the love God has for us. God is love. Whoever lives in love lives in God, and God in them.

1 John 1:5 (NIV)This is the message we have heard from him and proclaim to you, that God is light and in him there is no darkness at all.

Matthew 5:16 (NRSV) "In the same way, let your light shine before others, so that they may see your good works and give glory to your Father in heaven."

John 10:10 (RSV) The thief comes only to steal and kill and destroy; I came that they may have life, and have it abundantly.

John 6:35 (KJV) And Jesus said unto them, I am the bread of life: he that cometh to me shall never hunger; and he that believeth on me shall never thirst.

Let us make bread together! Let's come together, bake and multiply the bread of LIFE here in America and all the Earth, so that we may all be filled and none will be hungry.

John 21:17 (RSV) The third time he said to him, "Simon son of John, do you love me?" Peter was hurt because Jesus asked him the third time, "Do you love me?" He said, "Lord, you know all things; you know that I love you." Jesus said, "Feed my sheep."

We will be combining the God-centered, holistic paradigm[395] with the third equation[396] noted above.

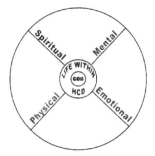

$$(1 + 1 + 1)^{GOD} = \textbf{Extraordinary Results}$$

First let's proof the yeast. With the warm water of our love and prayers, let us invite the Love of the I AM and His Christ into our daily lives. God's Love and LIFE are the substance of the Divine that raises the lives in all peoples, all in nature, all on our Earth into their Divine Purpose of abundant life. The I AM, God Our Father is at the center and is both the Source of LIFE and the Creator, through His Christ Word, of the manifest Universe, including our Earth.

John 1:1 (KJV) In the beginning was the Word, and the Word was with God, and the Word was God. ² The same was in the beginning with God. ³ All things were made by him; and without him was not any thing made that was made. ⁴ In him was life; and the life was the light of men. ⁵ And the light shineth in darkness; and the darkness comprehended it not.

Let's bring together the other ingredients. Let's get to know each other so we also can grow informed empathy, understanding, and respect. Notice that this does not mean coming together to submit a list of grievances or demands! Let's <u>listen</u> to each other, without fear, judgement, or ulterior motive. We need to commit to open, <u>civil dialogue</u> and not allow the insinuation of anger, resentment, hatred, or condemnation to enter. We can have genuine discussions that will build relationships of reciprocal love.

<u>1 John 4:18</u> (NIV) There is no fear in love. But perfect love drives out fear, because fear has to do with punishment. The one who fears is not made perfect in love.

<u>1 John 5:3</u> (NIV) In fact, this is love for God: to keep his commands. And his commands are not burdensome,

Let's blend it together. We'll have to mix all the ingredients of our bread together so that the special and essential qualities of each are spread throughout. We will all be both mentors and learners.

<u>Genesis 5:2</u> (NIV) When God created mankind, he made them in the likeness of God. ² He created them male and female and blessed them. And he named them "Mankind" when they were created. (note: "mankind" = "adam")

Each individual in all mankind, male and female, of all colors, created in the image of I AM are the essential ingredients in reciprocal love and justice. Let's call in the God's Love, Wisdom, and Power which are the Divine Yeast. Now, we will mix it all together in fellowship to make the intended Bread of LIFE expand to fulfill the Divine Intent.

<u>Matthew 25:45</u> (NRSV) "Truly I tell you, just as you did it to one of the least of these who are members of my family, you did it to me."

<u>Malachi 2:10</u> (NRSV) have we not all one father? Has not one God created us? Why then are we faithless to one another, profaning the covenant of our ancestors?

This is the conscious collaboration of the I AM Family joining in the manifestation of reciprocal Love to experience the joy of LIFE together with our Father God, the Christ, and the Holy Spirit. This creates reciprocal Justice sustainably.

And, as you can see, Love, LIFE, and Justice are not entitlement programs. We have to – and we get to – participate.

Let's make our relationships with God, Our Father, Jesus Christ, and each other all personal.

<u>Ecclesiastes 4:9-10, 12</u> (KJV) Two are better than one; because they have a good reward for their labour. ¹⁰ For if they fall, the one will lift up his fellow: but woe to him that is alone when he falleth; for he hath not another to help him up. ¹¹ And if one prevail against him, two shall withstand him; and a threefold cord is not quickly broken.

What if's!

What if, we started gathering people of one accord, people who strongly want Our Father's and Jesus' intervention in, and the restoration of, America? What if we bring together those who want the healing and raising of the whole earth and all our siblings in God's Family?

What if we prayed our intention, commitment, and request with mighty, unified power up to Our Father's ears and heart?

What if we learned to continue to live that way in everyday life, not only for our increased wellbeing, but to be examples and encouragement to every Child of God we contact, no matter what their current situation?

The 2018 census showed the population of United States of America to be 325,145,963. One percent (1%) of population equals 3,251,460 people.

What is the population of your community? How many people would make up one percent?

And in your church? Make the same kind of calculation for whatever groups in which you participate.

Now, let's expand the possibilities. In which of the groups you have chosen, would you like to see 100% engagement in the endeavor to save America by restoring acknowledgement of the Presence of God and use of God principles?

How would achieving a nearly 100% participation affect your family, group, church, or organization - and the individuals within it?

What would the healing and leadership impact be of those groups on a neighborhood or larger community?

Malachi 2:10 have we not all one father? Has not one God created us? Why then are we faithless to one another, profaning the covenant of our ancestors?

How much of the Love, Wisdom, and Power of the I AM could these 100% groups collectively send into the larger populations?

As a part of a broader group, how much of the 1% of the larger group could your 100% group – or many 100% groups – be? What if we consciously combined groups across a community?

Directing our love consciously and together back to the I AM WHO I AM, Our Father God often - as Jesus demonstrated – is a mighty, powerful, and constructive activity. We need all of Our Father's and Jesus' Love, Wisdom, and Power. And They already want us to have it! We need it right now in America! With this sustained activity, God's Creativity will build and come forth powerfully. Everything needed to awaken, heal, and galvanize We the Peoples will follow for the raising and saving of our beloved America – God's Way and for God's Purpose.

It is time for the multiplying of the loaves. It is time for all those with the Divine LIFE of the I AM WHO I AM within us to rise up and speak and act! It is time for us to rise up of one accord.

Luke 9:16 (NRSV) And taking the five loaves and the two fish, (Jesus) looked up to heaven, and blessed and broke them, and gave them to the disciples to set before the crowd. [17] And all ate and were filled. What was left over was gathered up, twelve baskets of broken pieces.

Ephesians 6:10-17 (NRSV) Finally be strong in the Lord and in the strength of his power. [11] Put on the whole armor of God, so that you may be able to stand against the wiles of the devil. [12] For our struggle is not against enemies of blood and flesh, but against the rulers, against the authorities, against the cosmic powers of this present darkness, against the spiritual forces of evil in the heavenly places.

[13] Therefore take up the whole armor of God, so that you may be able to withstand on that evil day, and having done everything, to stand firm. [14] Stand therefore, and fasten the belt of truth around your waist, and put on the breastplate of righteousness. [15] As shoes for your feet put on whatever will make you ready to proclaim the gospel of peace. [16] With all of these ([c] and in all circumstances) take the shield of faith, with which you will be able to quench all the flaming arrows of the evil one. [17] Take the helmet of salvation, and the sword of the Spirit, which is the (Word / Christ) and word (the Bible) of God.

One percent (1%) of population of the United States of America equals approximately 3,251,460 people.

In 2018, 65% of the US citizenry asserted they were Christian. One percent of the US population is 1.54% of those who claim Jesus Christ. So help us God, we can do this! And we'll invite all who want to join in!

What if we are armed with powerful prayer-decrees with which to begin, punctuate, and complete our frequent, regular gatherings to practice our commitment to unity in God's and Jesus' Love? What if we combine and focus our calls for Their Love, Wisdom, and Power to come down to us for the protection and restoration of America, home of the I AM race?

What if we became "experts" in calling to Our Father God and Jesus? The square root of 1% of the American people is 1,803 experts praying – together consciously.

What if at least 1% of the residents of your entire community were living consciously every day, even between prayer gatherings?

XX.
Making the call compels the answer

It is morning. As I awaken, my first thought is, *"I am so grateful, Father. I am so grateful. I am so grateful, for Your Love, for all You have given me and all that is yet to come!"* I notice that my voice is whispering this good morning prayer in unison with my mind and heart.

Heart, mind, and voice blended in expressing my Christ-consciousness, the song of God's I AM LIFE within me, I continue:

"Beloved I AM, my Father God, I love you. I bless You. I thank You. I face Thy eternal Light and receive Your Mighty Radiance, ever manifest in my being and world. I am Thine! I am Thy Child! I claim my Divine Birthright! I claim my essential place in Your I AM Family of Light! I stand serene in Thy Great Forever! I claim Thy Dominion, here, at this point in Your Universe, where you have placed me. I stand in the Radiance of God Eternal, ever looking Thee full in the face!

"How may I be of service to You and our God Family on earth today?" Silence, stillness, listening, communion.

Prayer is not just for supplication, asking for divine favors, or for confessing sins. The greatest blessing of prayer is as an invitation for dialogue. Prayer is an avenue for reciprocal love, for communion. The prayer avenue is a two-way street. It is a two-way conversation, if we will allow it. Prayer is a manifestation and opportunity provided through Grace.

Prayer helps us to remember the future God intends for us, who we really are, and our true relationship to each other.

"Sir, my concern is not whether God is on our side; my greatest concern is to be on God's side, for God is always right."
— Abraham Lincoln

Again, prayer is a two-way street - if we don't hog or block both lanes. Let's make sure that we give God and Jesus the courtesy of both anticipating and receiving Their responses to our prayers.

This courtesy is love and it is our extending justice to Them. It is reciprocity.

Holding our ego and its selfish busy-ness in check is more important than we can initially imagine. Ego was mankind's first mistake, the first sin against Our Lord God in the Fall. It is still what is keeping us in our own personal "separation-from-God experiment." As we all know, unavoidable facts of this existence are loneliness, fear, limitation, uncertainty, and mortality.

Collectively, this is the same sin/mistake that is keeping humanity separate, out of the garden of the wholeness, unity, joy, and the splendor of Our Father's Eternal Love and Presence.

It keeps us clawing at each other, in our desperation for substance to cure our incessant, crushing emptiness, and lack.

Only the Supreme Love of the I AM WHO I AM can satisfy and heal this hellish condition. This Love will heal us individually and collectively. It will heal our nation and the world. Every time we see something that is not love and justice, it is an opportunity! It is an opportunity to pray into that situation God's and Jesus' all wise and powerful intervention. Their intervention is always a blessing to all concerned. Let's not waste our precious life any longer on fear, anger, hate, criticism, condemnation, or judgment.

Beloved fellow Americans – all of us Children of God! All the I AM race throughout the world! Beloved Christian family! The familiar, predictable times we lived in in the past are ***gone!***

If we look on what is past, we, like Lot's wife, will calcify and never be part of the living future. Nor will we be of any use to it.

Jesus warned us, in _Luke 17:30-33_ (NRSV) ...*it will be like that on the day that the Son of Man is revealed.* [31] *On that day, anyone on the housetop who has belongings in the house must not come down to take them away; and likewise anyone in the field must not turn back.* [32] *Remember Lot's wife.* [33] *Those who try to make their life secure will lose it, but those who lose their life will keep it.*

To be saved we must run into the arms of Our Father and Jesus. We must want the Kingdom of God, the I AM, more than we want the things of the world and what makes up our mundane lives. We cannot love both God and mammon. We cannot serve two masters. The wannabe imposter master, that is NOT the I AM, is determined to take us into slaughter or enslavement.

Matthew 6:24 (NRSV) *"No one can serve two masters; for either he will hate the one and love the other, or he will be devoted to the one and despise the other. You cannot serve God and mammon.*

Mankind began to call on the name of the Lord, the I AM, a very long time ago!

Genesis 4:26 (NRSV) *At that time men began to call upon the name of the Lord.*

Today, many assert that it is heresy when we say that we humans are the ones who must make the call for God's Perfection to manifest here on earth. That is because they do not know who we ARE!

Genesis 1:26-27 (KJV) *And God said, Let us make man in our image, after our likeness: and _let them have dominion_ _...over all the earth,_...*[27] *So God created man in his own image, in the image of God created he him; male and female created he them.*

Prayer can also be a command! We must now use our God-given dominion <u>constructively</u>. We created this mess by our disobedience. We must choose and command that our lives be made anew in God's image. Once done, we can arise into our God-ordained office, take back our rightful power from the deceiver and his sinister force, and command the earth re-created up to God's original goodness and purpose.

We make the call from our Divine Birthright. God has promised to answer. He will.

It is the I AM WHO I AM, God Our Father Who will redeem our beloved America and the Earth, manifesting His re-creation, through the Word, His Christ.

It is time to make the dynamic, in-unison invitation to Our Father to intervene, like He did in the third episode of Washington's vision.

It is time for We the Peoples to become, by Free Will choice, We the People – again. What better time than as we lift our voices in unison calls to our God and Jesus?

Malachi 2:10 (NRSV) have we not all one father? Has not one God created us?

(Please note that the following vigorous, enthusiastic prayers are only samples!)

We have to get really, sincerely determined to dissolve and rise above our mistakes, to remove those habits from our minds and feelings. If we repeatedly <u>demand</u> of ourselves the change or action we want, it breaks through our mental and emotional resistance. In a prayer, let's combine the determined choice as a <u>demand on ourselves,</u> so that God knows we are committed and not lukewarm. We'll use the words: "I demand". . .

Then we will add the all-powerful name of God – I AM!

Think of God, Our Father, and say "I AM" many times in a row. Can you feel the tug in your own heart? That is where His LIFE in us is anchored! As we say His Name in the following "decree-prayers", we will know that He is with us and His LIFE in us is engaging.

Again, prayer is meant to be a two-way street. Let's pause about three heartbeats after each short prayer. Remember the baseball analogy earlier in this book? This pause is the "touch the base" with God and Jesus in action. After each larger section, consider a minute of silent love and communion.

Here we go!

"I demand and I AM full acceptance of God's and Jesus' Presences in my life!"

Let's ratchet up the power!

"Beloved I AM WHO I AM, Our Father God, in the name of the Ascended Jesus Christ, I demand and I AM full acceptance of Yours and Jesus' Presence in my life!"

"Beloved I AM WHO I AM, Our Father God, in the name of the Ascended Jesus Christ, I demand and I AM reclaiming my Divine Birthright!"

Do you have the feeling? Do you see why throughout the Bible from Genesis, in Exodus, through Psalms and Proverbs, throughout the whole New Testament, we are being advised concerning the name of God, which God Himself called "I AM"?

Genesis 4:26 (NRSV) ... At that time men began to call upon the name of the LORD.

Exodus 3:14 (NRSV) God said to Moses, "I AM WHO I AM." He said further, "Thus you shall say to the Israelites, 'I AM has sent me to you.' " ...This is my name forever, and this my title for all generations.

Proverbs 18:10 (NRSV) The name of the Lord is a strong tower; the righteous run to it and are safe.

John 8:58 (NRSV) "Very truly I tell you," Jesus answered, 'before Abraham was born, I AM!'

Do you begin to realize the incredible Power available to us, from the I AM and balanced with God's Love and Wisdom?

Numbers 11:23 (NRSV) The Lord said to Moses, "Is the Lord's power limited? Now you shall see whether my word will come true for you or not."

Matthew 17:20 (NRSV) "Truly I tell you, if you have faith as small as a mustard seed, you can say to this mountain, 'Move from here to there,' and it will move. Nothing will be impossible for you."

John 14:12-14 (NIV) Very truly I tell you, whoever believes in me will do the works I have been doing, and they will do even greater things than these, because I am going to the Father. 13 And I will do whatever you ask in my name, so that the Father may be glorified in the Son. 14 You may ask me for anything in my name, and I will do it.

Luke 11:9 (NIV) And I say unto you, "Ask, and it shall be given you; seek, and ye shall find; knock, and it shall be opened unto you."

Genesis 1:27-28 (NIV) So God created man in his own image, in the image of God he created him; male and female he created them. 28 And God blessed them, and God said to them, "Be fruitful and multiply, and fill the earth and subdue it;

The sinister force is only here and active by our deceived and "drugged" complicity.

Without vision we were perishing.

Proverbs 29:18 (KJV) Where there is no vision, the people perish: but he that keepeth the law, happy is he.

Our Assets – *again, in reverse order!*
1.There are way more of us than them (the sinister force).

2. We can consciously engage our Divine Birthright, then powerfully and continuously use our Divinely-given Free Will. We can:

- choose not to cooperate with their evil. We can refuse submission and obedience to the sinister force, globalists, or their minions. Here, "no decision" is a choice for enslavement;

- consciously and resolutely choose obedience to God and His Law of Love, as spoken and demonstrated by Jesus Christ,

- energetically pray and pray and pray, calling to Our Father for help and deliverance,

- actively cooperate with Our Father, Jesus, the angelic hosts, and each other, and

- we can gather together for our unison prayers to increase the Power - and speed - of God's Intervention.

Matthew 18:14 (NRSV) So it is not the will of your Father in heaven that one of these little ones should be lost.

Love must be reciprocal to experience its greatest fulfillment and power. Perfect Justice is an extension of perfect Love.

Justice requires reciprocity to be sustainable.

Once we choose conscious, active obedience to God, we can call on the I AM with full confidence in His Loving, Wise, and All-Powerful Response. **The more of God's Children, who call together consciously, the more powerful and fast-moving will be the Deliverance.**

When we pray in unison,
- it focuses a cohesive vision, a chalice for the request we are asking to become manifest, and
- as the increased love God, Jesus and we pour out together collects, it fills the chalice of the vision and compels it manifestation.

These together create exponential power, activating the accomplishment of Divine Yeast.

Mankind must be trained to access Christ-consciousness above the physical world if there is going to be mastery over the conditions human beings have generated here.

Arising in our Divine Birthright, let us use our Free Will consciously and declare the Dominion of the I AM WHO I AM, Our Father God on Earth fully manifest NOW and eternally sustained!

Every call we make to our ever-present Father and Christ Jesus compels a loving, powerful, wise, and constructive answer! This is the way the I AM, Our Father "wired" His Creation.

Again, calling in unison, together in groups of people, gathered in the same place, in-real-life, clearly activates "Divine Yeast"! This was scientifically proven by the Drs. Aron.

It may require creativity to reclaim our divinely given and constitutionally acknowledged and protected rights of worshipping together in sufficient numbers.

Let us accept God's Grace by our dynamic Free Will choice and live with joyful obedience within Our Father's Law of Love. Thereby we will enjoy reciprocal relationship and deliberate, conscious collaboration with Our Father and Jesus!

Let's not be lukewarm about it!!!

Revelation 3:15-17, 19-20 (NRSV) I know your deeds, that you are neither cold nor hot. I wish you were either one or the other! [16] So, because you are lukewarm—neither hot nor cold—I am about to spit you out of my mouth. [17] You say, 'I am rich; I have acquired wealth and do not need a thing.' But you do not realize that you are wretched, pitiful, poor, blind and naked

[19] Those whom I love I rebuke and discipline. So be earnest and repent. [20] Here I am! I stand at the door and knock. If anyone hears my voice and opens the door, I will come in and eat with that person, and they with me.

For our fullest experience and for the greatest power, we must start from that point of reciprocal, consciously-connected love with the I AM, Our Ever-Loving, Father God.

Before beginning, pause for at least a minute to place your attention on God, Our Father … on Jesus Christ … on Their Perfect Love and Unity. Accept, as God's Child, your participation in that Unity. Accept your essential place in God's Family of Light!

Psalm 46:10 (NRSV) He says, "Be still, and know that I am God; I will be exalted among the nations, I will be exalted in the earth."

Matthew 18:14 (NRSV)...it is not the will of your Father in heaven that one of these little ones should be lost.

Here are samples of some snappy short prayers, for starters. Make up some of your own, too! Pause for about three heartbeats of silence in between each.

Beloved Father God, in the Name of Jesus Christ...
(Begin with this before each line. Remember the three heartbeats between each short prayer.)

. . .with love and gratitude I reclaim my Divine Birthright!
. . .protect us and all Your Children!
. . .thank you for helping us to see your LIFE in everyone we meet!
. . .help us see Your LIFE in each other and love each other!
. . .help us to see Your LIFE in each other and forgive each other!
(Pause for a minute of love and communion.)

Beloved Father God, in the Name of Jesus Christ, I thank you!...
(Begin with this before each line. Remember the three heartbeats between each.

. . .I demand and I AM You are removing evil from our America and our World!
. . .I demand and I AM You are dissolving all hypnotic control of our people by the sinister force!
. . .I demand and I AM You are dissolving all misunderstanding, disunity, injustice, and all hate within Our Family of God!

. . .I demand and I AM the Victory of Your Love in _____! *(Repeat this prayer 3 times.)*
(Pause for a minute of love and communion.)

The Answer

Our earnest and determined Call to God from us His Children <u>compels</u> the answer, due to God's Love for us. Let us rise up in our love and full devotion to Our Father God, the I AM, and Jesus Christ by fulfilling Our Father's desire for our obedience and full acceptance of His Love, through our life lived and our calls. We consciously speak with and through our Divine Birthright as God's Children.

Now, let's go into dynamic action! Standing while speaking increases the power.

Remember: *Matthew 19:26 (KJV) Jesus looked at them and said, "With men this is impossible, but with God all things are possible."*

Beloved God, Our Father! In the Name of Jesus Christ! *(Put this line at the beginning of each prayer in this section. Say each second part three times, if you wish.)*

. . .I demand and I AM acknowledging and accepting that Your Love, Wisdom and Power - demonstrated through Jesus - are greater and more powerful than all my sins and mistakes — and those of all mankind.

. . .I demand and I AM full acceptance of Your unconditional and infinite Love.

. . .I demand and I AM seeking and fully accepting Yours and Jesus' forgiveness of my sins and mistakes.

. . .I demand and I AM <u>my</u> forgiveness of my sins and mistakes.

. . .I demand and I AM the forgiveness of the sins and mistakes of all others.

I AM so grateful! *(3 times)* Almighty I AM! *(3 times)*
(Pause for a minute of love and communion.)

Our Father does not withhold any of His Love from ANY of us! He loves infinitely and is never depleted. We are the only ones who limit our experience of the fullness of His Love and our every-moment encounter with the Divine.

In the same way, **we limit the manifestation of His intended response** if we put our attention on our own or others' failures. The same thing happens if, when we pray, we hold our attention on the evil we are asking God to remove, instead of on the miracle we desire!

This is the power of our God-given Free Will. It is also how Our Father is teaching us what is a constructive choice and what is unconstructive. This is how He and Jesus are teaching us to live willingly within the eternal Love of the I AM.

God and His Perfection are the only true reality. Anything less than that is a temporary resistance of disobedience to perfect, complete, and absolute Love.

Our Free Will choice, consciously and constructively used, is the reciprocal, love connection with Our Father God that opens the door for miracles manifest at our request. How many times did Jesus demonstrate this in his mission when he was embodied with mankind? He is still demonstrating it. Many, many of us are witnesses to this truth.

For this next section, try before each of these short prayers:
Beloved God, Our Father! In Thy Mighty Name I AM and in the name of the Ascended Jesus Christ! . . .

. . .I demand and I AM the healing of the Fall and the fulfillment of the separation experiment at this point in Your universe, where the You, Father have placed me!
(As we make this Call, the separation experiment, the Fall, is being healed, plus, the separation agreements and, thereby, the authority of the sinister force are being dissolved!)

. . .I demand and I AM is the Resurrection and the LIFE out of the serpentine context and into the freedom of the abundant life Jesus promised!

. . .I demand and I AM the Victory of my full, conscious reunification with You, our Father God, Jesus Christ, and our Family of God!
(This is a declaration that we have chosen Our Father, God the I AM, as number One in our lives.)

Let's add more power!

Beloved I AM WHO I AM! in the Name of the Ascended Jesus Christ!. . .
. . .I demand and I AM *(3 times),* Your annihilation – cause, effect, record and memory – of the separation agreements, and thereby, the dissolving of the authority of the entire sinister force and its leadership!

. . .I demand and I AM *(3 times),* You are replacing the new world order and all human nonsense with Yourself, Your Love, Perfection, and Infinite Protection!
(Pause for a minute of love and communion.)

Keep remembering: *Matthew 19:26* (KJV) *"With men this is impossible, but with God all things are possible."*

Beloved Father, I AM WHO I AM, in the Name of the Ascended Jesus Christ, by Thy Mighty Love, Wisdom, and Power!
. . .I demand and I AM reclaiming my Divine Birthright! *(3 times)* I choose to be the fulfillment of the separation experiment at this point in Your Universe where You have placed me!

. . .I thank you for removing of all the separation agreements, and thereby dissolving and consuming the authority of the entire sinister force and its leadership - from our lives, our nation, and from the earth!

. . .I demand and I AM You are returning America to God! *(9 times)*
(Pause for a minute of love and communion.)

With love and joy, let us humbly invite every Child of the I AM throughout America mankind to join in saying these prayer-decrees with us and claiming their immediate, complete, and eternal fulfillment.

In the Name of God, the I AM WHO I AM and the Ascended Jesus Christ!
. . .I demand and I AM *(3 times),* that through every one of Your Children throughout America and all mankind, this Illumination, choice, and decree – for the fulfillment of the separation experiment and the end of the authority of the sinister force and it leadership - is NOW expanding with the speed of lightning and joy of the angels! - Almighty I AM! *(3 times)*

Beloved I AM, Our Father and Beloved Jesus Christ!
. . . I demand and I AM Your return to us on Earth in your visible, tangible Presences! *(3 times)*

In the Name of the I AM WHO I AM and the Ascended Jesus Christ!
. . .I demand and I AM Your Command, Our Father God, is now going forth to the would-be pharaohs of Earth and their minions: "**Let - My – People - go!**" *(3 times)* Almighty I AM! *(3 times)*

Revelation 3:8-9 I know your deeds. See, I have placed before you an open door that no one can shut. I know that you have little strength, yet you have kept my word and have not denied my name. 9 I will make those who are of the synagogue of Satan, who claim to be Jews though they are not, but are liars—I will make them come and fall down at your feet and acknowledge that I have loved you.

In the Name of the I AM WHO I AM and the Ascended Jesus Christ!
. . . to the would-be pharaohs of Earth and their minions: I demand and I AM you **let – God's – People - Go!** *(3 times)* **Almighty I AM!** *(3 times)*

Revelation 3:10-13 Since you have kept my command to endure patiently, I will also keep you from the hour of trial that is going to come on the whole world to test the inhabitants of the earth.

11 I am coming soon. Hold on to what you have, so that no one will take your crown. 12 The one who is victorious I will make a pillar in the temple of my God. Never again will they leave it. I will write on them the name of my God and the name of the city of my God, the new Jerusalem, which is coming down out of heaven from my God; and I will also write on them my new name. 13 Whoever has ears, let them hear what the Spirit says to the churches.

Now we are true, fiery children of Our Father and disciples of Jesus Christ!

Now, we can claim the final stanza of our national anthem!

O thus be it ever when free (people) shall stand
Between their lov'd homes and the war's desolation!
Blest with vict'ry and peace may the heav'n rescued land
Praise the power that hath made and preserv'd us a nation!
Then conquer we must, when our cause it is just,
And this be our motto - "In God is our trust,"*
And the star-spangled banner in triumph shall wave
O'er the land of the free and the home of the brave.

*This is the source of our national motto.

1 Thessalonians 4:16 (NIV) For the Lord himself will descend from heaven with a cry of command, with the voice of an archangel and with the sound of the trumpet of God.

Matthew 13:41 (NIV) The Son of Man will send out his angels, and they will weed out of his kingdom everything that causes sin and all who do evil.

2 Chronicles 7: 14 (NRSV) I f my people who are called by my name (I AM) humble themselves, pray, seek my face, and turn from their wicked ways, then I will hear from heaven, and will forgive their sin and heal their land.

Isaiah 9:1-7 (NRSV) The Righteous Reign of the Coming King
... there will be no gloom for those who were in anguish. ....
² The people who walked in darkness have seen a great light;
those who lived in a land of deep darkness— on them light has shined.

³ You have multiplied the nation, you have increased its joy;
they rejoice before you as with joy at the harvest, as people exult when dividing plunder.
⁴ For the yoke of their burden, and the bar across their shoulders,
 the rod of their oppressor, you have broken as on the day of Midian.
⁵ For all the boots of the tramping warriors and all the garments rolled in blood shall be burned as fuel for the fire.

⁶ For a child has been born for us, a son given to us;
authority rests upon his shoulders' and he is named
Wonderful Counselor, Mighty God, Everlasting Father, Prince of Peace.
⁷ His authority shall grow continually, and there shall be endless peace for the throne of David and his kingdom.
 He will establish and uphold it with justice and with righteousness from this time onward and forevermore.

The zeal of the LORD of hosts will do this.

Revelations 5:5 (NRSV) Then one of the elders said to me, "Do not weep. See, the Lion of the tribe of Judah, the Root of David, has conquered, so that he can open the scroll and its seven seals."

The time has come, fellow Americans and all the Children of God throughout the Earth, to actively choose what is sacred, over what is convenient.

And now for the beginning! "The world is not coming to an end. It's coming to a start!" [397]

Appendix I:
Anything not attempted remains impossible...an invitation

Now you know more about the WHY and WHAT to do!
Thank you and God bless you for reading this book and for all you will be doing to accept Our Father's and Jesus' invitation to be part of Their Victorious Solution! They are the Source of America's Victory!

To just passively see what will happen by 'going with the flow' or 'sitting it out' bunkered are in the "no decision" category! No decision is a choice for enslavement. Again Grace is not an entitlement program. We get to collaborate, to choose to consciously and actively cooperate with what is the only true protection of our God freedoms.

The full return of Jesus Christ and God, Our Father into mankind's affairs and throughout the Earth will be the healing of the Fall. It will be our full conscious reunion with God and Jesus in God's Family eternally.

Author's contacts:
SecuringAmericasVictory@protonmail.com
http://www.outskirtspress.com/securingamericasvictory

If the message in this book was the only thing offered to you here, it might be only a long rant!

Do you want to focus and leverage your impact?

Would you like to personally experience an Inspired "HOW to"? Would you like to facilitate the experience with others?

Christ-Inspired, developed, tested, and proven over 25 years, the Living Consciously® system was created for these times. It guides and instills a simple step-by-step process toward living within Jesus' Great Command and His Golden Rule:

Matthew 22:37-40 *(NRSV)* He said to him, 'You shall love the Lord your God with all your heart, and with all your soul, and with all your mind.' [38] This is the greatest and first commandment. [39] And a second is like it: 'You shall love your neighbor as yourself.' [40]On these two commandments hang all the law and the prophets."

Luke 6:31 *(NRSV)* Do to others as you would have them do to you.

Because of this active, conscious alignment with God and Jesus Christ, experiencing the Living Consciously® program has been proven to shatter all matrixes.

These include:
- serpentine context
- victim mentality
- entitlement / poverty mentality
- criminality
- mental, emotion, and spiritual dependence on substances
- collectivism, herd mentality
- stop-think
- immobilizing fear
- ideological possession

Immunity to evil can only be achieved by shattering the matrixes holding our minds, emotions, and spirits captive. This experience restores us, the Children of God, to our original wiring, including greatly increasing our conscious awareness of our connection with God, Our Father and Jesus.

A "how to" for recognizing and shattering matrixes, this program is a major factor in sustainable healing of the effects of trauma, including:
- child abuse
- domestic violence
- indoctrination
- poverty
- substance abuse
- criminality
- battle fatigue

This is a "how to" experience for living within Jesus' Great Command and Golden Rule.

Based in the Love of God and Jesus Christ, and making innate God-principles practical, this program restores and builds:
- the holistic, balanced, healthy integrity of the individual Child of God within ourselves
    - and our conscious reciprocal relationship with God, Our Father
- wholesome, reciprocal relationships with others
- balanced, righteous unity within mankind's natural, God-appointed groupings
- Justice
- the armor of God

What if at least 1% of the residents of your entire community were living consciously every day? What if at least 1.54% of the Christians in your community were living consciously every day, even between prayer and worship gatherings?

How many people would you like to see equipped (trained) at the "expert level"?

"The world is not coming to an end. It's coming to a start!" [398]

Building the critical mass noted in the Divine Yeast chapter is essential. That means and requires a conscious, active, deliberate, resolute, strategic, and cohesive collaboration.

Do you agree that we need to build unifying critical mass as quickly as possible?

Overviewed below, is what I've been inspired to create since November 1994. It is implemented by others. The story of the inspiration that began, and still guides this endeavor, is shared in Appendix II.

By God's Grace, this program is...

Spiritual, Mental, and Emotional CPR!
The experience of this system of curricula:
- cracks apart indoctrination and other confusion,
- ends the "serpentine context,"
- restores God's original wiring, within each of us, His Children, and
- reestablishes unity and collaboration within groups of God's Children, no matter of size.

A multi-pronged, multi-level approach, geared to multiple perspectives, has been created for customized delivery. The process is statistically trackable in detail, through proprietary, online software. It provides both confidential, personal progress reports and custom, compiled reports that are confidentiality protected.

You've already had a taste! The core, solution elements within this book have been liberally borrowed from this inspired curricula system called Living Consciously®. These core elements are in Chapters V through IX. This program is non-competitive with any other training or process with which it is implemented. It acts as a catalyst, enhancing the process, results, and sustainability of any endeavor. Living Consciously simply acts as a stabilizing, balancing foundation within every person. The implementation also creates a collaboratively-created, God-based (integrity-based), shared, core value system within every group that uses it.

It is significant that all and every group, no matter its makeup, has chosen exactly the same God-centered, inner core values. This is a confirmation to me that this program is truly from God.

Both openly Christian-based and secularly- harmonious versions are available. Please also know that every manual in the Living Consciously family, from the fifth-grade reading level up, has the full text of the Declaration of Independence, the Constitution of the United States of America, the Bill of Rights, and all the subsequent Amendments to the Constitution.

The system is licensed to only two organizations for outreach and implementation.

The first is Conscious Community Inc., a 501(c)3. Its mission is: *"Healing trauma. Restoring wellbeing. Building justice and unity."* This organization serves in churches, K-12 education, youth transitioning into adulthood, and other human service areas, including healing poverty, chronic disease, homelessness, domestic violence, substance abuse, and criminality. Leadership and staff development for nonprofit organizations and community leadership curricula are also available.

The second is Conscious Company Inc. It's offerings have been called "a quantum leap in leadership and employee development." This company provides seminars for organizational leadership and staff in the for-profit sector.

Open enrollment seminars are available for:
- *individuals for their personal experience with Living Consciously,*
- *training of staff facilitators in your organization through both nonprofit and for-profit avenues, and*
- *community leadership.*

Both Christian and non-religious groups will be offered.

A more thorough overview of the offerings follows, including each sector's purpose and intentions. It's a lot of detail! But I've noticed since 1994, most of us cannot immediately grasp the possibilities and needs of a situation. Heaven knows, it took me twenty-five years – and I'm still learning!

The mission of Living Consciously

This is a causal intervention to bring individuals, groups, and communities into clear and harmonious attunement with Jesus' Great Command and Golden Rule.

Matthew 22:37-40 (NRSV) He said to him, "You shall love the Lord your God with all your heart, and with all your soul, and with all your mind."[38] This is the greatest and first commandment. [39] And a second is like it: 'You shall love your neighbor as yourself.' [40] On these two commandments hang all the law and the prophets." Similar: Mark 12:29-31.

Luke 6:31 (NRSV) .Do to others as you would have them do to you.

These can be summed up as living in attunement with these principles:
- love God with all our hearts, minds, and strength;
- love our neighbor as ourselves, and
- treat others as we would have them treat us.

This is accomplished by:
- focusing on changing the way we make choices at the smallest level - and not just intellectual processing. It encompasses our emotions, engaging our spirits, and, of course, physical applications as well;

- weeding out what is unconstructive and growing the constructive choices,

- creating clarity, self-esteem, reasoning, long-term thinking, and self-responsibility and reliance;

- detailed statistical tracking, for individual and group coaching, plus proof of efficacy.

All this is truly causal, not just symptomatic. The process empowers individuals to respond constructively and creatively to life situations and opportunities. It puts aside memorizing prescribed, behavioral responses and depending on others to think for us.

This process can be implemented simultaneously across three main pillars of society, which have their own primary goals when functioning at their highest levels. These include:

Faith-Based/Christian Sector	**Non-Profit Sector**	**Business Sector**
Goal: Restoration	Goals: Learning, Rehabilitation, Community Leadership	Goal: Prosperity

***

First Special Opportunities!
Become a certified Conscious Community staff facilitator, working remotely in your community! Flexible hours; good base pay; commissions; other add-ons

We are especially looking for individuals with interest in these focused areas:

- inner-city *(neighborhood residents encouraged)*

- young adults, ages 18-23 *(college-aged facilitators welcome!), plus*

- general adult population facilitators (Create your own niche!)

For more information, please contact us at info@ConsciousCommunityInc.org

For those interested in collaborating with us in leadership and employee development in business and non-profit arenas, please contact us at info.ConsciousCompanyInc@protonmail.com.

***

Here are the Christian community arenas where we are ready to serve with you:

Christian Sector Goals
Restoration:
- return to conscious unity with God, Our Father, the Creator

- enter into harmonious, grateful collaboration with Jesus in His mission to mankind

Aspiration:
Living in attunement with these principles, as contained in Jesus' Great Command and Golden Rule.
- love God with all heart, mind, and strength
- love neighbors as ourselves
- treat others as we would have them treat us

Also building:
- constructive relationships within ourselves and with others
- stewardship – engagement – collaboration
- spiritual wholeness and health.

Current Antitheses and Opposition:
- spiritual poverty (which is the cause of economic poverty and all human malady)
- selfishness and egotism
- fear
- non-engagement, disaffection
- Grace as an entitlement program
- strong secular movement to put state/government in place of God
- human tendencies to either:
  - idolize, which steals from the idolater the responsibility and desire to refine themselves and their relationship with God, or
  - set oneself up as an idol , to dominate others for power, prestige, and money,
- addiction to unconstructive behavior (out of attunement with principles of Jesus Great Command)
- enslavement

IMPLEMENTATION SERVICES:

Seminars/Curricula
These are Bible studies, *wrapped around the inspired*
Living Consciously® core program, that is a practical "how to"
for living every day within Jesus Great Command and Golden Rule.
Curriculum is available for ages 4-adult.

Reinvigorating the Church
Living Consciously, Christian
version (pilots, adults)

Church Outreach Services
Living Consciously, secular
version (pilots, adults)

Serving Consciously™
(staff & congregation)

Serving Consciously
(outreach volunteers)

Leading Consciously™
(core program & verses, plus
deep-dive into current issues
affecting churches & communities)

Statistical Tracking

Reinvigorating the Church

Tracking accounts:
Class, group, or individual

Compiled reports
Customized groups

Church Outreach Services

Personal tracking accounts

Compiled reports
Customized groups

Ancillary Services

Reinvigorating the Church

Personal coaching
(staff or members)

Training new staff

Consulting

Church Outreach Services

Personal coaching
(staff or outreach
participants)

Consulting

Training Certified Staff & Volunteer Facilitators

Reinvigorating the Church   Church Outreach Services
4-day certification trainings in seminar facilitation & coaching
annual re-certification & development required

for Sunday school facilitators
& coaches (for groups age 4-adult)
plus youth & adult activities leaders;
Living Consciously, Christian version

facilitators & coaches
(for participants in outreach)
Living Consciously,
secular setting version

The above services provided by Conscious Community Inc. (a 501(c)3);
info@ConsciousCommunityInc.org, 866.849.2615
www.ConsciousCommunityInc.org

Preface to "secular" implementations:

Jesus likened himself to a shepherd. As we all know, the Children of God are a lot harder to herd than sheep, because we have the unique Breath of God in us, with the attribute of God-given free will.

Here are the attributes he enumerated for a true shepherd:
- enters through the gate, i.e. Jesus' Great Command
- provides food and water for his sheep (spiritual nutrition)
- protects his sheep
- goes out to where anyone becomes lost to rescue, redeem, and bring that one safely back into the fold

So, as does Our Good Shepherd, we go out to where the members of God's Family are wandering. This includes going into the kingdoms of virtual reality where people think there is such a reality as "secular" – a place where God is not. And we go humbly and kindly.

The restoration of We the People to conscious choice of God's Love and the use of our free will to create and sustain constructive change. This is necessarily a kind, gentle, and respectful process, accomplished in small, interactive groups or one-on-one. The exchange of reciprocal love is an essential ingredient of success. <u>This cannot be truly accomplished in a virtual environment</u>, where participants and the facilitator are physically separated from each other.

Each person must be given full freedom to choose what his or her relationship with God will be. They must also be given the freedom to not choose God.

Here is a sampling of the results in solely or largely secular settings:
- 460 families off TANF and food stamps due to income

- 29% reduction in trauma in adults with generational poverty, plus
    o 37% newly hired and 32% with improved employment

- 30% reduction in trauma for those with BOTH generational poverty and generational homelessness

- recidivism rates less than 9% for prison reentries, and an
    o 87% employment rate for individuals previously incarcerated

- 85% reduction in disciplinary incidents, with students marked for permanent expulsion

- for staff in business and nonprofits: 15%-25% more value for wages/salaries already being paid. Similar increases in production, quality, and collaboration; plus decreases in non-engagement, disaffection, and turnover are usual.

When allowed to introduce God, even at a cautious level, the results are generally 30% greater. Nearly all the participants, of both faith-based and secular groups, have either come to God for the first time, returned to God, or increased their faith exponentially.

Our Father loves us so much, He wants us to be a family of consciously-shared love, joy, and unity – eternally. And we often have great pride in what we see as our godliness and understanding of Jesus' Message. This kind of pride can be problematic. Humble love is a very special attribute. It is also much more productive in helping to bring the freedom and protection of God's Kingdom to our brothers and sisters.

Here are the secular arenas we are ready to serve with you:

Non-Profit Sector
Goals:
Collaborative community action toward:

Learning: healthy, balanced, enriched education, including K-12, higher education, and continuing, adult education

Rehabilitation: compassionate healing and rehabilitation, including:
- raising people out of poverty and its sidekicks (These include many forms of unconstructive choices, addiction, criminality, and trauma)
- This intervention removes victim mentality and poverty / entitlement mindset, while reducing fear, anxiety, ignorance, and confusion.

Community leadership: wise, balanced, and just community leadership

Current Antitheses and Opposition:
- ignorance of true history, plus revisionist history
- selfishness, fear, resentment against injustice
- traditions of largely symptomatic approaches
- heavily polarizing political environment
- toxic charity, including long-term government subsidies

For typical program results, please see previous list.

IMPLEMENTATION SERVICES:

Seminars/Curricula
The core curricula are the same, but without the Bible verses or openly Christian language. The concept of Highest Power / Supreme Being is included in the curricula. It is also included in America's foundational documents in the Appendix of each participant manual. Facilitation of each group is customized to their needs.

Education
Living Consciously®,
ages PK-12 (pilots)

Human Services
Living Consciously,
 ages PK-adult (pilots)

Serving Consciously™ – staff

Serving Consciously - staff

Leading Consciously™
 for Educators

Leading Consciously
 for Non-Profits

We also have Leading Consciously™ for Community Leaders.

Statistical Tracking
Education
Tracking accounts:
Class or individual

Human Services
Personal tracking
accounts

| Compiled reports | Compiled reports |
| Customized groups | Customized groups |

Ancillary Services

Education	Human Services
Personal coaching	Personal coaching
(staff or students)	(staff or clients)

Training for Certified Staff Facilitators

Education   Human Services
4-day certification trainings in seminar facilitation & coaching
Annual re-certification & development required

PLEASE NOTE: For Christian schools and homeschooling, our K-12 curricula with Bible verses is available. Homeschoolers may also purchase our general curricula.

The above services provided by Conscious Community Inc. (a 501(c)3);
info@ConsciousCommunityInc.org, 866.849.2615
www.ConsciousCommunityInc.org

Here are the business and for-profit areas where we are ready to serve with you:

Business Sector
Goal: Prosperity

Creation of wealth through entrepreneurism
- individual efforts and abilities justly rewarded
- benefits society at large
    - an alternative to acquiring wealth by conquest

Providing individuals a platform for satisfying building of character, self-respect, and achievement; also
- means to economic self and family support and sustainability
- raising personal quality of life
- self-expression and improvement
- building legacy
- being part of improving own community and nation
- making the world a better place

Strengthen individuals, families, communities, nations; providing for:
- security
- discovery
- innovation
- advancement
- higher quality of life

Current Antitheses and Opposition:
- selfishness from

- o   those who want to monopolize or steal from consumers and/or employees
- o   those who demand the fruits/wealth without adding to the production
- fear
- non-engagement, disaffection, high turnover
- over regulation, over taxation
- socialism, communism, fascism, corporatism, globalism
- current government educational system damaging the character of children, and thereby weakening the future citizenry and workforce
- ongoing government subsidies to those able, but not working, thereby, significantly reducing workforce and potential

Typical program results with staff in business, include 15%-25% more value for wages/salaries already being paid. Similar increases in production, quality, and collaboration; plus decreases in non-engagement, disaffection, and turnover are usual.

IMPLEMENTATION SERVICES:

Seminars/Curricula
Leading Consciously™ for Business
Two versions for:
- executive leaders & middle management
- 1st line supervisors and emerging leaders

Working Consciously™
For general company employees

Statistical Tracking
Customized tracking tool of choices supportive to company goals, plus custom survey schedule

Personal statistical tracking accounts, online; using unique, coded entry for data upload and download of personal progress reports. Gives each employee a personalized tool for self-improvement.

Compiled reports, at all new data uploads; for work teams, departments, locations, overall company, etc.

Customized ROI tracking, of germane production, work environment, workforce factors, to complement tracking of choices
- These ROI factors are selections from what the company is already tracking.

Ancillary Services
Personal Coaching, usually used for:
- fast-tracking leaders
- additional assistance to at-risk or new employees

Training new hires

Consulting

Training of Certified Client Staff Facilitators

5-day certification trainings in seminar facilitation, coaching, and other uses
of ongoing, statistical reports. Annual re-certification and development required.

The above services provided by Conscious Company Inc.
info.ConsciousCompanyInc@protonmail.com; 866.849.2615
www.ConsciousCompanyInc.com

Thank you for your interest, prayer, thought, and serious consideration.

Appendix II:
The inspiration

Here's the story that preceded the curricula which I noted in the previous appendix. This experience ignited the impetus that has brought this system into full readiness. It has also inspired this book.

On November 19, 1994, after seven months of persistent, demanding prayers to God and the Christ for something that would help stop the suffering of mankind, They answered my ardent prayers. In a brief encounter with Their angelic messenger, the Inspired and specific components of a process to use toward the ending of suffering were given.

The most magnificent part of the encounter by far, was the experience of overwhelming, unconditional LOVE. My heart nearly bursts with gratitude and my tears flow every time I think of it. And since then, every time another helping of life-changing Grace is given, I have the same experience.

Fully engaged in a financially rewarding career at that time, I started finding time to get the Inspiration on paper. The angel remained patiently and quietly present.

He counseled me, "Child, for the people to return to Our Father, they must also return to living within the I AM's Law of Love. ... Jesus spoke, embodied, and demonstrated the Way. ... This Gift with which you have been entrusted is a way to live consciously in attunement with Jesus' Great Command. ... This must be accomplished within people gathered together. They will also be instructed in the use of their use of their personal, God-given Free Will.

"Mankind must be trained to use Christ-Consciousness above the physical world if there is going to be mastery over the conditions human beings have generated here."

It took four years to create the first master curriculum. The next step was to test it. In 1998, two groups, of about twenty community leaders each, attended day-long seminars.

The response from the focus-group seminars was astounding. The participants came carrying the usual stress of their lives and with curiosity. The seminar is not presented. Rather, it is facilitated. The answers nearly all come through the participants' input. Soon their faces were registering surprise and they relaxed. By the end of the day, the expressions were peace, hope, gratitude, enthusiasm, and eagerness.

The participants were saying such things as, "I haven't felt so peaceful, confident, and hopeful in a long time" and "You gave me my life back!"

The teachers in the groups ganged up on me, saying this had to be brought into the schools. They asserted that six-year olds would handle the concepts well. "Even better than the adults," an educator insisted, "because they don't have the baggage!" Another added, "Wouldn't it be great if they didn't make the baggage?"

Shortly after these first tests of the Gift, while in prayer, I got the message, 'Well done, Child. Now you get to do this full time." I was astonished!

There was no pressure! Truly! I knew I was given total free-will choice in the matter. A few moments of silent review and I knew there was only one choice that held any love, truth, or honor. Our Father and the Christ let me rest peacefully there for a few days. Then I made my commitment.

My spouse knew that the Gift came from God. When I shared the Command / Invitation, the reaction was one of anger and resistance. Acceptance of God's Invitation would immediately and severely affect my ability to provide a very comfortable lifestyle. Aggressive language and physical violence was delivered on me as well. It ended with divorce, with a generous settlement. I sold my house and put everything, including all my time, into the development, testing, and readiness of the Gift, while awaiting God's appointed time.

When the Gift was given, I was also told that it would be a while before mankind, in large numbers, would be ready for it. I'm really glad that the angel didn't tell me it would be twenty-five-plus years! I honestly don't know if I would have had the courage to make it! As it was, I have gladly invested the equivalent of $2.61 million so far, and all the talent, time, and treasure with which God has blest me. I've suffered homelessness twice and uncountable rejections; waves of attacks ranging from jealousy to wrath from leadership – including from those active in the church.

I've also been blessed daily with the steadfast, unconditional, and ever-present Love and Presence of Our Father God, Jesus Christ, and the angelic host, plus the love, help, encouragement, and friendship of many Christians. I don't believe I could hold more gratitude. And yet again, as I key these words to you, my tears are overflowing.

Now, with all the love, hope, and blessings of my heart, I float the loaves that God, Jesus, the angel, and I have baked together out on the water to you … and through you to God's Family, America, and all mankind.

Author's contacts:
SecuringAmericasVictory@protonmail.com
http://www.outskirtspress.com/securingamericasvictory

Appendix III:
Input from people who have gone before and other information

PRELUDE: This information represents collected input from thousands of participants in Living Consciously seminars since 1998. The remarkable – no, astonishing – dimension to these responses is that, at the core, they have been always the SAME across <u>every</u> and all groups. Of course, they differed in expression according to the age, background, and education of the individuals in each group. But the content, the meaning of the responses, has been the same. The groups and participants varied widely, from 4 years old to 85, across the range of American racial and social economic groups. These results include groups experiencing generational homelessness, poverty, drug addiction, and criminal backgrounds to the wide expanse of general life in America, and representatives of most major religions.

And still, when asked "what qualities are constructive/helpful and which are unconstructive/ hurtful?", the core responses are the same. They are not just similar, though people with more education offer more descriptors. Individuals that began the course while stuck in difficult, unconstructive lives internally knew the constructive qualities, even though they had not been choosing to live them. Learning how to incorporate constructive choices into their lives and leaving the unconstructive choices behind, about 95% made major, positive changes in the quality of their lives by the conscious, deliberate use of their own free will.

The preceding question to these responses is always something like: "What would be (or are) the qualities of…"

A "Perfect" World
Love, Justice, Harmony, Self-control, Abundance, Peace, Joy, Opportunity, Safety/Security, Respect, Tolerance, Forgiveness, Courage, Balance, Happiness, Honor, Kindness, Health, Honesty, Integrity, Reliability, Beauty, Inclusiveness, Purity, Innocence, Goodwill, Empathy, Compassion, Understanding, Illumination, Responsibility, Work ethic, Trustworthiness, Trust, Virtue/Morality, Optimistic, Hopeful, Cheerful, Confidence

Justice
Love, Full perception, Truth/All facts, Fairness/Balance, Forgiveness, Power, Empathy, New opportunity, Illumination, Understanding, Good intention, Healing, Accountability, Humility, Integrity/Honesty, Wisdom, Compassion, Restoration, No partiality, Meaningful apology, Personal responsibility

Constructive versus Unconstructive Qualities

Builds	Destroys
Positive	Negative
Collaboration	Apathy or sabotage
Encouraging	Discouraging
Optimistic	Pessimistic
Inspiring	Shaming
Can do / Will try	Won't do / Won't try
Expecting best/success	Expecting worst/failure

Thought "Drugs" (All "drugs" are unconstructive choices gone toxic and addictive.)
Excuses, If only, then…, Denial, "No" to everything, Blame, I can't, I won't, Guilt, No time, Putting off, Chip on shoulder, Avoiding, Only my way right, Focus on what's wrong, Low self-esteem, Know-it-all, Victim mentality, Poverty / Entitlement mindset, Criminality. *Most toxic: Self-deception, Selfishness, Blame*

Feeling Choices
<u>Constructive</u>: Loving, Happy, Accepting, Peaceful, Giving, Forgiving, Thankful, Kind, Patient, Hopeful, Flexible, Respectful, Gentle, Faithful, Eager, Helpful, Open, Understanding

<u>Unconstructive</u>: Angry, Afraid, Stingy, Guilty, Hopeless, Sad, Hateful, Mean, Doubtful, Confused, Worried, Uncaring, Critical, Rejecting, Frustrated, Cowardly, Sarcastic

Feeling "Drugs"
Anger, Being a victim, Fear, Confusion, Disappointment, Not being thankful, Giving up, Hate, Criticism, Not caring/Apathy, Stressed out, Vanity, Not cooperating, Shame. *Most toxic: Self-pity*

Physical "Drugs"
Vaping, Drinking, Smoking, Sex, TV / Movies, Gossip, Social media, Video games, Stop listening, Swearing, Lying, Stealing, Cheating, Phone, Junk food, Too much / too little sleep, Internet, Too much / too little exercise, Put downs, Designer clothes, Power trips. *Most toxic: Illegal, street drugs; Misuse of prescription pharmaceuticals, Social media, Violence, Sugar*

Spirit "Drugs"
Mocking, Better than everybody else, Prejudice, Narrow minded, Racism, Fanaticism, Stingy, Judgmental, Violence / War, Deceit, Treachery, Treason, Cheating, Defamation, Using others, Getting even / revenge, Sexism, Bullying, Withholding our best, Intolerance, Criticism, Condemnation, Judgment, Mocking, Abuse, Prejudice, Dishonesty, Cheating, Manipulation, Coercion, Tyranny, Narrow minded, Stinginess, Entitlement, Withholding and/or manipulating, of information. *Most toxic: Self-righteousness, Self-justification, Entitlement, Resentment against injustice, Misuse of Information, Violence / War, Deceit, Treachery, Treason against God*

Power: Constructive vs Unconstructive

God, the I AM / LIFE	vs	worldly power
Peaceful	vs	suppressing
Calm	vs	agitated
Unifying	vs	dividing
Deep	vs	superficial
Powerful	vs	forceful, shocking
Empowering	vs	weakening
Inside toward outer	vs	outer toward inner
Gives	vs	demands
Joyful	vs	frantic
Infinite	vs	finite
Creates from within itself	vs	steals power, resources, & energy
Abiding	vs	hurried
Steadfast	vs	unfaithful
Clear	vs	distorted
True	vs	false
Dependable	vs	untrustworthy
Expansive	vs	limiting
Delivers	vs.	promises
Unconditional	vs	conditional
Free	vs	costly
Supplying	vs	depleting
Satisfies	vs	creates appetite
Fulfills	vs	creates addiction
Freeing	vs	controlling, jealous
Is	vs	uses salesmanship
Love	vs	plays on fear & selfishness
Assuring	vs	creates fear
Comforting	vs	agitating
Effortless	vs	struggling
Accepting	vs	critical
Clear	vs	confused
Honest	vs	dishonest
Patient	vs	impatient
Permanent	vs	temporary
Always there	vs	never sure

Cooperate with What Is Constructive

- See each person you meet as their Highest Common Denominator (their LIFE inside)
- Deliberately choose constructive thoughts, feelings, words, and actions personally
- Encourage constructive traits and actions in others - Encourage constructive activities
- Give to or join constructive activities - Stand up for / protect what is constructive

- Be kind, helpful, and generous - Be optimistic and stay balanced - Think, speak, and act justly
- Be courageous - Think for yourself - Stay awake, alive, and alert

Stop Cooperating with What Is Unconstructive
- Stop gossiping, supporting it, or staying where it is done
- Stop laughing at jokes that belittle a person, persons, or groups
- Do not collaborate with or support any form of injustice, including by inaction
- Do not ignore injustice - Do not ignore extreme lack or suffering
- Stop allowing yourself to be manipulated, deceived, coerced, or misused
- Stop living on "autopilot" or "cruise control"- Do not let yourself go or stay "unconscious"

Symptoms of Social Media Addiction
- Inability to turn it off
- FOMO (acute fear of missing out)
- Constant undercurrent of anxiety, inability to concentrate, very short attention span
- Overwhelmed by deluge of empty or twisted information,
- Isolation from others, shredding of IRL (real) relationships,
- Dificultly expressing love,
- Depression; feelings of inadequacy, low self-worth,
- Denying themselves love, while desperately seeking / needing it;
- Drama, increasing need to be validated

(Note that, greedy grasping for attention and affirmation is not love. It turns others into "marks" from whom to get/take affirmation.)

Other Addictions Created by Overuse of Social Media
- Acute need for constant, varied, entertaining input, (a form of attention deficit disorder)
- Expectation of ongoing rewards
    - not for excellence, but for the fundamentals of engagement
    - i.e. showing up, staying on task, actually producing something, anything
- Getting sucked into a raging, fragmented, chaotic social justice war
- Starving for reassurance of worth, for love, meaning
- Acute depression
- Feelings of inadequacy, low self-worth

Antidotes to Social Media Addiction
- Hard break - turn it off for increasingly longer times
- Ease off compulsively having to immediately answer every post, tweet, etc.
- Spending more face-to-face time in real life with real people
- Find other things that give you meaning and satisfaction that aren't connected to social media, and have mental, emotional, physical, and spiritual input with "nutritional" value

RESPONDING TO INJUSTICE

How often do you hear about, see, or experience injustice? In current times, for most of us, it is every day. Being part of creating justice requires that we learn to make constructive choices consciously and deliberately – especially in highly polarized situations of conflict. Here we have used historic and present day examples that are polar opposite ways of responding to injustice.

Constructive Response - Gandhi, as example

Thought	+ Feeling	+ Spirit/HCD	= Outcomes
All are God's Child Humility	Self-worth	See HCD & God in all	
Non-violence, Non-cooperation with evil	Humility	Inspired	Recognize truth
Get involved	Hope, Joy	Conviction	Fully engaged
Goodwill	Love, Joy	Each asked to pray Forgiveness	
Respect for all, including enemies	Empathy	Generosity	Courage,
All human life is sacred	Valued	Strength	Restraint
Inclusive	Belonging	Call to HCD of enemies	Unity, Worthiness
Goal is Justice,	Moved, Eager	Self-restraint	Means in harmony with ends
Peace for all	Meaningful,	Compassion	
Discernment	Courage		
Led by example	Assured	Inspired	Commitment
			Brits left India as friends. Unity w/ former enemies

Unconstructive Response – Terrorist as example

Thought	+ Feeling	+ Spirit/HCD	= Outcomes
Violence as modus operandi	Fear, blame,	Resentment against ....injustice	Disunity w those not "like" you
Incite violent actions	Hatred	Revenge	Destruction, Death
Deceit Secrecy	Distrust	Judgmental	Fear in in "targets"
Only those of one religion acceptable	Self-righteous	Condemning Disinherit	Demonization of others; see as enemy
Religious fanaticism	Suspicion	Deny HCD	Division
Contempt for all "outsiders"	Distrust	Exclusivity	Conflict
Human life expendable/cheap	Anger, Fear	Turmoil	Destroy and desecrate, Terrorist acts
Lead by coercion and manipulation	Increases hate	Promotes all of above	Devastation and death, Enemies created
Leaders not harmed, They send others to risk and die.	Promise Guilt	Coercion Fanaticism	Blood sacrifices
Goal: defeat, overcome, annihilate the enemy	Blind hate and rage	Terror	End justifies means, Increasing chaos, destruction, death

What more common scenarios are very much the same dynamic as the unconstructive example? Bullying - domestic violence - child abuse -profiling - tyranny and violence of any kind, including in families, corporations, organizations, communities, nations, and worldwide

Why is it imperative to be FOR what is RIGHT instead of AGAINST what is WRONG?
Once the perceived, mutual "enemy" is overcome, the tendency is to return to fighting and conflict with those with whom only a temporarily, expedient alliance was formed. What is unconstructive is not corrected. What is constructive is not yet fully created or established.

***

PUBLIC EDUCATION: Additional Information Related to Supreme Court Rulings
Consider the following information, and form your own responses to the questions.

Amendment I: Congress shall make no law respecting an establishment of religion, or prohibiting the free exercise thereof; or abridging the freedom of speech....

Amendment X: The powers not delegated to the United States by the Constitution, nor prohibited by it to the States, are reserved to the States respectively, or to the people.

US Department of Education: Traditionally in the United States, education has been primarily the responsibility of parents and local and state government. The US Constitution says nothing about education, and therefore, according to the 10th Amendment, the role of the federal government is limited.[398]

The purpose of the Supreme Court is to guard and interpret the Constitution. It does not have the power to enforce its decisions. It may not make laws. For example, it has taken generations to end segregation and race hatred. We're still working on it.

Yet, in multiple landmark decisions regarding prayer in the public schools, immediate and immeasurable change was made, not only in education, but also in moral landscape of the United States of America. Here is the most famous ruling:

- Engel v. Vitale[400], case in which the US Supreme Court ruled on June 25, 1962, that voluntary prayer in public schools violated the US Constitution's First Amendment prohibition of state establishment of religion.

They objected to this "state written" prayer:
"Almighty God, we acknowledge our dependence upon Thee, and we beg Thy blessings upon us, our parents, our teachers and our Country."[401]

With this prayer, did the government establish a religion?

There is no doctrinal bias in the language in this prayer. Therefore, it upholds the 1st Amendment's "separation of church and state." "Church" refers to a specific religious doctrine, not separation of the God and the state. "God" is the English word for Supreme Being, Creator.

A similar prayer is said at the beginning of every Congressional meeting and Court session. Its language is similar to that used in the Declaration of Independence and the Bill of Rights, Amendment I.

A complaint for ten students removed 1st Amendment rights for millions. (Not even all the students, in whose name this action was initiated, wanted it. Some had even volunteered to lead the prayers prior to the filing.

- Abington School District v. Schempp. The US Supreme Court, on July 17, 1963, ruled Bible reading in public schools to be unconstitutional.[402]

Other similar rulings are listed at the end of this section.

The ramifications of these decisions and the actions enforcing them have created tremendous changes in both our state and local education systems. Teaching standards became radically divergent to the cultural norms, overriding significant majority parental choice and consent. It began to befuddle the value base and morals of students. No Supreme Being could be acknowledged. Thereby, all ethics, previously associated with America's Judeo-Christian culture (and the same values of other major religions), were no longer accepted as valid.

Certain powers within our federal and state governments colluded with the National Education Association (NEA) and others to remove the right to teach religious and moral living to our children within public schools and their forums in America. Public schools became , very quickly, infiltrated with atheism, materialism, socialism/communism, collectivism, propaganda, and indoctrination. Our children have been directed away from the God-centered principles on which the United States of America is founded. What other governmental power, which is evident in every state in the union, was complicit?

Virtually all other, prior decisions by the Supreme Court upheld majority moral code. These two did not.[403]

Would a Supreme Court decision similar to the laws upheld by New York State have been sufficient to protect the rights of the minority, while assuring the rights of the majority? The lower courts that heard the case upheld the power of New York to allow the prayer to be said each day as long as no student was forced to participate or if the student was compelled to do so over the parents' objection.[404]

Why did the Supreme Court take away the first Amendment rights of the vast majority of US citizens to support a tiny majority?

By whose power were these rulings implemented so quickly? Again, other sweeping Supreme Court decisions have taken decades, even generations to be implemented, such as desegregation.

***

An Outline History of Religion in American Schools[405]

Comment: This overview of history documents a huge paradigm shift, not supported by the vast majority of the American people. Please heed Abraham Lincoln's wise warning below.

"The Philosophy of the school room in one generation. . .will be the Philosophy of Government in the next." - Abraham Lincoln

1620 Mayflower Compact signed: "Having undertaken for the glory of God and advancement of the Christian faith . . . furtherance of the ends aforesaid." The Pilgrims taught their children the Bible and the Christian faith.

1642 Compulsory School law passed in Massachusetts, called the "Old Deluder Satan Law ." This law was passed to assure that children could read their Bibles.

1690 Connecticut Law passed that children be taught to read so they can read Holy Scriptures.

1690 First New England Primer is published. The Alphabet is taught using Bible verses for each letter, and has questions on Bible moral teachings. The Primer contains children's prayers, the Lord's Prayer, the Ten Commandments, the Shorter Catechism, and questions on the Bible by Mr. Cotton. The New England Primer will be in wide use in American schools of all types public, private, home or parochial, for the next 200 years.

1781 Congress approves the purchase of Bibles to be used in schools.

1783 First Noah Webster (Blue Book) Speller is published, with its opening sentence declaring: "No man may put off the law of God." This speller is widely used in American schools and is peppered throughout with Bible verses. Later versions stated, "Noah Webster who taught millions to read but not one to sin."

1784 Jedediah Morse, father of American Geography, publishes the first Geography text book which contains references to Christianity.

1787 Congress passes the Northwest Ordinance which outlines requirements for governments of new territories so they can qualify for statehood. Article 3 of the Northwest Ordinance directs the people of the territories to establish schools "to teach religion, morality, and knowledge." Nearly every state admitted to the Union after this has written in their State Constitution wording that the schools are to teach morality and religion and they all use the Bible as the basis for their teachings.

1808 Washington's Farewell Address is published as a separate text book. Washington's Address is looked upon as one of the most important political documents in American history. In the speech Washington emphasizes that for America to succeed it must have a moral society which can only come from roots in the Christian faith. This text book is used until 1960's.

1830 Dr. Benjamin Rush signer of the Declaration of Independence, letter is published in support.

1836 First McGuffey reader is published which teaches the ABC's along with Bible verses. This reader is looked at as an "eclectic reader" which combine instructive axioms and proverbs, fundamentals of grammar and selections of the finest English literature.

1844 Girard proposes to teach morals without the Bible. The Supreme Court rules that American schools are to teach Christianity using the Bible. The case is argued and won by Daniel Webster. (Videl v. Girard)

1890 Supreme Court rules that America "is a religious people. . . . this is a Christian nation" as such it is fitting that its people would teach their children the Christian faith. (The Trinity Case)

1892 The American Teachers Union declare that schools should continue to teach morals from the Bible as schools are turned over to the various States from the Christian Churches. Prior to this many schools had been run by churches of various denominations. Many state Constitution's mandate the teaching of morals, religion and knowledge.

1900 Virtually all school text books published to date have contained Biblical references or teachings.

1925 Tennessee governor signs law forbidding the teaching of evolution in public schools. ACLU Lawyers take a school district to court in the famous Scopes Monkey Trial in an effort to have evolution taught in Tennessee Public Schools.

1925 Florida State legislators pass law requiring daily Bible reading in public schools.

1946 Dallas schools publish textbook titled "Bible Studies Course for New Testament." This book has many questions and answers about the life of Jesus Christ.

1948 Supreme Court rules that time set aside for prayer in public schools is unconstitutional. (McCollum v. Board of Education)

1954 The words "One Nation Under God" are add to the Pledge of Allegiance.

1962 Supreme Court rules that children may not recite a state written prayer in school (Engel v. Vitale).

1963 Supreme Court bans individual school prayer (Murry v. Curlett) and Bible reading in public schools (Abington Township School District v. Schempp.

1965 Supreme Court rules that a child may pray silently to himself if no one knows he is praying and his lips do not move.

1980 US schools report the lowest S.A.T. scores ever, after 18 straight years of decline following the 1962 ban on school prayer.

1980 Supreme Court rules that the Ten Commandments cannot be posted in classrooms, "for a child might read them, reflect upon them and then obey them." (Stone vs. Graham)

1985 Supreme Court strikes down Alabama law requiring schools to have a moment of silent meditation at the beginning of the day.

1987 Supreme Court overturns a State Law requiring a balanced treatment of creation science and evolution. (Edwards vs. Aguillard)

1992 Supreme Court rules Clergy may not offer prayer at graduation ceremonies. (Lee vs. Weisman)

1999 Two Students at Littleton, Colorado High School shoot eleven students. None of the students have ever seen the Ten Commandments, "Thou shall not Kill" in a public school.

2000 Supreme Court rules student initiated or student led prayer at football games is unconstitutional. (Doe vs. Santa Fe Independent School District)

2004 Supreme Court affirms the words "One Nation Under God" in the Pledge of Allegiance.

2008 Christian run schools and most home schooling programs continue to produce students with higher academic test results than secular public schools.

Comment regarding 1980 Supreme Court ruling on the Ten Commandments: Every major religion has an equivalent to the Ten Commandments in the Judeo-Christian religions. The fundamental difference is in the 9th Commandment "Thou shalt not bear false witness against thy neighbor." The other religions say fundamentally, "Do not lie."

Endnotes

A note on the endnotes! *This book conveys my own perceptions and understandings. These notes reflect facts and other confirmations of what I have written. They are not the source of the observations, opinions, or writings. References noted here were selected for their concise, competent, and calm presentation of information and opinion, which has also been confirmed from multiple other sources.*

Please, you are humbly asked to search out with your own prayers and research, the validity and truth of all presented in this book. I encourage you to think for yourself.

Also note that the same references may be used in multiple parts of this book where they are germane.

Attribution of Bible verses:

[Scripture quotations marked *(NRSV)* are from] New Revised Standard Version Bible, copyright © 1989 National Council of the Churches of Christ in the United States of America. Used by permission. All rights reserved worldwide.

Scripture quotations marked *(NIV)* are taken from the Holy Bible, New International Version®, NIV®. Copyright © 1973, 1978, 1984, 2011 by Biblica, Inc.™ Used by permission of Zondervan. All rights reserved worldwide. www.zondervan.com.The "NIV" and "New International Version" are trademarks registered in the United States Patent and Trademark Office by Biblica, Inc.™

[Scripture quotations marked *(RSV)* are from] Revised Standard Version of the Bible, copyright © 1946, 1952, and 1971 National Council of the Churches of Christ in the United States of America. Used by permission. All rights reserved worldwide.

The King James Version (*KJV*) of the Bible is in public domain.

I. Prologue

Mainstream media owned by 6 corporations All are multi-national
[1] Ashley Lutz, *"These 6 Corporations Control 90% of The Media In America."* Infographic created by Jason at Frugal Dad.com, posted June 14, 2020 by BusinessInsider.com (website), last accessed September 4, 2020, https://www.businessinsider.com/these-6-corporations-control-90-of-the-media-in-america-2012-6?op=1.

Definition of God
[2] www.dictionary.com, assessed May 12, 2020.

General Washington's Vision
[3] Wesley Bradshaw, *General Washington's Vision;* Reprinted, *National Tribune,* Vol. 4, No. 12, December 1880.

Speech of the Unknown
[4] George Lippard, *"The Speech of the Unknown,"* Washington and His Generals: or, Legends of the Revolution, published in 1847. (Also: *i-uv.com/the-speech-of-the-unknown/* and http://www.reversespins.com/signthatdocument.html.)

II. America is key

Why is America a Christian nation?
[5] Dinesh D' Souza (website), "#TruthStraightUp: America Is a Christian Nation," posted June 25, 2019, last accessed September 3, 2020, https://www.dineshdsouza.com/news/america-is-a-christian-nation/.

Conquest ethic:
[6] Dinesh D'Souza, Bruce Scholley, John Sullivan, writers; Dinesh D'Souza, John Sullivan, diredtors. *America: Imagine the World without Her*. 2013; Santa Monica, CA: Lions Gate, 2014. DVD.

Forms of Law:
[7] "Natural Law: The Ultimate Source of Constitutional Law," National Center for Constitutional Studies (website), last accessed September 3, 2020, https://nccs.net/blogs/our-ageless-constitution/natural-law-the-ultimate-source-of-constitutional-law.

Practical examples of living within governmental systems:
Cuba:
[8] "Cuban who windsurfed 90 mile to escape socialism warns America," ForbiddenKnowledgetv.net, posted September 13, 2019, last accessed September 3, 2020, https://forbiddenknowledgetv.net/cuban-who-windsurfed-for-90-miles-to-escape-socialism-warns-america/?utm_source=newsletter&utm_medium=email&utm_campaign=Cuban+Who+Windsurfed+for+90+Miles+to+Escape+Socialism+Warns+America.

Chinese subject surveillance:
[9] Melissa Dykes, "What's Your Social Credit Score?" Truthstream Media , ForbiddenKnowledgetv.net, posted December 29, 2019, last accessed September 3, 2020, https://forbiddenknowledgetv.net/whats-your-social-credit-score/?utm_source=newsletter&utm_medium=email&utm_campaign=What%27s+Your+Social+Credit+Score%3F.

Chinese using ethnic and religious prisoners to for organ transplants:
[10] Saporah Smith, "China forcefully harvest organs from detainees, tribunal concludes," NBC News, June 18, 2019, last accessed September 3, 2020, https://www.nbcnews.com/news/world/china-forcefully-harvests-organs-detainees-tribunal-concludes-n1018646.

Current communist worldwide agenda:
[11] Gina Shakespeare, "Is Your Country Actually Communist?" The Epoch Times, ForbiddenKnowledgetv.net, posted, July 6, 2019, last accessed September 3, 2020, https://forbiddenknowledgetv.net/is-your-country-actually-communist/.

Communism rose out of the writings of Karl Marx and is called Marxism:
Paul Kengor, *The Devil and Karl Marx: Communism's Long March of Death, Deception, and Infiltration,* (Gastonia, North Carolina: TAN Books, 2020)

Eyewitness account of communist take-over of Ethiopia, once the oldest Christian nation in the world:
[12] Marta Gabre-Sadick, *Sheltered by the King,* (United States of America; self-published, 2008), pp. 57-80, 127.

Corporatism:
[13] Friedrich Moser and Matthieu Lietaert, "The Brussels Business – Who Runs the EU?," ForbiddenKnowledgetv.net, posted July 6, 2019, last accessed September 3, 2020, https://forbiddenknowledgetv.net/the-brussels-business-who-runs-the-eu/.

Alexandra Bruce, John Chambers, "Corporate Communism and the Deep State," MSOM, ForbiddenKnowledgetv.net, October 1, 2020, last accessed October 4, 2020, https://forbiddenknowledgetv.net/corporate-communism-and-the-deep-state/, or https://www.youtube.com/watch?v=-PzZ1TdQZN8

Techno fascism:
[14] Dr. Robert Epstein, "Big Tech Censorship testimony to Judiciary Subcommittee SD 226 of the Senate on their influencing voting," ForbiddenKnowledgetv.net, posted July 20, 2019, last accessed September 3, 2020, Video and transcript: https://forbiddenknowledgetv.net/dr-robert-epstein-on-big-tech-censorship/.

Peter Svab, *"Facebook and Its CEO Emerge as Powerful Influence on 2020 Elections," The Epoch Times, Nation,* September 16-22, 2020, pp. A1, A4-A5.

More on Google:
BitChute, posted June 24, 2019, last accessed September 3, 2020, video:
https://www.bitchute.com/video/re9Xp6cdkro/?utm_source=newsletter&utm_medium=email&utm_campaign=Techno-Fascism+Revealed
Back up, posted June 24, 2019, last accessed September 3, 2020:
https://www.projectveritas.com/2019/06/24/insider-blows-whistle-exec-reveals-google-plan-to-prevent-trump-situation-in-2020-on-hidden-cam.

China's social surveillances of their people:
[15] Melissa Dykes, "What's Your Social Credit Score?", Truthstream Media, ForbiddenKnowledgetv.net, posted Dec. 29, 2019, last accessed September 3, 2020, https://forbiddenknowledgetv.net/whats-your-social-credit-score/?utm_source=newsletter&utm_medium=email&utm_campaign=What%27s+Your+Social+Credit+Score%3F.

Brain implants from Elon Musk's company:
[16] Greg Reese, "Neurolink: The War Against Humanity Goes Mainstream," NewsWars.com, ForbiddenKnowledgetv.net, posted July 20, 2019, last accessed September 3, 2020, https://forbiddenknowledgetv.net/neuralink-the-war-against-humanity-goes-mainstream/?utm_source=newsletter&utm_medium=email&utm_campaign=Neuralink%3A+The++Against+Humanity+Goes+Mainstream.

Democracy or republic?
[17] James D. Best, *"A Republic, if you can keep it,"* What Would the Founders Think (website), last accessed September 3, 2020, http://www.whatwouldthefoundersthink.com/a-republic-if-you-can-keep-it.

Abraham Lincoln quote:
[18] AZ Quotes, last accessed September 4, 2020, https://www.azquotes.com/author/8880-Abraham_Lincoln.

Definition of "stewardship:"
[19] www.dictionary.com.

Ben Franklin quote acknowledging God doing the building:
[20] "Benjamin Franklin, quotes by this author," Our Republic (website), last accessed September 5, 2020, http://www.ourrepubliconline.com/Author/21.

III. Where we are now

Pandemic related:
Pandemic medical experts' connections:
[21] Greg Reese, "Medical Tyranny 2020," InfoWars.com; ForbiddenKnowledgetv.net, posted Apr. 10, 2020, last accessed September 3, 2020, https://forbiddenknowledgetv.net/medical-tyranny-2020/.

COVID-19 morbidity facts:
[22] Tony Robins with Dr. Michael Levitt, "The Truth About Mortality Rates," ForbiddenKnowledgetv.net, posted June 1, 2020, last accessed September 3, 2020, https://www.youtube.com/watch?v=sEbcs37aaI0&feature=emb_rel_end.

Dr Reiner Fuellmich, "Crimes against Humanity: Class Action Lawsuits Incoming," ForbiddenKnowledgetv.net, October 6, 2020, https://forbiddenknowledgetv.net/crimes-against-humanity/.

Daniele Pozzati, "German Official Leaks Report Denouncing Corona as 'A Global False Alarm'," Strategic Culture Foundation, May 29, 2020, last accessed October 6, 2020 https://www.strategic-culture.org/news/2020/05/29/german-official-leaks-report-denouncing-corona-as-global-false-alarm/

Informed medical knowledge related to COVID-19 vaccines:
[23]Dr. Carrie Madjed, *"The most important video you'll every watch,"* ForbiddenKnowledgetv.net, posted July 13, 2020, last accessed September 3, 2020, https://www.youtube.com/watch?v=8kpJESKPqCo

Mandatory vaccine policy:
[24]Y. Tony Yang and Dorit Rubinstein Reiss, "A federal COVID-19 vaccine mandate: Dubious legality, faulty policy," The Hill, July 23, 2020, last accesses September 12, 2020, https://thehill.com/opinion/healthcare/508773-a-federal-covid-19-vaccine-mandate-dubious-legality-faulty-policy.

Contact tracing:
[25] Ashkan Soltani, Ryan Calo, and Carl Bergstrom, "Contact-tracing apps are not a solution to the COVID-19 crisis ," Bookings Institute, *Tech Streams* (blog), April 27, 2020, last accessed September 12, 2020, https://www.brookings.edu/techstream/inaccurate-and-insecure-why-contact-tracing-apps-could-be-a-disaster/

First Amendment:
[26]Tom Head, "The First Amendment: Text, Origins, and Meaning," Thoughtco (website), updated January 30, 2018, last accessed September 13, 2020, https://www.thoughtco.com/the-first-amendment-p2-721185.

The Bill of Rights, Constitutional Amendment #4:
[27]"The Bill of Rights (Amendments 1 - 10)," National Center for Constitutional Studies (website), last accessed September 7, 2020, https://nccs.net/blogs/americas-founding-documents/bill-of-rights-amendments-1-10.

Armen Nikogosian, *"Body Autonomy – the Core of Personal Freedom," The Epoch Times, April 30-May 6,2020.*

The Bill of Rights, Constitutional Amendment #5:
[28]"The Bill of Rights (Amendments 1 - 10)," National Center for Constitutional Studies (website), last accessed September 7, 2020, https://nccs.net/blogs/americas-founding-documents/bill-of-rights-amendments-1-10.

Pandemic control overreach:
[29]Naom, "DOCTORS IN BLACK – PlanDemic, a film about the global plan to take control of our lives, liberty, health & freedom," Videotube, last accessed September 3, 2020, https://bannedvids.com/doctors-in-black-plandemic/.

Dr Reiner Fuellmich, "Crimes against Humanity: Class Action Lawsuits Incoming," ForbiddenKnowledgetv.net, October 6, 2020, https://forbiddenknowledgetv.net/crimes-against-humanity/.

Brave Doctors speak out about COVID-19:
Austen Fletcher of the Fleccas Talks, "Brave Doctors Breakdown COVID Response and Demonization HCQ," ForbiddenKnowledgetv.net, posted June 19, 2020, last accessed September 3, 2020, https://forbiddenknowledgetv.net/doctors-break-down-covid-response-and-the-demonization-of-hcq/.

Financial incentives to perpetuate coronavirus response:
Carly Ortiz-Lytle, "Tucker Carlson shocked when guest explains 'profound' financial incentives to perpetuate coronavirus response," Fox News (website), September 08, 2020, https://www.washingtonexaminer.com/news/tucker-carlson-shocked-and-embarrassed-to-hear-coronavirus-has-become-big-business-on-air.

Health costs of COVID lockdown:
[30]Andrew Glen, Ph.D. and James D. Agresti , *"Anxiety From Reactions to Covid-19 Will Destroy At Least Seven Times More Years of Life Than Can Be Saved by Lockdowns,"* ForbiddenKnowledgetv.net, posted June 19, 2020, last accessed September 3, 2020, https://www.justfacts.com/news_covid-19_anxiety_lockdowns_life_destroyed_saved.

[31]*Mental Health Crisis due to lockdown:*

Bowen Xiao, *"Shutdown Spur Mental Health Crisis in US, Experts Say,"* The Epoch Times, No. 318, August 26-September 1, 2020, page 1.

Dr Reiner Fuellmich, "Crimes against Humanity: Class Action Lawsuits Incoming," ForbiddenKnowledgetv.net, October 6, 2020, https://forbiddenknowledgetv.net/crimes-against-humanity/.

Daniele Pozzati, "German Official Leaks Report Denouncing Corona as 'A Global False Alarm'," Strategic Culture Foundation, May 29, 2020, last accessed October 6, 2020 https://www.strategic-culture.org/news/2020/05/29/german-official-leaks-report-denouncing-corona-as-global-false-alarm/

Jack Phillips, *"Judge Rules Pennsylvania Governor's Shutdown Orders Unconstitutional,"* US NEWS. September 14, 2020 Updated: September 14, 2020,
https://www.theepochtimes.com/judge-rules-pennsylvania-governors-shutdown-orders-unconstitutional_3499183.html?ref=brief_News&utm_source=morningbrief&utm_medium=email&utm_campaign=mb

Plea for the voiceless victims – and for essential freedoms:
[32]Henna Marie, "Voiceless Victims of the COVID," ForbiddenKnowledgetv.net, posted Aug. 17, 2020, last accessed September 3, 2020, https://forbiddenknowledgetv.net/voiceless-victims-of-the-covid-lockdowns/.

Uncovered massive child trafficking by satanists
Massive child trafficking by satanists:
[33]Mabel P. Bronson, "The Tunnel Children"; David Zublick, producer, on Dark Outpost; posted June 26, 2020, last accessed September 3, 2020, https://timothycharlesholmseth.com/the-tunnel-children-featured-on-dark-outpost/.

Tunnels (Deep Underground Military Bunkers aka DUMBS – NOT US military) Q Info January 2020
 Coloseneil64@gmail.com , "The Underground War, Happening Now," posted Jan. 8, 2020, last accessed September 3, 2020, https://www.youtube.com/watch?v=yoQUrXzbvf4\.

"Raca" definition
[34]Got Questions: Your Questions. Biblical Answers. https://www.gotquestions.org/raca.html.

Who is funding the rioting?
[35]Spiro Skouras, *"Who Is Funding Black Lives Matter and Why?"* ; ForbidenKnowledgetv.net, posted June 26, 2020, last accessed September 4, 2020, https://forbiddenknowledgetv.net/who-is-funding-black-lives-matter-and-why-the-answer-may-shock-you/.

Individual asserts he is paid to riot – and so are many others - by George Soros:
[36]This link was last accessed in July 2020, The YouTube account associated with it has been "terminated."
https://www.youtube.com/watch?v=UnqasusPW70.

Where does your donation to Black Lives Matter go?
Alexandra Bruce, John Chambers, "Corporate Communism and the Deep State," MSOM, ForbiddenKnowledgetv.net, October 1, 2020, last accessed October 4, 2020, https://forbiddenknowledgetv.net/corporate-communism-and-the-deep-state/, or https://www.youtube.com/watch?v=-PzZ1TdQZN8. [time: 12:48-13:08]

On the early morning of October 5, 2020 , a query for this link, www.antifa.com , was redirected to https://joebiden.com/ [A battle ensued to change it beginning at 10:26 AM.]

Important opinions not given mass-media coverage
Muhamad Ali, Jr. speaks out against BLM:
[37]Erika Marie, *Muhammad Ali's Son Says Boxer Would Have Hated BLM Protests: They're Terrorists!,"* HotNewHipHop.com, posted June 22, 2020, last accessed September 4, 2020,

https://www.hotnewhiphop.com/muhammad-alis-son-says-boxer-would-have-hated-blm-protests-theyre-terrorists-news.113062.html.

Excellent overviews of the dynamics of the George Floyd riots (profanity alert on first one!):
[38]Seraphim Hanisch, "Soros, Clinton Foundation behind Antifa and Black Lives Matter" *[Video],* Sergeant StickItTooYa, The Duran posted June 10, 2020, last accessed September 4 2020, https://theduran.com/soros-clinton-foundation-behind-antifa-and-black-lives-matter-video/.

Candace Owens joins Glenn Beck, "Candace Owens: This Is What's Really Driving the Race Riots in America," ForbiddenKnowledgetv.net posted June 26, 2020, last accessed September, 4, 2020, https://forbiddenknowledgetv.net/candace-owens-this-is-whats-really-driving-the-race-riots-in-america/. [start at 11:30]

The historic roots of Black Lives Matter:
Reagan, "The White Man Behind Black Lives Matter," ForbiddenKnowledgetv.net, October 2, 2020, last accessed October 4, 2020, https://forbiddenknowledgetv.net/the-secret-origins-of-black-lives-matter/, or https://www.youtube.com/watch?v=Sq1m_PJtu5o.

Terry Turchie, "Attack & Dethrone God' Is Goal of Protests, Says Former FBI Agent Terry Turchie," *The Ingraham Angle,* Fox News, posted on Heavy on June 2020, last accessed October 9, 2020, https://heavy.com/news/2020/06/attack-and-dethrone-god/.

More funding sources make themselves known
269 corporations who have voiced support and made donations to rioters' funds and Black Lives Matter, etc. :
[39]Tim Brown, *"List of 269 Companies Supporting ANTIFA, Black Lives Matter,"* (list by Ashley Rae Goldenberg), Conservative Firing Line.com (website), posted June 9, 2020, last accessed September 4, 2020, https://conservativefiringline.com/list-of-269-companies-supporting-antifa-black-lives-matter/.

How have large corporations used their financial support historically?
Alexandra Bruce, John Chambers, "Corporate Communism and the Deep State," MSOM, ForbiddenKnowledgetv.net, October 1, 2020, last accessed October 4, 2020, https://forbiddenknowledgetv.net/corporate-communism-and-the-deep-state/, or https://www.youtube.com/watch?v=-PzZ1TdQZN8.

China declared war on the United States publically in May 2019
[40]Joshua Phillipp, "Tracking Down the Origin of the Wuhan Virus," The Epoch Times, ; ForbidenKnowledtetv.net posted April 7, 2020, last accessed September 4, 2020, https://forbiddenknowledgetv.net/tracking-down-the-origin-of-the-wuhan-coronavirus/, [Chinese expert, toward end of video, states source for declaration of war - time: 41:43].

Chinese involvement in US unrest
Previously unknown prelude to rioting: Chinese military on US soil:
[41]Joshua Phillipp, *Cross Roads*, broadcast August, 21, 2020; ForbidenKnowledtetv.net posted Aug. 23, 2020, last accessed September 3, 2020, https://forbiddenknowledgetv.net/nothing-to-eat-goes-viral-in-china/. Time: 9:15-12:15.

Fake IDs throughout US first six months of 2020:
[42]Gregory Hoyt (posted by), "CBP Seized Nearly 20K Fake IDs in First Six Months of 2020 – and That's Just Chicago Alone," Law Enforcement Today, posted August 9, 2020, last accessed Sept 3, 2020, https://www.lawenforcementtoday.com/cbp-have-seized-nearly-20k-fake-ids-in-first-six-months-of-2020-and-thats-just-chicago-alone/,

Protests expand

[43]Bowen Xiao, "After Weeks of Violent Protests, Some Now Call for Toppling of Jesus Statues," *The Epoch Times*, June 24, 2020 (online),
https://www.theepochtimes.com/some-activists-call-for-toppling-of-jesus-statues-amid-unrest_3400160.html?ref=brief_News&__sta=vhg.uosvpxbljqoa.luesp%7CUYJ&__stm_medium=email&__stm_source=smartech.

[44]Xiao, *Toppling of Statues*.

[45]Xiao, *Toppling of Statues*.

[46]Michael Walsh, "The Left Pushes to Finally Take Down America," The Epoch Times, June 24, 2020, (online)
https://www.theepochtimes.com/the-left-pushes-to-finally-take-down-america_3400013.html?ref=brief_Opinions&__sta=vhg.uosvpxbljqoa.luesp%7CUYJ&__stm_medium=email&__stm_source=smartech.

What is the source and strategy of the riots?
Alexandra Bruce, John Chambers, "Corporate Communism and the Deep State," MSOM, ForbiddenKnowledgetv.net, October 1, 2020, last accessed October 4, 2020, https://forbiddenknowledgetv.net/corporate-communism-and-the-deep-state/, or https://www.youtube.com/watch?v=-PzZ1TdQZN8. [time: 11:00-12:33]

[47]*Mainstream media owned by 6 corporations. All are multi-national:*
Ashley Lutz, "These 6 Corporations Control 90% of the Media In America." (Infographic created by Jason at Frugal Dad.com), posted June 14, 2020 by BusinessInsider.com (website), last accessed September 4, 2020, https://www.businessinsider.com/these-6-corporations-control-90-of-the-media-in-america-2012-6?op=1.

Floyd's family gets United Nations involved:
[48]Penny Star, "George Floyd's Family Petitions United Nations to Help Disarm Police in the United States" Breitbart (website), June 8 2020, last accessed September 4, 2020, https://www.breitbart.com/politics/2020/06/08/george-floyds-family-petitions-united-nations-help-disarm-police-united-states/.

Facts and statistics regarding black males being targeted by the police:
[49]C. Douglas Golden, "Stats" Systemic Police Racism Is a Myth," *(*featuring Heather Mac Donald, the Thomas W. Smith Fellow at the Manhattan Institute), The Western Journal (website) published June 4, 2020, last accessed September 4, 2020,
https://www.westernjournal.com/stats-systemic-police-racism-myth/.

Ron Hosko, "The Truth about Fatal Shootings by Police," Fox News (website) published January 14, 2018, last accessed September 4, 2020, https://www.foxnews.com/opinion/ron-hosko-the-truth-about-fatal-shootings-by-police.

Calls for UN Peacekeepers to replace police
US Constitution forbids foreign military on American soil:
[50]By Daniel V. McGonigle III, "Why Can't Foreign Troops Occupy American Soil?—Answers Through Analysis of Constitutional Language, Intent and Word Meanings," Camp Constitution (website), posted
August 22, 2012, last accessed September 4, 2020, http://campconstitution.net/why-cant-foreign-troops-occupy-american-soil-answers-through-analysis-of-constitutional-language-intent-and-word-meanings/.

To what end have UN peace keepers been used in the past:
Alexandra Bruce, John Chambers, "Corporate Communism and the Deep State," MSOM, ForbiddenKnowledgetv.net, October 1, 2020, last accessed October 4, 2020, https://forbiddenknowledgetv.net/corporate-communism-and-the-deep-state/, or https://www.youtube.com/watch?v=-PzZ1TdQZN8. [time: 12:33-12:47]

2016 Executive order allow UN to use force on American people:
[51]Aaron Kesel, "Executive Order: United Nations allowed to Use Force on US Citizens," *WeAreChange* (blog), posted July 13, 2016, last accessed September 4, 2020,
https://wearechange.org/executive-order-united-nations-allowed-use-force-us-citizens/.

2016 President Obama approves UN use of force within America:
Edith M. Lederer, "US approves UN use of force to protect civilians in conflict," Associated Press (website), posted May 11, 2016, last accessed September 4, 2020,
https://apnews.com/e91e15f98a8b4050ba71834b6865931a.

Find out how many UN troops currently in USA:
"*Troop and Police Contributors*" United Nation's Peacekeeping (website), https://peacekeeping.un.org/en/troop-and-police-contributors [NOTE: When I first last accessed this website in June 2020, it listed over 2,000 UN troops on US soil. Last accessed on September 4, 2020, the number given was 29.]

Use of UN peace to overthrow governments:
Alexandra Bruce, John Chambers, "Corporate Communism and the Deep State," MSOM, ForbiddenKnowledgetv.net, October 1, 2020, last accessed October 4, 2020, https://forbiddenknowledgetv.net/corporate-communism-and-the-deep-state/, or https://www.youtube.com/watch?v=-PzZ1TdQZN8. [time: 12:33-12:47]

Spiro Skouras "The Hidden Agenda Behind the Planned Destruction of America with Rosa Koire,"ForbiddenKnowledgetv.net, posted Jun 12, 2020, accessed last September 24, 2020, https://www.youtube.com/watch?v=EGA18p_XerE&feature=emb_title.

Video: projected ramifications of executive order:
Citizen Rogue "Foreign Troops In America - Pres Obama's Executive Order That changed U.S. Law" Conspiracy Files/Rogue Underground posted September 4, 2016, last accessed September 4, 2020, https://www.youtube.com/watch?v=D9CuF0Ww0V0.

Noted in executive order article:
[52]Myron C. Fagan, Internet Archive (website), posted? Dated June 11, 1951, last accessed September 4, 2020, https://archive.org/stream/MyronC.Fagan/Fagan,%20Myron%20C.-CEG-HQ-18_djvu.txt;
Very short excerpts from 1951 UN invasion plan in America:
"Well, I will concede that Kuchel was correct on one point:
Mr. Jackman, a dedicated American patriot, WAS the Paul
Revere who first sounded that "alarm!* But in all other respects,
Mr. Jackman was correct: The 'WATER MOCCASIN" maneuvers
was to have been the first of a series of similar projects
planned for every state in the Union. It was to have been
the perfect camouflage {the plotters hoped) for infiltration
into the United States of at least two million foreign troops
from various pro-Communist nations and from the new Afro-
Asian "nations** created by the UN, The idea behind it was the
creation of a "United Nations** army within the U. S. . . . the
same kind of an "army** that transformed Katanga into a horrible
shambles. ... an "army** that was to be held in readiness for
the final sequence in the overall Great Conspiracy for the
take-over of America by the UN,...

[August & September 1951]
WORLD GOVERNMENT PLAN — ALIEN TROOPS TO POLICE U.S.A.

"In the preamble to the PLAN, it states that (A) the UN will proceed to provides for disarmament to be carried out by the One World Police. A revision of its Charter and (B) this revision will transform the UN into Force which is provided for in proposal (2), viz., "this force to be a Federated World Government in conformity with proposals which responsible only to the One World Government and the various provide in part (1) "once a State (nation) has been admitted into Agencies of the U.N." It also provides that each Province (nation) has been admitted into Agencies of the U.N. It also provides that each Province (nation)
membership it shall have no right of secession." This proposal also within the One World Government would be policed by foreign troops.

"The map shows what alien troops would occupy and police the six regions into which the United States and Canada would be divided. Thus, you will note, the United States, according to their diabolical plan, would be policed by Mongolians, Belgians, Russians, Irish, Venezuelans and Colombians. No native Americans would be allowed to police American citizens."
...full file goes through October 6. 1966

Orthodox Jews in New York city sue its mayor and the state's governor
[53]VINnews, "Orthodox Jews Sue Cuomo And de Blasio Over 'Blatant Double-Standard'," Vos Iz Nelas? (website) posted June 12, 2020, last accessed September 4, 2020, https://vosizneias.com/2020/06/12/orthodox-jews-sue-cuomo-and-de-blasio-over-blatant-double-standard/.

First Amendment:
Tom Head, "The First Amendment: Text, Origins, and Meaning," Thoughtco (website), Updated January 30, 2018, last accessed September 13, 2020, https://www.thoughtco.com/the-first-amendment-p2-721185.

[54]In author's community

[55]In author's community

United States relationship with China shifts
[56]Bowen Xiao, "US Will No Longer Be Passive Toward China, White House Adviser Says," The Epoch Times, June 25, 2020, online, last accessed September 4, 2020, https://www.theepochtimes.com/us-officials-escalate-warnings-of-threat-posed-by-chinese-communist-party_3401764.html?ref=brief_News&__sta=vhg.uosvpxbljqoa.luesp%7CTYJ&__stm_medium=email&__stm_source=smartech.

[57]Isabel Van Brugen, "China is Biggest Threat to US, Over 2,000 Investigations Tied to Communist Regime," The Epoch Times, June 25, 2020, last accessed September 4, 2020,https://www.theepochtimes.com/fbi-china-is-biggest-threat-to-us-over-2000-investigations-tied-to-communist-regime_3401327.html.

Chinese companies backed by the Chinese military:
[58]Frank Fang, "Pentagon Lists 20 Chinese Companies as Backed by Chinese Military, Including Huawei The Epoch Times (website), updated June 26, 2020, last accessed September 4, 2020, https://www.theepochtimes.com/pentagon-names-20-chinese-companies-as-backed-by-chinese-military_3401480.html.

Protests continue
US on evolutions and rebellion listing:
[59]Wikipedia lists George Floyd protests on their worldwide list of "List of revolutions and rebellions"
"2020-present: George Floyd protests in the US.," Wikipedia, last accessed September 4, 2020, https://duckduckgo.com/?t=ffab&q=wikipedia+list+or+revolutions+and+revolts&ia=web. [11/12/2020: content for this page has been changed.]

Black Lives Matter: genuine, grassroots leaders quit:
[60]Timcast,"...BLM Leaders QUITTING Due To Far Left And Antifa," timcast.net, posted by ForbiddenKnowledgetv.net, July 5, 2020, last accessed on September 8, 2020, https://www.youtube.com/watch?time_continue=588&v=zgsbhUtGypU&feature=emb_title; [START ~9:40].

Torture in worldwide PsyOp?
[61]Greg Reese, "Worldwide Population Being Tortured in Deep State PsyOps," InfoWars.com, posted by ForbiddenKnowledgetv.net July 6, 2020, last accessed September 8, 2020, https://forbiddenknowledgetv.net/worldwide-population-being-tortured-in-deep-state-psyop/.

Signs of Americans rising together
[62]*Father of CHOP murdered son:*

Shawn Hannity, "Father of teen killed in Seattle's CHOP has heartbreaking plea to the public," Fox News / Hannity (website), July 1, 2020, last accessed September 4, 2020) https://www.youtube.com/watch?v=NORWxPQz0eI&feature=emb_rel_end.

Churches leading discussions toward racial community harmony and unity:
[63]In author's community

#WalkAway movement expands enough to attract resistance:
[64]Bob Price, "VIDEOS: BLM Attacks #WalkAway Event in Texas," Breibart, September 5, 2020, last accessed September 13, 2020,https://www.breitbart.com/border/2020/09/05/videos-blm-attacks-conservative-group-in-texas/.

#WalkAway: founder Brandon Straka's early speech:
"WalkAway March – Brandon Straka,"ForbiddenKnowledgetv.net, posted October 30, 2018, last accessed September 8, 2020, https://forbiddenknowledgetv.net/walkaway-march-brandon-straka/.

V. Back to the heart of all good

Ben Franklin quote:
[65]"Benjamin Franklin, quotes by this author," Our Republic (website), last accessed September 5, 2020, http://www.ourrepubliconline.com/Author/21.

VI. Love or fear?

[66]*A Course in Miracles,* (China: Barnes & Noble Inc., 2007). printed in China.

[67]Dr. Jordon Peterson, "Pathology of Ideological Possession Definition," Caige Mang, post and comments by Chris Caige, December 5, 2018, last accessed September 7, 2020, https://www.youtube.com/watch?v=rBDXpFei3KE.

VII. Shifting the paradigm

[68]*Definition of "paradigm":*
www.dictionary.com (website)

Illustrations:,

[69] Spoked wheel model, © 1998-2020 Living Consciously® LLC., printed by permission.

[70]Dominant paradigm, © 1998-2020 Living Consciously® LLC., printed by permission.

Definition of "egoism":
[71]Huber Gray Buehler, *Practical Exercises in English*, (New York: Harper & Brothers Publishers, 1896).

[72]Illustration:
[72]God-centered paradigm, © 1998-2020 Living Consciously® LLC., printed by permission.

Abraham Lincoln quote:
[73]AZ Quotes, last accessed September 4, 2020, https://www.azquotes.com/author/8880-Abraham_Lincoln.

VIII. Focusing the lenses of clarity

[74]"Wisdom" or "Wisdom of Solomon" is one of the Apocryphal /Deuterocanonical Books of Scripture .

[75]Rev. Al Duyck, circa 1995. Quoted with his permission.

Illustrations:
[76]Aspects of LIFE, © 1998-2020 Living Consciously® LLC., printed by permission.

[77]Dynamics of Change, © 1998-2020 Living Consciously® LLC., printed by permission.

All other content used with permission from the curricula of Living Consciously®, Serving Consciously™, Working Consciously™, Leading Consciously™. © 1998-2020 Living Consciously® LLC. All rights reserved. Published by Living Consciously® LLC.

IX. Constructive vs unconstructive power

Illustrations:
[78]Concerning power, © 1998-2020 Living Consciously® LLC., printed by permission.

Increasing rates of entitlement and narcissism in high school seniors:
[79]Jean Twenge, PhD, *Generation Me,* (New York: Simon & Schuster, 2017).

Eye-witness account to use of unconstructive power by communists:
[80]Marta Gabre-Sadick, *Sheltered by the King,* (United States of America; self-published, 2008), pp. 57-80, 127.

 All other content used with permission from the curricula of Living Consciously®, Serving Consciously™, Working Consciously™, Leading Consciously™. © 1998-2020 Living Consciously® LLC. All rights reserved. Published by Living Consciously® LLC.

X. An historic flyover

Jesus and the Pharisees, practitioners of the Babylonian Talmud (not to be confused with the Jerusalem or Palestinian Talmud):
"The Babylonian Talmud: The Jews Most Unholy Book," Esau Today, posted September 11, 2017, last accessed October 5, 2020, http://esau.today/the-babylonian-talmud/.

Cohen G. Reckart, Pastor, "The Babylonian Talmud," Apostolic Messianic Fellowship, last accessed October 5, 2020, http://jesus-messiah.com/apologetics/jewish/talmud.html.

Constantine and church doctrine:
[81]David Potter, *The Emperors of Rome,* (New York: Metro Books, 2011) pp. 189, 191-192.

[82]Potter, *Emperors,* p. 192.

Slavery and oppression in Europe
Serfdom:
[83]"History of Serfdom," Wikipedia, last accessed September 7. 2020, https://en.wikipedia.org/wiki/History_of_serfdom.

The Inquisition:
[84]Editors, "Inquisition," History.com, updated Aug. 21,2018, last accessed September 4, 2020, https://www.history.com/topics/religion/inquisition.

"Inquisition," Wikipedia, last accessed September 4, 2020, https://en.wikipedia.org/wiki/Inquisition.

Wikipedia, *Inquisition*

Ottoman Empire invasion in Europe:
[85]"Ottoman wars in Europe," Wikipedia, last accessed September 4, 2020, https://en.wikipedia.org/wiki/Ottoman_wars_in_Europe.

[86]Editors, "Ottoman Empire," Britannica (website), last accessed September 4, 2020, https://www.britannica.com/place/Ottoman-Empire/Ottoman-institutions-in-the-14th-and-15th-centuries.

Atrocity focused on women and free-thinkers:
[87]"Malleus Maleficarum," Wikipedia (website), last accessed September 6, 2020, https://en.wikipedia.org/wiki/Malleus_Maleficarum.

[88]Editors, "Malleus Maleficarum," Britannica (website), last accessed September 6, 2020, https://www.britannica.com/topic/Malleus-maleficarum.

[89]Jone Johnson Lewis, *"Malleus Maleficarum, the Medieval Witch Hunter Book,"* Thought Co. (website), updated Feb. 16, 2019, last accessed September 4, 2020, https://www.thoughtco.com/malleus-maleficarum-witch-document-3530785.

Witches Hammer death toll:
[90]Morgan L. Stringer "A War on Women? The Malleus Maleficarum and the Witch-Hunts in Early Modern Europe," a thesis, Oxford, p. 1, May 2015, last accessed September 4, 2020, http://thesis.honors.olemiss.edu/459/1/Malleus%20Maleficarum%20Final.pdf.

First common language translation of the Bible
[91]Editors, "Translation of the Bible," Britannica, last accessed September 4, 2020, https://www.britannica.com/biography/John-Wycliffe/Translation-of-the-Bible.

Paul F. Pavao, *"The Martin Luther Bible Translation,"* Christian History for Everyman, last accessed September 4. 2020, https://www.christian-history.org/martin-luther-bible.html,

Protestant Reformation:
[92]"Reformation," Wikipedia, last accessed September 4 , 2020, https://en.wikipedia.org/wiki/Protestant_Reformation.

[93]Pavao, *Martin Luther Bible.*

[94]Amanda Casanova, "10 Things Everyone Should Know about Mennonites and Their Beliefs," Christianity.com, last accessed September 5, 2020, https://www.christianity.com/church/denominations/10-things-everyone-should-know-about-mennonites-and-their-beliefs.html.

Illuminati
[95]"Illuminati," Wikipedia, accessed September 14, 2020,https://en.wikipedia.org/wiki/Illuminati.

Declaration of Independence
Speech of the Unknown:
[96]George Lippard, *Washington and His Generals: or, Legends of the Revolution*, published in 1847.

Frederick Douglass:
[97]Jimmy Sengenberger, "Stop Misquoting the Great Abolitionist Frederick Douglass to Slander America," The Federalist (website), posted July 8, 2020, last accessed September 5, 2020, *https://thefederalist.com/2020/07/08/stop-misquoting-the-great-abolitionist-frederick-douglass-to-slander-america/.*

[98]National Archives, last accessed September 6, 2020. https://www.archives.gov/founding-docs/declaration-transcript .

Constitution of the United State of America
[99]"Constitution Annotated,"Constitution.Congress.gov, last accessed September 6, 2020, https://constitution.congress.gov/constitution/.

What is America? Ben Franklin's quote on the USA being a republic:
[100]"Benjamin Franklin, quotes by this author," Our Republic (website), last accessed September 5, 2020, http://www.ourrepubliconline.com/Author/21.

[101]"The day the Constitution was ratified," National Constitution Center, *Constitution Daily* (blog), February 27, 2015, last accessed September 7, 2020, https://constitutioncenter.org/blog/the-day-the-constitution-was-ratified/

[102]Dinesh Souza (website), "#TruthStraightUp: America Is a Christian Nation," posted June 25, 2019, last accessed September 3, 2020, https://www.dineshdsouza.com/news/america-is-a-christian-nation/.

[103]Douglass, *Stop Quoting.*

1830-1850: Enslavement of Native Americans
[104]"Trail of Tears," Wikipedia, last accessed September 7, 2020, https://en.wikipedia.org/wiki/Trail_of_Tears.

[105]"One drop rule," Wikipedia, accessed September 4, 2020, https://en.wikipedia.org/wiki/One-drop_rule.

Dinesh D'Souza, Bruce Scholley, John Sullivan, writers; Dinesh D'Souza, John Sullivan, diredtors. *America: Imagine the World without Her.* 2013; Santa Monica, CA: Lions Gate, 2014. DVD.

"Native Americans," Wikipedia, last accessed September 5, 2020, https://en.wikipedia.org/wiki/One-drop_rule#Native_Americans.

1837-today: Urban plantations:
[106]D'Souza, Dinesha and Scholley, Bruce, writers and directors. *Death of a Nation, Can We Save America a Second Time?* 2018; Calabassa, CA: Quality Flix, 2018. DVD.

Lincoln elected and his views on slavery
[107]"1860 United States presidential election," Wikipedia, last accessed September 5, 2020, https://en.wikipedia.org/wiki/1860_United_States_presidential_election.

[108]D'Souza, Dinesha and Scholley, Bruce, writers and directors. *Death of a Nation, Can We Safe America a Second Time?* 2018; Calabassa, CA: Quality Flix, 2018. DVD.

[109]"Interview with Dr. Allen Guelszo," *Death of a Nation*, dir. by Dinesh D'Souza and Bruce Scholley (2018; Calabassa, CA: Quality Flix, 2018) DVD.

[110]Guelszo, *Death of a Nation.*

[111]"George Fitzhugh," Wikipedia, last accessed September 5, 2020, https://en.wikipedia.org/wiki/George_Fitzhugh.

[112]George Fitzhugh, *"Horace and his Lost Book,"* Southern Literary Messenger," Volume 31, Issue 3, 1860.

1861-1865 The Civil War
[113]D'Souza, Dinesha and Scholley, Bruce, writers and directors. *Death of a Nation, Can We Save America a Second Time?* 2018; Calabassa, CA: Quality Flix, 2018. DVD.

[114]Timcast,"...BLM Leaders QUITTING Due To Far Left And Antifa," timcast.net, posted by ForbiddenKnowledgetv.net, July 5, 2020, last accessed on September 8, 2020,

1865: 13th Amendment
[115]"The Thirteenth Amendment, Passage by the House," Harp Week (website), last accessed September 5, 2020, https://13thamendment.harpweek.com/HubPages/CommentaryPage.asp?Commentary=05HousePassage.

Spielberg, Steven, director, *Lincoln*, 2013,DreamWorks II Distribution Co., LLC, and Twentieth Century Fox Film Corporation, 2013, DVD.

1865 – current: Ku Klux Klan
[116]"Interview with Carol Swain, Ph.D.," *Hillary's America, the Secret History of the Democratic Party*, dir. by Dinesh D'Souza and Bruce Scholley (2016; Santa Monica, CA: Lions Gate, 2016) DVD.

[117]Swain, *Hillary.*

Rep. Hind assassinated by KKK:
[118]"Assassination," Wikipedia, last accessed September 5, 2020, https://en.wikipedia.org/wiki/James_M._Hinds#Assassination.

KKK still active:
[119]Spencer Platt, "Still a Threat to Society," RT.com, June 22. 2017, updated 2000, last accessed September 5, 2020, https://www.rt.com/usa/393638-kkk-active-adl-report-us/.

Nancy Pelosi:
[120]Pete Strocker, "Fact Check: Was Pelosi's Great-Grandfather a Founding KKK Member?" FreedomFictions.com, last accessed September 5, 2020, https://freedomfictions.com/fact-check-was-pelosis-great-grandfather-a-founding-kkk-member/.

Senator Robert Byrd:
[120]Scott Walker, "Party of Slavery and Jim Crow Has a Short Memory". Washington Times, June 19, 2020, RealClearPolitics.com reposted, last accessed September 5,2020, https://www.realclearpolitics.com/2020/06/19/party_of_slavery_and_jim_crow_has_a_short_memory_514744.html#.

Byrd was Hillary Clinton's mentor and friend, from her lips:
D'Souza, Dinesha and Scholley, Bruce, writers and directors. *Hillary's America, the Secret History of the Democratic Party*. 2016; Santa Monica, CA: Lions Gate, 2016. DVD.

Bill Clinton's comments on Byrd:
D'Souza, *Hillary.*

Resistance to African American freedom
Jim Crow laws:
[122]Scott Walker, **"Party of Slavery"**

Blacks and other "coloreds" – one drop rule:
[123]"One drop rule," Wikipedia, accessed September 4, 2020, https://en.wikipedia.org/wiki/One-drop_rule.

Defunct, never federal law:
[124]Wikipedia, One drop.

Dr. Carol Swain regarding Jim Crow and 2nd Amendment rights denied African Americans:
[125]"Interview with Carol Swain, Ph.D.," *Hillary's America, the Secret History of the Democratic Party*, dir. by Dinesh D'Souza and Bruce Scholley (2016; Santa Monica, CA: Lions Gate, 2016) DVD.

Enforcement of Jim Crow and lynching:
[126]John Fund, "Setting the Record Straight on Jim Crow," National Review (website), posted July 22, 2014, last accessed September 5, 2020,
https://www.nationalreview.com/corner/setting-record-straight-jim-crow-john-fund/.

Who owned slaves?
[127]"The Democratic Party's History of Slavery, Jim Crow, and the KKK," Social Justice Survival Guide (website), accesses September 5, 2020, https://www.socialjusticesurvivalguide.com/2018/01/08/the-democratic-partys-history-slavery-jim-crow-kkk/.

Dinesh D'Souza, Bruce Scholley, John Sullivan, writers; Dinesh D'Souza, John Sullivan, diredtors. *America: Imagine the World without Her.* 2013; Santa Monica, CA: Lions Gate, 2014. DVD.

Quora (website), accessed September 12, 2020, https://www.quora.com/What-percentage-of-the-Southern-population-owned-slaves-at-the-beginning-of-the-American-Civil-War?share=1.

1866: 14th Amendment
[128]Annonymous, "How come not a single Democrat voted for the 14th Amendment, which granted full citizenship to blacks?" Yahoo! Answers, 2012, last accessed September 5, 2012https://answers.yahoo.com/question/index?qid=20120901155829AAbVwka&guccounter=1&guce_referrer=aHR0cHM6Ly9kdWNrZHVja2dvLmNvbS8_dD1mZmFiJnE9d2hhdCt3YXMrdGhlK3ZvdGUrYnkrcGFydHkrb24rdGhlKzE0dGGrQW1lbmRtZW50JTNGJmlhPXdlYg&guce_referrer_sig=AQAAAKOxpRYZmQrEBK2RyNIbnNRkqZoXE6XVKLhLizIpv5zcHyjhcTI9q1gl2fJSLMCz6HbqS9Oudg--H1Z8sW8o1q8vflBsJ9NL711jCCYxyCbebSauqmvcqFrhmi0SQ9tFsVJJTIddJ3qoa5Bw2-SXyQGImTGpQGdl_fQiPM03Wu9g.

[Author's Note: researching the details of the voting record in 2019 was easy. Many sites had the details. This is the only one I've been able to find in 2020 that has the correct outcome. Now the sites I had from 2019 no longer carry this information. This is true for many other facts.]

Late 1800s – current: Eugenics
[129]"Eugenics in the United States," Wikipedia, last accessed September 5, 2020, https://en.wikipedia.org/wiki/Eugenics_in_the_United_States,

[130]Wikipedia, *Eugenics.*

[131] Wikipedia, *Eugenics.*

78% of Planned Parenthood clinics in minority neighborhoods:
[132]"Planned Parenthood," BlackGenocide.org, last accessed Sept, 5, 2020, http://www.blackgenocide.org/planned.html.

PP is the largest provider of abortions in America:
Mary Margaret Olohan, "New Planned Parenthood Report Shows Increase in Abortions," The Daily Signal (website), January 06, 2020, last accessed September 5, 2020, https://www.dailysignal.com/2020/01/06/new-planned-parenthood-report-shows-increase-in-abortions/.

US leading cause of death:
[133]"Abortion," All American Life League (ALL) (website), last accessed September 5, 2020, https://www.all.org/learn/abortion/abortion-statistics/.

Katia Lervasi , "What are the leading causes of death in the US?," Finder.com, updated Apr 27, 2020, last accessed September 5, 2020, https://www.finder.com/what-are-the-top-20-causes-of-death-in-united-states.

Worldwide leading cause of death:

[134]Steven Ertelt, Micaiah Bilger "Abortion Was the Leading Cause of Death Worldwide in 2019, Killing 42 Million People," LifeNews.com, Dec 31, 2019, last accessed September 5, 2020, https://www.lifenews.com/2019/12/31/abortion-was-the-leading-cause-of-death-worldwide-in-2019-killing-42-million-people/.

Blacks 12% of the population, 36% of the abortions:
[135]Planned Parenthood," Black Genocide, http://www.blackgenocide.org/planned.html.

[136]D'Souza, Dinesha and Scholley, Bruce, writers and directors. *Death of a Nation, Can We Safe America a Second Time?* 2018; Calabassa, CA: Quality Flix, 2018. DVD.

Progressives forced sterilization:
[137]"The Supreme Court Ruling That Led To 70,000 Forced Sterilizations," heard on "Fresh Air," NPR, March 24, 2017, last accessed September 5, 2020, https://www.npr.org/2017/03/24/521360544/the-supreme-court-ruling-that-led-to-70-000-forced-sterilizations.

"Interview with Jonah Goldberg," *Hillary's America, the Secret History of the Democratic Party*, dir. by Dinesh D'Souza and Bruce Scholley (2016; Santa Monica, CA: Lions Gate, 2016) DVD.

More on Carrie Buck – why they declared her incompetent:
Brendan Wolfe, "Buck v. Bell (1927)," Encyclopedia Virginia (website), last accessed September 5, 2020, https://www.encyclopediavirginia.org/Buck_v_Bell_1927.

1869: 15th Amendment
[138]"Fifteenth Amendment to the United States Constitution," Wikipedia, last accessed September 5, 2020,https://en.wikipedia.org/wiki/Fifteenth_Amendment_to_the_United_States_Constitution#cite_note-13.

[139]"Interview with Carol Swain, Ph.D.," *Hillary's America, the Secret History of the Democratic Party*, dir. by Dinesh D'Souza and Bruce Scholley (2016; Santa Monica, CA: Lions Gate, 2016) DVD.

Blacks in Congress:
[140]Wikipedia, *Fifteenth*..

Blocking of black's voting rights:
[141]Rick Jervis, "Black Americans got the right to vote 150 years ago, but voter suppression still a problem," USA Today (website), published Feb. 2, 2020, last accessed September 5, 2020, https://www.usatoday.com/story/news/nation/2020/02/03/black-voting-rights-15th-amendment-still-challenged-after-150-years/4587160002/.

1886: The Statue of Liberty
[142]"Statue of Liberty," National Park Service, last accessed September 5, 2020, https://www.nps.gov/stli/index.htm.

Inscription:
Jill, "Inscription on the Statue of Liberty," Scrapbook.com, last accessed September 5, 2020, https://www.scrapbook.com/poems/doc/3061.html.

1895: Fabian Society
[143]"Who Founded Fabian Socialism in the United States?" *ProgressingAmerica* (blog), posted February 2, 2012, last accessed September 6, 2020,https://progressingamerica.blogspot.com/2012/02/who-founded-fabian-socialism-in-united.html.

Scott Boyd, "How Fabian socialism explains modern day American socialism," Truth Stream Media, January 19, 2020,posted by *The NOQ Report*, (podcast), September 6, 2020, last accessed September 6, 2020, https://noqreport.com/2020/01/19/how-fabian-socialism-explains-modern-day-american-socialism/.

Alexandra Bruce, John Chambers, "Corporate Communism and the Deep State," MSOM, ForbiddenKnowledgetv.net, October 1, 2020, last accessed October 4, 2020, https://forbiddenknowledgetv.net/corporate-communism-and-the-deep-state/, or https://www.youtube.com/watch?v=-PzZ1TdQZN8.

1913: Federal Reserve
[144]David All Rivera, Final Warning: A History of the New World Order Illumunism and the master plan for world domination, Modern History Project, 1994, last accessed September 5, 2020, https://modernhistoryproject.org/mhp?Article=FinalWarning&C=1.1.

[145]ReallyGraceful, "The Richest Family You've Never Heard of…House of Schiff," posted by ForbiddenKnowledgetv.net on Mar. 25, 2020, last accessed September 5, 2020, https://forbiddenknowledgetv.net/the-richest-family-in-america-youve-never-heard-of/.

Alexandra Bruce, John Chambers, "Corporate Communism and the Deep State," MSOM, ForbiddenKnowledgetv.net, October 1, 2020, last accessed October 4, 2020, https://forbiddenknowledgetv.net/corporate-communism-and-the-deep-state/, or https://www.youtube.com/watch?v=-PzZ1TdQZN8.

LORDDREADNOUGHT , "Communist China was created by Jewish infiltrators working for the *International Banking Cartel,* Communist China was created by the Jews and serves their interests / Communist China was created by Rothschilds and their agents'," The Millennium Report, July 6, 2019, last accessed October 5, 2020, http://themillenniumreport.com/2019/07/communist-china-was-created-by-jewish-infiltrators-working-for-the-international-banking-cartel/.

1914, British foreign policy and the Rothschild Banking family foreign policy became one and the same:
[146] "Twas a long, long Money Trail awinding…." Revisionist.net, last accessed September 5, 2020, http://www.revisionist.net/hysteria/bankers.html.

1917: Russia falls to communism
[147]"Communism in Russia," Wikipedia, Nov. 2019, last accessed September 5, 2020, https://en.wikipedia.org/wiki/Communism_in_Russia.

Source of Karl Marx's inspiration for communism:
William F. Marshall, *"Are Karl Marx and Satan Taking Over America?" Epoch Times, September 8-20, p. B7.*

Paul Kengor, *The Devil and Karl Marx: Communism's Long March of Death, Deception, and Infiltration,* (Gastonia, North Carolina: TAN Books, 2020)

Interview with Paul Kengor by Glenn Beck, "Hear the HORRIFYING words Karl Marx wrote about Satan, Evil | THIS is the Origin of BLM, Marxism," Glenn Radio, September 9, 2020, last accessed October 5, 2020, https://www.youtube.com/watch?v=_ItS_df8GIQ.

Here is from where the funding for the communist revolution in Russia came:
Alexandra Bruce, John Chambers, "Corporate Communism and the Deep State," MSOM, ForbiddenKnowledgetv.net, October 1, 2020, last accessed October 4, 2020, https://forbiddenknowledgetv.net/corporate-communism-and-the-deep-state/, or https://www.youtube.com/watch?v=-PzZ1TdQZN8.

1919: 19th Amendment Women's suffrage in USA beg 1878, finally ratified 1920
[148]David Catron "Dems Revise History Regarding the 19th Amendment" The American Spectator (website), June 5, 2019, last accessed September 5, 2020, https://spectator.org/dems-revise-history-regarding-the-19th-amendment/.

[149]D'Souza, Dinesha and Scholley, Bruce, writers and directors. *Hillary's America, the Secret History of the Democratic Party.* 2016; Santa Monica, CA: Lions Gate, 2016. DVD.

[150]D'Souza, *Hillary.*

1920: American Civil Liberties (ACLU)

[151]David All Rivera, Final Warning: A History of the New World Order Illumunism and the master plan for world domination, Modern History Project, 1994, last accessed September 5, 2020, https://modernhistoryproject.org/mhp?Article=FinalWarning&C=1.1.

[152]Rivera, *Final Warning.*

[153]Rivera, *Final Warning.*

[154]Rivera, *Final Warning.*

1922-1945: Fascism

[155]"Italian Fascism," Wikipedia, last accessed September 5, 2020, https://en.wikipedia.org/wiki/Italian_Fascism.

Italy:
[156]Editors,"Benito Mussolini," History.com, October 29, 2019, last accessed September 5, 2020, https://www.history.com/topics/world-war-ii/benito-mussolini.

Germany: How Nazism differed from original Italian fascism:
[157]Jagran Josh, "What is the difference between Fascism and Nazism?," jagranjosh.com, last accessed September 5,2020, https://www.jagranjosh.com/general-knowledge/what-is-the-difference-between-fascism-and-nazism-1553251239-1.

Hitler's rule:
[158]"Adolf Hitler," Wikipedia, last accessed September 5, 2020, https://en.wikipedia.org/wiki/Adolf_Hitler.

[159]D'Souza, Dinesha and Scholley, Bruce, writers and directors. *Death of a Nation, Can We Save America a Second Time?* 2018; Calabassa, CA: Quality Flix, 2018. DVD.

[160]Dinesh D'Souza, *Death of a Nation.*

[161]D'Souza, *Death of a Nation.*

The Nazis were funded by huge corporations in America and Germany:
Blogman-Blacksmith of Truth, "Wall Street Funded The Nazi Party," *Auric media* (blog), October 29, 2015, last accessed October 5, 2020, https://www.auricmedia.net/wall-street-funded-the-nazi-party/.

Stephanie Smith, "Who funded the Nazis?" Journalist Smith is website owner, Updated October 18, 2019, last accessed October 5, 2020, https://www.quora.com/Who-funded-the-Nazis?share=1

Ciara Torres-Spelliscy, "How Big Business Bailed Out the Nazis," Brennan Center for Justice, Updated October 18, 2019,last accessed October 5, 2020, https://www.brennancenter.org/our-work/analysis-opinion/how-big-business-bailed-out-nazis.

[162]"Externmination camp," Wikipedia, last accessed September 5, 2020, https://en.wikipedia.org/wiki/Extermination_camp.

Relationships of President Franklin Roosevelt and America with Benito Mussolini and Adolf Hitler:
[163]"Interview with Jonah Goldberg," *Hillary's America, the Secret History of the Democratic Party*, dir. by Dinesh D'Souza and Bruce Scholley (2016; Santa Monica, CA: Lions Gate, 2016) DVD.

Roosevelt opinion of Mussolini and FDR advisors' trip to Italy:
[164]D'Souza, Dinesha and Scholley, Bruce, writers and directors. *Death of a Nation, Can We Save America a Second Time?* 2018; Calabassa, CA: Quality Flix, 2018. DVD.

[165]D'Souza, *Death of a Nation.*

Formation of Hitler's leftist ideology:
[166]D'Souza, *Death of a Nation.*

[167]D'Souza, *Death of a Nation.*

[168]D'Souza, *Death of a Nation.*

Hitler and Lenin playing chess:
[169]Reporter, "Sketch of young Adolf Hitler playing chess with Lenin put up for auction... but does it capture a genuine historical event?," MailOnline, posted September 4, 2009, last accessed September 5, 2020, https://www.dailymail.co.uk/news/article-1210950/Pictured-Young-Adolf-Hitler-playing-chess-Lenin.html.

[170]D'Souza, *Death of a Nation.*

"The Nazi Party 25 Points",(1920), Alpha History, last accessed October 7, 2020, https://alphahistory.com/nazigermany/nazi-party-25-points-1920/.

[171]D'Souza, *Death of a Nation.*

Nazis eugenics programs drawn from US Progressives:
[172]D'Souza, *Death of a Nation.*

Dinesh D'Souza, "Exclusive – D'Souza: The Hitler-Sanger Connection," Breibart (website), posted September 1, 2017, last accessed September 5, 2020, https://www.breitbart.com/politics/2017/09/01/exclusive-dsouza-the-hitler-sanger-connection/.

German eugenicists beating US eugenicists at their own game:
[173]"Interview with *Edwin Black*," *Death of a Nation*, dir. by Dinesh D'Souza and Bruce Scholley (2018; Calabassa, CA: Quality Flix, 2018) DVD.

[174]D'Souza, *Death of a Nation.*

1933: Stealing of the US Gold Reserves
[175] David All Rivera, Final Warning: A History of the New World Order Illumunism and the master plan for world domination, Modern History Project, 1994, last accessed September 5, 2020, https://modernhistoryproject.org/mhp?Article=FinalWarning&C=1.1.

[176]Rivera, *Final Warning.*

Keynes:
[177]Rivera, *Final Warning.*

[178]Rivera, *Final Warning.*

[179]Rivera, *Final Warning.*

What did US progressives do when Hitler was defeated?
[180]D'Souza, Dinesha and Scholley, Bruce, writers and directors. *Death of a Nation, Can We Safe America a Second Time?* 2018; Calabassa, CA: Quality Flix, 2018. DVD.

1945: United Nations
Lenin's call for a global government:
[181]*The Socialist Democrat,* issue 40, 1915.

After WW II, push for toward an organization, around which to form a new world order:
Alexandra Bruce, John Chambers, "Corporate Communism and the Deep State," MSOM, ForbiddenKnowledgetv.net, October 1, 2020, last accessed October 4, 2020, https://forbiddenknowledgetv.net/corporate-communism-and-the-deep-state/, or https://www.youtube.com/watch?v=-PzZ1TdQZN8. [time: 7:13-8:00]

[182] David All Rivera, Final Warning: A History of the New World Order Illumunism and the master plan for world domination, Modern History Project, 1994, last accessed September 5, 2020, https://modernhistoryproject.org/mhp?Article=FinalWarning&C=1.1.

What the UN says it does:
[183]P. Altıok, "United Nations Mission and Vision statements Analysis," last accessed September 5, 2020, mission-statement.com, 2011, last accessed September 5, 2020, https://mission-statement.com/united-nations/.

How have the United Nations "peacekeeping" troops been used in the past?
Alexandra Bruce, John Chambers, "Corporate Communism and the Deep State," MSOM, ForbiddenKnowledgetv.net, October 1, 2020, last accessed October 4, 2020, https://forbiddenknowledgetv.net/corporate-communism-and-the-deep-state/, or https://www.youtube.com/watch?v=-PzZ1TdQZN8. [time: 12:33-12:47]

[184]United Nations (website),last accessed September 15, 2020, https://www.un.org/en/sections/what-we-do/.

[185]United Nations (website).

Incoming class action lawsuit against director-general of World Health Organization:
Dr Reiner Fuellmich, "Crimes against Humanity: Class Action Lawsuits Incoming," ForbiddenKnowledgetv.net, October 6, 2020, https://forbiddenknowledgetv.net/crimes-against-humanity/.

Chisolm quote:
[186]Rivera, *Final Warning.*

UN 2020 Budget and goals:
[187]United Nations (website),last accessed September 5, 2020, https://news.un.org/en/story/2019/12/1054431.

Agenda 21, 2030, and 2050 goals:
[188]United Nations (website),last accessed September 5, 2020, United Nations (website),last accessed September 5, 2020, https://news.un.org/en/story/2019/12/1054431.

[189]Artikel 7, "Agenda 30/Agenda 21 NOT Sustainable," posted by ForbiddenKnowledgetv.net February 2, 2020, last accessed September 7, 2020, https://forbiddenknowledgetv.net/un-agenda-21-and-modern-monetary-theory/.

Democrats Against UN Agenda 21,last accessed September 24, 2020, https://www.democratsagainstunagenda21.com/.

Global Research, Centre for Research on Globalization, Rosa Koire video, last September 24, 2020, https://www.globalresearch.ca/video-un-agenda-2030-exposed/5717356

Who pays the tab?
[190]"United Nations Budget Contribution by Country 2019," howmuch.net, 2019, last accessed September 5, 2020, https://howmuch-net.myshopify.com/products/united-nations-budget-contribution-by-country-2019?variant=33489975804043.

Voting in the UN:
[191]Rivera, *Final Warning.*

US military concessions sought by UN:
[192]Rivera, *Final Warning.*

Rep. John Rankin (D MS):
[193]Rivera, *Final Warning.*

Orson Wells:
[194]Rivera, *Final Warning.*

George Bush:
[195]Rivera, *Final Warning.*

Bill Clinton:
[196]Rivera, *Final Warning.*

1949: China becomes communist
Mao's announcement of People's Republic of China:
[197]"The day China became communist," BBC News (website), (videos also), September 29, 2019, last accessed
September 5, 2020, https://www.bbc.com/news/av/stories-49829435.

Who funded the Chinese communists?
LORDDREADNOUGHT , "Communist China was created by Jewish infiltrators working for the *International Banking
Cartel,* Communist China was created by the Jews and serves their interests / Communist China was created by
Rothschilds and their agents," The Millennium Report, July 6, 2019, last accessed October 5, 2020,
http://themillenniumreport.com/2019/07/communist-china-was-created-by-jewish-infiltrators-working-for-the-
international-banking-cartel/; and https://lorddreadnought.livejournal.com/37272.html.

Tiananmen Square demonstrations for democracy in 1989 (witness video):
[198]"How the Tiananmen Square protests changed my life," (video also), BBC News (website), May 30, 2019, last
accessed September 5, 2020, https://www.bbc.com/news/av/stories-48448564.

Chinese declaration of war against the US:
[199]Joshua Phillipp, "Tracking Down the Origin of the Wuhan Virus," The Epoch Times, ForbidenKnowledtetv.net posted
April 7, 2020, last accessed September 4, 2020, https://forbiddenknowledgetv.net/tracking-down-the-origin-of-the-
wuhan-coronavirus/, [Chinese expert, toward end of video, states source for declaration of war - time: 41:43].

Chinese social credit score:
[200]Melissa Dykes, "What's Your Social Credit Score?," Truthstream, posted by ForbiddenKnowledgetv.net Dec. 29,
2019, last accessed September 5, 2020,
https://forbiddenknowledgetv.net/whats-your-social-credit-
score/?utm_source=newsletter&utm_medium=email&utm_campaign=What%27s+Your+Social+Credit+Score%3F.

Chinese using live ethnic and religious prisoners to for organ transplant donors:
[201]Saphora Smith, "China forcefully harvests organs from detainees, tribunal concludes," NBC News (website), June
18, 2018, last accessed September 5, 2020,
https://www.nbcnews.com/news/world/china-forcefully-harvests-organs-detainees-tribunal-concludes-n1018646.

CCP complicit in Coronavirus pandemic:
[202]Simone Gao, "Cover up of the Century, Zooming In, Jun 28, 2020, last accessed September 5, 2020,
https://www.youtube.com/watch?v=MZ74NhEUY-w.

Joshua Phillipp, "Tracking Down the Origin of the Wuhan Virus," The Epoch Times, ForbidenKnowledtetv.net posted
April 7, 2020, last accessed September 4, 2020,
https://forbiddenknowledgetv.net/tracking-down-the-origin-of-the-wuhan-coronavirus/.

Current communist worldwide penetration and agenda:
[203] Gina Shakespeare, "Is Your Country Actually Communist?" The Epoch Times, ForbiddenKnowledgetv.net, posted,
July 6, 2019, last accessed September 3, 2020, https://forbiddenknowledgetv.net/is-your-country-actually-
communist/.

Alexandra Bruce, John Chambers, "Corporate Communism and the Deep State," MSOM, ForbiddenKnowledgetv.net, October 1, 2020, last accessed October 4, 2020, https://forbiddenknowledgetv.net/corporate-communism-and-the-deep-state/, or https://www.youtube.com/watch?v=-PzZ1TdQZN8.

LORDDREADNOUGHT , "Communist China was created by Jewish infiltrators working for the *International Banking Cartel,* Communist China was created by the Jews and serves their interests / Communist China was created by Rothschilds and their agents'," The Millennium Report, July 6, 2019, last accessed October 5, 2020, http://themillenniumreport.com/2019/07/communist-china-was-created-by-jewish-infiltrators-working-for-the-international-banking-cartel/.

1960s: Alinski community organizing

[204]Dinesh D'Souza, Bruce Scholley, John Sullivan, writers; Dinesh D'Souza, John Sullivan, diredtors. *America: Imagine the World without Her.* 2013; Santa Monica, CA: Lions Gate, 2014. DVD.

Alinsky mentor:
[205]D'Souza, *America.*

Alinski students:
[206]D'Souza, *America. (long list)*

Gary North, "Saul Alinsky: Mentor to Hillary and Obama," Gary North (website), June 20, 2019, last accessed September 5, 2020, https://www.garynorth.com/public/19627.cfm.

1964: Civil Rights Act

[207]John Fund, "Setting the Record Straight on Jim Crow," National Review (website), July 22, 2014, last accessed September 5, 2020, https://www.nationalreview.com/corner/setting-record-straight-jim-crow-john-fund/.

[208]Brad Sylvester, "Fact Check: 'More Republicans Voted for the Civil Rights Act as a Percentage Than Democrats Did', "The Daily Signal (website), December 17, 2018, last accessed September 5, 2020, https://www.dailysignal.com/2018/12/17/fact-check-more-republicans-voted-for-the-civil-rights-act-as-a-percentage-than-democrats-did/.

[209]Sylvester, Fact Check.

1964: War on Poverty

[210]Rachel Sheffield and Robert Rector, "The War on Poverty After 50 Years," The Heritage Foundation, September 15, 2014, last accessed September 15, 2020, https://www.heritage.org/poverty-and-inequality/report/the-war-poverty-after-50-years.

[211]"Interview with Carol Swain, Ph.D.," *Hillary's America, the Secret History of the Democratic Party*, dir. by Dinesh D'Souza and Bruce Scholley (2016; Santa Monica, CA: Lions Gate, 2016) DVD.

Robert Rector, "How Welfare Undermines Marriage and What to Do about It," The Heritage Foundation (website), November 27, 2014, https://www.heritage.org/welfare/report/how-welfare-undermines-marriage-and-what-do-about-it.

Daniel Patrick Moynihan, *The Moynihan Report, "African American family structure,"* Wikipedia, last accessed September26, 2020, https://en.wikipedia.org/wiki/African-American_family_structure.

Daniel P. Moynihan, "The Negro Family: The Case for National Action," Washington, D.C., Office of Policy Planning and Research, U.S. Department of Labor, 1965, last accessed September 26, 2020, https://en.wikipedia.org/wiki/The_Negro_Family:_The_Case_For_National_Action.

National Review, April 4, 1994, p. 24, posted by Wikipedia, last accessed September 26, 2020, https://en.wikipedia.org/wiki/National_Review.

Jesse Washington, "Blacks Struggle with 72 Percent Unwed Mothers Rate", Jesse NBC News, July 11, 2010, last accessed September 26, 2020, hhttp://www.nbcnews.com/id/39993685/ns/health-womens_health/t/blacks-struggle-percent-unwed-mothers-rate/#.URXHo80hclk.

Jason Riley, "For Blacks, the Pyrrhic Victory of the Obama Era,"The Wall Street Journal, November 4, 2012, last accessed September 26, 2020, https://www.wsj.com/articles/SB10001424052970204712904578090483678801780.

Paul Bedard, "77% Black Births to Single Moms, 49% for Hispanic Immigrants" Washington Examiner, May 5, 2017, last accessed September 26, 2020, https://www.washingtonexaminer.com/77-black-births-to-single-moms-49-for-hispanic-immigrants.

Single Mother Guide, updated August 22, 2020, last accessed September 26, 2020, https://singlemotherguide.com/single-mother-statistics/.

[212] *Thomas Sowell on the Myths of Economic Inequality:*
Thomas Sowell hosted by Peter Robinson, "Thomas Sowell on the Myths of Economic Inequality," *Uncommon Knowledge with Peter Robinson*, Hoover Institution, recorded November 15, 2018, last accessed September 9, 2020, https://www.youtube.com/watch?v=mS5WYp5xmvI.

Sowell, *Robinson*.

1970s-current: Political Correctness
Definition of "politically correct" and its surface origins:
[213]www.dictionary.com, accessed on September 4, 2020.

[214]Jack Evans, *"The Rise of Progressive Orthodoxy," The Oxford Review*, February 15, 2016.

From where did the PC "Hate America First" indoctrination come?
[215]Kent Clizbe, *Willing Accomplices*, posted February 4, 2012, last accessed September 6, 2020, http://www.willingaccomplices.com/willing_accomplices/videos.

2010: Gates advocates zero carbon emissions - drastic depopulation
[216]Bill Gates, "Innovating to Zero,"TED2010, Feb. 2010, last accessed September 5, 2020, https://www.ted.com/talks/bill_gates_innovating_to_zero.

February 2015: FEMA recruits pastors to be in Clergy Response Team
[217]Wishful, "The Pastors who signed up to help lure Americans into FEMA camps; The Secret Clergy Response Team," THEYIG (website), Feb. 8, 2020, last accessed September 5, 2020, https://theyig.ning.com/front-page-news/the-pastors-who-signed-up-to-help-lure-americans-into-fema-camps-.

[218]David Hodges, "Pastors to Help DHS in Arrests and Detention of Americans in FEMA Camps," Freedom Outpost, (web archived), posted Feb. 28, 2015, last accessed September 5, 2020, https://freedomoutpost.com/pastors-to-help-dhs-in-arrests-and-detention-of-americans-in-fema-camps/, [only available through link on the above noted website. It has been hacked, i.e. videos removed, which were available in winter of 2019.]

National Defense Authorization Act (NDAA):
[219]"President Obama Signs Indefinite Detention Bill Into Law," ACLU (website), posted December 31, 2011, last accessed September 5, 2020, https://www.aclu.org/press-releases/president-obama-signs-indefinite-detention-bill-law.

2015: Gates claims global vulnerability to pandemic

[220]Bill Gates, "The next outbreak? We're not ready."TED2015, March 25, 2015, last accessed September 5, 2020, https://www.ted.com/talks/bill_gates_the_next_outbreak_we_re_not_ready, unsuccessful on September 7, 2020; try: https://www.youtube.com/watch?v=6Af6b_wyiwI, successfully last accessed.

May 2018 #WalkAway Campaign begun
Brandon Straka's early speech
[221] "WalkAway March – Brandon Straka,"ForbiddenKnowledgetv.net, posted October 30, 2018, last accessed September 8, 2020, https://forbiddenknowledgetv.net/walkaway-march-brandon-straka/.

January 2019: Dangers of 5G reported on UN floor
[222]Claire Edwards, "UN Staff Member: 5G Is War on Humanity," Take Back Your Power (website), posted January 4, 2019, last accessed September 5, 2020, https://www.takebackyourpower.net/un-staff-member-5g-is-war-on-humanity/ [Recommend personal research for additional information on dangers of 5G.].

May 2019: China declares war on US
[223]   Joshua Phillipp, "Tracking Down the Origin of the Wuhan Virus," The Epoch Times, ForbidenKnowledtetv.net posted April 7, 2020, last accessed September 4, 2020, https://forbiddenknowledgetv.net/tracking-down-the-origin-of-the-wuhan-coronavirus/, [Chinese expert, toward end of video, states source for declaration of war - time: 41:43].

October 2019: Event 201
[224]Event 201, a global pandemic exercise, last accessed September 6, 2020, https://centerforhealthsecurity.org/event201/,

[225]Event 201 disclaimer: "Statement about nCoV and our pandemic exercise," last accessed September 6, 2020, https://www.centerforhealthsecurity.org/news/center-news/2020-01-24-Statement-of-Clarification-Event201.html.

January 2020: In China, leaks regarding the Wuhan virus begin; CCP complicit in Coronavirus pandemic
[226]Simone Gao, "Cover up of the Century, Zooming In, Jun 28, 2020, last accessed September 5, 2020, https://www.youtube.com/watch?v=MZ74NhEUY-w.

Joshua Phillipp, *"Tracking Down the Origin of the Wuhan Virus," The Epoch Times,* ; ForbidenKnowledtetv.net posted April 7, 2020, last accessed September 4, 2020, https://forbiddenknowledgetv.net/tracking-down-the-origin-of-the-wuhan-coronavirus/.

Pandemic in America
[227]Matt Margolis, "TIMELINE: The Trump Administration's Decisive Actions To Combat the Coronavirus Pandemic" PJ MEDIA (website), March 19, 2020, last accessed September 6,2020, By Matt Margolis Mar 19, 2020, https://pjmedia.com/news-and-politics/matt-margolis/2020/03/19/timeline-the-trump-administrations-decisive-actions-to-combat-the-coronavirus-pandemic-n382699.

Travel bans support and opposition:
Matt Margolis, "SHAME: Democrats Opposed Travel Bans Now Being Implemented Worldwide to Slow Coronavirus" PJ MEDIA (website), March 19, 2020, last accessed September 6,2020, https://pjmedia.com/news-and-politics/matt-margolis/2020/03/19/shame-democrats-opposed-travel-bans-now-being-implemented-worldwide-to-slow-coronavirus-n382711.

Spring 2020: the US riots and the "Philosopher of Antifa"
[228]Dinesh D'Souza, *"The Philosopher of Antifa," The Epoch Times,* June 11-17, 2020, *Opinion, pp Q18-19.* [D'Souza is author of *United States of Socialism,* and a contributor to The Epoch Times.].

Roots, history, and objectives of Black Lives Matter:
Reagan, "The White Man Behind Black Lives Matter," ForbiddenKnowledgetv.net, October 2, 2020, last accessed October 4, 2020, https://forbiddenknowledgetv.net/the-secret-origins-of-black-lives-matter/, or https://www.youtube.com/watch?v=Sq1m_PJtu5o.

Terry Turchie, "Attack & Dethrone God' Is Goal of Protests, Says Former FBI Agent Terry Turchie," *The Ingraham Angle*, Fox News, posted on Heavy.com, June 2020, last accessed October 9, 2020, https://heavy.com/news/2020/06/attack-and-dethrone-god/.

The "new" socialism
[229]The Candace Owens Show: Dinesh D'Souza, premiered July 26, 2020, last accessed September 6, 2020, https://www.youtube.com/watch?v=X5_DBg31ZWU&feature=emb_rel_end.

Regarding using the pandemic to create fear for subjugation:
Dr Reiner Fuellmich, "Crimes against Humanity: Class Action Lawsuits Incoming," ForbiddenKnowledgetv.net, October 6, 2020, https://forbiddenknowledgetv.net/crimes-against-humanity/.

Daniele Pozzati, "German Official Leaks Report Denouncing Corona as 'A Global False Alarm'," Strategic Culture Foundation, May 29, 2020, last accessed October 6, 2020 https://www.strategic-culture.org/news/2020/05/29/german-official-leaks-report-denouncing-corona-as-global-false-alarm/

As the call for a second lockdown goes out:
[230] "Plandemic II: Indoctrination," PlandemicSeries.com, posted by ForbidenKnowledgetv.net, August 18, 2020, last accessed September 6, 2020, https://forbiddenknowledgetv.net/plandemic-ii-indoctornation/,[See also plandemicseries.com.].

Lou Dobbs with Alex Benenson,"The Politics of the Global Pandemic," *FoxBusiness LIVE*, September 11, 2020, last accessed September 16, 2020. https://duckduckgo.com/?t=ffnt&q=calls+for+second+lockdown&iax=videos&ia=videos&iai=https%3A%2F%2Fwww.youtube.com%2Fwatch%3Fv%3DkX9bpWuotdM.

Vaccine warning from doctor, with attendance in planning meetings. who has been studying vaccines for 20 years:
[231]Dr. Carrie Madjeg, "'Human 2.0'? A Wake Call to the World," posted by ForbiddenKnowledgetv.net, August 18, 2020, last accessed September 6, 2020, https://forbiddenknowledgetv.net/human-2-0-a-wake-up-call-to-the-world/.

Unmasking the masks agenda:
[232]James Grundvig, "Unmasking the Masks Agenda," presented by John Michael Chambers in *Making Sense of the Madness* (YouTube channel), posted by ForbidenKnowledgetv.net, August 13, 2020, last accessed September 6, 2020, https://forbiddenknowledgetv.net/unmasking-the-masks-agenda/.

Mental health crises due to lockdowns:
[233]Bowen Xiao, *"Shutdown Spur Mental Health Crisis in US, Experts Say," The Epoch Times, No. 318, August 26-September 1, 2020, page 1.*

Costs of life lost due to lockdown:
[234]Andrew Glen, Ph.D. and James D. Agresti , "Anxiety From Reactions to Covid-19 Will Destroy At Least Seven Times More Years of Life Than Can Be Saved by Lockdowns," ForbiddenKnowledgetv.net, posted June 19, 2020, last accessed September 3, 2020, https://www.justfacts.com/news_covid-19_anxiety_lockdowns_life_destroyed_saved.

Dr. Reiner Fuellmich, "Crimes against Humanity: Class Action Lawsuits Incoming," ForbiddenKnowledgetv.net, October 6, 2020, https://forbiddenknowledgetv.net/crimes-against-humanity/.

Daniele Pozzati, "German Official Leaks Report Denouncing Corona as 'A Global False Alarm'," Strategic Culture Foundation, May 29, 2020, last accessed October 6, 2020 https://www.strategic-culture.org/news/2020/05/29/german-official-leaks-report-denouncing-corona-as-global-false-alarm/

Plea for the voiceless victims – and for essential freedoms:

[235]Henna Marie, "Voiceless Victims of the COVID," ForbiddenKnowledgetv.net, posted Aug. 17, 2020, last accessed September 3, 2020, https://forbiddenknowledgetv.net/voiceless-victims-of-the-covid-lockdowns/.

Forces pressing toward communism and a new world order from the Russian communist revolution to an immediate communist revolution in America:
Alexandra Bruce, John Chambers, "Corporate Communism and the Deep State," MSOM, ForbiddenKnowledgetv.net, October 1, 2020, last accessed October 4, 2020, https://forbiddenknowledgetv.net/corporate-communism-and-the-deep-state/, or https://www.youtube.com/watch?v=-PzZ1TdQZN8.

The spread of satanism
[236]Lily Rothman, The Evolution of Modern Satanism in the United States," TIME, History - Faith (website), July 27, 2015, last accessed September 6, 2020, https://time.com/3973573/satanism-american-history/.

[237]"The Satanic Temple," Wikipedia, last accessed September 6, 2020, https://en.wikipedia.org/wiki/The_Satanic_Temple.

"The Church of Satan," Wikipedia, last accessed September 6, 2020, https://en.wikipedia.org/wiki/Church_of_Satan.

Q Anon calls attention to satanic practices and sexual exploitation among the elite:
[238]Dr. Michael Salla, "Epstein Arrest Supports Q Anon Claims of Global Satanic Cult blackmailing Political Elites," posted in Featured, US Politics, and here ExoPolitics.org, written by Salla July 10, 2019, last accessed September 6, 2020, https://exopolitics.org/epstein-arrest-supports-q-anon-claims-of-global-satanic-cult-blackmailing-political-elites/.

Jeffery Epstein and Ghislaine Maxwell:
[239]60 Minutes Australia, "Inside the Wicked Saga of Jeffrey Epstein: the arrest of Ghislaine Maxwell," posted by ForbiddenKnowledgetv.net, July 11, 2020, last accessed September 16, 2020, https://forbiddenknowledgetv.net/inside-the-wicked-saga-of-jeffrey-epstein-the-arrest-of-ghislaine-maxwell-60-minutes-australia/.

Frank Parlato,"More Than Just Pedophilia? Insights Into Epstein's Island Temple and Its Purported Use for Satanic Worship," FrankReport (website), August 22, 2019, last accessed September 16, 2020, https://frankreport.com/2019/08/22/more-than-just-pedophilia-insights-into-epsteins-island-temple-and-its-purported-use-for-satanic-worship/.

Satanism in international banking:
[240]Ronald Bernard, "Illuminati Satanic Bankers (Dutch international banker), video interview embedded in above link, last accessed September 6, 2019, [first interview from Bernard].

ReallyGraceful, "The Richest Family You've Never Heard of...House of Schiff," posted by ForbiddenKnowledgetv.net on Mar. 25, 2020, last accessed September 5, 2020, https://forbiddenknowledgetv.net/the-richest-family-in-america-youve-never-heard-of/.

"A conversation with ex illuminati insider Ronald Bernard and Sacha Stone," May 2, 2018, last accessed September 6, 2020, https://youtu.be/uA1Ut-K1FsU.

Satanic child trafficking:
[241]John Paul Rice, "A Child's Voice, the real story of a hidden network," Hollywood filmmaker, personal appeal, posted August 7, 2020, last accessed September 6, 2020, https://youtu.be/dztir94oaOo.

Carol M. Swain, *"Netflix's 'Cuties' the Latest Instance of Sacrificing Our Children," The Epoch Times, Opinion,* September 18-22, p. A13.

US military cleaning out underground tunnel systems, where trafficked children imprisoned:
[242]Tunnels (Deep Underground Military Bunkers aka DUMBS – NOT US military) January 2020

Coloseneil64@gmail.com , *"The Underground War, Happening Now,* posted Jan. 8, 2020, last accessed September 3, 2020, https://www.youtube.com/watch?v=yoQUrXzbvf4\.

"Adrenochrome, the Elites Super Drug," ForbiddenKnowledgetv.net, February 16, 2019, last accessed October 5, 2020, https://forbiddenknowledgetv.net/adrenochrome/.

DUMB survivor – WARNING! Graphic descriptions of violence against children:
[243]Katie Grove "Child Snuf Survivor Speaks Out," posted by Yig Wilson Aug. 10, 2018, last accessed Sep. 3, 2020, https://theyig.ning.com/generalvideos/tw-cia-child-snuff-survivor-speaks-out.

Illuminati-escaped daughter confirms satanic child trafficking:
Mabel P. Bronson, "The Tunnel Children"; David Zublick, producer, Dark Outpost; posted June 26, 2020, last accessed September 3, 2020, https://timothycharlesholmseth.com/the-tunnel-children-featured-on-dark-outpost/.

XI. Targeting of vulnerable populations

Our children in government schools
[244] Alex Newman, *"Big Foundations Unleashed 'Revolution' Via US Schools,"* The Epoch Times, May 14-20, p A19.

[245]Newman, *"Big Foundations".*

[246] Newman, *"Big Foundations".*

[247] Newman, *"Big Foundations".*

[248]Newman, *"Big Foundations".*

[249]Newman, *"Big Foundations".*

[250]Newman, *"Big Foundations".*

[251] AZ Quotes, last accessed September 4, 2020, https://www.azquotes.com/author/8880-Abraham_Lincoln.

[252]Newman, *"Big Foundations".*

Corporations who have voiced support and made donations to rioters' funds and Black Lives Matter and Antifa:
[253]Ashley Rae Goldenberg, "279 Companies Supporting Violent Antifa & Black Lives Matter, *"Reality and Denial* (blog), June 3, 2020, last accessed September 18, 2020, https://realityanddenial.wordpress.com/2020/06/09/279-companies-supporting-violent-antifa-black-lives-matter/.

Tim Brown, *"List of 269 Companies Supporting ANTIFA, Black Lives Matter,"* (list by Ashley Rae Goldenberg), Conservative Firing Line.com (website), posted June 9, 2020, last accessed September 4, 2020, https://conservativefiringline.com/list-of-269-companies-supporting-antifa-black-lives-matter/.

The globalist agenda or the National Education Association (NEA)
[254] Alex Neman, *"How Socialists Used Teachers Unions Such as the NEA to Destroy Education, The Epoch Times,* May 21-27, 2020, Opinion, pp A19-20.

[255]Newman, *NEA.*

[256]Newman, *NEA*

[257]Newman, *NEA*

[258]Newman, *NEA*

Sex-education and fluid gender issues
Facebook gender options:
[259]Russell Goldman, "Here's a List of 58 Gender Options for Facebook Users," NBC News (website), posted February 13, 2014, last accessed September 6, 2020, https://abcnews.go.com/blogs/headlines/2014/02/heres-a-list-of-58-gender-options-for-facebook-users.

Sample of films being created for adolescents:
[260]"MENstruation." Thinx, posted by ForbiddenKnowledgetv.net, October 25, 2019, last accessed September 6, 2020, https://forbiddenknowledgetv.net/MENstruation/.

[261]Catherine Yang, *"Cathy Rouse on the Fight Parents Face in Public Schools,"* The Epoch Times, June 11-17, p B3 .

[262]Yang, *Fight Parents Face*

[263]Cathy Rouse's brochure on sex-education in public schools
bit.ly/2XPojWK.

[264]Yang, *Fight Parents Face*

Definition of psychoneurosis:
[265]The Free Dictionary, *last accessed August 30, 2020, https://www.thefreedictionary.com/psychoneurosis.*

Common Core curricula
Gates Foundation involvement in Common Core curricula:
[266]Newman, *Big Foundations, p A20.*

Where did the focused impetus for Common Core start?
[267]Allie Bidwell, "The History of Common Core State Standards," U.S. News & World Report (website),   Feb. 27, 2014, last accessed September 6, 2020, https://www.usnews.com/news/special-reports/articles/2014/02/27/the-history-of-common-core-state-standards.

How is Common Core affecting student test scores?
[268]Joy Pullmann, "9 Years Into Common Core, Test Scores Are Down, Indoctrination Up," The Federalist (website), published November 5, 2018, last accessed September 6, 2020, https: //thefederalist.com/2018/11/05/9-years-common-core-test-scores-indoctrination/.

Lauren Camera, Senior Education Writer, "Across the Board, Scores Drop in Math and Reading for U.S. Students," U.S. News & World Report (website), Oct. 30, 2019, last accessed September 6, 2020, https://www.usnews.com/news/education-news/articles/2019-10-30/across-the-board-scores-drop-in-math-and-reading-for-us-students.

Current education tactics compared to practices in Nazi Germany:
[269]Catherine Yang, "Karen Siegemund on the Fight to Preserve American Culture," *The Epoch Times*, May 21-27, 2020, page B3.

War on the most vulnerable
[270]Right to Life, the Option Line: (866) 993-0794 (24/7), Decision Line: (866) 993-0794; peer support: STANDUPGIRL.com, a place where women share the truth about their own unexpected pregnancies, last accessed September 6, 2020, https://www.nrlc.org/help/.

US leading cause of death:
[271]"Abortion," All American Life League (ALL) (website), last accessed September 5,2020, https://www.all.org/learn/abortion/abortion-statistics/.

Katia Lervasi , "What are the leading causes of death in the US?," Finder.com, updated Apr 27, 2020, last accessed September 5, 2020, https://www.finder.com/what-are-the-top-20-causes-of-death-in-united-states.

Worldwide leading cause of death:
[272]Steven Ertelt, Micaiah Bilger "Abortion Was the Leading Cause of Death Worldwide in 2019, Killing 42 Million People," LifeNews.com, Dec 31, 2019, last accessed September 5, 2020, https://www.lifenews.com/2019/12/31/abortion-was-the-leading-cause-of-death-worldwide-in-2019-killing-42-million-people/.

Expanded abortion statistics for US:
[273]"Abortion," All American Life League (ALL) (website), last accessed September 5,2020, https://www.all.org/learn/abortion/abortion-statistics/.

[274]ALL, *Abortion.*

Abortion clinics open during COVID-19 lockdown:
[275]Ema O'Connor, "Abortion Clinics Are Staying Open During The Coronavirus Outbreak. Here's Why," Buzz Feed (website), March 20, 220, last accessed September 6, 2020, https://www.buzzfeednews.com/article/emaoconnor/coronavirus-abortion-clinics-open-planned-parenthood.

Candace Owens, a woman born in the inner city, speaks on abortion and the PP:
[276]Candace Owens, "Liberty University Convocation," September 26, 2018. Last accessed September 6, 2020, https://duckduckgo.com/?t=ffab&q=candace+owens+at+liberty+university+youtube&iax=videos&ia=videos&iai=https%3A%2F%2Fwww.youtube.com%2Fwatch%3Fv%3DT-OtQx5mLrY.

Planned Parent applied for and received coronavirus relief intended for struggling small businesses:
[277]Jordon Sekulow, "Planned Parenthood Improperly Applied for and Unlawfully Received $80 MILLION of Coronavirus Relief Funds Meant for Struggling Small Businesses," ACLJ.org, last accessed September 6, 2020, https://aclj.org/pro-life/planned-parenthood-improperly-applied-for-and-unlawfully-received-80-million-dollars-of-coronavirus-relief-funds-meant-for-struggling-small-businesses.

Abortion is 95% of PP's "pregnancy resolution" service:
[278]Mary Margaret Olohan, "New Planned Parenthood Report Shows Increase in Abortions," The Daily Signal (website), January 6, 2020, last accessed September 6, 2020, https://www.dailysignal.com/2020/01/06/new-planned-parenthood-report-shows-increase-in-abortions/.

PP income and profit:
[279]Olohan, *Planned Parenthood.*

NPR poll of American opinions on abortion:
[280]Domenico Montanaro, "Poll: Majority Want To Keep Abortion Legal, But They Also Want Restrictions," NPR (website), June 7, 2019, last accessed September 6, 2020, https://www.npr.org/2019/06/07/730183531/poll-majority-want-to-keep-abortion-legal-but-they-also-want-restrictions.

Pew Research Center overview of where Christian doctrines and other religions stand on abortion:
[281]"Major religious groups' positions on abortion," Pew Research Center, June 20, 2016, last accessed September 6, 2020, https://www.pewresearch.org/fact-tank/2016/06/21/where-major-religious-groups-stand-on-abortion/ft_16-06-22_churchabortion/.

The statistics of poverty
[282]"World Poverty Rate 1981/2020," Macro Trends (website), last accessed September 18, 2020, https://www.macrotrends.net/countries/WLD/world/poverty-rate.

"What is the current poverty rate in the United States?", Center for Poverty Research, University of California, Davis (website), last accessed September 18, 2020, https://poverty.ucdavis.edu/faq/what-current-poverty-rate-united-states.

Bob Pfeiffer, a CPA ," US poverty and the welfare programs of the federal government," Federal Safety Net, federalsafetynet.com/us-poverty-statistics.html.

Children and seniors in poverty:
[283]"Who lives in Poverty USA?" Poverty USA (website),2018, last accessed September 6, 2020, https://www.povertyusa.org/facts.

Black children in poverty:
[284]"Poverty in Black America," Black Demographics (website, excellent graphs, last accessed September 6, 2020, https://blackdemographics.com/households/poverty/.

Poverty USA.

Poverty by ethnicity:
[285]Poverty USA.

Population by Race 2018:
[286]"Quick Facts," US Census, 2018, last accessed September 7, 2020, https://www.census.gov/quickfacts/fact/table/US/IPE120218.

Enslavement of Native Americans
Removal of Native Americans from their traditional homelands on the "Trail of Tears":
[287]"Trail of Tears," Wikipedia, last accessed September 7, 2020, https://en.wikipedia.org/wiki/Trail_of_Tears.

Dinesh D'Souza, Bruce Scholley, John Sullivan, writers; Dinesh D'Souza, John Sullivan, diredtors. *America: Imagine the World without Her.* 2013; Santa Monica, CA: Lions Gate, 2014. DVD.

[288]Wikipedia, *Trail*

Enslavement of Africans
History of slavery in West Africa before, during, after slavery of West Africa in America:
[289]"Slavery in Africa," Wikipedia, last accessed September 6, 2020, https://en.wikipedia.org/wiki/Slavery_in_Africa#Atlantic_slave_trade, https://en.wikipedia.org/wiki/Slavery_in_Africa#West_Africa (portion of the above*).*

[290]Sandra Greene, "The Curious History of Slavery in Africa," Cornell Research (cornell.edu), last accessed September 6, 2020, https://research.cornell.edu/news-features/curious-history-slavery-west-africa.

The slavery of Africans in America:
[291]David Eltis & David Richardson, *Atlas of the Transatlantic Slave Trade,* (New Haven & London: Yale University Press, 2010), pp 17-19, 21.

[292]Eltis, *Transatlantic*

[293]Eltis, *Transatlantic*

Glenn Loury & John McWhorter "Critical Look at the 1619 Project," The Glenn Show, Sep 11, 2019,last accessed October 7, 2020, https://www.youtube.com/watch?v=8hWQmzgiKXQ. (time: start at 3:35]

"The 1619 Project Exposed: A Special Edition of the American Mind Podcast" Claremont Institute, April 27, 2020, last accessed October 7, 2020, https://www.youtube.com/watch?v=tPSyBcIfyFw.

"Revisionists at it again: The '1619 Project' is bad history fueled by bad motives," Washington Post, May 24, 2020, last accessed October 7, 2020. https://www.washingtontimes.com/news/2020/may/24/editorial-1619-project-bad-history-fueled-bad-moti/.

Willie Lynch, full text of his letter (warning vile and evil):
[294]"Full text of 'willie lynch letter 1712," Internet Archive (website), last accessed September 7, 2020, https://archive.org/stream/WillieLynchLetter1712/the_willie_lynch_letter_the_making_of_a_slave_1712_djvu.txt.

Wikipedia proposes Willie Lynch letter is a hoax, but does not deny slave treatment:
[295]"William Lynch speech," Wikipedia, last accessed September 7, 2020, https://en.wikipedia.org/wiki/William_Lynch_speech.

African American freemen owning black slaves in the South:
[296]Dinesh D'Souza, Bruce Scholley, John Sullivan, writers; Dinesh D'Souza, John Sullivan, diredtors. *America: Imagine the World without Her.* 2013; Santa Monica, CA: Lions Gate, 2014. DVD.

Urban plantations:
[297] D'Souza, Dinesha and Scholley, Bruce, writers and directors. *Hillary's America, the Secret History of the Democratic Party.* 2016; Santa Monica, CA: Lions Gate, 2016. DVD.

War on poverty:
[298]Rachel Sheffield and Robert Rector, "The War on Poverty After 50 Years," The Heritage Foundation, September 15, 2014, last accessed September 15, 2020, https://www.heritage.org/poverty-and-inequality/report/the-war-poverty-after-50-years.

[299]"Interview with Carol Swain, Ph.D.," *Hillary's America, the Secret History of the Democratic Party*, dir. by Dinesh D'Souza and Bruce Scholley (2016; Santa Monica, CA: Lions Gate, 2016) DVD.

Candace Owens growing up black and what politicians expect of blacks, plus much more:
Candace Owens, "Liberty University Convocation," September 26, 2018. Last accessed September 6, 2020, https://duckduckgo.com/?t=ffab&q=candace+owens+at+liberty+university+youtube&iax=videos&ia=videos&iai=https%3A%2F%2Fwww.youtube.com%2Fwatch%3Fv%3DT-OtQx5mLrY.

Robert Rector, "How Welfare Undermines Marriage and What to Do about It," The Heritage Foundation (website), November 27, 2014, https://www.heritage.org/welfare/report/how-welfare-undermines-marriage-and-what-do-about-it

Daniel Patrick Moynihan, "The Moynihan Report, "African American family structure," Wikipedia, last accessed September 26, 2020, https://en.wikipedia.org/wiki/African-American_family_structure.

Daniel P. Moynihan, *"The Negro Family: The Case for National Action,"* Washington, D.C., Office of Policy Planning and Research, U.S. Department of Labor, 1965, last accessed September 26, 2020, https://en.wikipedia.org/wiki/The_Negro_Family:_The_Case_For_National_Action.

National Review, April 4, 1994, p. 24, posted by Wikipedia, last accessed September 26, 2020, https://en.wikipedia.org/wiki/National_Review.

Jesse Washington, "Blacks Struggle with 72 Percent Unwed Mothers Rate", Jesse NBC News, July 11, 2010, last accessed September 26, 2020, hhttp://www.nbcnews.com/id/39993685/ns/health-womens_health/t/blacks-struggle-percent-unwed-mothers-rate/#.URXHo80hclk.

Jason Riley,"For Blacks, the Pyrrhic Victory of the Obama Era,"The Wall Street Journal, November 4, 2012, last accessed September 26, 2020, https://www.wsj.com/articles/SB10001424052970204712904578090483678801780.

Paul Bedard, "77% Black Births to Single Moms, 49% for Hispanic Immigrants" Washington Examiner, May 5, 2017, last accessed September 26, 2020, https://www.washingtonexaminer.com/77-black-births-to-single-moms-49-for-hispanic-immigrants.

Single Mother Guide, updated August 22, 2020, last accessed September 26, 2020, https://singlemotherguide.com/single-mother-statistics/.

78% of Planned Parenthood clinics in minority neighborhoods:
[300]"Planned Parenthood," Black Genocide (website), last accessed September 7, 2020, http://www.blackgenocide.org/planned.html.

Dr. Alveda King believes the abortion mill still maintains Margret Sanger's racist eugenics beliefs are still part of Planned Parenthood, https://lidblog.com/alveda-king-planned-parenthood/.

[301]Dr. Jerry Newcombe, "Dr. Alveda King: Planned Parenthood Targets Blacks For Abortion," *The Lid* (blog), Jan 24, 2019, last accessed September 7, 2020, https://lidblog.com/alveda-king-planned-parenthood/.

Dr. Jerry Newcombe, "Dr. Alveda King: Planned Parenthood Targets Blacks For Abortion," *The Lid* (blog), Jan 24, 2019, last accessed September 7, 2020, https://www.lifenews.com/2020/08/04/alveda-king-slams-planned-parenthood-its-been-working-to-annihilate-blacks-for-100-years/.

Black Americans comprise 13.4% of the U.S. population, they accounted for 36.0% of the abortions in US:
[302]Emily War, "CDC: 36% of Abortions Abort Black Babies" CNS News (website), posted November 28, 2018, last accessed September 7, 2020, https://www.cnsnews.com/news/article/emily-ward/blacks-make-134-population-36-abortions.

"Planned Parenthood," Black Genocide (website), last accessed September 7, 2020, http://www.blackgenocide.org/planned.html.

Thomas Sowell on the Myths of Economic Inequality , includes quote:
[303]Thomas Sowell hosted by Peter Robinson, "Thomas Sowell on the Myths of Economic Inequality," *Uncommon Knowledge with Peter Robinson*, Hoover Institution, recorded November 15, 2018, last accessed September 9, 2020, https://www.youtube.com/watch?v=mS5WYp5xmvl.

[304]Sowell, *Robinson.*

Former NFL player Jack Brewer at RNC: I'm lifelong Democrat, but I support Donald Trump:
Republican National Convention, August 26, 2020, last accessed September 9, 2020, https://www.youtube.com/watch?v=wqPpz7gL_Wk.

Is Trump a racist?
"What you need to know about Trump," The Hidden Things in Front of Your Eyes, posted June 1, 2020, last accessed September 7, 2020, https://youtu.be/o2krYAU87to.

White slavery and serfdom
When did Western Europeans start immigrating to America?
[306]"History of Immigration to the United States," Wikipedia, last accessed September 7, 2020, https://en.wikipedia.org/wiki/History_of_immigration_to_the_United_States.

Ottoman Empire enslaves whites:
[305]*"Ottoman wars in Europe,"* Wikipedia, last accessed September 4, 2020, https://en.wikipedia.org/wiki/Ottoman_wars_in_Europe.

Editors, *"Ottoman Empire,"* Britannica (website), last accessed September 4, 2020, https://www.britannica.com/place/Ottoman-Empire/Ottoman-institutions-in-the-14th-and-15th-centuries.

"Indentured Servitude," Wikipedia, last accessed October 10, 2020, https://en.wikipedia.org/wiki/Indentured_servitude

D'Souza, Dinesha and Scholley, Bruce, writers and directors. *Hillary's America, the Secret History of the Democratic Party.* 2016; Santa Monica, CA: Lions Gate, 2016. DVD.

When did Western Europeans start immigrating to America?
[306]"History of Immigration to the United States," Wikipedia, last accessed September 7, 2020, https://en.wikipedia.org/wiki/History_of_immigration_to_the_United_States

What was serfdom and how long did it last in Europe?
Western European serfdom:
[307]"History of Serfdom," Wikipedia, last accessed September 7. 2020, https://en.wikipedia.org/wiki/History_of_serfdom.

[308]"Serfdom in Europe," Khan Academy (website), last accessed September 7, 2020, https://www.khanacademy.org/humanities/world-history/medieval-times/european-middle-ages-and-serfdom/a/serfdom-in-europe.

Eastern European serfdom:
[309]Boris B. Gorshkov, Serfdom: Eastern Europe, encyclopedia.com, updated August 31, 2020, last accessed September 7, 2020, https://www.encyclopedia.com/international/encyclopedias-almanacs-transcripts-and-maps/serfdom-eastern-europe.

Video describing feudalism and serfdom:
[310]"Serfs and Manorialism," Khan Academy (website), last accessed September 7, 2020, https://www.khanacademy.org/humanities/world-history/medieval-times/european-middle-ages-and-serfdom/v/serfs-and-manorialism.

XII. The road out and away from global enslavement

Fabian Society in America
[311]"Who Founded Fabian Socialism in the United States?" *ProgressingAmerica* (blog), posted February 2, 2012, last accessed September 6, 2020,https://progressingamerica.blogspot.com/2012/02/who-founded-fabian-socialism-in-united.html. [This page in this blog has been taken down. 9/29/2020.]

[312]Scott Boyd, "How Fabian socialism explains modern day American socialism," Truth Stream Media, January 19, 2020,posted by *The NOQ Report*, (podcast), September 6, 2020, last accessed September 6, 2020, https://noqreport.com/2020/01/19/how-fabian-socialism-explains-modern-day-american-socialism/. [This site is under attack. You may have to try a number of times to get it up. 9/29/2020.]

[313]George Bernard Shaw (on video above) explaining what life would be like for those who lived in the new world order they were creating through the Fabian Society, [time: 18:40-20:00]

Spiro Skouras, "Henry Kissinger and Bill Gates Call for Mass Vaccination and Global Governance," posted by ForbiddenKnowledgetv.net April 6, 2020, last accessed September 7, 2020, https://forbiddenknowledgetv.net/henry-kissinger-and-bill-gates-call-for-mass-vaccination-and-global-governance/ [If this gets censored from YouTube, check www.truthecomestolight.com/author/skouras.]

"Montage of "New World Order" Quotes," last accessed September 7, 2020, https://duckduckgo.com/?t=ffab&q=quotes+from+leaders+about+new+world+order&iax=videos&ia=videos&iai=https%3A%2F%2Fwww.youtube.com%2Fwatch%3Fv%3DI3zgsJEm5dQ. [Google is now tracking views of this video. The duckduckgo address above is safe.]

UN attempt at taking over the United States in 1951
[314] Myron C. Fagan, Internet Archive (website), posted? Dated June 11, 1951, last accessed September 4, 2020, https://archive.org/stream/MyronC.Fagan/Fagan,%20Myron%20C.-CEG-HQ-18_djvu.txt

Communist agenda
[315]Curtis Bowers, writer and director, *Agenda, Grinding America Down*, last accessed September 6, 2020, self-distributed, www.AgendaDocumentary.com.

"New socialism"
[316]The Candace Owens Show: Dinesh D'Souza, premiered Jul 26, 2020, last accessed September 6, 2020, https://www.youtube.com/watch?v=X5_DBg31ZWU&feature=emb_rel_end.

Definition of fascism:
[317]www.dictionary.com, accessed September 6, 2020.

Definition of oligarchy::
[318]www.dictionary.com, accessed September 6, 2020.

Legend of Hercules and the hydra
[319]Gregory R. Cane, Editor-in-Chief, "The Labors of Hercules,:" The Perseus Project, Perseus Digital Library, Tufts University, last update April 24, 2019, last accessed September 6, 2020, https://www.perseus.tufts.edu/Herakles/hydra.html.

Black Lives Matter's historic source and their objectives:
[320]Reagan, "The White Man Behind Black Lives Matter," ForbiddenKnowledgetv.net, October 2, 2020, last accessed October 4, 2020, https://forbiddenknowledgetv.net/the-secret-origins-of-black-lives-matter/, or https://www.youtube.com/watch?v=Sq1m_PJtu5o.

George Floyd: suppressed police body-cam
[321]Cristina Laila, "George Floyd Police Bodycam Footage Released – Floyd Resisted Arrest, Said He 'Couldn't Breathe' While Standing and Breathing (VIDEO)," Gateway Pundit (website), posted August 3, 2020, last accessed September 8, 2020, https://www.thegatewaypundit.com/2020/08/george-floyd-police-bodycam-footage-released-floyd-resisted-arrest-said-couldnt-breathe-standing-breathing-video/.

Autopsy and independent review opinion:
"George Floyd: Full autopsy report reveals cause of death," New Zealand Herald (nzherald.co.nz), published June 4, 2020, accessed September 6, 2020, https://www.nzherald.co.nz/world/news/article.cfm?c_id=2&objectid=12337305

Ideological possession
[322] Dr. Jordon Peterson, "Pathology of Ideological Possession Definition," Caige Mang, post and comments by Chris Caige, December 5, 2018, last accessed September 7, 2020, https://www.youtube.com/watch?v=rBDXpFei3KE.

Candace Owens on riots
[323] Candace Owens joins Glenn Beck, *"Candace Owens: This Is What's Really Driving the Race Riots in America,"* ForbidenKnowledtetv.net posted June 26, 2020, last accessed September 4, 2020, https://forbiddenknowledgetv.net/candace-owens-this-is-whats-really-driving-the-race-riots-in-america/. [Start at 11:30.]

The devil's goals and tactics
[324]C.S. Lewis, *"The Screwtape Letters,"* The Screwtape Letters, Mere Christianity, Surprised by Joy**,** Trilogy Edition, New York: Quality Paperback Book Club, 1982, 5-160.

Paul Kengor, *The Devil and Karl Marx: Communism's Long March of Death, Deception, and Infiltration,* (Gastonia, North Carolina: TAN Books, 2020)

Interview with Paul Kengor by Glenn Beck, "Hear the HORRIFYING words Karl Marx wrote about Satan, Evil | THIS is the Origin of BLM, Marxism," Glenn Radio, September 9, 2020, last accessed October 5, 2020, https://www.youtube.com/watch?v=_ItS_df8GlQ.

Reagan, "The White Man Behind Black Lives Matter," ForbiddenKnowledgetv.net, October 2, 2020, last accessed October 4, 2020, https://forbiddenknowledgetv.net/the-secret-origins-of-black-lives-matter/, or https://www.youtube.com/watch?v=Sq1m_PJtu5o.

Terry Turchie, "Attack & Dethrone God' Is Goal of Protests, Says Former FBI Agent Terry Turchie," *The Ingraham Angle,* Fox News, posted on Heavy on June 2020, last accessed October 9, 2020, https://heavy.com/news/2020/06/attack-and-dethrone-god/.

Alexandra Bruce, John Chambers,"Corporate Communism and the Deep State," MSOM, ForbiddenKnowledgetv.net, October 1, 2020, last accessed October 4, 2020, https://forbiddenknowledgetv.net/corporate-communism-and-the-deep-state/, or https://www.youtube.com/watch?v=-PzZ1TdQZN8.

XI. Preview of intended coming attractions

Machiavelli
[325]Harvey Mansfield, "Niccolò Machiavelli, Italian statesman and writer," Britannica (website), updated June 17, 2020, last accessed September 7, 2020, https://www.britannica.com/biography/Niccolo-Machiavelli.

[326] Marta Gabre-Sadick, *Sheltered by the King, (*United States of America; self-published, 2008), p. 127.

Funders and supporters of rioters
269 corporations who have voiced support and made donations to rioters' funds and Black Lives Matter:
[327]Tim Brown, *"List of 269 Companies Supporting ANTIFA, Black Lives Matter,"* (list by Ashley Rae Goldenberg), Conservative Firing Line.com (website), posted June 9, 2020, last accessed September 4, 2020, https://conservativefiringline.com/list-of-269-companies-supporting-antifa-black-lives-matter/.

Alexandra Bruce, John Chambers, "Corporate Communism and the Deep State," MSOM, ForbiddenKnowledgetv.net, October 1, 2020, last accessed October 4, 2020, https://forbiddenknowledgetv.net/corporate-communism-and-the-deep-state/, or https://www.youtube.com/watch?v=-PzZ1TdQZN8.

Rioters paid by Soros:
This YouTube account has been terminated, https://www.youtube.com/watch?v=UnqasusPW70.

Ashley Rae Goldenberg, "279 Companies Supporting Violent Antifa & Black Lives Matter, *"Reality and Denial* (blog), June 3, 2020, last accessed September 18, 2020, https://realityanddenial.wordpress.com/2020/06/09/279-companies-supporting-violent-antifa-black-lives-matter/.

Nuremberg Code full text:
[328]Evelyne Shuster, Ph.D., "Fifty Years Later: The Significance of the Nuremberg Code," The New England Journal of Medicine, published November 13, 1997, last accessed September 7, 2020, https://www.nejm.org/doi/full/10.1056/NEJM199711133372006.

Armen Nikogosian, *"Body Autonomy – the Core of Personal Freedom," The Epoch Times,* April 30-May 6,2020.

European Union
[329]Friedrich Moser and Matthieu Lietaert, "The Brussels Business – Who Runs the EU?," ForbiddenKnowledgetv.net, posted July 6, 2019, last accessed September 3, 2020, https://forbiddenknowledgetv.net/the-brussels-business-who-runs-the-eu/.

Alexandra Bruce, John Chambers, "Corporate Communism and the Deep State," MSOM, ForbiddenKnowledgetv.net, October 1, 2020, last accessed October 4, 2020, https://forbiddenknowledgetv.net/corporate-communism-and-the-deep-state/, or https://www.youtube.com/watch?v=-PzZ1TdQZN8.

Gates: depopulation
[330] Bill Gates, "Innovating to Zero,"TED2010, Feb. 2010, last accessed September 5, 2020, https://www.ted.com/talks/bill_gates_innovating_to_zero.

Propaganda ban on American citizens lifted
[331]John Cable, "U.S. Repeals Propaganda Ban, Spreads Government-Made News to Americans," The Cable, posted by FP (foreighpolicy.com) July 14, 2013, last accessed September 2020, https://foreignpolicy.com/2013/07/14/u-s-repeals-ban-spreads-government-made-news-to-americans/

Gates: pandemic
[332] Bill Gates' 2015 TED Talk, https://www.youtube.com/watch?v=6Af6b_wyiwI
Bill Gates, "The next outbreak? We're not ready."TED2015, March 25, 2015, last accessed September 7, 2020, https://www.youtube.com/watch?v=6Af6b_wyiwI.

Mainstream media owned by 6 corporations. All are multi-national.
[333]Ashley Lutz, *"These 6 Corporations Control 90% of The Media In America."* (Infographic created by Jason at Frugal Dad.com), posted June 14, 2020 by BusinessInsider.com (website), last accessed September 4, 2020, https://www.businessinsider.com/these-6-corporations-control-90-of-the-media-in-america-2012-6?op=1.

California wildfires not burning like natural fires
[334]*Aerial drone footage after "wildfire" burned "through" California residential neighborhood (language alert!),* Jake, "California Wildfires EXPOSED," YouTube, posted November 12, 2018, last accessed September 7, 2020, https://www.youtube.com/watch?v=Mzxdks6ZnXs. (Start at 5:57)

"Callfornia Directed Energy Weapon (DEW) – Color-Enhanced View," posted by ForbiddenKnowledgetv.net, September 10, 2020, last accessed September 15, 2020, https://forbiddenknowledgetv.net/california-directed-energy-weapon-dew-color-enhanced-view/

Joseph P. Farrell, "The Strangeness of the California Fires Just Became Stranger,"Giza Death Star (website), last accessed September 7, 2020, https://gizadeathstar.com/2017/10/strangeness-california-fires-just-became-stranger/.

Maps of northern California wildfires coincide s with Agenda 21 map with same area marked as future "no human habitation" areas:
Artikel 7, "Agenda 30/Agenda 21 NOT Sustainable," posted by ForbiddenKnowledgetv.net February 2, 2020, last accessed September 7, 2020, https://forbiddenknowledgetv.net/un-agenda-21-and-modern-monetary-theory/.

Pandemic related
COVID-19 morbidity facts:
[335]Tony Robins with Dr. Michael Levitt, "The Truth About Mortality Rates," ForbiddenKnowledgetv.net, posted June 1, 2020, last accessed September 3, 2020, https://www.youtube.com/watch?v=sEbcs37aaI0&feature=emb_rel_end.

Regarding use of face masks:
[336]James Grundvig, "Unmasking the Masks Agenda," presented by John Michael Chambers in *Making Sense of the Madness* (YouTube channel), posted by ForbidenKnowledgetv.net, August 13, 2020, last accessed September 6, 2020, https://forbiddenknowledgetv.net/unmasking-the-masks-agenda/

Pandemic control overreach:
[337]Naom, "DOCTORS IN BLACK – PlanDemic, a film about the global plan to take control of our lives, liberty, health & freedom," Videotube, last accessed September 3, 2020, https://bannedvids.com/doctors-in-black-plandemic/

"Plandemic II: Indoctrination," PlandemicSeries.com, posted by ForbiddenKnowledgetv.net, August 18, 2020, last accessed September 6, 2020, https://forbiddenknowledgetv.net/plandemic-ii-indoctornation/.

Influential leaders expose their agendas
[338]Spiro Skouras, "Henry Kissinger and Bill Gates Call For Mass Vaccination and Global Governance," posted by ForbiddenKnowledgetv.net April 6, 2020, last accessed September 7, 2020, https://forbiddenknowledgetv.net/henry-kissinger-and-bill-gates-call-for-mass-vaccination-and-global-governance/ (If this gets censored from YouTube, check www.truthecomestolight.com/author/skouras.

Samples of protests against "COVID hoax" in Europe August 2020
[339]David Icke (London), "Freedom Protests in Europe," Alexandra Bruce (comments), posted by ForbiddenKnowledgetv.net March 30, 2020, last accessed September 7, 2020, https://forbiddenknowledgetv.net/david-ickes-speech-at-the-unite-for-freedom-rally-trafalgar-sq-london-aug-29-2020/.

Tom Williams, "10,000 anti-lockdown protesters gather in London to claim coronavirus is 'a . hoax'" MetroUK (website), posted Saturday 29 Aug 2020, last accessed September 2020, https://metro.co.uk/2020/08/29/anti-lockdown-protesters-calling-coronavirus-hoax-gather-london-13195529/.

"German police arrest 300 in Berlin and disband protest against coronavirus curbs," CNBC News (website), posted August 30, 2020, last accessed September 7, 2020, https://www.cnbc.com/2020/08/30/german-police-arrest-300-in-berlin-and-disband-protest-against-coronavirus-curbs.html , [Official reports of Berlin numbers range from 18,00-38,000, Eyewitnesses say 100s of thousands.]

Dr. Reiner Fuellmich (German), "Crimes against Humanity: Class Action Lawsuits Incoming," ForbiddenKnowledgetv.net, October 6, 2020, https://forbiddenknowledgetv.net/crimes-against-humanity/.

Daniele Pozzati, "German Official Leaks Report Denouncing Corona as 'A Global False Alarm'," Strategic Culture Foundation, May 29, 2020, last accessed October 6, 2020 https://www.strategic-culture.org/news/2020/05/29/german-official-leaks-report-denouncing-corona-as-global-false-alarm/

Strategic importance of the COVID vaccine
[340]Dr.Carrie Madjeg, "'Human 2.0'? A Wake Call to the World," posted by ForbiddenKnowledgetv.net, August 18, 2020, last accessed September 6, 2020, https://forbiddenknowledgetv.net/human-2-0-a-wake-up-call-to-the-world/.

Charlotte Cuthbertson, *"With Vaccine on Horizon, Push for Mandatory Shots Expected to Build,"* The Epoch Times, Nation, pp. 1, A8-A9.

[341] Dr. Carrie Madjeg, *"The most important video you'll every watch,"* ForbiddenKnowledgetv.net, posted July 13, 2020, last accessed September 3, 2020, https://www.youtube.com/watch?v=8kpJESKPqCo

[342]Madjeg, *Human 2.0.*

[343]Madjeg, *Human 2.0.*

Charlotte Cuthbertson, *"With Vaccine on Horizon, Push for Mandatory Shots Expected to Build,"* The Epoch Times, Nation, pp. 1, A8-A9.

European restrictions on GMO:
[344]"Restrictions on Genetically Modified Organisms: European Union." Library of Congress LAW, law.gov, last accessed September 7, 2020, https://www.loc.gov/law/help/restrictions-on-gmos/eu.php.

Lorraine Chow, "It's Official: 19 European Countries Say 'No' to GMOs," EcoWatch.com, October 5, 2015, last accessed September 7, 2020, https://www.ecowatch.com/its-official-19-european-countries-say-no-to-gmos-1882106434.html.

[345]Madjeg, *Human 2.0.*

Charlotte Cuthbertson, *"With Vaccine on Horizon, Push for Mandatory Shots Expected to Build,"* The Epoch Times, Nation, pp. 1, A8-A9.

Definition of "genome"
[346]www.dictionary.com, last accessed September 11, 2020.

[347]Madjeg, *Human 2.0.*

Supreme Court allowing patents on genetically modified organisms:
[348]"Diamond v. Chakrabarty, 447 U.S. 303 (1980)," Justia, US Supreme Court, June 26, 1980, last accessed September 7, 2020, https://supreme.justia.com/cases/federal/us/447/303/.

GMO plants take over genomes of other plants; patent holders successful suits:
[349]Paul Harris, "Monsanto sued small famers to protect seed patents, report says," The Guardian (website), February 12, 2015, last accessed September 7, 2020, https://naturalsociety.com/monsanto-sued-farmers-16-years-gmos-never-lost/.

[350]"Agricultural Giant Battles Small Farmers," CBS News (website), posted April 26, 2008, last accessed September 7, 2020, https://www.cbsnews.com/news/agricultural-giant-battles-small-farmers/.

[351]Madjeg, *Human 2.0.*

Armen Nikogosian, *"Body Autonomy – the Core of Personal Freedom,"* The Epoch Times, April 30-May 6,2020.

[352]Madjeg, *Human 2.0 .*

[353]Madjeg, *Human 2.0.*

[354]Madjeg, *Human 2.0.*

Facebook manipulates mood in secret experiment:
[355] Hill, "Facebook Manipulated 689,003 Users' Emotions For Science," Forbes (website). Posted June 28, 2014, last accessed September 7, 2020, https://www.forbes.com/sites/kashmirhill/2014/06/28/facebook-manipulated-689003-users-emotions-for-science/#69f1dd0d197c.

[356]Madjeg, *Human 2.0.*

Additional facets of the vaccine issue
Vaccine manufacturer not legally responsible for damages:
[357]"42 U.S. Code § 300aa-22 - Standards of responsibility," Legal Information Institute, Cornell University (website), last accessed September 7, 2020, https://www.law.cornell.edu/uscode/text/42/300aa-22.

Emergency Preparedness legislation:
[358]Madjeg, *Human 2.0.*

May government mandate vaccinations?
[359]Laura Beltz, "Where does the government's right to require vaccinations come from?" National Constitution Center, *Constitution Daily* (blog), February 27, 2015, last accessed September 7, 2020, https://constitutioncenter.org/blog/where-does-the-governments-right-to-require-vaccinations-come-from/.

"Regulations and Laws That May Apply During a Pandemic," Centers for Disease Control and Prevention (CDC), last accessed September 7, 2020, https://www.cdc.gov/flu/pandemic-resources/planning-preparedness/regulations-laws-during-pandemic.htm.

Protection for our rights
Nuremberg Code:
[360]Evelyne Shuster, Ph.D., "Fifty Years Later: The Significance of the Nuremberg Code," The New England Journal of Medicine, published November 13, 1997, last accessed September 7, 2020, https://www.nejm.org/doi/full/10.1056/NEJM199711133372006.

Armen Nikogosian, *"Body Autonomy – the Core of Personal Freedom,"* The Epoch Times, April 30-May 6,2020.

The Bill of Rights, Constitutional Amendment #4:
[361]"The Bill of Rights (Amendments 1 - 10)," National Center for Constitutional Studies (website), last accessed September 7, 2020, https://nccs.net/blogs/americas-founding-documents/bill-of-rights-amendments-1-10.

The Bill of Rights, Constitutional Amendment #5:
[362]Ibid.

Pathology of ideological possession
[363]Dr. Jordon Peterson, "Pathology of Ideological Possession Definition," Caige Mang, post and comments by Chris Caige, December 5, 2018, last accessed September 7, 2020, https://www.youtube.com/watch?v=rBDXpFei3KE.

XIV. The globalist intentions

[364]Clifford Humphrey, *"The Dangerous Naivety of Narratives We Tell Ourselves,"* The Epoch Times, Opinion, June 4-10, 2020 edition, p A20.

[365]"Benjamin Franklin, Quotes by This Author," Our Republic (website), last accessed September 6, 2020, http://www.ourrepubliconline.com/Author/21.

More on China
Chinese "Quit the Party" movement:
[366]Editorial team, *"How the Specter of Communism Is Ruling Our World,"* Chapter 13, The Epoch Times, Opinion, May 21 -27, 2020 edition, p A21.

Chinese Communist Party tyrannizing surveillance of their people; signs of it spreading into America:
[367]Melissa Dykes, "What's Your Social Credit Score?" Truthstream Media , ForbiddenKnowledgetv.net, posted December 29, 2019, last accessed September 3, 2020, https://forbiddenknowledgetv.net/whats-your-social-credit-score/?utm_source=newsletter&utm_medium=email&utm_campaign=What%27s+Your+Social+Credit+Score%3F.

Who financed the Chinese Communist Party at its inception:
LORDDREADNOUGHT , *"Communist China was created by Jewish infiltrators working for the International Banking Cartel, Communist China was created by the Jews and serves their interests / Communist China was created by Rothschilds and their agents',"* The Millennium Report, July 6, 2019, last accessed October 5, 2020, http://themillenniumreport.com/2019/07/communist-china-was-created-by-jewish-infiltrators-working-for-the-international-banking-cartel/; and https://lorddreadnought.livejournal.com/37272.html

Chinese "Quit the Party" movement:
Editorial team, *"How the Specter of Communism Is Ruling Our World,"* Chapter 13, The Epoch Times, Opinion, May 21 -27, 2020 edition, p A21.

Federation of China:
[368]Steven Bannon reads, "The New Federal State of China Declaration," posted June 3, 2020, las accessed September 7, 2020, https://youtu.be/hsv3OWUp0YU.

What the CCP is doing to force Hong Kong under their communist system:
[369]Diana Zhang, Ph.D., staff writer, *"Why Beijing, in Act of Desperation Wants to Completely Take Away Hong Kong's Freedom,"* Opinion, *The Epoch Times,* May 28-June 3, 2020 edition, p A13

China enacts "national security law" in Hong Kong
Frank Fang, "Hong Kong Police Fire Tear Gas, Arrest More Than 350 Protesters as They March Against Beijing's Security Law," The Epoch Times, updated July 8, 2020, last accessed September 27, 2020, https://www.theepochtimes.com/hong-kong-police-enforce-national-security-law-against-local-protesters_3408121.html.

Frank Fang, "Hong Kong Authorities Ban Popular Protest Song in Schools as City's Freedoms Are Further Eroded," The Epoch Times, July 8, 2020 Updated: July 8, 2020, last accessed September 27, 2020, https://www.theepochtimes.com/hong-kong-authorities-ban-popular-protest-song-in-schools-as-citys-freedoms-are-further-eroded_3416520.html.

Yinyin Liao, "What Transpired in the First Week of Beijing's Security Law Taking Effect in Hong Kong," The Epoch Times, Updated: July 8, 2020, last accessed September 27, 2020, https://www.theepochtimes.com/what-transpired-in-the-first-week-of-beijings-security-law-taking-effect-in-hong-kong_3413850.html.

Forced demolition of homes in Beijing:
[370]Wang Jing and Fang Jing, "Beijing Homeowners Pepper Sprayed by Police When Defending Their Homes," The Epoch Times, July 8, 2020, last accessed September 27, 2020, https://www.theepochtimes.com/beijing-homeowners-pepper-sprayed-by-police-when-defending-their-homes_3416779.html.

Bilderberg
Bilderberg connections to everything in the world:
[371]Ashley Lutz, "This Chart Shows The Bilderberg Group's Connection To Everything In The World," Business Insider (website), June 12, 2012, last accessed September 7, 2020, https://www.businessinsider.com/this-chart-shows-the-bilderberg-groups-connection-to-everything-in-the-world-2012-6.

Bilderberg membership:
David All Rivera, Final Warning: A History of the New World Order Illumunism and the master plan for world domination, Modern History Project, 1994, last accessed September 5, 2020, https://modernhistoryproject.org/mhp?Article=FinalWarning&C=1.1.

[372]George Bernard Shaw (on video above) explaining what life would be like for those who lived in the new world order they were creating through the Fabian Society, https://noqreport.com/2020/01/19/how-fabian-socialism-explains-modern-day-american-socialism/. [This site is under attack. You may have to try a number of times to get it up. 9/29/2020. Time of clip: 18:40-20:00].

Scientific proof of God
[373]Geoffrey Levy, *"There must be a God,"* Daily Express in London, August 14, 1981.

[374]"Fred Hoyle," Wikipedia, last accessed September 24, 2020, https://en.wikipedia.org/wiki/Fred_Hoyle#Rejection_of_Earth-based_abiogenesis

Hoyle, Fred, *Evolution from Space*, Omni Lecture, Royal Institution, London, 12 January 1982; *Evolution from Space* (1982) pp. 27–28 ISBN 0-89490-083-8; *Evolution from Space: A Theory of Cosmic Creationism* (1984) ISBN 0-671-49263-2

*Hoyle, Fred (1984). The Intelligent Universe, Holt, Rinehart, and Winston. ISBN 978-0-03-070083-5*1.

Globalists tracks
Map of North America proposed megaregions:
[375]IrvingPlNYC, "The 11 Emerging Mega-Regions Of The United States," Brilliant Maps (website), posted November 24, 2017, last accessed September 7, 2020, https://brilliantmaps.com/usa-mega-regions/.

Global Research, Centre for Research on Globalization, Rosa Koire video, last September 24, 2020, https://www.globalresearch.ca/video-un-agenda-2030-exposed/5717356.

Democrats Against UN Agenda 21, last accessed September 24, 2020, https://www.democratsagainstunagenda21.com/.

Spiro Skouras "The Hidden Agenda Behind The Planned Destruction of America with Rosa Koire,"ForbiddenKnowledgetv.net, posted Jun 12, 2020, accessed last September 24, 2020, https://www.youtube.com/watch?v=EGA18p_XerE&feature=emb_title.

Inventory and control:
[376]Global Research, Centre for Research on Globalization, Rosa Koire video, last September 24, 2020, https://www.globalresearch.ca/video-un-agenda-2030-exposed/5717356

Spiro Skouras "The Hidden Agenda Behind The Planned Destruction of America with Rosa Koire,"ForbiddenKnowledgetv.net, posted Jun 12, 2020, accessed last September 24, 2020, https://www.youtube.com/watch?v=EGA18p_XerE&feature=emb_title, https://forbiddenknowledgetv.net/what-is-the-real-agenda-behind-defunding-and-dismantling-the-police/

"Unsustainables" in the new world order :
[377]Artikel 7, "Agenda 30/Agenda 21 NOT Sustainable," posted by ForbiddenKnowledgetv.net February 2, 2020, last accessed September 7, 2020, https://forbiddenknowledgetv.net/un-agenda-21-and-modern-monetary-theory/.

George Bernard Shaw (on video above) explaining what life would be like for those who lived in the new world order they were creating through the Fabian Society, https://noqreport.com/2020/01/19/how-fabian-socialism-explains-modern-day-american-socialism/. [This site is under attack. You may have to try a number of times to get it up. 9/29/2020; time of clip: 18:40-20:00]

Plan for depopulation and other "agenda" items:
[378]Global Research, Centre for Research on Globalization, Rosa Koire video, last September 24, 2020, https://www.globalresearch.ca/video-un-agenda-2030-exposed/5717356

Edward Morgan, "Agenda 21 (Reinvented as Agenda 2030 and Agenda 2050) is a Plan to Depopulate 95% of the World Population by 2030," Prepare for Change (website), April 8, 2018, last accessed September 2020, https://prepareforchange.net/2019/04/08/agenda-21-reinvented-as-agenda-2030-and-agenda-2050-is-a-plan-to-depopulate-95-of-the-world-population-by-2030/ .

Spiro Skouras "The Hidden Agenda Behind The Planned Destruction of America with Rosa Koire,"ForbiddenKnowledgetv.net, posted Jun 12, 2020, accessed last September 24, 2020, ttps://www.youtube.com/watch?v=EGA18p_XerE&feature=emb_title, https://forbiddenknowledgetv.net/what-is-the-real-agenda-behind-defunding-and-dismantling-the-police/

Bill Gates, "Innovating to Zero,"TED2010, Feb. 2010, last accessed September 5, 2020, https://www.ted.com/talks/bill_gates_innovating_to_zero.

What can you do to stop the globalist?
Global Research, Centre for Research on Globalization, Rosa Koire video, last September 24, 2020, https://www.globalresearch.ca/video-un-agenda-2030-exposed/5717356

[380]Democrats Against UN Agenda 21,last accessed September 24, 2020, https://www.democratsagainstunagenda21.com/.

Global Research, Centre for Research on Globalization, last accessed September 24, 2020, https://www.globalresearch.ca/global-reset-unplugged/5716178

Educate Yourself, "What to Do to STOP the Globalist Takeover of America?" https://educate-yourself.org/lte/fightingtakeover05feb09.shtml

The John Birch Society, click "Action Projects," https://jbs.org.

This is just a sample. Please search yourself, including locally.

Follow the recommendations in Chapter XX. Making the call compels the answer.

XV. What are our choices?

[381]"Benjamin Franklin, Quotes by This Author," Our Republic (website), last accessed September 6, 2020, http://www.ourrepubliconline.com/Author/21.

Videos of recent world leaders supporting a new world order:
[382] "Montage of "New World Order" Quotes," last accessed September 7, 2020, https://duckduckgo.com/?t=ffab&q=quotes+from+leaders+about+new+world+order&iax=videos&ia=videos&iai=https%3A%2F%2Fwww.youtube.com%2Fwatch%3Fv%3DDI3zgsJEm5dQ.

Historic quotes regarding a new world order:
Wes Penre, "World Leaders and Famous People Promoting a New World Order and a One World Government," Illumati-new.com, February 20, 2004, last accessed September 7, 2020, illuminati-news.com/worldleaders-quote-nwo.htm.

Current, Influential leaders' agendas exposed:
Spiro Skouras, "Henry Kissinger and Bill Gates Call For Mass Vaccination and Global Governance," posted by ForbiddenKnowledgetv.net April 6, 2020, last accessed September 7, 2020, https://forbiddenknowledgetv.net/henry-kissinger-and-bill-gates-call-for-mass-vaccination-and-global-governance/ , (If this gets censored from YouTube, check www.truthecomestolight.com/author/skouras.

Alexandra Bruce, John Chambers, "Corporate Communism and the Deep State," MSOM, ForbiddenKnowledgetv.net, October 1, 2020, last accessed October 4, 2020, https://forbiddenknowledgetv.net/corporate-communism-and-the-deep-state/, or https://www.youtube.com/watch?v=-PzZ1TdQZN8.

Reagan, "The White Man Behind Black Lives Matter," ForbiddenKnowledgetv.net, October 2, 2020, last accessed October 4, 2020, https://forbiddenknowledgetv.net/the-secret-origins-of-black-lives-matter/, or https://www.youtube.com/watch?v=Sq1m_PJtu5o.

The parable of the lost son:
[383]Luke15:11-32

For important information and illumination
Dinesh D'Souza movies: *Obama's America, love him, hate him, you don't know him; America, imagine the world without her; Hillary's America, the secret history of the democratic party;* and *Death of a Nation* and his books, including *United States of Socialism.*

Chris Bowen, *AGENDA: Grinding America Down*, www.AgendaDocumentary.com.

Ronald Reagan's full speech:
[384]Ronald Reagan, "Time for Choosing" (October 27,1964),"The Reagan Presidential Library, posted April 2, 2009, last accessed September 7, 2020, https://www.youtube.com/watch?v=qXBswFfh6AY.

XVI. Quick discernment guide

Illustrations:
[385]Dominant Paradigm Worldwide, © 1998-2020 Living Consciously® LLC., printed by permission.

Illustrations:
[386]God-Centered Paradigm, © 1998-2020 Living Consciously® LLC., printed by permission.

XVII. Was the fall meant to be permanent?

Illustrations:
[387]Serpentine context paradigm, © 1998-2020 Living Consciously® LLC, printed by permission.

[388]God-Centered Paradigm, © 1998-2020 Living Consciously® LLC, printed by permission.

[389]Serpentine context paradigm, © 1998-2020 Living Consciously® LLC, printed by permission.

[390]God-Centered Paradigm, © 1998-2020 Living Consciously® LLC, printed by permission.

XVIII. Reclaiming our divine birthright

The current-day battle lines
[391] Spiro Skouras "The Hidden Agenda Behind The Planned Destruction of America with Rosa Koire,"ForbiddenKnowledgetv.net, posted Jun 12, 2020, accessed last September 24, 2020, https://www.youtube.com/watch?v=EGA18p_XerE&feature=emb_title, https://forbiddenknowledgetv.net/what-is-the-real-agenda-behind-defunding-and-dismantling-the-police/

Joshua Phillipp, Cross Roads, broadcast August, 21, 2020; ForbidenKnowledtetv.net posted Aug. 23, 2020, last accessed September 3, 2020, https://forbiddenknowledgetv.net/nothing-to-eat-goes-viral-in-china/, [Time: 9:15-12:15.]

Joshua Phillipp, "Tracking Down the Origin of the Wuhan Virus," *The Epoch Times,* ; ForbidenKnowledtetv.net posted April 7, 2020, last accessed September 4, 2020, https://forbiddenknowledgetv.net/tracking-down-the-origin-of-the-wuhan-coronavirus/, [Chinese expert, toward end of video, states source for declaration of war - time: 41:43]

[392] Spiro Skouras, "Henry Kissinger and Bill Gates Call For Mass Vaccination and Global Governance," posted by ForbiddenKnowledgetv.net April 6, 2020, last accessed September 7, 2020, https://forbiddenknowledgetv.net/henry-kissinger-and-bill-gates-call-for-mass-vaccination-and-global-governance/ (If this gets censored from YouTube, check www.truthecomestolight.com/author/skouras.

Infringement on freedom of religion
[393]Wishful, "The Pastors who signed up to help lure Americans into FEMA camps; The Secret Clergy Response Team," THEYIG (website), Feb. 8, 2020, last accessed September 5, 2020, https://theyig.ning.com/front-page-news/the-pastors-who-signed-up-to-help-lure-americans-into-fema-camps-.

February 28, 2015 Pastors to help Department of Homeland Security in arrests and detention of parishioners in FEMA camps:
David Hodges, "Pastors to Help DHS in Arrests and Detention of Americans in FEMA Camps," Freedom Outpost, (web archived), posted Feb. 28, 2015, last accessed September 5, 2020, https://web.archive.org/web/20161202181910/https://freedomoutpost.com/pastors-to-help-dhs-in-arrests-and-detention-of-americans-in-fema-camps/,

XIX. Divine Yeast

"Equation" content used with permission from the curricula of Living Consciously®, Serving Consciously™, Working Consciously™, Leading Consciously™. © 1998-2020 Living Consciously® LLC. All rights reserved. Published by Living Consciously® LLC.

Scientific proof and measurement of "divine yeast"
[394]Elaine and Arthur Aron, **The Maharishi Effect: A Revolution through Meditation**, (Walpole NH: Stillpoint Publishing, 1986), ISBN 0-913299-26-X (There are two books by the same name.)

[395]God-centered paradigm, © 1998-2020 Living Consciously® LLC., printed by permission.

[396]Equation for Divine Yeast, © 1998-2020 Living Consciously® LLC., printed by permission.

Instructions for expansion campaign to activate Divine Yeast:
Gayle Wisner, *Leading Consciously™: integrity-based, servant leadership for sustainable prosperity, Nonprofit Edition,* Grand Rapids MI: Living Consciously® LLC., 2019), beginning, p 140.

XX. Making the call compels the answer

The world is not coming to an end. It's coming to a start!
[397]*"Purlie"* (the song), *Purlie* (1981), (Broadway musical), Showtime Entertainment, (full movie, 'Purlie' is also the name of one of the songs) Robert R. Thiel in association with CBS Video Enterprises, May 24, 2016, last accessed September 7, 2020, https://duckduckgo.com/?t=ffab&q=Purlie&iax=videos&ia=videos&iai=https%3A%2F%2Fwww.youtube.com%2Fwatch%3Fv%3DABFVcH5WJDM.

Appendix I. Anything not attempted remains impossible...an invitation

[398]*Purlie (1970 Original Broadway Cast),* https://www.amazon.com/Purlie-1970-Original-Broadway-Cast/dp/B000003EWA.

Appendix III.

All content used with permission from the curricula of Living Consciously®, Serving Consciously™, Working Consciously™, Leading Consciously™. © 1998-2020 Living Consciously®LLC. All rights reserved. Published by Living Consciously® LLC.

Supreme Court rulings regarding prayer in schools
Legal Limits to US Federal and Department of Education Powers:

[399]https://www2.ed.gov/about/overview/fed/role.html, [This link can no longer be reached with a secure connection. It is likely that views are being tracked. Content from this US Department of Education site is directly quoted in the book at this footnote number. It was copy/pasted directly from the site in the Spring of 202, when the site was secure.]

The ruling removing prayer from public schools, ligated by the ACLU.
[400]Editors, "Engel v Vitale," Britannica, last accessed September 26, 2020, , https://www.britannica.com/event/Engel-v-Vitale.

To what prayer did they object?
[401]Ibid.

The ruling prohibiting the reading of the Bible:
[402]Stephen R. McCullough,"The School District of Abington v Schempp," Britannica, last accessed September 26, 2020, https://www.britannica.com/topic/School-District-of-Abington-Township-v-Schempp.

[403]Corinna Barrett-Lain, "God, Civic Virtue, and the American Way: Reconstruction of Engel," University of Richmond, UR Scholarship Repository, Law Faculty Publications, School of Law, 2015, last accessed September 26, 2020, https://scholarship.richmond.edu/cgi/viewcontent.cgi?referer=https://www.google.com/&httpsredir=1&article=2153 &context=law-faculty-publications

New York law regarding prayer in public schools:
[404]The original source used for this information - https://www.pbs.org/jeffer son/enlight/prayer.htm - has been removed from the internet. The sources below are offered in its place

"Facts and Case Summary - Engel v. Vitale," United States Courts (website), last accessed September 26, 2020, https://www.uscourts.gov/educational-resources/educational-activities/facts-and-case-summary-engel-v-vitale

Rabbi Menachem M. Schneerson, "Letter on the Question of the Regents Prayer," Chabad,org, November 21,1962, last accessed September 26, 2020, https://www.chabad.org/therebbe/letters/default_cdo/aid/1274011/jewish/Non-Denominational-Prayer-in-Public-Schools.htm.

An outline history of religion in American Schools:
[405]Written by 10 reformed Protestant ministers, "Outline History of Religion in American Schools," Free Republic (website)posted on March 8, 2009, last accessed September 26, 2020, www.freerepublic.com/focus/religion/2201818/posts.

Acknowledgements

There are many – specifically and broadly – whom deserve acknowledgement as being part of this book's contents, revelations, understandings, inspiring and provocative thoughts, and its actual manifestation in print.

These include:

The I AM WHO I AM, God, the Creator, and miraculously, also my Father.

Jesus Christ and the Angelic Host, who have loved and cherished me, protected, befriended, taught, and inspired me from the very beginning of my lifetime. Even when I was at-risk, vulnerable, incorrigible, courageous but stupid, and when I was defeated, broken, and alone.

You never left me. You always love, encourage, heal, and uplift me. And I am very grateful.

To those who have striven mightily to build, nurture, and honorably protect the United States of America and all the promise, hope, and possibility She represents.

To all who love, honor, steward, and protect Her still.

To all my life's teachers and enrichers:
- all who taught me what <u>not</u> to do by their own choices and actions
- all who have demonstrated love, honor, integrity, and steadfast courage and goodwill
- all the leaders, researchers, writers, servers, all who care enough about the truth and the wellbeing of mankind, America, and our world to find the true facts and share their constructive observations and understandings with courage, clarity, and poise. I'd especially like to call out, not only for their assistance to me, but for what they are doing for America and us all: President Donald Trump, Dinesh D'Souza, *The Epoch Times*, Alexandra Bruce of *ForbiddenKnowledgetv.net*, and
- all who live consciously and constructively.

To all my family – of blood and of love and friendship – who have stood in that love and relationship, with courage and with me, regardless of outer or internal circumstances.

To Nick and Suzie Chester, Susan Graham, John Harvey, Victoria Hanania-Raphael, Jean Franz, Cathy Keiser, Gindy Gray, Susan Heartwell, Larry Babcock, Nancy Flint Schambaugh, Ellen Mann, Sondra Waite, and countless others who chose to, at this time, remain unnamed.

To the publishing team at Outskirts Press, who brought this synthesis of a lifetime into a real and beautiful book, and are helping me to share it widely.

To all who will read it and find something of value that enhances the substance, clarity, and purpose of their lives.

Thank you all. And may God give you return blessings, expanded a billion-fold.

Author contacts:
SecuringAmericasVictory@protonmail.com
http://www.outskirtspress.com/securingamericasvictory

CPSIA information can be obtained
at www.ICGtesting.com
Printed in the USA
FSHW021711040121
77329FS